Orders:
Box 20725
Birmingham, AL 35216

Editorial Address:
3601 Westbury Road
Birmingham, AL 35223

CONTINUATIONS

CONTINUATIONS

Essays on Medieval French Literature and Language

In Honor of John L. Grigsby

Edited by

Norris J. Lacy and Gloria Torrini-Roblin

SUMMA PUBLICATIONS, INC.
Birmingham, Alabama
1989

Copyright 1989
Summa Publications, Inc.

ISBN 0-917786-74-2
Library of Congress Catalog Number 89-62174

Printed in the United States of America

Frontispiece photo by courtesy of Carol Grigsby

Contents

Contents (Cont'd)

II. THE OLD FRENCH EPIC

III. MISCELLANEOUS

Foreword

With the death of John L. Grigsby, on February 14, 1988, the academic world lost a most uncommon scholar and teacher, and a great many people lost a very good friend. This volume is a tangible expression of the respect he commanded.

Medievalists who know his work are invariably impressed, and occasionally surprised, by the diversity of his interests and the variety of his work. Rare are the scholars who remain as committed as he was to tradition while embracing innovation. Even less common are those who not only accept the legitimacy of the full scholarly spectrum but work comfortably and productively on both ends of it, ranging from textual criticism and genre studies to semiotics, hermeneutics, and grammatology. He was a scholar and critic of extraordinary solidity and breadth.

His bibliography might suggest that he evolved gradually from an interest in philology and editing—the two critical editions for which he is known date from 1967 and 1972—to a later concern for critical theory. Yet it is clear that for him theory complemented philology; it never supplanted it. At his death, he left, alongside important critical and theoretical articles recently out or awaiting publication, both a weighty manuscript on genre and a nearly completed edition of the *Voeux du héron*.

Jack himself might well have been surprised that what he did should surprise anyone else. Central to all his work was his unwavering respect for texts, for *the* text, and he surely would have seen no contradiction in his work: only a reliable text can be reliably interpreted. The theorist and critic deal with the principles and methods of literature, the editor and philologist provide the textual base for critical activity. Surely these are—must be!— complementary activities, in scholarship and teaching alike. And central to both is the text itself.

A devotion to the text was also a personal trait of Jack's. Many of his friends will have noted that he was a somewhat reserved man who often expressed himself more openly in letters than in personal conversations.

The written word was, both personally and academically, central to his world.

The title of our volume expresses a triple intent. First, of course, it is an allusion to Jack Grigsby's specific and enduring interest in the Continuations of Chrétien de Troyes's last romance. Second, it refers to the evolution of his own work and interests. Finally, and fundamentally, it points to the continuity inherent in the study of literature, as scholars train students, discuss with colleagues, and provoke thought through publication. And in regard to Jack Grigsby, is not a book an appropriate "continuation" of a life devoted to books?

The variety of subjects treated in our collection provides some reflection of the range of Jack's own interests and emphases. When we began to plan the book, we quickly realized that if we wanted to retain such a reflection, we could hardly impose either a strict thematic (or generic) organization or a methodology on the contributors. Jack Grigsby's own work produced important publications in several areas, and the work of his friends and admirers is inevitably, and fittingly, no less varied. In addition to a bibliographical essay devoted to his work, we have groups of essays on two of his principal interests (the Old French epic and the medieval—especially Arthurian—romance), but the remaining contributions still exhibit remarkable diversity of approach and subject matter (fabliaux, theater, philology). We hope that readers will agree with us that a "miscellaneous" rubric, while often inevitable in such a volume, is by no means inappropriate in this one.

Scholars both traditional and nontraditional responded enthusiastically to our plans to produce this volume. That gratifying reaction produced, however, one regret: that the number of responses and the limitations of space made it impossible to accommodate essays offered by a good many respected scholars and longtime friends of Jack Grigsby. We have expressed that regret to them personally; here we repeat our apologies, to them and to any others among Jack's friends and admirers who were inadvertently overlooked in our invitations and announcements of the project.

Many persons, both contributors to this volume and others, have offered support and encouragement, accompanied in every case by expressions of extraordinary admiration for John Grigsby—for the scholar, the critic, the editor, the teacher, and especially the person. To all of them (who must go unnamed here, although many have had their names recorded in the *tabula* to follow), we express our gratitude.

It is a pleasure to acknowledge our very great debt to Washington University in St. Louis, which provided material support for this publication, and in particular to James F. Jones, Jr., Chairman of the Department of Romance Languages and Literatures at Washington University, who procured that support, encouraged the project, and prepared the bibliographical essay. And finally, as we dedicate this volume to the memory of Jack Grigsby, we also dedicate it to Carol Grigsby, his constant companion through his career, his equally constant support during his illness, and a good and valued friend to all of us, editors and contributors alike.

—*N. J. L.*
—*G. T.-R.*

Publications of John L. Grigsby

Books:

The Middle French Liber Fortunae. A Critical Edition. University of California Publications in Modern Philology, Volume 81. Berkeley, 1967. Pp. 276.

Joufroi de Poitiers, roman d'aventures du XIIIe siècle. Edition critique (in sequential collaboration with Percival B. Fay). Textes littéraires français 183. Geneva: Droz, 1972. Pp. 268.

Articles:

"A New Manuscript of the French *Liber Fortunae*," *Romania,* 80 (1959), 447-60.

"Miroir des Bonnes Femmes" (Part I), *Romania,* 82 (1961), 458-81. *"Miroir des Bonnes Femmes"* (Part II), *Romania,* 83 (1962), 30-51.

"The Goddess Fortuna in the *Liber Fortunae,*" *L'Esprit Créateur,* 2 (1962), 110-13.

"Wanted: An Edition of Marquard Vom Stein's *Ritter vom Turn,*" *Archiv für das Studium der neueren Sprachen und Literaturen,* 114 (1962), 325-29.

"A New Source of the *Livre du Chevalier de La Tour Landry,*" *Romania,* 84 (1963), 171-208.

"The Historicity of *Joufroi de Poitiers,*" *Year Book of the American Philosophical Society 1967,* 537-39.

"The Narrator in *Partonopeu de Blois, Le Bel Inconnu* and *Joufroi de Poitiers,*" *Romance Philology,* 21 (1967-68), 536-43.

"Louis-Ferdinand Céline," *Encyclopedia of World Literature in the Twentieth Century,* ed. W. B. Fleischman, Volume I. New York: Ungar, 1967.

"Realism and Legend in *Joufroi de Poitiers,*" *Kentucky Romance Quarterly,* 17 (1970), 325-34.

"Narrative Voices in Medieval French Romance," *Year Book of the American Philosophical Society, 1973,* 585-87.

"Justice Neale Carman," *Bibliographical Bulletin of the International Arthurian Society,* 26 (1974), 215-16. [necrology]

"More on the Shortwave Radio in the Classroom," *French Review,* 50 (1977), 557-61.

"Sign, Symbol and Metaphor: Todorov and Chrétien de Troyes," *L'Esprit Créateur,* 18 (1978), 28-40.

"Narrative Voices in Chrétien de Troyes: A Prolegomenon to Dissection," *Romance Philology,* 33 (1979), 261-73.

"The Ontology of the Narrator in Medieval French Romance," in *The Nature of Medieval Narrative,* ed. Minnette Grunmann-Gaudet and Robin F. Jones, French Forum Monographs 22 (Lexington, Ky., 1980), pp. 159-71.

"L'Empire des signes chez Béroul et Thomas," in *Mélanges offerts à Charles Foulon,* II (Liège, 1981), 115-25.

"A Note on the Genre of the *Voyage de Charlemagne,*" in *Essays in Early French Literature Presented to Barbara M. Craig,* ed. Norris J. Lacy and Jerry C. Nash. York, S.C.: French Literature Publishing Co., 1982, pp. 1-8.

"Perceval devant l'herméneutique et la grammatologie," *L'Esprit Créateur,* 23 (1983), 25-37.

"*Gab* épique, mais *gab* lyrique?" *Marche Romane,* 83 (1983), 109-22. [appeared 1986]

Dictionary of the Middle Ages (New York: Scribner's): "ballette," II (1983), 61; "Blondel de Nesle," II (1983), 276; "Golden Legend," V (1985), 74; "Guiot de Provins," VI (1986), 26; "Jean de Thuim," VII (1986), 53-54.

"Le *Gab* dans le roman arthurien français" in *Actes du Quartorzième Congrès International Arthurien,* (Rennes: Presses Universitaires de Rennes, 1985), pp. 257-72.

"Le Conflit des théories: Eagleton devant la critique de la littérature médiévale" in *Mittelalterbilder aus neuer Perspektiv,* Würzberger Kolloquium 1984 (Munich: Fink, 1958), pp. 402-19.

"Courtesy in *Les Voeux du Paon,*" *Neuphilologische Mitteilungen,* 86 (1985), 566-75.

"The Relics' Role in *Le Voyage de Charlemagne,*" *Olifant,* 9 (1981), 20-34. [appeared 1985]

For *The Arthurian Encyclopedia,* ed. Norris J. Lacy (New York: Garland, 1986): *"Caradoc, Livre de"* (pp. 82-83), "The Continuations of Chrétien de Troyes's *Perceval"* (pp. 118-20), "The Didot-*Perceval"* (pp. 136-37), "Jean Frappier" (pp. 186-87), "The International Arthurian Society" (pp. 292-93), "Kay (Cei, Keu, Cayous)," (pp. 313-14).

"Le Voyage de Charlemagne: A(n Un)likely source for *Joufroi de Poitiers,*" *Romance Notes,* 27 (1986), 95-102.

"Gadamer's Hermeneutics and Medieval French Literature (with an Excursus on *Les Voeux du Héron*)," *Œuvres et Critiques,* 11 (1986), 117-26.

"Le Voyage de Charlemagne, pèlerinage ou parodie?" *Au Carrefour des routes d'Europe: La Chanson de geste.* Xᵉ Congrès international de la Société Rencesvals pour l'étude des épopées romanes, Strasbourg 1985. *Senefiance* 20-21 (1987), 567-84.

"Manuscripts and Editions of *Les Voeux du héron,*" *Manuscripta* 32 (1988), 28-35.

"Heroes and Their Destinies in the *Perceval Continuations.*" In *The Legacy of Chrétien de Troyes,* ed. Norris J. Lacy, Douglas Kelly, and Keith Busby. Amsterdam: Rodopi, 1988; II, 41-53.

"Les Diables d'aventures dans Manessier et *La Queste del Saint Graal,*" in *Contemporary Readings of Medieval Literature,* ed. Guy Mermier (Ann Arbor, Mich., 1989), pp. 1-20. [Vol. 8 of *Michigan Romance Studies*]

"L'Intertextualité interrompu par l'histoire: le cas des *Voeux du héron.*" In the proceedings of the 5th triennial congress, International Courtly Literature Society, Dalfsen, The Netherlands (August 1985), ed. Erik S. Kooper and Keith Busby. Amsterdam: John Benjamins; forthcoming.

Review Articles:

"A Defense and Four Illustrations of Textual Criticism," *Romance Philology*, 20 (1967), 500-20.

"Symbolism and Source-Hunting vs. the Creative Spirit," *Romance Philology*, 31 (1978), 321-43.

"Editing Medieval French Texts," *Romance Philology*, 34 (1981), 64-73.

"Narrative in Three Garbs: *roman courtois, lai, chanson de toile*," *Romance Philology*, 34 (1981), 74-87.

"Truth and Method in Arthurian Criticism," *Romance Philology*, 38 (1984), 53-64.

"Remnants of Chrétien's Esthetics in the Early *Perceval* Continuations and the Incipient Triumph of Writing," *Romance Philology*, 41 (1988), 379-93.

"Three Exercises in Edification," *Romance Philology*, 42 (1988), 174-78.

Reviews:

Textos medievais portugueses e seus problemas, by Serafim de Silva Neto, *Hispanic Review*, 26 (1958), 362-63.

Dicionario técnico poliglota, by Manuel de Silva de Medeiros, *Word*, 15 (1959), 224-29.

Le Livre du roy Rambaux de Frise, ed. Barbara N. Sargent, *Romance Philology*, 18 (1965), 502-04.

L'Espinette amoureuse de Jean Froissart, ed. Anthime Fourrier, *Romance Philology*, 19 (1966), 510-12.

Le Moyen Français, by Pierre Guiraud, *Romance Philology*, 20 (1967), 224-30.

Le Roman de Helcanus, ed. H. Niedzielski, *Speculum* 43 (1968), 185-87.

The Education of the Hero in Arthurian Romance, by Madeleine P. Cosman, *Romanic Review*, 60 (1969), 188-89.

La Destruction des Mythes dans les Mémoires de Ph. de Commynes by Jean Dufournet, *Romance Philology*, 22 (1968-69), 643-49.

Li Proverbes au vilain: Untersuchungen zur romanischen Spruchdichtung des Mittelalters, by Eckhard Rattunde, *Romance Philology*, 26 (1972-73), 192-96.

Guiron le Courtois: Etude de la tradition manuscrite et analyse critique, by Roger Lathuillère, *Romance Philology,* 26 (1972-73), 726-31.

The Narreme in the Medieval Romance Epic, by Eugene Dorfman, *Symposium,* 27 (1973), 172-76.

The Book of the Knight of the Tower, William Caxton trans., ed. by M. Y. Offord, *Speculum,* 48 (1973), 349-50.

Villehardouin, Epic Historian by Jeanette M. A. Beer in *Romance Philology,* 28 (1974), 244-48.

The Memoirs of Phillippe de Commynes, I, Isabelle Cazeaux trans., ed. by Samuel Kinser, *Romance Philology,* 28 (1975), 406-08.

L'Ancien Français. Points de vue. Programmes by R.-L. Wagner, *Speculum,* 52 (1977), 444-48.

A Poet at the Fountain: Essays on the Narrative Verse of Guillaume de Machaut by William Calin, *Comparative Literature,* 29 (1977), 185-88.

L'Espinette amoureuse par Jean Froissart. rev. ed. by Anthime Fourrier, *Romance Philology,* 30 (1977), 687.

Le Haut Livre du Graal: Perlesvaus, A Structural Study by Thomas E. Kelly, *Zeitschrift für romanische Philologie,* 94 (1978), 410-14.

Chrétien's Jewish Grail: A New Investigation of the Imagery and Significance of Chrétien de Troyes' Grail Episode based upon Medieval Hebraic Sources by Eugene J. Weinraub, *Zeitschrift für romanische Philologie,* 95 (1979), 168-72.

Girart de Vienne, ed. Wolfgang Van Emden, *Olifant,* 8 (1980), 181-85.

The Romance of Tristan and Isolt, tr. Norman Spector; and *Le Charroi de Nîmes,* tr. Fabienne Gégou, *Romance Philology,* 35 (1982), 532-35.

Versions of Medieval Comedy, ed. Paul Ruggiers; and *Façons de sentir et de penser: les fabliaux français* by Marie-Thérèse Lorcin, *Romance Philology,* 36 (1982-83), 584-91.

Allegorical Imagery by Rosemond Tuve, *Romance Philology,* 36 (1982), 113-15.

Le Pèlerinage de Charlemagne/La Peregrinación de Carlomagno, ed. and trans. Isabel de Riquer, *Olifant,* 12 (1987), 155-64.

Le Somme abreiget de theologie: Kritische Edition der französischen Uebersetzung von Hugo Ripelins von Strassburg "Compendium theologicae veritatis," ed. Christa Michler, *Romance Philology,* 42 (1989), 491-93.

Tabula

Alison Adams
Judith Admussen
Mr. and Mrs. James E. Armstrong
Milica Banjanin
Mme Emmanuèle Baumgartner
Jeanette M. A. Beer
Larry D. Benson
Jean Blacker
R. Howard Bloch
Renate Blumenfeld-Kosinski
Gerard J. Brault
Elizabeth J. Brucker
Matilda Tomaryn Bruckner
Keith Busby
William Calin
Carleton W. Carroll
Suzanne Chamier
Carol J. Chase
Ruth Harwood Cline
Alice M. Colby-Hall
Robert Francis Cook
Raymond J. Cormier
Larry S. Crist
Nina Cox Davis
Mildred Leake Day
Peter F. Dembowski
Maria S. De Weer-D'Hooghe

David A. Dinneen
Armel H. Diverres
Joseph J. Duggan
Sigmund Eisner
Patrick K. Ford
Charles Foulon
David C. Fowler
Maureen Fries
John F. Garganigo
Judith K. Greene
Robert W. Greene
Alice Grellner
Peter R. Grillo
Minnette Grunmann-Gaudet
Solange Saragea Guberman
Emily Riddle Guignon
Basil Guy
Peter Haidu
William and Sue Hendrickson
Tony Hunt
Pascal A. Ifri
Leonard W. Johnson
James F. Jones, Jr.
Marianne E. Kalinke
Martin and Eveline L. Kanes
Hans-Erich Keller
Douglas Kelly

Thomas E. Kelly
Elspeth Kennedy
William W. Kibler
Roberta L. Krueger
Raymond C. La Charité
Norris J. Lacy
Hannah Langsam
William Thomas Little
Donald Maddox
Yakov Malkiel
William H. Matheson
Philippe Ménard
Guy R. Mermier
Stamos Metzidakis
Don A. Monson
Daniel P. Nastali
Roger A. Noël
Richard O'Gorman
Wendy Pfeffer
Jean-Louis G. Picherit
Rupert T. Pickens
John F. Plummer
James F. Poag
Randolph D. Pope
Susan Rava
Annalee Rejhon
William Roach
Michael J. Ruggerio
Hans R. Runte
Theodore H. Rupp
Michel and Maya Rybalka
William Merritt Sale, III
Barbara Nelson Sargent-Baur
Joseph Schraibman
Elizabeth Schreiber
Eric Sellin
Christina N. Sharp
Michael Sherberg

Edith and Isidore Silver
David Staines
Harriet Stone
François Suard
Toshiyuki Takamiya
Jane H. M. Taylor
Raymond H. Thompson
Ann and Rudy Torrini
Gloria Torrini-Roblin
Madeleine Tyssens
Colette-Anne Van Coolput
Stephanie Cain Van D'Elden
Kenneth Varty
Mark and Irmgard Whitney
Sumner and Charity Cannon
   Willard
Gerhild Scholz Williams
Raymond Leslie Williams
Suzanne Wilson
Colette H. Winn
E. Paige Wisotzka
Lenora D. Wolfgang
Friedrich E. Wolfzettel
Michel Zink

The Works of John Lambert Grigsby: A Bibliographic Essay

James F. Jones, Jr.

At the end of "Perceval devant l'herméneutique et la grammato-logie," which Professor Grigsby published in 1983, we read:

> Ce qui ressort de notre brève excursion c'est une conscience du "progrès" des études médiévales. [Quoting Gadamer] "Le naïf méthodo-logisme de la recherche historique ne domine plus seul le champ. Le progrès de l'enquête n'est plus universellement vu dans le cadre de l'expansion et de la pénétration dans de nouveaux champs ou de nou-velles matières, mais plutôt comme l'arrivée à un niveau plus haut de la réflexion. . . ." Il faut continuer, bien sûr, la poursuite de nouvelles informations, l'édition et l'amélioration des textes, la recherche des sources. . . , mais cette "pénétration dans de nouvelles matières" doit être accompagnée de l'examen de nos méthodes d'interprétation et de compréhension.[1]

These sentences might have well served as an epigraph to this volume in Professor Grigsby's memory, for they most assuredly define his own career. I do not know if he had himself in mind when he put these thoughts to paper, but I do recall—at some point in the early eighties—that he spoke over and again about how medieval studies had evolved over the past three decades and how his own professional career had spanned such divergent swings in critical methodology that he hardly could recognize the Grigsby of the early sixties anymore. His comment in the Perceval essay makes this clear, for whereas he underscored the tried and true traditions of medieval scholarship in which he had been intellectually reared, he also held up the ideal of always entering into uncharted waters in hopes that new vistas might be made discernable to the extent that such new vistas could be shared with others.

Looking critically at the Grigsby bibliography, one is, I think, accordingly struck by two poles of endeavor: one exemplified by the traditionalist and the other assumed by the literary scholar interested to the point of fascination in a wide variety of modern, theoretical possibilities of interpreting literature. It is almost as if two, or maybe even three, medievalists were residing under the medievalist known by the Grigsby patronym. As proof of the rarity of the combination, one need only list the major medievalists of his generation in this country, and certainly abroad, those who came of scholarly age in the late 1950s and early 60s (he took his doctoral degree from the University of Pennsylvania in 1960 with a dissertation on the *Liber fortunae*). While it may not be totally uncommon to find one or two who dabbled in structuralism and its aftermath(s), it is indeed difficult to think of anyone who, having begun his research career in an intellectual world dwarfed by Paris, Holmes, Bédier, Curtius, Frappier, Pidal, *et al.,* to say nothing of the host of textual critics of medieval literature (including especially William Roach to whom he was most indebted), actually launched into a plethora of scholarly investigations about medieval literature using as theoretical constructs the works of Todorov, Derrida, Gadamer, Habermas, Lacan, Eagleton, Lentricchia, Barthes, Foucault, Genette, Greimas, Kurzweil, Ricœur, Greisch, Jauss, Donoghue, Hartman, and all the rest, whose names are part and parcel of the literary "Social Register" of our time. As Professor Grigsby phrased it with characteristic brevity of expression a year after the Perceval essay was published, "If interpreters of medieval literature expect to retain, better still, to increase their audience, unexplored paths must be part of their quest" (review article entitled "Truth and Method in Arthurian Criticism," *Romance Philology,* [1984] 64). During the last fifteen years of his career, Professor Grigsby did indeed go down unexplored paths, but he started three decades ago by taking those which have long been acknowledged to be the domain of the traditional medievalist.

Let us begin our review of his bibliography, therefore, with those works of traditional medieval scholarship. It all started when the Rare Books Division of the University of Pennsylvania Library fortuitously purchased in rapid succession two medieval manuscripts: that text labeled the *Liber fortunae* and a second one containing two different fragments, one brief passage from the *Somme le roi* and the first half of an unnoticed prose work entitled the *Miroir des bonnes femmes.* The young Grigsby, then seeking a dissertation subject, quickly realized that these purchases offered him an unparalleled opportunity, a perfect case—as he loved to say—of serendipity.[2] His find at the University of Pennsylvania occasioned his first six articles and his first book.

In 1959 *Romania* published his first scholarly piece, a relatively short (fourteen-page) description of the *Liber fortunae* manuscript. This article is noteworthy for two traits that would come to mark the rest of his critical *œuvre:* on one hand there is a meticulous, objective attention to the literary text at hand, and on the other there is certain evidence of clear, unadorned, and indeed at times parsimonious language. His goal is descriptive. Comparisons with the other two manuscripts of the *Liber fortunae* first appear, followed by a history of this particular manuscript, with every detail given due comment in the best of medieval textual tradition. After the description of the manuscript, we find the customary prose paraphrase of the Middle French verses, with the variants amply noted. The essay concludes with some mention of the work's originality and with a remark that serves as a presage of the book-length study that will follow several years later in 1967, to wit that scholars had passed much too quickly over the *Liber fortunae*'s importance to medieval studies and that a critical edition was sorely needed. A companion piece to this first article was published in *L'Esprit Créateur* in 1962, and in this particular essay, the shortest one (four pages) in his bibliography, the influence of Curtius is most readily apparent, for the guiding principle is that of the latter's *toposforschung.* From Boethius's Philosophy came the model for the goddess Fortuna in the *Liber fortunae,* her textual presence having in fact resulted in the title by which medievalists know and refer to the work. Citing the pertinent passage at length from the University of Pennsylvania manuscript, Grigsby displayed here as well that same frugality of expression that had already betokened a developing, personal scholarly style in his first essay and that would later characterize all his writings.

From approximately 1959 until 1967, the major project of his life was the critical text of the *Liber fortunae.* He digressed here and there along the way, primarily on issues dealing with the second of the University of Pennsylvania acquisitions—the *Miroir des bonnes femmes,* to which we shall return later in this essay—but for the most part he devoted his energies first to the completion of his dissertation and then to the recasting and polishing of the thesis into book form. Steadily encouraged primarily by William Roach and then later by his colleagues at the University of California, Berkeley, where he taught from 1962 until his 1967 move to Washington University, Professor Grigsby at long last brought out the edition upon which he had been working for eight years, with the customary delays in actual publication with which most humanists are unfortunately more than casually acquainted. One delay he experienced was, however, something of a disaster. The original typescript of the book and all the supporting material for the project burned, along with most of their personal belongings, in a moving van when the Grigsbys left Oklahoma for California. To the modern generation of scholars, born into the comfortable world of copying machines, computer-age technology, and word processing, such an event might not have the significance it would for a slightly older generation which depended entirely upon typewriters and messy sheets of carbon paper. Undaunted by the total loss of his work, he persevered, and the edition, which appeared as volume eighty-one of the University of California Publications in Modern Philology, was finally published in 1967.

The edition comprises some 276 pages. Divided into nine main divisions, to which were added separate textual notes, a glossary, and a very detailed bibliography, the *Liber fortunae* was almost immediately heralded by reviewers as a model of medieval textual criticism at its best. Prefatory information is quickly and, in due fashion, tersely provided: a summary of the work, a discursus on the author and the narrator, one on the prosopopoeia of Fortuna that reflects the earlier essay published in *L'Esprit Créateur,* a discussion of the work's sources, then of the manuscripts, an extremely detailed section on the orthography and language of the scribes, one on the language of the text, a final, all-too-brief note on the manner of the textual method applied, and the text itself. The sections beginning with the orthography and concluding with the note on textual method are denoted by individual paragraph numbers so that, as is customary, the references in the *vario lectio* follow smoothly to previous points of importance.

The second manuscript at the University of Pennsylvania that had interested the young scholar was the *Miroir des bonnes femmes,* obtained by that institution at approximately the same time as the manuscript of the *Liber fortunae,* which took so much of Professor Grigsby's time and energy during the early years of his career. What tempted him most was apparently the fact that this second text had gone completely unnoticed. He found only one mention of the title, and that was "buried" in the *Catalogue général des manuscrits des bibliothèques de France*. He was here, therefore, dealing with that virgin text about which textual critics of medieval literature dream, and from this interest would stem four essays, all written and published within a span of only slightly more than two years (1961-63). Alongside the *Liber fortunae* project, which was continuing at the same time, the *Miroir des bonnes femmes* efforts betoken a sustained period of intense activity that shows the degree to which Professor Grigsby was dedicated to his chosen field. A single, exceedingly long essay on the *Miroir* had to be divided by the editors of *Romania* into two parts for publication. It follows the traditional patterns of textual presentation. First we find the description of the manuscript itself, then a section on its composition, authorship, date, analogues, and sources. A third section provides a summary of the two separate series in the text: one on "les mauvaises femmes" and the second on "les bonnes femmes." The series are *exempla* from the Bible, and for each (the bad unfortunately outnumber the good, thirty-five to thirty) the biblical reference and a prose rendering of the exemplum appear. Textual interpretation is virtually nonexistent in this two-part *Romania* essay, a fact that would later play a decided role in Professor Grigsby's changing attitudes towards medieval studies.

From his descriptive reduction of the *Miroir,* however, and again according to his "theory" of the importance of pure serendipity in scholarship, he extended his reading of this manuscript to the *Livre du Chevalier de La Tour Landry* where he found quite by chance that the *Miroir des bonnes femmes* had served as a principal source for the later work. The editors of *Romania* once more published his paper, which made public his findings. Here we may note a stronger critical voice in its development, for we advance far beyond mere descriptions and prose renderings of medieval verse. The *Chevalier de La Tour Landry* borrowed to the extent of actually copying entire sections from the *Miroir,* without any textual indication on his part of the source. A comparison of the *Miroir* base text with that of *La Tour Landry* provides more than requisite proof of the rapport between the two works. Professor Grigsby then wandered into interpretation by remarking (pp. 204 ff.) that the salient question concerning *La Tour Landry*'s obvious borrowings from the *Miroir* did not deal with what was directly copied but with what had been purposely omitted from its source.

Grigsby's reflections on the matter result in some of the most cogently argued and most expertly wrought pages from his early period as a medieval scholar. The *Romania* essay on *La Tour Landry* led then to a brief piece of literary history on Marquard von Stein's *Ritter vom Turn,* the title given in 1493 by the governor of Mömpelgart to his translation of *Le Livre du Chevalier de La Tour Landry.* Here Professor Grigsby made a plea for a critical edition of the *Ritter vom Turn* so that research into the *Miroir des bonnes femmes-Livre du Chevalier de La Tour Landry-Ritter vom Turn* triangle might continue unabated.[3]

The move to California in the summer of 1962 brought Grigsby into contact with Percival B. Fay, who, years and indeed decades before, had begun work in collaboration with Charles H. Livingston on a critical edition of *Joufroi de Poitiers.* Their collaborative efforts to advance the cause of such a needed scholarly tool had been stifled, however, by the publication by Walter Streng-Renkonen in 1930 of *Joufroi, roman françois du XIIIe siècle.*[4] This edition was, unfortunately for its Finnish editor, marred by serious faults, which were quickly identified by reviewers in Europe and in America. Be that as it may, the Livingston-Fay collaboration apparently was shelved, and the issue dropped for almost four decades until Professor Grigsby met Fay in California in the early sixties, at which time, and being completely unaware himself of all that had transpired concerning a critical edition in the twenties and thirties, he decided that medievalists badly needed a proper text of the work. Grigsby called upon the more senior figure who at once told him all that had occurred between 1924 and 1932 and who, in a gesture of admirable generosity, turned over all the notes, transcriptions, source and bibliographical references, and the like, according the younger medievalist full permission to use the material in any way necessary, with the proviso that Livingston's permission be sought. This Mr. Grigsby did, and only a short while before Livingston's death, permission was granted, and an exceedingly fruitful collaborative effort between Fay and Grigsby replaced the earlier one between Livingston and Fay, which had regrettably been halted by external events. The result was the publication in 1972 of *Joufroi de Poitiers, roman d'aventures du XIIIe siècle,* brought out by the Droz press as part of its "Textes Littéraires Français" series.[5] What remained of Livingston's contributions from decades before was, however, largely subjective and cursory and was not used. Fay's contribution was of course substantive and in the 1972 edition is appropriately acknowledged. Fay died before the work appeared and therefore never lived to see in print something he had dreamed about for the better part of four decades. He had, however, most wisely entrusted the mission to an extremely dedicated scholar.

If the reader were to stop merely at the end of the introduction to the *Joufroi,* the difference between the first major scholarly effort undertaken by Professor Grigsby and the second would be readily apparent. His voice no longer is content with pure description. Nuances, subtleties, astute reflection upon the literary aspects of the text enter at every turn. He is concerned by the humorous, and by the textual sources, by narratological problems, and by comparisons with other similar works such as the *Flamenca.* These more "literary" traits notwithstanding, the presentation remains traditional. Following the introduction, there are sections on the *princeps* and variant manuscripts, on the author's language, on that of the copyist, a detailed bibliography, the text, the "Leçons non conservées et notes" which comprise the unpublished textual commentaries by Fay and the corrections, the index of proper nouns, and the glossary. Reviews of this edition show without hesitation that the serious lacunae of the 1930 Streng-Renkonen publication had been met and dispensed with properly. This *Joufroi* remains the standard text of the work.

Not only in the introduction to the edition but also in articles dealing with the *Joufroi* do we find some evidence—albeit not yet definitive—that a different Grigsby is arising from the previous producer of editions and literary history essays. He brought out a note for the *Year Book of the American Philosophical Society* on the role of historicity in the work and a longer, companion piece for the *Kentucky Romance Quarterly* on realism and legend. Yet in both, he remains in the secure frame of the literary, fictive text and its rapport with the real world. (Witness, for example, the informative digression in the *KRQ* essay on patronyms in the *Joufroi* and their scarcely cloaked allusions to historical personages [331-33].) More substantive signs of nascent, wider interests begin to appear, however, with the *Romance Philology* essay on the comparative narrators of the *Partonopeu de Blois, Le Bel Inconnu,* and *Joufroi de Poitiers* brought out in 1968.

The date is obviously significant for all sorts of reasons, not the least of which is the fact that at this point *Communications 8* had been in circulation for two years and that the Hopkins conference on structuralism was still the subject of the most intense enthusiasm, debate, argument, suspicion, and indeed openly vitriolic hostility.[6] The pseudo-science of narratology as Todorov and company would soon thereafter conceive of it did not yet fully exist as a methodological underpinning for the study of literature, and yet presciently Professor Grigsby had stumbled—surely he would bring up the issue of serendipity here—upon a vast domain of intellectual inquiry. The essay is pivotal, in my view, for its position in the Grigsby bibliography. At one and the same time, he was towards the end of the sixties and at the beginning of the seventies straddling two scholarly worlds: one the stable, certain environment of textual editing and medieval literary history, and the other a new and totally uncharted arena of different vistas and of different goals for literary criticism. The juxtaposition of the two worlds is everywhere evident during these years. He could pen a solidly grounded "Defense and Four Illustrations of Textual Criticism" in May of 1967 for the same *Romance Philology* that would, but one year later, publish his piece on the narrator's role in the *Partonopeu de Blois, Le Bel Inconnu,* and *Joufroi de Poitiers.* That he never lost his admiration for, and sincere interest in, the traditions of medieval textual criticism is resolutely borne out by his beautifully honed review article ("Editing Medieval French Texts") to be found in the 1981 special issue of *Romance Philology* and by the fact that among the papers left at his untimely death is a draft of an edition of the *Voeux du Héron.* The more traditionalist side of his critical nature appears prominently in the thematic pieces that he wrote throughout his career, beginning with the "Goddess Fortuna" essay in 1962 and continuing through "Courtesy in *Les Voeux du Paon,*" in 1985 and "The Relics' Role in *Le Voyage de Charlemagne,*" written for a 1981 number of *Olifant* but which did not appear until 1985.

A glimpse of what had transpired in Professor Grigsby's own approach to things literary, and of what was indeed occurring in the world of literary criticism at large, can be adroitly perceived by comparing three of his pieces on the subject of the narrator. The 1968 essay to which we made reference above remained in what we might label the "Wayne Booth" model of narratological inquiry. The short contribution to the *Year Book of the American Philosophical Society* for 1973 already shows a decidedly marked difference, and his 1979 essay entitled "Narrative Voices in Chrétien de Troyes: A Prolegomenon to Dissection" demonstrates without a doubt that he has fully digested the theoretical works of Todorov, Genette, Bremond, Jakobson, Scholes, and Kellogg, and that he has become well versed in the applications of the various narratological theoreticians to be found in the works of Marcel Mueller, Susan Suleiman, and others. Discarding what he believed to be remnants of chaff in some of Genette's terminological neologisms, he advanced an ingenious system of dividing narratological "intrusions" (his term) into twelve categories: announcements, exclamations, exhortations (to include imperatives and vocatives), formulaic expressions, opinions, protestations of insufficiency, claims of insufficiency, assertions of fidelity to truth, reminders, refusals, rhetorical questions, and allusions or attributions to source (267-72). His "control romances" are, significantly enough, those three which had served him several years earlier as base texts for the 1968 *Romance Philology* article on the narrator: *Partonopeu de Blois, Le Bel Inconnu,* and *Joufroi de Poitiers.* Reading the 1968 article from the viewpoint of the 1979 essay with its incomparably broader theoretical base shows the radical distinction that can be discerned in the two critical voices and one of which Professor Grigsby was himself more than just casually aware.

Towards the end of the 1979 essay, he promises to return to the problem of the ontology of the narrator in medieval romances, and this he does, true to his word, two years later in a special number of the French Forum Monographs entitled *The Nature of Medieval Narrative.* Each of his many admirers undoubtedly has a favorite piece. I shall state here, quite unabashedly, that "The Ontology of the Narrator in Medieval French Romance" would be my choice for place of pride among the article-length publications that came forth from Mr. Grigsby's many-faceted interests. As Auerbach taught that literary commentary should ideally do, the subject here sweeps far beyond those always artificial constructs like nationality, chronology, themes, or whatever, that we impose upon literature in order to speak about it. Mr. Grigsby's ideas on the nature of the ontological *situs* of the medieval romance narrator touch upon Stendhal, Homer, José Martí, Proust, Croce, Paz, the Canadian poet Jacques Brault, Julien Gracq, the various theories of Curtius, the latter's acerbic opponent Alberto Vàrvaro, Foucault, Spitzer, and Zumthor. The narrator is conceived of as a "fragmentable being, in imitation of his creator," and "surgery on the text to uncover manifestations of the narrator is always justifiable" (169). And, in another of these insights that always kept Professor Grigsby on the forefront of his profession, his concluding words presage most aptly the Reception Theory that has come to mark so decisively the last few years of the eighties:

> Because the narrative components derive from multiple sources, because they may represent or misrepresent the author, because they may function on several levels, *every analyst will surely discover diverse accents*

> *in each voice he examines and each analyst's interpretation will*
> *undoubtedly reflect the succession of beings which fragment his own*
> *life* (169, emphases ours).

It is telling indeed that, having completed the essay on the ontology of the narrator, he never again returned to the subject.

Alongside the narratological essays are also pieces cast within the frame of semiotics: first with "Sign, Symbol, and Metaphor: Todorov and Chrétien de Troyes" for *L'Esprit Créateur* in 1978 and then "L'Empire des signes chez Béroul et Thomas," brought out in a two-volume set of essays by distinguished medievalists published in honor of Charles Foulon in 1981. (Again, without insisting too much on this point, such sweeping activity on Professor Grigsby's part during these years evidences the new, ever-advancing role of theory in literary circles and the multiple possibilities of theory's application to medieval studies, which were not—to be sure— always receptive to the modern, and certainly different, trends of viewing and articulating discussions of literature.) Tzvetan Todorov's *Théories du symbole* had a profound effect upon much of what Professor Grigsby wrote and taught in the years immediately following the publication of this study in 1977, insofar as his nascent interest in semiotics was concerned.[7] In his survey of Todorov's book, and before he applied the latter's theories to Chrétien de Troyes's *œuvre,* he took Todorov to task for having completely swept past the medieval rhetoricians in the development of Todorov's analyses from the age of Quintilian to the plethora of eighteenth-century treatises on the subject. Naming especially Matthew of Vendome, Geoffroy of Vinsauf, and John of Garland, Professor Grigsby expressed some degree of righteous indignation, as he would later in his remarks on Gadamerian hermeneutics, that his beloved Middle Ages had been blithely ignored. Once he had made his point, however, he used Todorov's survey of the symbolic process to elucidate Chrétien's manipulations of signs, symbols, and metaphors. By the time Professor Grigsby undertook the second of the two semiological essays (actually written in 1979 and early 1980 although not published until the following year), that on Béroul and Thomas, Todorov had published the second volume of his study, this tome entitled *Symbolisme et interprétation* (1978), and our critic dissected with stunning clarity the multiple facets of the sign system at work in the Tristan legend by a provocative, and always rigorous, handling of the theoretical construct being applied.[8]

Three other articles may be logically grouped together for our purposes here in this bibliographical essay on the works of John Lambert Grigsby before we reach the *matière* of his final years: the Perceval piece referred to at the outset ("Perceval devant l'herméneutique et la grammatologie"), "Le Conflit des théories: Eagleton devant la critique de la littérature médiévale," and "Gadamer's Hermeneutics and Medieval French Literature (With an Excursus on *Les Voeux du Paon*)." Three figures tend to replace Todorov *et al.* in these two essays: Derrida, Gadamer, and Eagleton. Odd bedfellows, these, but they do share one trait that links them, in addition to their stance at the center of current debates about literary theory, and that is the perplexing, and unavoidable, question of how post-modernist theory (a term I employ—*faute de mieux*—despite the dangers with which its use is fraught) can elucidate and illuminate a medieval text. Mr. Grigsby's late research was, in effect, dominated by this last issue, as if he had indeed become transfixed, if not obsessed, with the application of critical methodologies, still themselves in relatively nascent states, to medieval literature. The sweeping titles he ascribed to these articles betoken his thrust: "Gadamer's Hermeneutics *and Medieval French Literature. . . ,*" ". . . Eagleton *devant la critique de la littérature médiévale. . . .*" His observations in these forums reached far beyond Chrétien de Troyes, Arthur, and all the rest and dealt more generally with the confrontation of medieval literature and post-modernist critical theory. Here without hesitation, among those of his scholarly generation, he was an exceptional example of breadth and scope of enterprise.

The springboard for the Perceval essay was Jean Greisch's 1977 *Herméneutique et grammatologie,* a not always successful and unfortunately often pedantic and ponderous early attempt to juxtapose the world vistas of Jacques Derrida with those of Hans-Georg Gadamer. Readily acknowledging the decided weaknesses of Greisch, our critic pursued his goal of comparing the two "systems" of thought by sketching differences and similarities in five areas (conceptions of the past, conceptions of writing, the status of the text, the role of the author, and finally, the role played by meaning), while employing the Perceval legend in its various transformations as the working, textual basis upon which the theories are to be applied. The pages of the Perceval essay are so convincing that they could easily be used by neophytes seeking a brisk, thumbnail sketch of modern hermeneutics and Derridean grammatology, as well as by budding medievalists pondering whether modern methodological systems can pertain to the vast literature that stretches from the fall of Rome to the beginning of the Renaissance.

The same theoretical juxtapositioning of hermeneutics and grammatology inaugurates the article on Gadamer. Then, as an example of how Gadamer's corpus might be easily assimilated, Mr. Grigsby ingeniously used—in order to prove one of the major principles of hermeneutics—the history of the term "moyen âge" from the Neo-Latinate periphrases of *media tempestas, media aetas, media antiquas, medium saeculum,* and *media tempora* through the neologism's first actual appearance in 1640. We follow the term through the successive ages, until we reach those echoes to be perceived in the late twentieth century in *Excalibur, Star Wars, The Natural,* etc. Then, pulling upon Gadamer for support, our critic takes on the prejudices against the *Middle* Ages by reminding us that essential to hermeneutics is the notion that we must treat our prejudices especially with due respect, for the prejudices themselves tell us more about ourselves than we might wish to know (the "conditions of understanding" principle). The "fusion of horizons" therefore functions as an exemplum when applied to the *Voeux du Paon,* for in this case are co-mingled the Northern rituals of boasting, pagan antiquity, the epic, themes and characters from the Alexander romances, and chivalry. And in a final *tour de force,* Professor Grigsby argued that by seeing the *Voeux du Paon* as suggested, we might begin to realize the integration of our own horizons. Should we not, he asks rhetorically (123), simply abolish those terms like "medieval," "moyen âge," "Middle Ages," etc., which literally drip indictment? Should we not then propose that the old, worn-out by cliché, "Grand Modèle" of the French canon of literature from the sixteenth to the eighteenth centuries be relabeled the "Middle Ages," recasting the nineteenth century as "la Renaissance," while assigning the former "Middle Ages" to a more fitting category, "the Age of the Rose," taking the lead from Eco? To end his article, Professor Grigsby proffers one final comparison: Ordericus Vitalis, who in 1143 reminded his readers of the value of writing so that the deeds of the ancients would not pass into oblivion, and Geoffrey Hartman, who in 1980 urged us to recover "forgotten voices, arguments, and artifacts" (p. 123). Only someone who understood the true, intrinsic possibility of fusing horizons, who understood the worlds of both Ordericus Vitalis and Geoffrey Hartman, could have imagined the comparison.

A fervent disciple of Walter Benjamin, the Eagleton of the third article in this trilogy uniting post-modernist theory and medieval literature is one whose contribution is recognized but whose current popularity is somewhat disturbing. Eagleton's *Literary Theory* is somehow too facile; the chapters too simplistically laid out for us; the assertions too limiting (doctoral students should write only on truly major figures, literary criticism should always be politically swayed, etc.). Our critic's greatest fear concerning the application of Eagleton's ideologically grounded criticism is that, were one to push Marxist analysis to its most extreme consequences, no one would ever have need to study medieval literature, and this conclusion brought Professor Grigsby to several pages of ruminations on what it is to be a critic of medieval literature at the end of the twentieth century, a subtext which runs throughout this trilogy of articles. Who, he asks in retort to Eagleton, would then choose to work on Renaut de Beaujeu or Geoffroi de Vinsauf (p. 416)? Must one be a certifiable schizophrenic to wish to write on figures such as these rather than on Sartre, Derrida, or whomever? Literary critics, Mr. Grigsby concludes, cannot be slaves to a theory which does not itself allow an unbounded freedom within which the mind can play (*ibid.*). He ends borrowing from Gadamer, for whom he now has more than a little affection.

All of which brings us, over the twenty-five years from the *Liber fortunae* in 1959 to Eagleton in 1984, directly to the *gab*. One might be easily tempted to apply to the Grigsby bibliography that sort of evolutionist enthusiasm espoused by Brunetière and company almost a century ago at the Sorbonne. The first works were preparatory and traditional. The intervening ones more innovative, expansive, and creative. The final ones majestic and towering, except here the Brunetiérian evolutionism would abruptly stop, for Brunetière and his colleagues were none too well disposed to the Middle Ages, which Professor Grigsby obviously loved and which he sought to defend from disdain and from neglect. His interest in the *gab* dates—at least formally—from the 1982 essay "A Note on the Genre of the *Voyage de Charlemagne*," extends through the 1983 *Marche Romane* article "*Gab* épique, mais *gab* lyrique?" and through the 1985 "*Gab* dans le roman arthurien français," culminating in the thick, book-length manuscript which he completed in the late summer of 1987 and to which he added a few final footnotes only three weeks before his death in February of 1988. The first piece sets the context for the ensuing argument (pp. 1-3). We simply do not have a sufficient label to pin upon the *Voyage de Charlemagne*. In fact, as opposed to the inherently useful and concise *Karlsreise,* we cannot even come to a consensus about what title to give to this *récit* of

Charlemagne's *gabs* (*Chanson du Pèlerinage, Chanson du Pèlerinage en Orient,* the longer titles that add "à Jérusalem et à Constantinople," etc.). Our essential difficulty is that the work is of indeterminate genre. No one knows where to put it, so to speak. These thoughts lead our critic to a discussion of genres in general. Do genres exist? If they do, who creates them? Why should we study literature under generic headings? The replies to these questions from contemporary theorists he finds troubling and for the most part discouraging (pp. 2-3). And then, after developing the theme in this particular poem, finally he solves his own riddles by returning to the beginning of the article and by stating that the solution to the *Voyage* is that the poem created its own genre, which was that of the *gab*. The 1982 article was written almost concomitantly with the "*Gab* épique. . . ." piece which, for various reasons, did not appear until late in 1986. In this second study, Professor Grigsby was much more expansive, offering his readers a far more detailed inquiry into how the *gab* functions in the *Voyage de Charlemagne* and suggesting (see esp. pp. 117-18) that this leitmotif defines an important element hitherto unrecognized as a latent genre in precursor texts such as *Beowulf* and the *Heimskringla* and successor works such as the *Voeux du Paon,* the *Voeux du Héron,* and the *Voeux de l'Epervier.* This notion he then later sketched within the context of the Arthurian romances in the paper he published in the proceedings of the fourteenth meeting of the International Arthurian Society held at Rennes. These pieces point to what will surely be acknowledged as the *magnum opus* of Professor Grigsby's career: a vast, sweeping study of the *gab* in medieval literature. And, furthermore, evolutionist or not, we may safely conclude that the various voices that made up the patronym Grigsby will all be found: the traditional textual critic is here present in a study of the *Voeux du Héron* (a critical edition of which he prepared at the same time); the modernist critic is here present in the discussions of orality where he borrows heavily from Derrida and Father Ong and in his reliance upon Gadamer for support on all sides. The admirer of Curtius can be perceived alongside the admirer of Dilthey.

     And throughout the entire bibliography can be witnessed that admixture of tremendous dedication to the task at hand and of equally tremendous love for the *matière* chosen, that rare, inspiring combination to which *res severa, res gaudia* refers. The admixture for which the medieval expression was aptly coined is one that Professor Grigsby's career perfectly embodied.

Notes

[1]John L. Grigsby, "Perceval devant l'herméneutique et la grammatologie," *L'Esprit Créateur*, 22, No. 1 (1983), 36-37. All subsequent references are to Professor Grigsby's works, unless otherwise noted, and will be included parenthetically in abbreviated form; the reader is referred to the list of his published titles found at the beginning of this volume.

[2]When confronted by an anxious graduate student seeking a doctoral dissertation subject many years later, Mr. Grigsby used to relate his own experience as an example. He related it, however, with a purely Grigsbian twist, telling the student first to find the etymology of "serendipity" and then to search in the Bible for the verse "Seek and Ye shall find." Unless the student came back to his office with a full explanation of Horace Walpole's neologism and its rapport with the biblical line, the individual was promptly dispatched again to the library to continue the inquiry.

[3]In 1979 a Kraus Reprint of the 1903 edition originally published by J. H. Ed. Heitz in Strasbourg appeared in *Studien zur deutschen Kunstgeschichte*, volume 44, thanks to Rudolf Kautzsch.

[4]See Walter O. Streng-Renkonen, *Joufroi, roman français du XIIIe siècle* (Turku: Annales Universitatis Aboensis, 1930). Exactly as had Fay and Livingston, Streng-Renkonen had taken his lead from negative comments expressed by the eminent Charles-Victor Langlois [*La Vie en France au moyen âge, de la fin du XIIe au milieu du XIVe siècle. I, La Société française au XIIIe siècle d'après dix romans d'aventure* (Paris: Hachette, 1924)] of the earlier Hofmann-Muncker edition [*Joufroi, altfranzösisches Rittergedicht zum ersten Mal herausgegeben* von Konrad Hofmann und Franz Muncker (Halle: Niemeyer, 1880)]. See also Fay, review article in *Romania*, 58 (1932), 114-20. In an exceedingly rare slip, Mr. Grigsby once described bibliographically this review as pertaining to the Hofmann-Muncker edition when it in fact concerns the Streng-Renkonen 1930 publication. See the Fay-Grigsby *Joufroi de Poitiers*, p. 65.

[5]The earlier collaboration between Fay and Livingston had been at least for a while destined to be published by the "Classiques français du moyen âge" series (see Fay's *Romania* review, p. 120), so the 1972 edition, appearing as it did in the "Textes Littéraires Français," does fulfill in a way that which had been destined for the original effort.

[6]Tellingly, the review article in the *Romance Philology* issue that carried the piece on the narrators bore the title "Modernists Versus Traditionalists: A Confrontation in Continental Europe."

[7]The Grigsbys lived in Todorov's apartment during a long stint of research time in Paris, and, later, Professor Grigsby was wont to inform his graduate seminars with feigned unctuousness that he had become so enmeshed in Todorov's theories that he had had no choice but to make a solemn pilgrimage to the location of their creation.

[8]Worthy of some note is the fact that Umberto Eco's *A Theory of Semiotics* (1979) is characterized as "touffu" (115).

I. THE FRENCH ROMANCE

Le *Tristan* de Béroul en tant qu'intertexte

Keith Busby

Les fragments du *Tristan* de Béroul constituent l'une des plus belles énigmes de la littérature française médiévale. La difficulté qu'éprouve un lecteur moderne devant ce poème s'explique non seulement par l'état fragmentaire et corrompu du texte mais également, peut-être surtout, par la fluidité manifeste de ses affiliations génériques. L'ouvrage de Béroul est désigné comme *roman* par la critique moderne, bien qu'aucune appellation auto-référentielle ne se trouve dans le poème.[1] Il est certes difficile d'imaginer une autre dénomination, toujours est-il que si nous pouvions formuler une description des plus libérales qui soient de ce genre, fondée sur l'examen d'un corpus étendu, le *Tristan* n'y répondrait guère.[2] Si nous abordons ce texte avec des idées préconçues de ce que devrait être un roman courtois médiéval, celles-ci étant basées sur des données de l'époque, nous risquons, en premier lieu, de mal apprécier les intentions et les procédés du poète, et en second lieu de réagir tout autrement qu'un auditeur médiéval ne l'aurait fait.

L'histoire de Tristan et Iseut, avant sa véritable intégration dans le monde arthurien avec le *Tristan en prose,* diffère de la plupart de celles choisies par les romanciers du 12e siècle, surtout en ceci qu'elle ne consiste ni en véritables quêtes ni en un grand nombre d'aventures. Les protagonistes sont, par exemple, en général plus passifs que ceux de Chrétien de Troyes, et leurs actions semblent être contrôlées par le destin plutôt que par leur propre volonté.[3] Un lecteur qui aborde le *Tristan* de Béroul en s'attendant à un récit plein de péripéties sera quelque peu désorienté, et il est probable qu'il en était de même pour l'auditeur médiéval, habitué peut-être aux romans de Chrétien de Troyes et de ses contemporains. Nous ne pouvons pas attribuer à Béroul l'absence d'aventures ou de quêtes dans cette histoire, et la déception de ce que Hans Robert Jauss a appelé "l'horizon d'attente" est dans un certain sens fortuite.[4] Mais Béroul a, bien sûr, choisi sa propre matière et a choisi de présenter à son public une histoire d'amour qui différait sensiblement de la plupart des autres histoires qui circulaient à l'époque. Il aurait été possible, bien sûr, d'en faire un roman d'aventures, mais il ne me semble pas insignifiant qu'il nous faudra attendre le second quart du 13e siècle et le *Tristan en prose* avant que cela ne se réalise.

L'un des problèmes les plus graves ressortant de l'état fragmentaire du texte, c'est que nous ne connaissons l'auteur qu'à travers 4485 vv., tandis que les dimensions de l'œuvre de Chrétien de Troyes nous permettent de mieux cerner ses techniques et ses intentions.[5] Les prologues, les interventions d'auteur et de narrateur, où nous voyons le poète au travail, ne font pas défaut chez Chrétien, mais dans le cas de Béroul ils sont pratiquement absents.[6] Nous attribuons ainsi à juste titre au poète champenois un art dont le succès dépend non seulement de son propre talent mais aussi des connaissances de son public et par conséquent de leur réaction devant son texte, de leur réponse à ses intentions. Quand Chrétien écrit *Cligés,* pour ne citer qu'un seul exemple non sans importance ici, il sait que son public tirera des comparaisons avec l'histoire de Tristan et Iseut, et il les y invite même.[7] Nous hésitons, par contre, à attribuer à Béroul une telle intention, alors que rien ne nous autorise à penser qu'il diffère sensiblement de Chrétien à cet égard. Le manque d'interventions de ce genre en rend l'exemple unique plus précieux encore:

> Li contor dïent que Yvain
> Firent nïer, qui sont vilain;
> N'en sevent mie bien l'estoire,
> Berox l'a mex en sen memoire:
> Trop ert Tristran preuz et cortois
> A ocirre gent de tes lois.
>
> (vv. 1265-70)

Ce passage en effet n'est pas sans rappeler le début d'*Erec et Enide,* où un sentiment semblable exprime le topos rhétorique *ab adversariorum* de l'exorde cicéronien.[8] En ce qui concerne les romans de *Tristan,* on se rappellera également les vv. 835 et ss. du fragment Douce du poème de Thomas.[9] Ces vers de Béroul montrent en tout cas sa conscience artistique et son désir de faire autrement et mieux que ses concurrents.

Béroul renvoie constamment à la littérature de son époque et s'attend à ce que son public saisisse en écoutant le jeu littéraire intime qu'il mène avec eux. Il a remanié une histoire d'amour déjà bien connue à l'époque où il écrit, à en croire le témoignage onomastique des chartes,[10] mais ce qui prête à ce texte son caractère individuel et distinctif, c'est la façon dont il a fabriqué la texture de son poème par l'emploi d'éléments et de procédés propres à d'autres genres. Pierre Kunstmann a déjà, dans un article sur le *Tristan* de Thomas, donné une définition de la sorte d'intertextualité que j'envisage ici:

> L'accueil et la transformation par le texte centreur d'extraits ou d'échos
> de toute œuvre constituante de la tradition littéraire [...] dans la seconde
> moitié du douzième siècle.[11]

Paul Zumthor a pour sa part suggéré que nous pourrions avec profit considérer la production et la réception de la littérature médiévale comme un "encodage" par l'auteur menant au "décodage" par le public:

> Le texte du XIe, XIIe et XIIIe siècle, a été produit par une opération
> d'encodage, à partir d'éléments fournis par une situation personnelle et
> culturelle; mais ces éléments étaient polarisés par une certaine inten-
> tion, qui était, entre autres, pour les auditeurs ou lecteurs d'alors,
> destinée à orienter le décodage.[12]

Dans ce qui suit, je me propose d'examiner le *Tristan* de Béroul dans ses aspects intertextuels dans un essai de reconstruction de ces procédés d'encodage et de décodage, tout en admettant que cette reconstruction sera nécessairement imparfaite.

I

Si l'amour adultère se prête ailleurs à un traitement plus roma-nesque—n'oublions pas les parallèles remarquables entre l'histoire de Tristan et celle de Lancelot—Béroul nous le présente ici, malgré le cadre d'un poème narratif, comme essentiellement lyrique.[13] Il n'est pas sans intérêt de noter que les allusions à Tristan et Iseut dans la lyrique des trou-badours et des trouvères sont beaucoup plus nombreuses que celles se rapportant à d'autres couples d'amants célèbres.[14] Là où Lancelot passe le roman entier dans un état de rêve, l'intensité de la passion de Tristan et d'Iseut ne se laisse voir chez Béroul qu'à travers des moments d'effusion lyrique. Le vocabulaire est de temps en temps celui de la lyrique et l'on notera, entre autres, les différents qualificatifs de l'amour: "fol'amor" (301, 496), "amor vilaine" (502), "bone amor" (1365, 2416), et surtout "fine amor" (2722). Roger Dubuis a analysé l'emploi fréquent chez Béroul des mots "dru(e)" et "druerie," dont le réseau sémantique s'étend sur de nombreuses variantes du grand chant courtois.[15] Les éléments courtois du vocabulaire de Béroul ancrent le poème en effet dans une tradition lyrique en train de faire son entrée dans le roman.[16]

Le lyrisme de Béroul, qui n'aurait nullement étonné son public, se révèle aussi dans des exclamations et des plaintes amoureuses telles que: " 'Ahi! Yseut, fille de roi' " (101), " 'Ha! las, dolent, et moi que chaut?' " (981), " 'Lasse, dolente' " (2201), " 'Dex!' dist Tristran, 'quel departie! / Molt est dolenz qui pert s'amie' " (2681-82), etc., pour ne pas parler de tous les appels à Dieu et à sa merci qui ponctuent certaines parties du texte. Il y a également certaines phrases qui fonctionnent comme des refrains lyriques et qui reviennent à plusieurs reprises au cours du récit, le plus souvent lors de ces moments que j'ai qualifiés d'effusion lyrique. Les plus remarquables sont probablement constituées par les apostrophes de Tristan à Iseut: " 'Ahi! Yseut, fille de roi, / Franche, cortoise, bone foi!' " (101-02); " 'Roïne gent' " (2221), " 'Roïne franche' " (2249), " 'Roïne de parage' " (2279), " 'Roïne franche, debonere' " (3914), " 'Avoi!' fait il, 'roïne franche' " (3920). D'autres passages montrent le lyrisme incontestable de Béroul; les vv. 1777-78, par exemple, auraient pu former le début d'une reverdie: "Par un matin, a la rousee, / Li oisel chantent l'ainzjournee."[17] D'autre part, le jardin, lieu de rencontre des amants et où ils sont aperçus par les félons (581 et ss.), est un *locus* du grand chant courtois.

A un autre niveau, les personnages jouent des rôles déjà établis dans la lyrique: le couple et le triangle amoureux, les losengiers. Le poème entier, en effet, ressemble dans ce sens à une aube qui a subi une transposition de modalités, de lyrique en narrative, avec la réalisation concomitante au cours du récit de la virtualité inhérente de la lyrique.[18] Tristan et Iseut, comme les amants de l'aube, profitent de quelques rares moments d'amour idyllique, mais dont la fragilité se fait ressentir par la même menace constante de trahison par leurs ennemis. La dénonciation de leur amour par ces félons et la découverte par le roi Marc correspondent dans cette transposition narrative à la méchanceté des losengiers, à l'aube révélatrice, et à la découverte par les parents ou par le jaloux dans la lyrique. L'effet lyrique se trouve également renforcé par l'emploi régulier de phrases similaires par lesquelles sont désignés les opposants: "li felon de cest' enor" (26, 44), "li felon, li losengier" (427), "li felon losengeor" (1056), "li troi felon" (613, 4466), ou tout simplement "felons" (582).[19]

II

Si le rôle et la présentation des trois barons méchants prêtent d'un côté une résonance lyrique au poème, ils apportent de l'autre un écho intertextuel épique. Le traître en tant que personnage n'est pas propre à l'épopée, mais joue par contre un rôle assez important dans bon nombre de romans courtois. Le traître de l'épopée se distingue cependant assez nettement de celui du roman par sa provenance: dans la littérature héroïque il appartient normalement à la maison qu'il trahit tandis que dans le roman il est un étranger qui fait irruption dans la cour tout en trahissant les valeurs morales et éthiques de la société en général.[20] Le choix du nom Guenelon (3138, 3462, 3475, 4238), sans aucun doute le plus célèbre de tous les traîtres de la littérature française médiévale, pour l'un des trois félons, confirme les rapports avec l'épopée. Qu'il ne s'agit pas ici d'une coïncidence, mais bel et bien d'un renvoi de Béroul à la chanson de geste, est démontré par l'allusion au roi Otran, personnage sarrasin du cycle de Guillaume d'Orange (1406).[21]

En effet, l'intertextualité du *Tristan* de Béroul et de la chanson de geste est exceptionellement riche et subtile. L'esprit féodal visible dans les rapports entre les traîtres et les autres personnages s'articule souvent dans le texte, situant ainsi cette histoire d'amour dans un monde semblable à celui de l'épopée.[22] Citons à titre d'exemple les paroles de Marc adressées à ses hommes après avoir reçu la lettre de Tristan:

> "Seignors, un brief m'est ci tramis.
> Rois sui sor vos, vos mi marchis.
> Li briés soit liez et soit oïz;
> Et qant liz sera li escriz,
> Conseilliez m'en, jel vos requier;
> Vos m'en devez bien consellier."
> (vv. 2525-30)

Dans le sens inverse, les trois méchants barons justifient leur rancune ouverte envers les amants par les obligations du devoir féodal (3109 et ss.). L'attention consacrée à l'aspect légal du jugement d'Iseut et du comportement des personnages en général a été souvent remarquée par la critique et trahit la même vision du monde.[23] Ceci ne veut pas dire que le monde du roman courtois n'est pas un monde féodal. Au contraire, Köhler a montré l'importance des rapports entre seigneur et vassal pour la société arthurienne, mais la formalité et les obligations interpersonnelles s'y trouvent voilées derrière la fable tandis qu'elles constituent l'un des mobiles les plus évidents de la chanson de geste.[24]

Les combats singuliers abondent dans le roman courtois aussi bien que dans la chanson de geste, mais les variétés se distinguent d'abord par la perspective dans laquelle ils sont décrits (celui de l'épopée fait le plus souvent partie d'une lutte collective) puis par le style.[25] C'est cette deuxième caractéristique qui marque plusieurs passages du *Tristan* de Béroul comme appartenant à la tradition épique. Bien qu'il s'agisse de guet-apens plutôt que de véritables combats, le meurtre d'un des félons par les mains de Governal et celui de Denoalan par les mains de Tristan sont remarquables par leur sauvagerie quasi-épique:

> Governal saut de sen agait:
> Du mal que cil ot fait li menbre,
> A s'espee tot le desmenbre,
> Li chief en prent, atot s'en vet.
> > (vv. 1708-11)

> Sa mort queroit; cil s'en garda,
> Que le chief du bu li sevra.
> Ne li lut dire: 'Tu me bleces.'
> O l'espee trencha les treces,
> En sa chauce les a boutees.
> > (vv. 4387-91)

Même hors du contexte immédiat d'un combat, le sentiment épique apparaît, notamment dans les paroles de Girflet déclarant ses intentions vis-à-vis des trois félons:

"Ja ne me tienge Dex en sens,
Se vois encontre Goudoïne,
Se de ma grant lance fresnine
Ne pasent outre li coutel,
Ja n'en enbraz soz le mantel
Bele dame desoz cortine."
(vv. 3476-81)

Ajoutons à ces exemples Governal qui montre avec ostentation la tête de l'un des félons à Tristan (1735-46), et Tristan qui rapporte les tresses de Denoalan à Iseut tandis que Godoïne se cache derrière le rideau (4410 et ss.), deux scènes d' "épouvante épique."

Si Béroul a su donner une teneur épique à ses épisodes, le cas de la libération d'Iseut abandonnée par Marc aux lépreux est plus intéressant encore, puisqu'on peut y voir une parodie du combat épique.[26] Tout est là: le défi arrogant, la réponse, le sang, même le commentaire du narrateur, mais nous sommes les témoins d'un combat entre chevaliers et lépreux, non pas entre chrétiens et sarrasins, et les armes sont des béquilles et des bâtons de chêne et non des lances et des épées:

A qant qu'il puet s'escrie en haut:
'Ivain, asez l'avez menee;
Laisiez la tost, qu'a cest' espee
Ne vos face le chief voler.
Ivain s'aqeut a desfubler,
En haut s'escrie: 'Or as puioz!
Or i parra qui ert des noz.'
Qui ces meseaus veïst soffler,
Oster chapes et desfubler!
Chascun li crolle sa potence,
Li uns menace et l'autre tence.
Tristran n'en vost rien atochier
Ne entester ne laidengier.
Governal est venuz au cri,
En sa main tint un vert jarri
Et fiert Yvain, qui Yseut tient;
Li sans li chiet, au pié li vie[n]t.
(vv. 1246-62)

Vàrvaro a déjà suggéré que Béroul s'approche de temps en temps de la technique épique des *laisses similaires,* et qu'en général il emploie plusieurs formes de répétition.[27] Les observations de l'érudit italien soulignent mes propres remarques au sujet des refrains "lyriques" dans le poème et ajoutent en même temps une nouvelle dimension aux rapports entre ce texte et la tradition épique. Les deux exemples les plus frappants sont certainement ceux cités par Vàrvaro, c'est-à-dire la tentative des trois méchants barons d'apaiser Marc après leur demande d'un *escondit* (3101 et ss.) et la lecture de la lettre d'Ogrin devant Marc d'abord et ensuite devant le conseil des barons (2510 et ss.). Notons aussi les vv. 295-97 et 315-17, où le même sentiment est exprimé d'abord par le narrateur puis par Iseut, et les vv. 2167 et ss. et 2201 et ss., où Tristan et Iseut se lamentent l'un après l'autre au sujet de leur séparation de la vie de cour. En plus, l'emploi régulier de petites phrases, trop nombreuses à citer ici, dont les éléments syntaxiques varient légèrement (temps du verbe, ordre des mots, etc.), ressemble beaucoup aux procédés formulaïques qui constituent un aspect important de l'art épique.[28]

Mais l'affiliation du *Tristan* et de l'épopée se laisse le plus facilement voir dans les interventions d'auteur ou de narrateur. Tandis que le narrateur d'un roman courtois offre un commentaire sur son propre récit et indique indirectement des possibilités d'interprétation, celui de la chanson de geste montre une solidarité ouverte avec son public et ses personnages. Ces dispositions narratives ont été décrites ainsi par Hans Robert Jauss:

> E (Epos): Epische Formeln wie Wahrheitsbeteuerung, Teilnahme am Geschick des Helden, epischer Vorgriff stellen emotionale Einheit von Jongleur und Publikum her.

> R (Roman): Einschaltungen des Erzählers (signes du narrateur) dienen der Auslegung der Fabel (*matière et sens* treten auseinander).[29]

Le poème de Béroul contient de nombreux exemples de cette technique narrative. Le rapport intime entre le narrateur et son public s'établit en premier lieu par l'emploi fréquent des mots ou des phrases comme "Oez, seignors" (909), "Seignor" (948, 1065, 1303, 1637, 2765), "Seignors, molt avez bien oï" (1351), "Oez, seignors, quel aventure" (1835, 4351), "Seignors, du vin de qoi il burent / Avez oï, por qoi il furent / En si grant

paine lonctens mis; / Mais ne savez, ce m'est avis. . ." (2133-36),
"Seignors, oiez de la roïne" (2319). Ces apostrophes adressées au public et
l'emploi fréquent du verbe à la seconde personne du pluriel pour indiquer
les auditeurs constituent bien plus qu'une simple *captatio benevolentiae* pour
attirer leur attention. Comme l'a bien vu Vàrvaro,[30] et comme l'a décrit
Jauss pour l'épopée, il s'agit en effet des moments d'une empathie profonde
du narrateur et son public.

La solidarité du narrateur avec ses personnages s'effectue surtout
par la présentation de chaque événement et ses conséquences du point de
vue des protagonistes. Le commentaire sur les méchants barons est essentiellement le commentaire de Tristan et Iseut: "Un de ces trois que Dex
maudie" (1656), "Li troi felon, qui mal feu arde" (3788), etc. Les expressions de sympathie contribuent à ce même effet de solidarité: "Dex! quel
pechié! trop ert hardiz!" (700), "Ha! Dex, po[r]qoi ne les ocist? / A mellor
plait asez venist" (825-26), "Ses oceïst, ce fust grant deus" (1991-94), etc.
Mais ce sentiment de solidarité va plus loin encore, parce que la voix de
Béroul semble être la voix du peuple:

> Pleurent li grant et li petit,
> Sovent l'un d'eus a l'autre dit:
> "A! las, tant avon a plorer!
> Ahi! Tristran, tant par es ber! . . .
> Ha! roïne franche, honoree. . .
> Ha! nains, ç'a fait ta devinalle?"
> (vv. 831-34, 837, 840)[31]

Ce passage est suivi d'une autre intervention du narrateur qui élargit le
cercle de sympathisants pour y inclure Dieu lui-même:

> Oez, seignors, de Damledé,
> Conment il est plains de pité;
> Ne vieat pas mort de pecheor:
> Receü out le cri, le plor
> Que faisoient la povre gent
> Por ceus qui eirent a torment.
> (vv. 909-14)

Voilà donc réunis le narrateur, le public, Dieu, le peuple et Tristan et Iseut. En face se trouvent les trois "felons losengiers," et quelque part entre eux, le roi Marc.[32]

III

　　Le fabliau semble avoir connu sa plus large diffusion aux 13e et 14e siècles, mais il est probable que des "contes à rire en vers" existaient déjà à l'époque de Béroul. Exception faite des fabliaux d'auteurs connus (comme Jean Bodel, par exemple), il y a très peu d'indications qui permettent une datation positive des poèmes individuels. La date des manuscrits ne pose pas un problème sérieux puisque la plupart des œuvres du 12e siècle nous sont parvenues dans des copies des 13e et 14e siècles.[33] Il y a en tout cas suffisamment d'évidence de nature générale pour soutenir l'hypothèse de la circulation des fabliaux bien avant l'époque des manuscrits. Le cas déjà cité de Jean Bodel, dont l'adieu au monde, le *Congé,* date de 1202, n'est pas sans signification, et suffirait en lui-même à montrer qu'un poète respectable s'était accaparé vers la fin du 12e siècle de ce genre déjà existant.[34] Si nous ajoutons à cela la date proposée par Nykrog pour le fabliau de *La Plantez* (extrême fin du 12e siècle) et le témoignage de la seconde branche du *Roman de Renart,* où il est question de *fabliaus* dans un texte datant des environs de 1176, rien ne nous empêche de regarder le fabliau comme appartenant au corpus de littérature française qu'aurait connu Béroul, écrivant de toute probabilité pendant la dernière décennie du 12e siècle.[35] Il n'est pas dans mon intention de démontrer ici l'influence de fabliaux spécifiques sur le *Tristan* de Béroul, seulement de suggérer que plusieurs éléments du poème auraient pu rappeler chez un auditeur de la fin du 12e siècle le genre fabliau.

　　Au niveau le plus simple, plusieurs vocables dans le *Tristan* appartiennent plutôt au fabliau qu'à d'autres sortes de poème. La remarque d'Iseut qui vient de tromper le roi Marc vers le début du fragment, par exemple, serait également à sa place dans un fabliau: " 'Partie me sui du tripot' " (369). Iseut reproche au roi d'avoir soupçonné qu'elle aime Tristan " 'Par puterie et par anjen' " (408), et au cours de son *escondit* elle emploie la phrase peu courtoise " 'entre mes cuises' " (4205), reprise quelques vers plus tard par les témoins (4227).[36] Dans un article récent, Barbara Nelson Sargent-Baur cite plusieurs passages du poème (par exemple, les vv.

3962-80) où le détail réaliste, "this concern for the trivia of everyday life," incongrument mis dans la bouche d'Iseut, évoque également le fabliau.[37] Dans bon nombre de ces endroits où l'auditeur médiéval aurait ressenti la proximité du monde du fabliau, il s'agit directement d'une tromperie, d'une ruse, élément narratif autour duquel sont construits beaucoup de fabliaux.[38] La même chose vaut pour le commentaire du narrateur sur Brangien qui, elle aussi, vient de tromper le roi:

> Oiez que dit la tricherresse!
> Molt fist que bone lecherresse:
> Lores gaboit a esscïent
> Et se plaignoit de maltalent.
>   (vv. 519-22)

Point n'est besoin d'insister sur l'importance de la tromperie dans le récit de Béroul, et la critique a longuement discuté à ce sujet, surtout par rapport à la moralité des personnages. Presque toute histoire d'amour adultère, bien sûr, montre le mari trompé par les amants, mais l'accent mis sur la ruse dans le poème de Béroul est exceptionnel et fournit au récit une série de moments décisifs. Le fragment s'ouvre sur la scène célèbre du rendez-vous épié, le roi Marc caché dans l'arbre, témoin de la réunion des deux amants qui, avisés de sa présence, réussissent à le convaincre de leur innocence. Barbara Nelson Sargent-Baur a souligné que les rapports entre presque tous les personnages sont marquées par un égoïsme profond et par un désir de manipuler autrui qui est caractéristique de la moralité du fabliau.[39] On peut voir ici une situation typique du fabliau transférée à un tout autre contexte et modifiée pour mieux servir aux besoins du nouveau récit. Parmi les fabliaux qui tournent autour de cette sorte de tromperie, citons seulement à titre d'exemple ceux du *Vilain de Bailluel* de Jean Bodel, et du *Preste qui abevete* de Garin, dans lesquels un vilain est témoin de l'adultère de sa femme avec le prêtre.[40] L'allusion à l'histoire du nain Segoçon, châtré par l'Empereur Constantin pour avoir commis l'adultère avec sa femme, convient au contexte immédiat non seulement par un étrange quasi-parallélisme avec le triangle Tristan-Iseut-Marc (plus Frocin) mais aussi par ses rapports avec le fabliau, dont elle aurait pu très bien former un sujet.[41] Même pendant l'épisode sérieux où Tristan est pris en flagrant délit avec la reine, Béroul ajoute le détail du ronflement simulé par Tristan de sorte qu'il évoque chez son public la proximité du fabliau.

Avant de quitter les rapports intertextuels entre le *Tristan* de Béroul et le fabliau, il faut noter deux autres épisodes où les deux genres semblent se frôler. Quand Tristan porte la lettre au roi Marc à Lancien (2449 et ss.), il le fait subrepticement la nuit, et se présente devant la fenêtre de la chambre où dort le roi. Or, la nuit est dans le roman courtois le temps des rendez-vous amoureux tandis que dans le fabliau elle se prête à toutes sortes d'activités illégales, surtout au larcin. Dans ce sens-là, l'expédition nocturne de Tristan rappelle le fabliau plutôt qu'un autre genre.[42] Béroul laisse entrevoir de temps à autre un certain humour assez macabre qui appartient d'une part à la chanson de geste (comme nous l'avons déjà vu) et d'autre part au fabliau. Ce goût du macabre transforme parfois un motif qui aurait pu appartenir au fabliau. L'exemple le plus frappant est sans doute celui d'Iseut livrée aux lépreux, dont elle sera désormais la maîtresse commune. Le sort d'Iseut, tel que l'esquisse Ivain, est épouvantable:

"Veez, j'ai ci compaigno[n]s cent;
Yseut nos done, s'ert conmune;
Paior fin dame n'ot mais une.
Sire, en nos a si grant ardor
Soz ciel n'a dame qui un jor
Peüst soufrir nostre convers;
Li drap nos sont au cors aers. . .
                    (vv. 1192-98)

Dans le fabliau *D'une seule Fame qui a son con servoit .c. chevaliers de tous poins,* une femme se trouve obligée de devenir la maîtresse de cent chevaliers après avoir trahi une amie.[43] Là aussi, ce sort est présenté comme une punition. Je ne veux nullement suggérer qu'il y a un lien direct entre ces deux textes, mais plutôt démontrer que ce motif se prêtait en effet à l'emploi dans le fabliau aussi bien que dans le poème de Béroul; l'effet d'incongruïté qu'il produit dans le *Tristan* peut très bien s'expliquer du fait qu'il "convient mieux" au fabliau qu'à un roman d'amour.

IV

En fin de compte, cependant, le poème de Béroul se rapproche le plus du roman que de n'importe quel autre genre médiéval. Le seul fait d'être un long poème narratif d'amour situé dans un milieu courtois assure une affiliation fondamentale au roman. Cela étant dit, il faut signaler que les rapports du texte avec la lyrique, l'épopée, le fabliau et le roman ne sont pas continus et qu'ils varient au cours du récit. C'est certes dans la seconde partie du fragment, et surtout vers la fin, que les aspects romanesques deviennent au fur et à mesure plus évidents. Il y a d'abord une coloration arthurienne, visible pour la première fois aux vv. 649 et ss. dans les conseils de Frocin au roi; le monde arthurien joue un rôle dans le piège préparé pour Tristan en ceci que les rapports déjà existants entre les deux rois rendent plausible la ruse du nain. Le nain méchant, avec ses talents surnaturels, est lui-même un type du roman arthurien qui ne paraît presque jamais ailleurs; sa présence ici marque l'appartenance du récit, pour le moment du moins, au roman breton.[44] Ce premier cas d'intertextualité arthurienne, qui souligne le parallélisme structural des deux triangles amoureux, sert d'introduction au suivant, c'est-à-dire au piège lui-même, qui évoque irrésistiblement la scène d'amour nocturne de Lancelot et Guenièvre dans le *Lancelot* de Chrétien de Troyes. Vu la renommée de ces deux histoires et leur nature paradigmatique pour le public du moyen âge, il est presque certain qu'un auditeur du *Tristan* les aurait associées.[45]

L'un des éléments structuraux les plus importants du *Tristan,* c'est le contraste du monde de la cour avec celui de la forêt de Morois.[46] La vie dans la forêt, dénuée de splendeur, s'oppose à celle de la cour, si civilisée, si courtoise. Il n'est donc pas surprenant de constater que la première partie du fragment, dont l'action se déroule parfois loin du château, se distingue par une absence caractéristique de cette splendeur. Ce n'est qu'avec les préparations d'Ogrin pour la réconciliation d'Iseut et de Marc que le poème commence à se rapprocher de ce point de vue-là du roman. Ogrin se rend au Mont-Saint-Michel afin d'acheter des vêtements pour la reine (2733-44); une brève description courtoise d'Iseut se trouve tout au début de la scène de réconciliation (2879-88); la description du retour d'Iseut à Saint-Samson est des plus courtoises qui soient: la joie du peuple, les clochers qui sonnent, le pavoisement des rues, la présence des ecclésiastiques, la générosité du roi envers les pauvres, et l'adoubement de chevaliers, etc.[47]

Un mouvement semblable apparaît dans les préliminaires de *l'escondit.* Iseut invoque l'autorité d'Arthur, de Gauvain, Girflet et Keu le sénéchal en tant que témoins, préparant le terrain, pour ainsi dire, pour la réunion des deux cours, pour l'entrée dans le poème de Béroul du roman arthurien. L'arrivée de Perinis à la cour d'Arthur (3365 et ss.) ressemble au début traditionnel du roman arthurien si brillamment analysé par Beate Schmolke-Hasselmann.[48] Perinis, après avoir demandé le chemin à un berger, se présente devant la cour et annonce son message au roi Arthur; en réponse au récit esquissé de la situation en Cornouaille, Gauvain, Girflet et Yvain se lèvent et se proposent d'aller venger la reine. Dans un autre contexte, ce passage aurait pu fonctionner comme le début d'un roman: un messager venu de l'extérieur apporte la nouvelle d'une injustice et fait appel au sens de l'honneur des chevaliers de la Table Ronde, provoquant ainsi le départ de quelques-uns. L'arrivée de Perinis à la cour d'Arthur n'est pas simplement un cas d'intertextualité en vertu de la réunion des deux cours mais surtout grâce à l'introduction de toute une séquence narrative propre au roman arthurien.

C'est après l'arrivée d'Arthur et de ses chevaliers au Gué Aventureux que les descriptions si caractéristiques du roman courtois s'enchaînent rapidement. Il y a d'abord celle d'Iseut devant le Mal Pas (3903-11), puis celle du campement de la cour, des vêtements, de la musique, et finalement du tapis étendu devant le pavillon du roi (4093 et ss.). Entre ces deux passages se trouve la description du tournoi (3985 et ss.) pendant lequel deux personnages majeurs de l'histoire de Tristan se mêlent à ceux du roman arthurien. Dans ce tournoi, qui n'est pas sans ressembler à celui de Noauz dans le *Lancelot* de Chrétien,[49] nous retrouvons plusieurs éléments traditionnels: l'arrivée de chevaliers étrangers au milieu des rencontres déjà commencées, la discussion au sujet de leur identité par les spectateurs (trompés par le déguisement de Tristan et de Governal), les combats incognitos avec des amis, le sourire d'un seul des spectateurs qui connaît l'identité des étrangers, etc. Tout aussi significatif que la rencontre des personnages arthuriens et tristaniens dans un tournoi romanesque typique est le soin que prend Béroul de préserver une ligne de démarcation entre ces deux types. Leur déguisement amène Girflet et Gauvain à penser que Tristan et Governal sont des chevaliers de l'autre monde (4019, 4062), opinion partagée par les autres barons (4072). Egalement traditionnel est la fin du tournoi où les deux étrangers quittent soudain le champ de bataille sans se faire connaître. C'est comme si Béroul n'est pas encore prêt à présenter une intégration complète des deux matières; le roman arthurien a pour lui beaucoup de choses en commun avec l'histoire de Tristan et Iseut, mais les deux n'appartiennent pas encore au même monde.[50]

D'autres genres de la littérature française médiévale résonnent de temps en temps à travers le poème de Béroul, et mon enquête n'a pas été exhaustive. Le séjour des amants dans la forêt de Morois, par exemple, prête une apparence hagiographique au récit dont l'examen serait indispensable dans une étude complète des paramètres génériques du roman courtois et de la vie de saint.[51] J'ai discuté le thème de la tromperie ci-dessus surtout à propos du fabliau, mais il ne faut pas oublier que le fabliau est un genre ayant des rapports très étroits avec l'épopée animale, le *Roman de Renart*. Quand l'espion qui dénonce les amants vers la fin du fragment dit au v. 4285 que "Tristran set molt de Malpertis," Béroul évoque tout un corpus de littérature animale et invite son public à considérer la possibilité de juger le comportement de ses personnages selon les normes d'un autre genre.[52]

J'ai parfois employé le mot "genre" ci-dessus faute de mieux pour désigner une catégorie reconnaissable de la littérature française médiévale, mais cela sans croire que les genres littéraires constituent des espèces bien démarquées. Notre tendance moderne à vouloir tout définir n'est pas véritablement conforme à la réalité médiévale, mais une méthode de classification comme celle de Jauss a du moins le mérite d'imposer un peu d'ordre dans la masse de textes médiévaux qui nous sont parvenus. Qui plus est, le concept d'éléments pertinents et non-pertinents ainsi que celui de l'épreuve de commutation nous permet d'entrevoir la méthode du poète et une réaction historique devant son texte. Si le public du moyen âge n'avait pas de définitions du roman, de la chanson de geste, du fabliau, etc., et si l'usage médiéval de la terminologie littéraire peut nous sembler instable, ce public avait tout de même une perception de certains éléments qui indiquaient la position d'un texte dans le "Gattungssystem" entier. C'est cette perception qui conditionne l'horizon d'attente et ouvre le chemin de l'intertextualité. Presque chaque texte se révèle aujourd'hui comme intertexte, et il est facile de considérer la théorie de l'intertextualité comme une panacée universelle. Cependant, le *Tristan* de Béroul est un poème qui doit non seulement ses propres caractéristiques mais aussi son existence même à la confluence de plusieurs courants littéraires distincts de la fin du 12e siècle. C'est finalement de cette confluence que dépendent l'encodage et le décodage du texte médiéval.

Notes

[1]Voir, par exemple, les titres donnés aux deux éditions les plus utilisées par des médiévistes: Béroul, *Le Roman de Tristan*, éd. par Ernest Muret, 4ᵉ édition revue par L. M. Defourques (Paris: Champion, 1974), et *The Romance of Tristran* by Beroul, éd. par A. Ewert, 2 t. (Oxford: Blackwell, 1939, 1970). En ce qui concerne l'état du texte, l'on se rapportera à T. B. W. Reid, *The Tristran of Beroul. A Textual Commentary* (Oxford: Blackwell, 1972). Je cite le poème dans l'édition de Ewert.

[2]Voir, par exemple, l'article de Paul Zumthor, "Le Roman courtois: essai de définition," *Etudes Littéraires*, 4 (1971), 75-90.

[3]Pour une explication, voir Pierre Gallais, *Genèse du roman occidental. Essais sur 'Tristan et Iseut' et son modèle persan* (Paris: Têtes de Feuille/Sirac, 1974), pp. 12-24.

[4]Par exemple, dans son "Epos und Roman—eine vergleichende Betrachtung an Texten des XII. Jahrhunderts," *Nachrichten der Giessener Hochschulgesellschaft*, 31 (1962), 76-92; réimp. dans idem, *Alterität und Modernität der mittelalterlichen Literatur* (Munich: Fink, 1977), pp. 310-26.

[5]Le nombre des vers est celui de Muret-Defourques et de Ewert. Dans son édition de 1974 (*Tristan et Yseut* [Paris: Garnier]), Jean-Charles Payen ne compte que des vers complets et arrive à un total de 4452.

[6]Sur Chrétien, voir John L. Grigsby, "Narrative Voices in Chrétien de Troyes. A Prolegomenon to Dissection," *RPh*, 32 (1978-79), 261-73.

[7]Sur Chrétien et le *Tristan*, voir Gallais, *Genèse du roman occidental*, pp. 56-74, et Hubert Weber, *Chrestien und die Tristandichtung* (Bern/Frankfurt: Lang, 1976).

[8]Sur le prologue du roman arthurien, voir Tony Hunt, "The Rhetorical Background of the Arthurian Prologue," *FMLS*, 6 (1970), 1-23; réimpr. dans D. D. R. Owen (éd.), *Arthurian Romance. Seven Essays* (Edimbourg: Scottish Academic Press, 1970).

[9]Dans l'édition de Bartina H. Wind, *Les Fragments du Tristan de Thomas* (Leyde: Brill, 1950).

[10]Voir l'excellent article de Pierre Gallais, "Bleheri, la Cour de Poitiers et la diffusion des récits arthuriens sur le continent," dans *Moyen Age et littérature comparée* (Paris: Didier, 1967), pp. 47-79.

[11]Pierre Kunstmann, "Texte, intertexte et autotexte dans le *Tristan* de Thomas d'Angleterre," dans *The Nature of Medieval Narrative*, éd. par Minnette Grunmann-Gaudet et Robin F. Jones (Lexington, Ky.: French Forum, 1980), pp. 173-89, p. 175.

[12]Paul Zumthor, "Le Texte médiéval et l'histoire," *RR*, 64 (1973), 5-15, p. 8.

[13]Voir Jean-Charles Payen, "Lancelot contre Tristan: la conjuration d'un mythe subversif (réflexions sur l'idéologie romanesque au Moyen Age)," dans *Mélanges Pierre le Gentil* (Paris: SEDES, 1973), pp. 617-32, et Joan M. Ferrante, "The Conflict of Lyric Conventions and Romance Forms," dans *In Pursuit of Perfection: Courtly Love in*

Medieval Literature, éd. par Joan M. Ferrante et George D. Economou (Port Washington: the Kennikat Press, 1975), pp. 135-78.

[14]Voir Frank M. Chambers, *Proper Names in the Lyrics of the Troubadours* (Chapel Hill: Univ. of North Carolina Press, 1971), et François Pirot, *Les Connaissances littéraires des troubadours occitans et catalans des XIIe et XIIIe siècles* (Barcelone: Real Academia de Buenas Letras, 1972).

[15]Roger Dubuis, " 'Dru' et 'Druerie' dans le *Tristan* de Béroul," dans *Mélanges Pierre Jonin* (Aix-en-Provence: CUER MA, 1979), pp. 223-31.

[16]Ferrante, art. cit.

[17]Sur la reverdie, voir Pierre Bec, *La Lyrique française au moyen âge (XIIe-XIIIe siècles),* t. 1 (Paris: Picard, 1977), pp. 136-41. Cet aspect du lyrisme de Béroul a été l'objet d'une étude de Pierre Jonin, "Sur quelques ouvertures lyriques du *Tristan* de Béroul," *Mélanges Charles Rostaing,* t. I (Liège: Marche Romane, 1974), pp. 501-14, qui souligne "les affinités du jongleur normand avec les poètes lyriques" (p. 514).

[18]Sur l'aube, voir Bec, *La Lyrique française,* pp. 90-107.

[19]A Propos du mot "losengier," Jean-Charles Payen écrit: "Ce terme . . . dénote une influence de la poésie courtoise" (art. cit., p. 619, n. 11).

[20]Par exemple, le Méléagant du *Lancelot* de Chrétien.

[21]Voir, par exemple, le *Charroi de Nimes,* éd. par Duncan McMillan, 2e éd. revue et corrigée (Paris: Klincksieck, 1978).

[22]Pour l'importance de l'arrière-plan féodal du *Tristan,* voir Stephen G. Nichols, Jr., "Ethical Criticism and Medieval Literature: *Le Roman de Tristan*," dans *Medieval Secular Literature. Four Essays,* éd. par William Matthews (Berkeley et Los Angeles: Univ. of California Press, 1965), pp. 68-89.

[23]Pour l'aspect légal, voir R. Howard Bloch, "Tristan, the Myth of the State and the Language of the Self," *YFS,* 51 (1975), 61-81, et idem, *Medieval French Literature and Law* (Berkeley et Los Angeles: Univ. of California Press, 1977), pp. 238-48.

[24]Erich Köhler, *Ideal und Wirklichkeit in der höfischen Epik* (Tubingue: Niemeyer, 1956).

[25]Voir Renate Hitze, *Studien zur Sprache und Stil der Kampfschilderungen in den "chansons de geste"* (Genève: Droz, 1965).

[26]Y a-t-il besoin de rappeler les combats parodiques dans des textes comme *Aucassin et Nicolette* et *Audigier?* Les exemples ne manquent pas.

[27]Dans son étude magistrale, *Il 'Roman de Tristran' di Béroul* (Turin: Bottega d'Erasmo, 1963). Je renvoie à la traduction anglaise, *Beroul's 'Romance of Tristran'* (Manchester: Manchester Univ. Press, 1972), pp. 137-61, surtout les pp. 143-46.

[28]Le débat sur le caractère oral-formulaïque de l'art épique a provoqué des conflits scientifiques d'une vigueur digne de la chanson de geste elle-même. Voir en dernier lieu Joseph J. Duggan, "La Théorie de la composition orale des chansons de geste: les faits et les interprétations," *Olifant,* 8 (1981), 238-55, et William J. Calin, "L'Epopée dite vivante: réflexions sur le prétendu caractère oral des chansons de geste," ibid., 227-37.

[29]Hans Robert Jauss, "Theorie der Gattungen und Literatur des Mittelalters," dans *Grundriss der romanischen Literaturen des Mittelalters*, I (Heidelberg: Winter, 1972), pp. 103-38; réimpr. dans idem, *Alterität und Modernität der mittelalterlichen Literatur* (Munich: Fink, 1977), 327-58, p. 334.

[30]*Op. cit.*, pp. 50-72. Voir aussi Elisabeth J. Bik, "Les Interventions d'auteur dans le *Tristan* de Béroul," *Neophil.*, 56 (1972), 31-42.

[31]C'est ce que Vàrvaro (*op. cit.*, pp. 64-68) appelle "le chœur."

[32]Nous soulignons ainsi l'avis de Robert Bossuat: "Béroul est plus éloigné d'*Enéas* que des chansons de geste, dont il a gardé l'esprit clair et naïf, en respectant certains de leurs procédés techniques." *Histoire de la littérature française. Le Moyen Age* (Paris: del DUCA, 1955), p. 64.

[33]Sur la rareté de manuscrits littéraires français du 12e siècle, voir Michel Zink, *La Subjectivité littéraire. Autour du siècle de saint Louis* (Paris: PUF, 1985), pp. 18-19.

[34]L'importance de Jean Bodel dans le développement du fabliau a été récemment soulignée par Luciano Rossi, "Jean Bodel et l'origine du fabliau," dans *Formation, codification et rayonnement d'un genre médiéval: la nouvelle*, éd. par Michelangelo Picone, Giuseppe di Stefano et Pamela D. Stewart (Montréal: Plato Academic Press, 1983), pp. 45-63.

[35]Pour la date de la *Plantez*, voir Per Nykrog, *Les Fabliaux* (Genève: Droz, 2e éd., 1973), p. 4, qui conclut: "Il paraît probable que c'est vers l'an 1200 que le genre s'est constitué sous sa forme définitive, et que le monde littéraire en a pris conscience comme d'un phénomène particulier et distinct." Le texte du *Roman de Renart* est cité par Jauss (*Untersuchungen zur mittelalterlichen Tierdichtung* [Tubingue: Niemeyer, 1959], p. 178) d'après l'édition Martin: "fabliaus et chançon de geste." Dans la version éditée par Mario Roques, t. II (Paris: Champion, 1972), v. 3739, par contre, se trouve la leçon "fables et chançons de geste."

[36]En ce qui concerne le style des fabliaux, l'on se rapportera en dernier lieu à Charles Muscatine, *The Old French Fabliaux* (New Haven et Londres: Yale Univ. Press, 1986), pp. 55-72.

[37]Barbara Nelson Sargent-Baur, "Between Fabliau and Romance: Love and Rivalry in Béroul's *Tristran*," *R*, 105 (1984), 292-311, p. 307.

[38]Philippe Ménard a discuté la ruse dans les fabliaux dans son *Les Fabliaux. Contes à rire du Moyen Age* (Paris: PUF, 1983), pp. 183-96.

[39]Art. Cit., p. 310.

[40]Le texte du premier poème se trouve dans Jean Bodel, *Les Fabliaux*, éd. par Pierre Nardin (Paris: Nizet, 1965), pp. 77-84, et du second dans A. de Montaiglon et G. Raynaud, *Recueil général et complet des fabliaux*, 6 tomes (Paris: Librairie des Biblio-philes, 1872-90), t. III, pp. 54-57. Voir aussi Helaine Newstead, "The Tryst Beneath the Tree: an Episode in the Tristan Legend," *RPh*, 9 (1955-56), 269-84, pp. 280-81.

[41]Les références à l'histoire de Constantin données par Jean-Charles Payen à la p. 328 de son édition (n. 12) sont incorrectes.

[42]Voir Marie-Thérèse Lorcin, *Façons de sentir et de penser: les fabliaux français* (Paris: Champion, 1979), pp. 130-31.

[43]Texte dans Montaiglon et Raynaud, *Recueil général*, t. I, pp. 294-300.

[44]Dans la terminologie de Jauss, le nain serait "unvertauschbar" entre le roman breton et un autre genre; il résisterait ainsi à la "Kommutationsprobe." Voir, par exemple, "Theorie der Gattungen und Literatur des Mittelalters," p. 333.

[45]Voir Payen, "Lancelot contre Tristan."

[46]Sur les *loci* de Béroul, on lira avec profit Emmanuèle Baumgartner, *Tristan et Iseut. De la légende aux récits en vers* (Paris: PUF, 1987), pp. 47-51.

[47]Les exemples sont trop nombreux à citer, mais il est certain que la description de la cour plénière d'Arthur dans le *Brut* de Wace (basée sur Geoffroi de Monmouth) a joué un rôle capital dans la diffusion de ce *topos*. Il s'agit des vv. 10197 et ss. dans l'édition d'Ivor Arnold, t. II (Paris: SATF, 1940).

[48]"Untersuchungen zur Typik des arthurischen Romananfangs," *GRM*, nouvelle série, 31 (1981), 1-13.

[49]Surtout vv. 5515-6066 de l'édition Wendelin Foerster, *Der Karrenritter* (Halle: Niemeyer, 1899).

[50]Sur l'incompatibilité de l'histoire de Tristan et la matière arthurienne, voir Joan Ferrante, *The Conflict of Love and Honour. The Medieval Tristan Legend in France, Germany and Italy* (La Haye/Paris: Mouton, 1973), p. 16.

[51]Bien que la thèse centrale reste peu convaincante, il y a quelques remarques utiles dans Ulla Erika Lewes, *The Life in the Forest: the Influence of the St. Giles Legend on the Courtly Tristan Story* (Chattanooga, Tenn.: Tristania, 1978). On se rapportera également à l'article de Brigitte Cazelles, "*Alexis* et *Tristan:* les effets de l'enlaidissement," *Stanford French Review*, 5 (1981), 85-95.

[52]La question a été traitée par Nancy Freeman Regalado, "Tristan and Renart: Two Tricksters," *ECr*, 16 (1976), 30-38.

Amadas et Ydoine: The Problematic World of an Idyllic Romance

William Calin

Amadas et Ydoine[1] was written between 1190 and 1220, perhaps earlier. Considerable fragments have survived in two Anglo-Norman manuscripts, and a complete version in a Picard manuscript from Arras can be dated 1288. It is agreed that the original text was Anglo-Norman; the Picard copy represents a later redaction, a conscious rewriting in line with Continental taste.[2]

Ydoine is daughter to the Duke of Burgundy, Amadas the son of the duke's seneschal. Ydoine sends her suitor out into the world to win martial renown. When the duke marries his daughter to someone else, the Count of Nevers, Amadas falls into madness. However, with the assistance of three sorceresses, Ydoine manages to conserve her virginity. The countess eventually cures the young man of his insanity, and he rescues her after she has been abducted by a demon. Ydoine then arranges for her marriage to be annulled so that she can wed her true love.

Amadas et Ydoine differs markedly from the sort of narrative we find in Thomas and Chrétien, in Béroul and Hue de Rotelande. In my opinion, this text partakes of a special mode or subgenre within the tradition that has been called the idyllic romance. The chief representatives of this mode are *Floire et Blancheflor, Galeran de Bretagne, L'Escoufle* by Jean Renart, and the deservedly famous *Aucassin et Nicolette.*

Our Anglo-Norman-Picard romance shares with the other idyllic stories a nonmilitary, nonadulterous, and nonhierarchical erotic relationship. Except for his tourneys, rapidly "told" but never "shown," and except for his duel with Ydoine's abductor, Amadas performs no martial feats. Like

Lanval, like Thomas's Tristan, he is a hero of love, not war. Indeed, once the youth and maiden avow passion for each other, it alone dominates their lives, is their unique reason for existence. This reciprocal desire reduces if not eliminates the sexual differences between them. On the contrary, Amadas, like Aucassin, Guillaume, and Galeran, becomes all but totally passive, and like Blancheflor, Aelis, and Nicolette, Ydoine assumes an active role, more active than her lover's, in bringing about a happy ending.

In an idyllic romance, love is the center of the universe, the unique motivating force behind the action. The *Amadas* trouvère differs from other romancers by taking a number of love conventions literally, then pushing them to their extreme limits, exploring what, both as fact and as metaphor, they imply.

One such convention or metaphor is the Malady of Heroes, love sickness. This is a constant motif in medieval letters, originating in Ovid. Amadas falls ill three times: first when desire for Ydoine, the *coup de foudre,* seizes him; secondly, when Ydoine's imminent marriage is announced; thirdly, when he discovers that she has been kidnapped. Especially on the first occasion, he undergoes the standard Ovidian symptoms: pallor, trembling, sighing, weeping, swooning, unwillingness to speak or take nourishment, a complete wasting away. Each time that he offers his suit to Ydoine and she refuses, his illness increases, and he wastes away still more. This process of physical and psychological decline occupies some two and a half years. It goes without saying that the only *mire* capable of curing the patient is Ydoine herself, who does so, once she also has been wounded by Cupid's shot, by returning his love or, on the second occasion, by pronouncing her name along with his.

On the second occasion, Amadas's illness proceeds immediately to its logical terminus: insanity, also an Ovidian motif. To love, happily or unhappily, is to participate in the irrational, in a *folie* that is both folly and madness. Hearing that his beloved will wed, the youth immediately and instantaneously endures *fine fole caleur, derverie,* and *foursenerie* (1794-96) and dashes off into the wilds like a werewolf. Eventually, we find him in Lucca, in Italy, where, love's jester, he provides the daily afternoon distraction. Naked, he leads a parade up the high street pursued by the rabble of the town who mock him and beat him without pity.

Amadas's first madness, manifest during his apparently unsuccessful suit to win Ydoine, is of a different, more problematic order. At first, insanity is a metaphor or a rationalization to explain the fact that he dares to love the duke's daughter and to tell her that he loves her. Both the youth and the maiden agree that his outrage (*outrage*) is a manifestation of *folage, rage,* and *derverie.* Ydoine tosses at him the following epithets: "Leciere outrequidiés, / Gars anïeus, fox assotiés!" (736-37). These insults, which cover the semantic fields of folly and foolhardiness, as well as of lechery and churlishness, allude to the loss of reason in social life presumed endemic in a low-class churlish lecher. Social irrationality has a cause: love itself. Therefore, we are not surprised to discover that, in the course of his wooing, Amadas goes mad for real, that he falls into physical *derverie* and *folie* as a result of Ydoine's constant refusals. On the other hand, insane or not, he indulges in *fin'amor* casuistry, reasoning subtly in the following terms: rather than simply perish from love without doing anything about it, would it not be better for me to plead my cause one more time? Would it not be madness for me not to speak to her one more time?

> En cele angousse, en cele paine
> S'est pourpensés seneement
> Que langui a trop longement
> Par fol corage et par folie . . .
> Pour fol se tient au departir
> Qu'il ne requiert plus d'une fois
> La pucele. . . .
> (vv. 625-28, 635-37)

Love madness becomes problematic indeed. Amadas is love's fool.

Insanity is intimately associated with those subject to Venus but also born under the sign of Saturn, the Greater Infortune, for whom love manifests itself as an explosion of black bile (melancolia) or of choler (frenzy). Love violates the rational code of society: to feel and to express it go against the code and become a concrete manifestation of folly. Amadas becomes society's fool, a jester in Ydoine's court or on the streets of Lucca. Yet, in the court of Venus, this madness is a sacred madness, a higher wisdom; Amadas's *sancta stultitia* is a form of martyrdom, the greatest humiliation, the lowest degradation for a *miles* and a rational male who ought to occupy the highest place. Such is his sacrifice for the highest of all goods! To abandon all, to become the lowest of the low for the highest of the high! For, from the vantage point of Eros, acts or attitudes that block love's progress are foolish, and all that contributes to love is sane, healthy, and full of good sense.

As we know from other texts, especially *Tristan et Iseut,* the bond between Eros and Thanatos is a constant in medieval literature. For the people of the Middle Ages, insanity was considered a form of death because the madman was dead to social life and because the demise of the mind is the worst of all possible ends. Since man is a mortal animal, since reason is the quality that distinguishes him from all other creatures (except the angels) and therefore is the essence of his manhood, insanity is the equivalent of death. How appropriate then that Amadas's fit of madness in Lucca does render him dead to the world, and that Ydoine, by ending his mental alienation, restores him to life and to society, the rebirth heralded by a purifying, healing bath.

Earlier, at the Duke of Burgundy's court, Amadas was again close to death. Yet here, as with his insanity, death is problematic, and the trouvère explores the ambiguities inherent in our conceptualization of it. If love is or leads to illness, the latter can be mortal. The true lover, when his passion is not reciprocated, finds himself on the point of dying. Furthermore, in his despair, the lover will wish he were dead ("Riens ne couvoite fors morir," 832) and will contemplate suicide as an avenue of escape. This does not prevent Amadas from employing traditional male seduction arguments in the face of a recalcitrant female: If you do not respond favorably to my petition, I shall perish! You will be responsible for my death! Not only that: the youth also justifies to himself still another declaration on the grounds that if he kills himself or perishes from love madness, he will be damned; much better for him to try once more to seduce Ydoine. When she then has him killed, as she has threatened, at least there will be hope for the salvation of his soul! (933-55). To some extent, Amadas reasons in good faith; to some extent he is inauthentic and grasping at straws, rationalizing his repeated efforts at seduction with one object in mind: winning Ydoine. Similarly, the author explores with sympathy but also with amused detachment the youth's will to Eros and to Thanatos, as he explores the concrete and metaphorical connotations of death. In this romance, death is concrete and metaphorical, is real and is convention, often at the same time.

In the second half of the narrative, after the lovers have been reunited, a stranger Knight abducts Ydoine. She is recovered but then falls ill (not love sickness this time) and apparently dies. In the middle of the night, Amadas and the stranger fight a duel for Ydoine's corpse, as if she were a living damsel. Inspired by the sight of her tomb, Amadas wins and succeeds in breaking the enchantment. The couple then proceeds to a happy ending.

Our strange Knight is a standard motif in Celtic folklore: the fairy prince from the Other World. Within Celtic legend, the Other World constituted a realm of the dead as well as of the fays. And, in *Amadas et Ydoine,* the death theme is pervasive. The Knight, called a *maufé,* is himself immortal but associated with death. He makes Ydoine appear to die, has power over her when she is in a death-like trance. He acts at night, comes to her at night, will spirit her away in her coffin, and, like a vampire or an evil spirit, must not be surprised by the dawn. Whether Satanic devil or Celtic fay, this black Knight is the concrete embodiment of death. Nevertheless, Amadas does rescue Ydoine from death, the peril to the body ("Venue estes de mort a vie," 6576; "Car vous m'avés de mort garie," 6708), as she rescued him from madness, the death of the spirit. In what is truly *aventure fiere* (4733) they each return from their respective Other Worlds, they both conquer insanity and death, acts that symbolize coming to maturity, after which the youth and maiden are allowed to wed and to exert sovereignty.[3]

Fundamental aspects of love are thus scrutinized as reality and metaphor, as concrete behavior and literary convention. They are shown to be illusion or reality, illusion and reality, in sequence or at the same time. And this ambiguous, paradoxical reality, and our perception of it, are shaped by Ydoine at her will. For Ydoine, like Iseut, is a master manipulator, a genius at deceit: she masks her feelings and her inner reality while causing other people to act in ways that serve her ends.

For example, hearing that her beloved is playing the village idiot in Lucca, she convinces her husband to allow her to leave home—to subsidize her—on a pilgrimage to Rome. Stopping off at Lucca, she veils her anguish—she is *sage,* will not reveal her *rage*—then, at night, she finds the sleeping Amadas, cures him, and arranges for his purportedly coincidental arrival in town. Afterwards, she manipulates her own counselors into advising her to retain him in the vicinity, under her auspices and at her own expense, while she continues on the pilgrimage. Yvoine thus actively engineers her spectacle of wit—the dashing Amadas returning from a crusade; the embarrassed Ydoine seeking counsel from her men—corresponding to, and in antithesis with, Amadas's passive spectacle of madness as he is chased through the streets by the town rabble.

Two other performances are more significant still in their scrutiny of appearance and reality, truth and deception, and the functioning of sickness, insanity, and death. To preserve her virginity, Ydoine has three witches work on her prospective husband, the Count of Nevers. These mad creatures, *dervees,* are also full of *sens.* They come to the man at night, pretending to be the three Fates and announce to him that Ydoine is tabu, will never know love, and if he forces her he will die:

> Je vous voel de la mort garir.
> Vous volés Ydoine espouser,
> La fille au duc, o le vis cler;
> Mais saciés bien, se la prenés,
> Vous estes mors et afolés.
> Ja ne l'avrés despucelee
> Ausi tost que par destinee
> Ne muiriés a mult grant dolor
> Et a martire et a tristrour.
>   (vv. 2286-94)

They lie to the count, commit *mençongne* (2266), *par felounie* (2209), but in a good cause, that Ydoine remain true to Amadas. Significantly, the witches do not employ supernatural enchantments or transform the physical world. Although they lie and create illusion, a sort of play or happening, from another perspective, they only offer reality to the count, that is three women talking among themselves and to him. If he makes the error of taking their speech literally and then acts on it, that is his responsibility. Their intimidation of the count, and his willingness to be intimidated, are psychological in essence, not physical or metaphysical. This is true even though, given his state of intimidation, his fear of death, the count does go, in some sense of the term, insane (he is *tresafolé* 2156, and in *folour* 2322), and may well risk death were he in fact to possess his bride.

The bride rises to the occasion in a most ingenious manner. With *voisdie* she pretends to be ill, and her proclaimed illness compounded by the count's (his fear) assures her of a sound sleep on their wedding night. Thus she claims to be ill but is healthy; the count appears to be healthy, but inside he is ill. On the other hand, *apalie* and *descoulouree* (2404), suffering from psychological ills and, like her husband, very afraid (he dreads death, she dreads defloration), the countess soon declines physically and manifests all the symptoms of love sickness for Amadas that Amadas endured earlier for her (2549-68).

When Ydoine appears to be dying in Lucca, she confesses to her suitor that, before having made his acquaintance, she for seven years had been the mistress of three of her cousins and had had three babies by them, babies that, urged on by Satan, she slew at birth. If her account were true, she would have been guilty of lechery, infidelity, incest, and infanticide. The young countess claims that her appearance of virginity was a ruse to deceive others, but now she willingly unmasks in order to reveal reality to Amadas. In fact, just the opposite is true. She was chaste and is chaste. Her alleged lie in the past is true, her alleged confession of truth in the present is a lie. Paradoxically, Ydoine commits this lie, which ought to destroy her reputation for fidelity and Amadas's love for her, out of "Estrange loiauté d'amour" (4959) and "fine loiauté d'amie" (4964) for him. The reasoning is the following: if she dies pure in his eyes, he also will perish from love sickness or even commit suicide *a derverie* (5236). Because of the horrible story she has now told him, his life will be spared. Not that he will cease to love her. But, since he is her unique confessor, he must live on to offer prayers and alms in her name, in order to preserve her soul from hell. Part of the irony derives from the fact that, unbeknownst to Ydoine, she is not on the point of dying but is indeed menaced by a demon from hell. And it is true that her confession, her total sacrifice of self and honor, is as much an *aventure* as the kidnapping and subsequent rescue.

As a result of all this, Amadas, the *fin amoureus,* in a state of libidinal exaltation, remains committed to Ydoine and her love, regardless of illusion and reality, in spite of illusion and reality. He believes in her troth, her fidelity to him, also in the truth of her words. In spite of her *pecié,* the truth of which he accepts, he loves her, will obey her, and will stay alive to pray for her soul. He accepts the fact that she is dead, yet he refuses to leave her coffin; he remains there literally to ward off any devils that may turn up looking for her soul. When the *estrange cevalier* (5770), having lied and said that Ydoine is dead, also lies claiming that she was his mistress and that she betrayed Amadas with him, after a momentary hesitation the latter refuses to believe him. He refuses to accept "reality": Ydoine's state of infidelity, "proved" by the concrete evidence of the ring, Amadas's ring, that the Knight plausibly declares Ydoine had given to him as a token of her love:

"Ydoine, amie et dame,
Merci, que trop mesfais me sui,
Quant onques de rien vous mescrui.
Comment que cist eüst l'anel,
Tant aviiés le cuer loiel
Que croire ne peüsse pas
Que vous trecissiés Amadas
Qui de fin cuer vous amoit tant,
Plus c'omme de cest mont vivant."
(vv. 5958-66)

As it turns out, Amadas is right not to accept such evidence, such reality. Ydoine lied, the Knight also lied. She is not dead, and she has not been untrue to him. The real is false; and because of his *hardement* (6468) Amadas makes the ideal real.

Such distinctions are crucial in a text that scrutinizes appearance and reality, that exalts romantic, idealized love, yet, in so curious a way, also insists upon natural cause and effect, upon life in the concrete world of everyday, as opposed to enchantments, as opposed even to the Christian supernatural. Ydoine, in a series of invented Christian visions and in her dramatized recounting of them to the court, resembles the three sorceresses who, instead of metaphysical distortion, also invent a story and put on a play. Perhaps they, as women, using the physical weapons of women (speech, psychology, the body), have to be distinguished from the *maufé,* a male employing knowledge of the supernatural and masculine force and effecting or dealing in metaphysical transformation. They (Ydoine and the magicians) are authors, actresses, and theatre directors, manipulating their male audiences in a good cause. And when Amadas the man is rendered irrational and impotent because of Eros, the woman assumes power and employs reason in his stead. The women are good because they hurt no one, because they believe in sacrifice, and because they work on behalf of love. The Knight is evil because he willingly hurts others, thinks only of himself, and opposes true love and true lovers. Also, they win, and he loses.

We now perhaps are in a position to appreciate the ironies inherent in the Narrator's fascinating tirades against women, 3568-656 and 7037-97, by what he says and by what he leaves unsaid. In two approximately equal passages the Narrator denounces women for their power and proclivity to trick and deceive, to turn wise men into fools and fools into sages, to be disloyal at whim; and he exculpates good women in general and Ydoine in particular, commending the latter for her loyalty, for following reason and right and thus not adhering to her nature as a woman. Clerical clichés! Yet it is obvious to the reader, to any reader, to the implied twelfth-century audience and to the real author behind the scenes, that this is a half-truth at best and that the entire romance text of *Amadas et Ydoine* proves it. Yes, Ydoine has been loyal; but she has done so using all the ruse, trickery, deception, even *ingremance* (3586) and the capacity to *enfantosmer* (7044) denounced in others. Never does she adhere so well to her feminine nature as when she purportedly surpasses it. Furthermore, indeed she has supported, embodied *raison* and *droiture,* but reason and law in a particular sense, in the name of love, against the reason and law of family, marriage, and church. By her very changeableness, her unpredictability as a woman, is not Ydoine typically a woman? And does not her active, obtrusive, intelligent domination of the narrative, her function as *sujet actant,* not *objet, destinateur,* or *destinataire,* make of her story a text strongly, vociferously in praise of woman and of *fin' amor?* It is then fitting that directly after his second antifeminist tirade, the implied author makes his retraction and invokes "Le bien, la francise et l'ounour" (7089) also to be found in women. In addition, whatever he says, although he doesn't admit it outright, he admires their ruse and their wisdom! After all, he has created them! So, as a maker of attacks and of palinodes, this early trouvère anticipates the greatest makers of attacks and palinodes: Jean de Meun, Machaut, Chaucer.

In the end, through Ydoine's careful machinations, the marriage is annulled and Amadas weds his lady. Then, their parents gracefully dispatched, the couple obtains sovereignty as Duke and Duchess of Burgundy. A cliché dénouement! Yet the ending is, in its way, of the utmost significance. Ydoine succeeds not only in marrying her beloved; she also succeeds in imposing her will totally. She never had to yield her body to the count, whom she doesn't love; nor did she ever yield her body illicitly, before their wedding, to Amadas, whom she does love. She neither indulges in adultery nor submits to marital rape: *point de folor* (6955). In other words, the young woman remains pure throughout. She maintains social respectability and moral integrity, external and internal honor. In both a shame and a guilt culture she is exalted. Thus she "improves" upon her two chief forebears in the hoaxed husband line: Thomas's Iseut and Chrétien's Fénice. The trouvère can be said to have consciously authored an anti-*Tristan* and an anti-*Cligès* or, if you prefer, a hyper-*Tristan* and a hyper-*Cligès*. Furthermore, although some scholars consider the Count of Nevers to play a ridiculous role, I propose that, unlike Iseut's husband the king and Fénice's husband the emperor, this husband gets off easily. He is kind, understanding, and supportive of Ydoine. Therefore, after the annulment ("Par conscïence et par raison," 7325) he is allowed to wed the young daughter of the Count of Poitiers. Both couples live happily ever after.

The trouvère adheres to a tradition that dates back to Roman comedy, in which one blocking figure plays the role of scapegoat (the black Knight?) but, overall, the society of law opposing the young lovers is reformed, not overthrown, the parent or authority figures are not defeated but converted, and at least two couples are united in a dénouement of festivity and social integration. The trouvère also seeks to provide ideals for courtly conduct, for irreproachable courtly conduct, in order that the social code and its external forms be respected. This must take place yet, at the same time, allow love—*fin' amor*—to flourish and to triumph, in all its pathological manifestations of desire, in all its melodramatic extremes of sentiment.

Sentiment, desire, and social conformity—these are juxtaposed, balanced, fused, more or less harmoniously, more or less successfully, in a fascinating romance text in which ambiguity is the rule and paradox the norm. By the beginning of the thirteenth century, we find in literature something comparable to post-classical mannerism, the play with forms, the pushing of convention to its logical extremes. And we find something comparable to post-Romantic Biedermeier, a world view in which sentiment, domestic tranquillity, social order, and happiness stake their claim to a place in the universe. The medieval aristocracy also had its yearning for young love, a happy ending, the art of play, and the play of art.

Notes

[1] All references to *"Amadas et Ydoine," roman du XIIIe siècle,* ed. John R. Reinhard, Classiques Français du Moyen Age (Paris: Champion, 1974). For literary criticism, see John Revell Reinhard, *The Old French Romance of "Amadas et Ydoine": An Historical Study* (Durham, N.C.: Duke Univ. Press, 1927); C. B. West, *Courtoisie in Anglo-Norman Literature* (Oxford: Blackwell, 1928), pp. 106-22; M. Dominica Legge, *Anglo-Norman Literature and Its Background* (Oxford: Clarendon Press, 1963), pp. 109-15; Faith Lyons, *Les Eléments descriptifs dans le roman d'aventure au XIIIe siècle* (Genève: Droz, 1965), chap. 1; Philippe Ménard, *Le Rire et le sourire dans le roman courtois en France au Moyen Age (1150-1250)* (Genève: Droz, 1969); Pierre Le Gentil, "A propos d'*Amadas et Ydoine* (Version continentale et version insulaire)," *Romania,* 71 (1970), 359-73; Hans-Dieter Mauritz, *Der Ritter im magischen Reich: Märchenelemente im französischen Abenteuerroman des 12. und 13. Jahrhunderts* (Bern: Lang & Frankfurt/Main: Lang, 1974), pp. 101-03, 135-37; Alison Adams, "*Amadas et Ydoine* and Thomas' *Tristan,*" *Forum for Modern Language Studies,* 14 (1978), 246-54; Jean-Claude Aubailly, tr., *"Amadas et Ydoine," roman du XIIIe siècle,* Traductions des Classiques Français du Moyen Age (Paris: Champion, 1986).

[2] According to Gaston Paris, "Sur *Amadas et Idoine,*" in his *Mélanges de littérature française du Moyen Age,* ed. Mario Roques (Paris, 1912), pp. 328-36; and Le Gentil.

[3] For a Jungian reading of the text, see Aubailly, "Préface."

Oral Performance of Romance
in Medieval France

Joseph J. Duggan

The twelfth- and thirteenth-century romances, generally composed in rhyming couplets by authors the majority of whom identify themselves— Benoît de Sainte-Maure, Chrétien de Troyes, Robert de Boron, Thomas d'Angleterre, Gautier d'Arras, Béroul, Renaut de Beaujeu, Jean Renart— and reveal in their style and the references that they make to classical authors that they have been trained in the school, have seldom been linked with oral tradition except in as far as they draw upon it as a source. It is common-place to consider the romance as a genre created in writing primarily for direct aristocratic consumption and disseminated principally in manuscript form. Potential recipients had access to the romance, according to this view, in one of two ways: either ocularly, that is as readers of manuscripts, or aurally, listening to lectors who would read them aloud to audiences. Evelyn Vitz has called into question the dichotomy "oral epic vs. written romance," asking whether many a work composed in octosyllabic rhyming couplets did not also participate in the processes of oral tradition.[1]

The first alternative, private reading, is confirmed by the existence of numerous illustrated codices whose confection was so expensive that it could only have been justified economically if they were used by their owners directly.

The classic depiction of the second alternative is found in Chrétien de Troyes's *Chevalier au lion* (vv. 5354-90) in which the hero happens upon a domestic scene in the Château de Pesme Aventure: in an orchard, a sixteen-year-old girl is reading aloud to her mother and father from a *roman*; they listen while recumbent on a silk cloth.

[Yvains] . . . voit apoié desor son cote
un riche home qui se gisoit
sor un drap de soie; et lisoit
une pucele devant lui
en un romans, ne sai de cui;
et por le romans escoter
s'i estoit venue acoter
une dame; et s'estoit sa mere,
et li sires estoit ses pere;
si se porent molt esjoïr
de li bien veoir et oïr,
car il n'avoient plus d'enfanz;
ne n'ot mie plus de seize anz,
et s'estoit molt bele et molt gente,
qu'an li servir meïst s'antente
li deus d'Amors, s'il la veïst. . . .[2]

Although *roman* may designate any work written in the vernacular, the fact that the scene is found in a narrative by Chrétien de Troyes and that he launches immediately into a digression on the god of love leads to the reasonable assumption that the girl is indeed reading aloud what we would designate by the genre term 'courtly romance.' A passage in *Hunbaut,* an anonymous romance written sometime in the third quarter of the thirteenth century, confirms this practice: the lady of Gaut Destroit is having a romance read when Kay and Sagremor arrive at her castle:

La pucele est contre els levee
Si tost conme venir le[s] voit.
O li sis puceles avoit
Et chevaliers desi a dis;
D'un roumant oënt uns biaus dis,
La pucele le faissoit lire.[3]

Here the audience comprises seventeen people, and it is worth remarking that it includes more men than women. The romance was disseminated to a courtly public in such intimate settings, even to those who were incapable of reading or who, if they could read, were disinclined to spend their time perusing manuscripts. The reading of romances aloud in semi-public gatherings was practiced at least late into the thirteenth century, according to this testimony, and probably lasted far beyond that period.

Evidence is at hand, however, to show that material that is associated with the courtly romance was also disseminated in jongleurs' performances.

Several texts attest to the inclusion of material from the courtly romances among the works that jongleurs were expected to be capable of performing. In his well-known *ensenhamen,* assigned by Pirot to before 1165, the Catalan troubadour Guerau de Cabrera reproaches his jongleur Cabra for not knowing some seventeen chansons de geste, the poems of four troubadours, and the earliest known fabliau, *Richeut,* but also tales about King Arthur, Gauvain, Erec's conquest of the sparrowhawk, Alexander, Troy, Thebes, Narcissus, and Apollonius of Tyre.[4] The other *ensenhamens* provide similarly constituted repertories. In the poem addressed to his jongleur Fadet and composed between 1190 and 1220,[5] Guiraut de Calanso makes it clear that he assumes knowledge of, among others, stories concerning Troy, Dedalus and Icarus, Aeneas, Alexander the Great, and Lancelot. Bertran de Paris's "Gordotz, e·us fatz un sol sirventes l'an," dated between 1270 and 1290,[6] attests that a jongleur might be expected to tell tales about Arthur and his court; King Mark and Tristan; Merlin "the Englishman"; Priam king of Troy, Achilles, Agamemnon, and Hector from the *Roman de Troie;* Oedipus, Polynices, Actaeon, Adrastus, and possibly Tydeus from the *Roman de Thèbes;* Aeneas (*Roman d'Enéas*), Nectanebes (*Roman d'Alexandre*), Narcissus and Dedalus. He might perhaps also be called upon, like Cabra, to recount a (now lost) vernacular version of *Apollonius of Tyre.* These courtly tales far outnumber Bertran's allusions to chansons de geste.

The early dates of the first two *ensenhamens,* before 1220, render it likely that the tales they refer to would have been in verse. All three include in their ideal repertories subjects that we identify with romance, and all speak of the desirability of jongleurs *knowing (saber)* the tales in question, indicating that it was not a question of reading romances from books, as is the case in the circumstances portrayed in the *Chevalier au lion* and *Hunbaut,* but rather of performing them on the basis of mental processes. The book does not figure as a source of performances in any of the *ensenhamens.*

From northern France, the parodic series of three jongleurs' monologues entitled *De deus bordeors ribaus* begins with a poem in which a jongleur boasts of knowing how to sing (*savoir chanter*) twelve chansons de geste. He also pretends, however, to be able to perform *romans d'aventure.*

> Ge sai des romanz d'aventure,
> De cels de la Reonde Table,
> Qui sont a oïr delitable.
> De Gauvain sai le malparlier,
> Et de Quex le bon chevalier;
> Si sai de Perceval de Blois;
> De Pertenoble le Galois
> Sai ge plus de .lx. laisses.
> Et tu, chaitis, morir te laisses
> De mauvaitie et de paresce:
> En tot le monde n'a proesce
> De quoi tu te puisses vanter;
> Mais ge sai aussi bien chanter
> De Blancheflor comme de Floire;
> Si sai encor moult bone estoire. . . .[7]

The jongleur's claim to know these subjects is, of course, undercut by the fact that he consistently assigns the wrong epithets to the heroes he mentions: Gauvain "the evil-tongued" and Kay "the good knight," Perceval "of Blois," and Partenopeu "the Welshman." About this last-named hero the persona pretends to know sixty laisses, not realizing that he has mismatched form and genre. In his reply to the first jongleur's extravagant assertions, the second boasts a similar repertory, which includes *fabliaux, sirventois* and *pastourelles,* but also *contes,* the term that medieval romancers often use to designate their works. The second jongleur specifies, in fact, that he knows "de Parceval l'estoire."[8] That the possibility of a jongleur "knowing" such stories is not being undercut despite the ironic tone of the exchange is indicated by the fact that the persona of the second monologue attacks his opponent's mastery of his art but does not call into question either the extent of the supposed repertory or the types of works it represents.

That such repertories are not merely a fantasy to be satirized in humorous tones but rather reflect a medieval reality is demonstrated by the famous wedding scene in the Occitan masterpiece *Flamenca,* which sketches an impressively rich portrayal of jongleurs' performances:

Apres si levon li juglar: . . .
L'uns viola[·l] lais de Cabrefoil,
e l'autre cel de Tintagoil;
l'us cantet cel des Fins Amanz,
e l'autre cel que fes Ivans. . . .
Qui volc ausir diverses comtes
de reis, de marques et de comtes,
auzir ne poc tan can si volc;
anc null'aurella non lai colc,
quar l'us comtet de Priamus,
e l'autre diz de Piramus;
l'us comtet de la bell'Elena
com Paris l'enquer, pois l'anmena;
l'autres comtava d'Ulixes,
l'autre d'Ector et d'Achilles;
l'autre comtava d'Eneas
e de Dido consi remas
per lui dolenta e mesquina;
l'autre comtava de Lavina,
con fes lo breu el cairel traire
a la gaita de l'auzor caire;
l'us comtet de Pollinices
de Tideu e d'Etïocles;
l'autres comtava d'Apolloine,
consi retenc Tyr et Sidoine;
l'us comtet de rei Alexandri,
l'autre d'Ero e de Leandri;
l'us diz de Catmus can fugi
e de Tebas con las basti;
l'autre comtava de Jason
e del dragon que non hac son;
l'us comte[t] d'Alcide sa forsa,
l'autre com tornet en se corsa
Phillis per amor Demophon;
l'us dis com neguet en la fon
lo belz Narcis quan s'i miret;
l'us diz de Pluto con emblet
sa bella moillier ad Orpheu. . . .

L'us diz de la Taula Redonda,
que no i venc homs que no·il responda
le reis segon sa conoissensa;
anc nuil jorn no i failli valensa;
l'autre comtava de Galvain
e del leo que fon compain
del cavallier qu'estors Luneta;
l'us diz de la piucella breta
con tenc Lancelot en preiso
cant de s'amor li dos de no;
l'autre comtet de Persaval
co venc a la cort a caval;
l'us comtet d'Erec e d'Enida,
l'autre d'Ugonet de Perida;
l'us comtava de Governail
com per Tristan ac grieu trebail,
l'autre comtava de Feniza
con transir la fes sa noirissa;
l'us dis del Bel Desconogut,
e l'autre del vermeil escut
que l'yras trobet a l'uisset;
l'autres comtava de Guiflet.
l'us comtet de Calobrenan,
l'autre dis con retenc un an
dins sa preison Quec senescal
lo Deliez, car li dis mal,
l'autre comtava de Mordret.
L'us retrais lo comte Divet
con fo per los Ventres faiditz
e per Rei Pescador grazitz;
l'us comtet l'astre de Merli,
l'autre dis con fan l'Ancessi
per gein lo Veil de la Montaina;
l'us retrais con tenc Alamaina
Karles Maines tro la parti. . . .
l'autre comtet con Dedalus
saup ven volar, e d'Icarus
co[n] neguet per sa leujaria.

Cascus dis lo mieil[z] que sabia.
Per la rumor dels viuladors
e pel brug d'aitans comtadors
hac gran murmuri per la sala.[9]

The jongleurs who provide entertainment for the wedding guests present lyrics belonging to genres such as the *canso* and the *descort,* and a poem by Marcabru; they sing chansons de geste such as *Floovant* and *Guy de Nanteuil.* But above all, perhaps because of the high aristocratic status of many of those in attendance, including the king of France, and the fact that *Flamenca* was written well into the thirteenth century, that is to say in a period long after courtly materials had become the dominant fashion among the aristocracy, they recount courtly tales, among which are short pieces such as a *Lai du Chèvrefeuil,* perhaps Marie de France's famous work, and *Piramus et Tisbé,* but also versions of poems which, at least in their surviving forms, are much more ambitious, including all four of the great romances of antiquity. In their collective repertory are also found, among other romances, *Le Chevalier au lion, Lancelot, Le Conte del graal, Cliges, Le Bel inconnu,* and perhaps a *Roman de Tristan.* Most of the texts evoked in this passage are extant in Old French rather than in Occitan, although the author may in some cases be referring to now lost Occitan versions. If the works were indeed in French, they would be appropriate for an audience that included French nobles, and in any case French was no doubt readily intelligible to sophisticated speakers of Occitan in this period.

I do not believe that the author of *Flamenca* meant his readers to imagine the jongleurs presenting the works in question in their entirety or in an orderly fashion: the performers are said to be distributed among the wedding guests, and the poet notes that a great murmur filled the hall from all the storytelling. To judge from the fact that he mentions as the subjects of separate tales characters who figure in a single romance, such as Cadmus, the founder of Thebes, and Etiocles, who was its king, both characters in the *Roman de Thèbes,* and that he assigns, for example, to one jongleur the tale of Aeneas and Dido and to another that of Lavinia, it is a question of narrative lays and episodes from romances rather than long integral works. This interpretation can also be applied to the performances adumbrated in the *ensenhamens* and *De deus bordeors ribauz.* Viewed in this light, Chrétien's complaint in *Erec et Enide* may well reflect the practice of performing discrete parts of courtly tales:

D'Erec, le fil Lac, est li contes,
que devant rois et devant contes
depecier et corronpre seulent
cil qui de conter vivre vuelent.[10]

This passage is usually taken to refer to lays whose subjects would be various independent episodes about Erec and Enide, but the choice of the word *depecier* implies rather that "those who make their living from recounting tales" are disaggregating sections of a longer and more substantial narrative.

Elsewhere I have drawn a distinction between vocal performances, in which memory plays a dominant role, improvisation is minimal, and the text of the work being presented is substantially the same from performance to performance; and oral composition, in which the performer generates a text for the first time or reproduces, on the basis of his memory but usually calling upon the improvisational technique, a work that he has performed or heard someone else perform previously.[11] These are not two discrete and consistently separate types of performance, but rather tendencies at the opposite ends of an axis of presentation. Improvisation was rarely practiced without the aid of memory—could it conceivably ever have been?—and performance from memory was probably seldom exact. In actual practice virtually all performances incorporated elements of both.

The chansons de geste are marked by a particular narrative technique that is widely attested as facilitating the oral composition of heroic song in a variety of cultures and linguistic traditions. As this technique has not been associated with the romance, in the case of the topics drawn from courtly romance that are mentioned in *Flamenca, De deus bordeors ribauz,* and the *ensenhamens,* one is left with the likelihood that jongleurs' presentations of courtly material resembled vocal performances more than they did instances of oral composition.

The manuscript traditions through which courtly literature has been passed down to us appear to be relatively free of versions taken down from jongleresque performance. A famous passages of *Huon de Bordeaux,* for example, testifies clearly to a *mise par écrit* of this song on the basis of oral composition,[12] but I know of no text that provides analogous documentary evidence for the romance. That does not necessarily mean that it does not exist, however: the models generated by prior scholarship are so entrenched that evidence in support of a new paradigm may pass unnoticed for long periods.[13] The jongleresque qualities of Béroul's *Roman de Tristan* have often been noted, most recently by Vitz (pp. 318-19), and a rereading of the evidence in the light of possible oral presentation, concentrating first of all on romances such as *Robert le Diable* and *Witasse le Moine,*[14] might yield useful results. In any case, since most jongleurs must have been illiterate, their vocal performances of courtly materials are likely to have been based ultimately upon hearing tales read aloud. I stress that the axis of presentation is a continuum, so that improvisation undoubtedly marked some performances more than others, a state of affairs that perhaps justified, at least from his point of view as a writing poet, Chrétien's use of the verb *corronpre* to characterize performances.

Evelyn Vitz makes the case that the octosyllable, as a short line, is intrinsically apt for the transmission of oral poetry, and perhaps the example of *Gormont et Isembart,* a chanson de geste composed in octosyllabic verse, confirms this judgment. On the surface it would appear that longer lines, which are less likely to undergo enjambement and which provide for the listener more context within the poetic unit, would have lent themselves more easily to aural comprehension in the kinds of bustling milieux in which oral poets often performed. If it were, in fact, a question of the oral composition of romances rather than simply of their vocal performance—contrary to the views presented here—the rhyming octosyllabic couplet would not appear to be particularly appropriate, as it would presumably have been much easier to compose an extended passage on the same end-rhyme than to come up with a new rhyming combination every sixteen syllables. One might think again of *Gormont et Isembart,* composed in octosyllables but also in laisses, in this regard. Still Vitz's point that most early non-epic literature in French is couched from the start in accomplished octosyllabic lines, and often in rhyming couplets, lends weight to her contention that the octosyllable may well have had a prehistory and may indeed have been an important vehicle of orally transmitted and orally presented literature.

The evidence furnished by references to jongleurs performing tales whose subjects fall within the ambit of the courtly romance supports her views.

Notes

[1]Evelyn Birge Vitz, "Rethinking Old French Literature: The Orality of the Octosyllabic Couplet," *Romanic Review,* 77 (1986), 307-21.

[2]Ed. Mario Roques, *Les Romans de Chrétien de Troyes,* vol. 4: *Le Chevalier au lion* (Classiques Français du Moyen Age, 89; Paris: Champion, 1959), vv. 5354-90.

[3]Ed. Margaret Winters, *The Romance of Hunbaut: An Arthurian Poem of the Thirteenth Century* (Davis Medieval Texts and Studies, 4; Leiden: Brill, 1984), vv. 3048-53.

[4]Edited in François Pirot, *Recherches sur les connaissances littéraires des troubadours occitans et catalans des XIIe et XIIIe siècles* (Memorias de la Academia de Buenas Letras de Barcelona, 14; Barcelona, 1972), pp. 545-62. Pirot's conclusions on dating are on p. 196. See also Martín de Riquer, "L'*ensenhamen* de Guiraut de Cabrera," in *Les Chansons de geste françaises,* 2d ed., trans. Irénée Cluzel (Paris, 1967), pp. 332-51.

[5]See Pirot, *Recherches,* p. 261; he edits the text on pp. 563-95. See also Wilhelm Keller's edition, "Das Sirventes 'Fadet joglar' des Guiraut von Calanso," *Romanische Forschungen,* 22 (1908), 143.

[6]Pirot, *Recherches,* p. 318. Edited by Pirot, pp. 596-614 and by Frank M. Chambers, "The *ensenhamen-sirventes* of Bertran de Paris," *Mélanges de linguistique et de littérature romanes à la mémoire d'István Frank* (Annales Universitatis Saraviensis, 6; Saarbrücken, 1957), pp. 129-40.

[7]Vv. 82-97 of "La Gengle," in Edmond Faral, ed., *Mimes français du XIIIe siècle* (Paris, 1910). Vitz also recognizes the importance of *De deus bordeors ribauz* for the issue in question (p. 320).

[8]Vv. 107-24 of "La Réponse," in Faral, *Mimes.*

[9]Ed. Ulrich Gschwind, *Le Roman de Flamenca: Nouvelle occitane du 13e siècle* (2 vols.; Romanica Helvetica, 86A-B; Bern, 1976), vv. 592, 599-602, 617-49, 661-95, 703-09.

[10]Carleton W. Carroll, ed. and trans., Chrétien de Troyes, *Erec et Enide* (Garland Library of Medieval Literature, series A, vol. 25; New York, 1987), vv. 19-22.

[11]"Performance and Transmission, Aural and Ocular Reception in the Twelfth and Thirteenth-Century Vernacular Literature of France," to appear in *Romance Philology,* vol. 43, no. 1, a special issue dedicated to the memory of Alison Elliott.

[12]Pierre Ruelle, ed., *Huon de Bordeaux* (Université Libre de Bruxelles, Travaux de la Faculté de Philosophie et Lettres, 20; Brussels, 1960), vv. 4976-91 and 5512-19. On the significance of these passages, see Joseph J. Duggan, "La Théorie de la composition orale des chansons de geste: Les faits et les interprétations," *Olifant,* 8 (1980-81), 249-51, and "Le Mode de composition des chansons de geste: Analyse statistique, jugement esthétique, modèles de transmission," *Olifant,* 8 (1980-81), 299-304.

[13]Thus some of the texts assembled by Edmond Faral in the appendix to his *Les*

Jongleurs en France au moyen âge (Paris, 1910) support conclusions that contradict Faral's findings in the study itself. Manfred Günter Scholz's *Hören und Lesen: Studien zur primären Rezeption der Literatur im 12. und 13. Jahrhundert* (Wiesbaden: Steiner, 1980), while it concentrates on Germany, reviews key secondary treatments on the manner in which the medieval literature of France was disseminated and received, but never takes into account *De deus bordeors ribaus* or the *ensenhamen* of Guerau de Cabrera or the wedding scene in *Flamenca,* apparently because his sources do not mention them. In the light of the evidence from the works analysed here, Martín de Riquer's statement that "le roman courtois est un genre narratif qui, détaché complètement de la récitation jongleresque, ne se transmet que par le livre. . . ," cited by Scholz, is puzzling but typical of the received view. See Riquer's "Epopée jongleresque à écouter et épopée romanesque à lire," *La Technique littéraire des chansons de geste: Actes du colloque de Liège (septembre 1957)* (Publications de la Faculté de Philosophie et Lettres de l'Université de Liège, 150; Paris, 1959), pp. 78-79. Likewise Paul Meyer's remark (cited by Gschwind [see note 9 above], note to v. 601) that the reference in *Flamenca* to "cel dels Fins Amanz" cannot be to Marie de France's *Lai des deux amants* because her lays were meant for reading or recitation rather than singing begs the question.

[14]At one point Witasse disguises himself as a jongleur, and to the question "Ses tu ore nule chançon?" answers

> "O je. D'Agoullant et d'Aimon;
> Je sai de Blanchandin la somme,
> Si sai de Flourenche de Romme
> Il n'a el mont nule chançon
> Dont n'aie oï ou note ou son."

Denis Joseph Conlon, ed., *Li Romans de Witasse le Moine: Roman du treizième siècle* (University of North Carolina Studies in the Romance Languages and Literatures, 126; Chapel Hill, 1972), vv. 2205-09. I have emended v. 2205.

De l'amour dans le *Roman de Brut*

Hans-Erich Keller

Les critiques ne sont toujours pas unanimes dans leur jugement du *Roman de Brut:* tandis que V.-L. Saulnier le qualifie de "simple adaptation de l'*Historia* de Gaufrei de Monmouth,"[1] Robert Bossuat est de l'avis qu'il faut le considérer "comme un poème narratif."[2] Or, Paul Zumthor[3] soutient que

> la narration historiographique ne diffère de la narration romanesque que (parfois) au niveau de la composition d'ensemble, les parties du "roman" s'intégrant mieux dans le tout; mais les séquences ou séries de séquences, "romanesques" ou "historiques", ont la même fonction textuelle, les mêmes règles d'enchaînement et emploient les mêmes moyens verbaux.

D'autre part, Zumthor souligne également le fait que, dans les romans avant le XVe siècle, "l'image génératrice relève de la tradition: mais elle surgit dans une double lumière: celle de l'érotisme et celle du combat."[4] Que le *Roman de Brut* fourmille de scènes de combat est bien connu: mais pourrait-on y trouver aussi de l'érotisme? C'est ce que nous allons examiner dans les pages qui suivent, examen qui nous permettra de vérifier la définition de Zumthor mais aussi de confirmer si Wace avait raison lorsqu'il qualifiait son œuvre de "roman":

> Puis que Deus incarnatiun
> Prist pur nostre redemptiun
> Mil e cent cinquante e cinc anz,
> Fist mestre Wace cest *romanz*.
>   (vv. 14863-66)[5]

Dès le début, Vénus trouve sa place dans l'*Historia regum Britanniae* de Geoffroy de Monmouth, car le fondateur de la race bretonne, Brutus, naît des amours d'un des fils d'Ascagne, lui-même fils d'Enée, avec une nièce de Lavinie. Mais tandis que Geoffroy exprime son désaccord sur l'aventure amoureuse de Silvius ("*Furtivae veneri* indulgens") et lui fait épouser la jeune fille, l'affaire est beaucoup plus romantique chez Wace:

> Il out amee une meschine
> *Celeement,* niece Lavine;
> Od li *parla,* cele *conçut.*
>
> (vv. 115-17)

Là, aucune question de mariage; au contraire, l'auteur insiste sur l'aspect sexuel de l'affaire par le parallélisme *parla - conçut* et suggère ainsi l'illégitimité de l'enfant.

Le même goût pour l'amour secret se manifeste dans l'épisode de Locrin, fils aîné de Brutus, et de Corineüs, camarade d'armes de Brutus et père de Guendoliene, que Locrin avait promis d'épouser avant d'avoir vu Hestrild, jeune fille ravie par des pirates en Allemagne, et que Corineüs force Locrin à accepter en mariage. Tandis que Geoffroy se contente de la phrase très brève "Volebat saltem *furtivam venerem* cum illa agere"[6] pour indiquer que Locrin a continué à aimer Hestrild malgré son mariage avec Guendoliene, Wace développe le thème d'une manière plus romantique:

> Dunc ad Locrin par itel guise
> Guendoliene a feme prise,
> Mais il nen ad mie obliee
> Hestrild, qu'il out *asoinantee.*
> Par un suen bien familier
> Fist fere a Lundres un celier
> Desoz terre parfundement,[7]
> La fud Hestrild *celeement.*
> Set anz la tint issi Locrin
> *Celeement* el sozterrin.
>
> (vv. 1381-90)

De nouveau, nous observons chez Wace une étonnante insistance sur le rapport sexuel (*asoinanter* 'traiter en concubine') et son caractère secret, trait sur lequel nous aurons à revenir un peu plus tard.

Un autre aspect de pure sexualité apparaît à nouveau dans le passage consacré au roi Eldol, passage qui, chez Geoffroy, consiste en une simple énumération ("Post illum regnavit Arthinail, frater suus. Post Arthinail Eldol. Cui successit Redion").[8] Wace enrichit cette liste plutôt sèche en y ajoutant des détails provenant de sa propre imagination:

> Emprés fu reis sis fiz Eldol,
> Ki mult se fist tenir pur fol
> Pur ceo, trop fu luxurius
> E de femes trop coveitus;
> Ja gentil feme n'i eüst,
> Que de si haut parage fust,
> Fust espuse, fust damisele,
> Pur ceo qu'ele li semblast bele,
> Que il ne vulsist purgesir.
> A mainte gent se fist haïr.
> > (vv. 3713-22)

Voici donc le parfait portrait du coureur de jupons!

Dans ces circonstances, il n'est pas étonnant que Wace se plonge avec délice dans l'épisode entre le roi breton Vortiger et Ronwen, fille du chef saxon Henguist, épisode où même Geoffroy sort de sa réserve habituelle:

> Vortegirnus autem diverso genere potus inebriatus, intrante Sathana in corde suo, amavit puellam et postulavit eam a patre suo. Intraverat, inquam, Sathanas in corde suo, quia, cum Christianus esset, cum pagana coire desiderabat.[9]

Toutefois, Wace traite cet épisode beaucoup plus élégamment en insistant avant tout sur les qualités délibérément séductrices de la jeune fille:

> La meschine ot *le cors mult gent,*
> E *de vis fu bele forment;*
> *Bele* fu mult e avenant,

De *bele* groisse e de *bel* grant;
Devant lu rei fu, *desfublee,*
Qui merveilles l'ad esgardee.
Tuz fu haitiez, bien ot beü,
Grant talent ad de li eü.
Tant l'ad Diables timoné,
Ki maint home ad a mal turné,
D'amur e de rage l'esprist
De prendre la fille Henguist.
                    (vv. 6981-92)

Voici donc les mots-clés de l'amour, passion destructrice: *amur e rage.*
C'est la sexualité de Vortigern qui va conduire finalement à la chute du
royaume des Bretons en Angleterre, excellent exemple choisi par notre auteur pour démontrer jusqu'où l' "amour-rage" (amour-passion) peut mener.

Wace reprend cette idée tout en la renforçant dans l'épisode traitant
de l'amour adultère entre Guenièvre et Modred, amour qui mettra fin au
monde arthurien: tandis que Geoffroy se contente de signaler d'une façon
brève qu'Artur confiait le royaume à Modred et Guenièvre lors de sa guerre
contre les Romains en Gaule ("Arturus Modredo, nepoti suo, atque Gue-
nuuerae reginae Britanniam ad conservandum permittens cum exercitu suo
Portum Hamonis adivit"),[10] Wace met l'accent sur cette erreur de jugement
de la part d'Artur en insistant sur le caractère particulièrement hideux de cet
amour-passion mais aussi adultère, où tout se passe en cachette, et d'autant
plus rébarbatif dans ce cas-ci qu'il s'agit d'amours entre tante et neveu. De
nouveau, notre auteur relève—ce qu'il abhorre par-dessus tout—la nécessité
du secret dans cet amour:

A Modred, un de ses nevuz,
Chevalier merveillus e pruz,
Livra en guarde Artur sun regne
E a Ganhumare, sa feme.
Modred esteit de grant noblei
Mais n'esteit pas de bone fei.
Il aveit la reïne amee,
Mais ço esteit chose *celee;*
Mult s'en *celout;* e ki quidast
Que il feme sun uncle amast,

Maïsmement de tel seinnur
Dunt tuit li suen orent enur;
Feme sun uncle par putage
Amat Modred si fist huntage.
A Modred e a la reïne,
Deus! tant mal fist cele saisine,
Comanda tut fors la corune.
(vv. 11173-89)

Ce long passage développé par Wace à partir de la demi-phrase citée par Geoffroy reflète toute son indignation de moraliste envers l'amour-passion, qui ne respecte rien, même pas les liens de famille; cette passion, fatale par excellence, est déjà condamnée dû au fait que Modred a osé toucher à la femme du roi ("maïsmement de tel seinnur / Dunt tuit li suen orent enur"). L'amour ici représente donc un triple crime—qu'on se souvienne de l'importance du nombre trois au moyen âge!—puisqu'il doit être secret, qu'il implique la femme de l'oncle de Modred et qu'il viole les rapports entre roi et vassal. L'indignation de Wace envers la monstruosité de cette passion le pousse jusqu'à saisir l'occasion offerte par Geoffroy lorsque celui-ci mentionne enfin le crime de Modred à la conclusion de la campagne victorieuse d'Artur contre l'empereur romain Lucius Hiber:[11]

En esté [Artur] volt Mungyeu [= le Grand-Saint-Bernard] passer
E a Rome voleit aler,
Mes Modred l'en ad returné.
Deus, quel hunte, Deus, quel vilté!
Sis niez, fiz sa surur, esteit,
E en guarde sun regne aveit;
Tut sun regne li ot livré
E en guarde tut cumandé.
E Modred li volt tut tolir
E a sun ués tut retenir;
De tuz les baruns prist humages
E de tuz les chastels hostages.
Emprés ceste grant felunie
Fist Modred altre vilainie,
Kar cuntre cristïene lei
Prist a sun lit femme lu rei,

Femme sun uncle e sun seignur
Prist a guise de traïtur.
                    (vv. 13013-30)

De nouveau, il est possible de discerner ici le triple crime entrevu par Wace: non seulement Modred s'est-il emparé du pouvoir royal, mais il couche aussi avec la reine qui, de plus, est la femme de son oncle. On n'aura probablement pas tort de supposer que Wace a voulu suggérer à son public que c'était l'amour-passion pour Guenièvre qui a amené Modred ("chevalier merveillus e pruz," v. 11174) à se saisir de la couronne, de façon à mettre fin, une fois pour toutes, au caractère secret de leur liaison.[12]

Wace reprend le même thème une troisième fois dans l'épisode où Geoffroy rapporte que Guenièvre, apprenant l'arrivée d'Artur à Winchester pour y assiéger Modred, se réfugie dans le centre religieux du royaume, Caerleon dans le pays de Galles du Sud,[13] et se retire dans le temple de Jules le Martyr. L'auteur se sert de cet événement pour faire les réflexions suivantes:

La reïne sot e oï
Que Modred tantes feiz fuï;
Ne se poeit d'Arthur defendre
Ne ne l'osot en champ atendre.
A Everwic [= York] iert a sujor,
En pensé fud e en tristur;
Membra lui de la vilainie
Que pur Modred s'esteit hunie,
Lu bon rei aveit vergundé
E sun nevou Modred amé;
Cuntre lei l'aveit espusee
Si en esteit mult avilee;
Mielz volsist morte estre que vive.
Mult fud triste, mult fud pensive;
A Karliun s'en est fuïe,
La entra en une abeïe,
Nune devint iloc velee,
En l'abeïe fud celee.
Ne fud oïe ne veüe,
N'i fud trovee ne seüe,

Pur la verguine del mesfait
E del pechié qu'ele aveit fait.
                    (vv. 13201-22)

Il fallait citer tout ce passage consacré à Guenièvre, car—à part un autre cas dont nous parlerons plus loin—c'est la seule fois dans tout ce roman de 14.866 vers que Wace décrit les sentiments d'une femme éprise d'amour, et seulement dans le cas où il s'agit d'amour-passion néfaste, à l'origine de la ruine de tout un empire, voire même de la disparition totale de l'âge d'or des Bretons sous Artur. Ce qui choque le plus notre auteur, ce n'est pas tellement que la reine ait aimé le neveu d'Artur, mais qu'elle a commis un adultère: pour un autre homme, elle s'est *hunie* et a *vergundé* son mari; c'est cette *verguine* que Wace qualifie de *mesfait* et de *pechié*. Voilà pour lui jusqu'où peut mener l'amour-passion: notre moraliste n'a pas assez de mots pour le condamner.

Afin de faire comprendre à son public à quel point l'amour-passion est faux et peut devenir même criminel, Wace a déjà décrit plus tôt dans le roman l'amour conjugal idéal. Il profite de l'énumération des rois qui, chez Geoffroy, suit l'histoire de Belin et Brennius,[14] pour peindre la vignette suivante:

Emprés Urian, Eliud
Ad le regne en grant pais tenud;

. . . .

Puis Merian, ki mult fu bels,
Ki de chiens sout mult e d'oiseals,
Mult sout de rivere e de bois;
Quant qu'il vuleit perneit a chois;
A altre deduit n'entendeit
E cist deduiz mult li plaiseit.
De dames ert mult desirrez
E mult requis e mult amez,
Mais il n'out de feme talent
Fors de la sue sulement.
                    (vv. 3669-82)

Cette description provient entièrement de la plume de Wace; Geoffroy n'en sonne mot. Selon notre moraliste, le mari idéal reste toute sa vie exclusivement amoureux de sa femme, en dépit de sa mâle beauté qui suscite l'admiration et l'amour de bien d'autres femmes; la seule passion, la chasse, à laquelle il s'adonne entièrement, sport noble par excellence, l'éloigne forcément de la compagnie de ces dernières. Wace préconise donc l'amour dans le mariage tout comme Chrétien une génération plus tard, à la seule différence que Wace combine amour et chasse, alors que Chrétien ne considère pas celle-ci comme suffisante pour un chevalier accompli (cf. la chasse d'Erec au cerf blanc).

De plus, Wace favorise l'amour entre amants non mariés mais inévitablement destinés l'un à l'autre. Geoffroy raconte que Brennius, pour obtenir l'appui du roi de Norvège contre son frère Belinus, se rend chez le roi, dont il épouse la fille. Cependant, lors de son retour en Grande-Bretagne, il se trouve poursuivi par Guichtlacus, roi du Danemark, qui *"aestuaverat namque amore puellae* quam Brennius duxerat."[15] Après maintes aventures, et grâce à Belinus, Guichtlacus obtient enfin l'amie désirée "et cum amica sua in Daciam reversus est" (*HRB,* p. 112). Or, Wace fait de ce récit tout un petit roman sentimental en insistant sur l'amour mutuel entre Gudlac, roi du Danemark, et la fille du roi de Norvège:

> Brennes. . . . .
> . . . .
> Feme out prise e fait sun afaire;
> Od grant gent se mist el repaire.
> La dame ert assez bele e gente.
> *Mais li plaiz li desatalente.*
> *Ele out, lunc tens aveit passé,*
> *Le rei de Danemarche amé,*
> *Gudlac, qui mult rout li amee*
> *Si li deveit estre dunee,*
> Mais Brennes l'en ad desturbé;
> E ele ad a Gudlac mandé
> E tut le conseil descovert
> Que Brennes l'ad e il la pert,
> E, si forment ne se purchace,
> Jamais ne girrat en sa brace.
> Gudlac, li reis des Daneis, sout
> Que Brennes s'amie en menout.
> O tant de nefs cum aver pout

> Le repaire Brenne guaitout;
> S'amie li vuldreit tolir
> S'il en poeit en liu venir.
> Il l'eüst, ceo diseit, eüe,
> Se par lui ne l'eüst perdue.
>
> (vv. 2435-58)

Notre auteur termine cet épisode par ces quatre vers:

> Gudlac issi s'en departi
> E en sa terre reverti;
> S'amie en ad od sei menee
> Que par grant peinne out achatee.
>
> (vv. 2595-98)

Cette fois, Wace place l'initiative pleinement du côté de la jeune fille qui, grâce à un certain chantage, fait appel à son amant pour lui demander aide, car autrement "jamais ne girrat en sa brace." Mais l'auteur raconte tout cet épisode avec bonne humeur et grande sympathie pour ce couple non marié, de race noble et égale et dont l'amour irréprochable dure depuis longtemps. Selon Wace donc, les amants avaient le droit de leur côté, et Brenne a fait irruption dans un ordre divin préétabli, où toutes les conditions exigées pour un amour parfait avaient déjà été remplies.

Dans ces circonstances, on comprendra que Wace se trouve mal à l'aise confronté à l'amour d'Uther Pendragon pour Igerne, la femme du comte de Cornouailles,

> cujus pulchritudo, nous dit Geoffroy,[16] mulieres omnes Britanniae superabat. Cumque inter alias inspexisset eam rex, subito incaluit amore illius, ita ut, pospositis ceteris, totam intentionem suam circa eam verteret. Haec sola erat cui fercula incessanter dirigebat, cui aurea pocula familiaribus internuntiis mittebat. Arridebat ei multotiens, jocosa verba interserebat. Quod cum comperisset maritus, confestim iratus ex curia sine licentia recessit.

Voici donc pour Wace un cas typique d'amour-passion, qu'il dénonce avec d'autant plus de véhémence que la passion d'Uther conduira à une guerre contre le comte, qui y sera tué. Seulement, de ce même amour naîtra grâce

aux enchantements de Merlin, le grand roi Artur, à l'insu d'Igerne, il est
vrai, puisqu'Uther, tel Amphitryon, s'introduira auprès d'elle à Tintagel
sous la forme de son mari. Tout cela met notre moraliste dans le plus grand
embarras. Il décide donc, une fois de plus, de changer les données de sa
source en recourant à l'enseignement des troubadours et leur *amor de lonh*
pour une dame mariée:[17]

> Li reis en ot oï parler
> E mult l'aveit oï loer;
> Ainz que nul semblant en feïst,
> Veire *assez ainz qu'il la veïst,*
> *L'out il cuveitee e amee,*
> *Kar merveilles esteit loee.*
>   (vv. 8577-82)

Ce n'est pas la première fois que Wace fait usage de l' "amour de
loin": il l'avait déjà introduit dans l'histoire du roi Leïr et de sa fille
Cordeïlle, où le roi Aganippus de France propose à Leïr d'épouser Cordeïlle
après avoir entendu parler d'elle:

> [Cordeïlle] mult esteit e bele e gente,
> E mult en ert grant reparlance.
> Aganippus, uns reis de France,
> *Oï Cordeïlle loer*
> E que ele ert a marier.
> Briefs e messages enveia. . .
>   (vv. 1796-1801)

Et Aganippus ne se laisse nullement détourner de son intention même
lorsque Leïr lui fait savoir qu'il lui accordera sa fille mais sans dot:

> Cil [Aganippus] quida qui l'aveit rovee
> Que pur chierté li fust vehee;
> *De tant l'ad il plus desirree,*
> *Kar merveilles li ert loee.*
> Al rei Leïr de rechief mande
> Que nul aveir ne li demande;
> Sa fille sule li otreit,

Cordeïlle, si li enveit.
E li peres li otreia. . .
　　　(vv. 1815-23)

Le comportement d'Uther à table devient alors plus compréhensible:
il s'agit ici de la réaction classique d'un homme sérieusement épris, depuis
longtemps, et non d'un coup de foudre:

Mult l'ad al mangier esguardee,
S'entente i ad tute turnee.
Se il mangout, se il beveit,
Se il parlout, se il taiseit,
Tutes eures de li pensot
E en travers la regardot.
En regardant, li surrieit,
E d'amur signe li faiseit.
Par ses privez la saluot
E ses presens li enveot,
Mult li ad ris e mult clunied
E maint semblant fait d'amistied. . .
　　　(vv. 8583-94)

Pour sa part, Igerne agit en parfaite dame courtoise:

Ygerne issi se conteneit
Qu'el n'otriout ne desdiseit.
　　　(vv. 8595-96)

Cette attitude exemplaire rejette tout le blâme de la brouille entre le roi et le
comte de Cornouailles sur ce dernier, qui, en véritable *gilos,* se fâche de
l'attention du roi envers sa femme et quitte la cour abruptement avec sa
femme, donc d'une façon très peu courtoise: Uther peut alors s'ériger en
champion de la courtoisie et justifier ainsi ses intentions hostiles envers le
comte:

Li reis li [au conte] ad emprés mandé
Qu'*il li fait huntë e vilté*
Ki senz congié vait de sa cort;

> Face li dreit, arriere turt.
> E se il de ço se defaut.
> Deffie le, quel part qu'il aut,
> Ne se puet mais en lui fier.
> (vv. 8607-12)

N'importe quel chevalier courtois de Chrétien de Troyes aurait pu tenir un tel discours. Chrétien, et déjà avant lui les auteurs du *Roman de Thèbes* ou du *Roman d'Eneas,* sans oublier évidemment Ovide, nous viennent aussi à l'esprit lorsqu'on entend comment Uther confie son amour à son ami Ulfin:

> "Ulfin, dist il, conseille mei,
> Mis conseilz est trestut en tei.
> L'amur Ygerne m'ad suspris,
> Tut m'ad vencu, tut m'ad conquis,
> Ne puis aler, ne puis venir,
> Ne puis veillier, ne puis dormir,
> Ne puis lever, ne puis culchier,
> Ne puis beivre, ne puis mangier,
> Que d'Ygerne ne me suvienge;
> Mais jo ne sai cum jo la tienge.
> *Morz sui* se tu ne me conseilles."
> (vv. 8657-67)

Cette idée de la mort d'amour se retrouve à nouveau dans les paroles qu'adresse Uther à Merlin sur le conseil d'Ulfin:

> Preié l'ad e merci crié
> Que conseil li dunt, se il puet,
> Kar senz cunfort *murir l'estuet*
> Se d'Igerne sun bon ne fait;
> Querë e face que il l'ait.
> Del suen li durra se il vuelt,
> Kar *mult ad mal* e *mult se delt.*
> (vv. 8684-90)

De toute évidence, Uther souffre du mal d'amour des troubadours, capable même d'entraîner la mort:[18] conquis et vaincu par l'amour, Uther "ne peut plus aller ni venir, ni se coucher ni se lever, ni dormir ni veiller, ni manger ni boire." Voilà l'image du parfait amant courtois. Mais Artur s'avère être le produit de cet amour; or, cela allait à l'encontre de cette impression et accentue, une fois de plus, l'aspect sexuel de l'amour: ". . . senz cunfort murir l'estuet / Se d'Igerne sun bon ne fait." Et, grâce aux enchantements de Merlin, Uther peut enfin coucher avec Igerne:

> Li reis od Ygerne se jut
> E Ygerne la nuit cunçut
> Le bon rei, le fort, le seür,
> Que vus oëz numer Artur.
> (vv. 8733-36)

Tout le charme d'une relation courtoise est rompu. Igerne, rejetée dans le rôle de femme-objet et trompée à son insu, croit coucher avec son mari, qui, au même moment, est tué par les hommes d'Uther. Wace, conscient de ce fait, après la reddition de Tintagel par les gens du comte, ajoute cette phrase, qui ne correspond en rien à son modèle:

> Li reis ot mult Ygerne amee,
> Senz ensuine l'ad espusee.
> La nuit ot un fiz conceü
> E al terme ad un fiz eü,
> Artur ot nun; de sa bunté
> Ad grant parole puis esté.
> (vv. 8813-18)

Wace reprend donc le sujet de l'amour d'Uther pour Igerne, sans pourtant mentionner les sentiments de la comtesse envers le roi; il se préoccupe uniquement du problème de la légitimation d'Artur, pour laquelle Uther épouse Ygerne "senz ensuine." Le fait même que le couple ait eu plus tard une fille, Anna, la future femme du roi Loth de Loëneis, ne jette aucune clarté sur les sentiments intimes d'Igerne, car au moyen âge—comme on le sait—rien ne peut prévaloir contre les intérêts dynastiques. La lueur d'un amour courtois qu'on croyait voir poindre chez Wace s'est de nouveau éteinte.

Dans cet épisode, le malaise qu'éprouve notre auteur envers "la nouvelle vague," en d'autres termes la *fin' amor,* est devenu évident: Wace en imite certaines manifestations extérieures, certes, mais il ne peut vraiment en saisir l'essence, et en accepte seulement ce qui lui semble logique. Ainsi, il souligne la position sociale et intellectuelle de certaines dames de la cour, par exemple celle de la reine Marcie:

> Lettree fu e sage dame,
> De buen pris e de bone fame.
> Sun enging mist tut e sa cure
> A saveir lettre e escriture.
>
> (vv. 3337-40)

Ici, Wace insiste ici sur le caractère lettré de la reine afin de pouvoir donner une étymologie populaire (*Marcie* + *laga* 'lois') des *Marcenelaga;*[19] cependant, on y sent un respect pour la femme instruite et cultivée qui est un "first" dans la littérature française, respect qu'on retrouve d'ailleurs à propos d'Hélène, mère de Constantin:

> De sa valur ne de sun sens
> Ne saveit l'om feme en sun tens,
> Ne de sun pris nule meschine. . .
>
> (vv. 5655-57)

Ce respect pour une dame noble de la part de l'auteur s'explique ici d'autant plus qu'il s'agit de l'Hélène qui trouvera la Croix à Jérusalem. Soulignons donc ici un trait important chez Wace: l'acceptation du rôle éminent joué par certaines femmes nobles dans la société,[20] élément totalement nouveau dans la littérature française.

A noter cependant que ces deux femmes remarquables ne sont en aucun cas liées à une histoire d'amour. Par conséquent, à l'exception de l'amour conjugal, il ne reste pour Wace aucune autre forme d'amour sinon l'amour-passion, qui aveugle l'homme et le mène à sa destruction. Et si la mort des amants résulte de l'adultère, péché mortel, ce n'en est que le juste châtiment.[21]

Pourtant, nous lisons aussi dans le même *Roman de Brut* à propos des fêtes à la cour d'Artur:

> Ja nul chevalier n'i eüst,
> De quel parage que il fust,

> Ja peüst aveir druerie
> Ne curteise dame a amie,
> Se il n'eüst treis feiz esté
> De chevalerie pruvé.
>   (vv. 10511-16)

Dans ce passage, on trouve des mots-clés de l'amour courtois, tels que
chevalerie en rapport avec *druerie, curteise dame* et *avoir a amie,* ce qui
suggère une ambiance de *fin' amor:* de plus, dames et chevaliers manifestent
leur sympathie mutuelle en portant des vêtements et des armes de la même
couleur:

> Ja ne veïssiez chevalier
> Ki de rien feïst a preisier
> Ki armes e dras e atur
> Nen eüst tut d'une culur;
> D'une culur armes faiseient
> E d'une culur se vesteient,
> Si rerent les dames preisiees
> D'une culur apareillees.
>   (vv. 10503-10)

Bref, du temps du bon roi Artur,

> De buens homes e de richesce
> E de plenté e de noblesce
> E de *curteisie* e d'enur
> Portout Engleterre la flur
> Sur tuz les regnes d'envirun
> E sur tuz cels que nus savum.
>   (vv. 10493-98)

Ici, Wace, semble-t-il, nous transporte dans un monde différent, où règne la
courtoisie, car

> Plus erent curteis e vaillant
> Neïs li povre païsant

> Que chevalier en altres regnes,
> E altresi erent les femes.
>   (vv. 10499-502)

Serait-il possible que Wace, dans ses rapports avec Aliénor d'Aquitaine, ait fait connaissance de la *fin'amor,* qu'il considérait impossible dans la vie réelle, et l'ait donc confinée au règne légendaire d'Artur? Le discours de Gauvain plaidant en faveur de la continuation de la *pax Arturiana* semble pointer vers une telle explication de l'attitude de Wace:

> Bone est la pais emprés la guerre,
> Plus bele e mieldre en est la terre;
> Mult sunt bones les gaberies
> E bones sunt les drueries.
> *Pur amistié e pur amies*
> *Funt chevaliers chevaleries.*
>   (vv. 10767-72)

Avec l'écroulement du monde arthurien, l'esprit courtois—et avec lui la *fin'amor*—serait alors arrivé à sa fin; il ne reste plus que la réalité de l'amour conjugal d'une part et de l'amour-passion de l'autre.

Si notre analyse est correcte, nous trouverions en Normandie le début de l'influence de l'idéologie courtoise du Midi lorsque Wace a terminé la composition du *Roman de Brut* (1155): Wace en aurait eu connaissance, mais ne croyant pas à la possibilité d'une réalisation de la *fin'amor* dans la vie réelle, il la relègue par conséquent au monde mythique d'Artur. Plus encore, il se serait servi du reste du roman pour démontrer qu'en réalité, il existe ou bien l'amour conjugal (ajoutons également l'amour entre fiancés, tel celui fort remarquable et fort louable entre le roi du Danemark et de la fille du roi de Norvège) ou bien l'amour-passion avec ses conséquences plus ou moins néfastes, tel qu'il est représenté dans les vignettes de Silvius, père de Brutus, de Locrin et Hestrild, d'Eldol, de Vortigern et Ronwen et surtout de Modred et Guenièvre, vignette par laquelle Wace termine sa discussion de l'amour dans son roman.

Aussi sommes-nous convaincus que, dans le *Roman de Brut,* Wace a voulu saisir l'occasion d'évaluer—une génération avant Chrétien de Troyes—sous forme de "roman" (Wace est un des premiers auteurs à se servir de ce terme) la nouvelle idéologie du Midi en la confrontant à la réalité de sa province, la Normandie, et comme André le Chapelain plus tard, il l'a fait en opposant à la *fin' amor* l'amour tel qu'il existait autour de lui aux environs de 1155. Cependant, tandis qu'André dédiera deux livres à la *fin' amor* et un livre à sa réfutation, Wace a inséré la sienne à la suite de ses vignettes sur les différentes variantes de l'amour "réel," en réléguant la *fin' amor* au monde mythique d'Artur, où, et uniquement dans ce dernier, "pur amistié et pur amies funt chevaliers chevaleries."[22]

Mais le même Wace n'écrit-il pas aussi: "En cele grant pais ke jo di, / Ne sai si vus l'avez oï, / Furent les merveilles pruvees / E les aventures truvees / Ki d'Artur sunt tant recuntees / Ke a fable sunt aturnees. / Ne tut mençunge, ne tut veir, / Tut folie ne tut saveir"?[23]

Notes

[1]V.-L. Saulnier, *La littérature française du moyen âge,* "Que sais-je?" 145 (Paris: P.U.F., 1962), p. 65.

[2]Robert Bossuat, *Le moyen âge* (Paris: Del Duca-De Gigord, 1955), p. 140. Jean Frappier, dans *Le roman jusqu'à la fin du XIIIe siècle,* éd. Jean Frappier et Reinhold R. Grimm, Grundriss der romanischen Litteraturen des Mittelalters, 4/1 (Heidelberg: Carl Winter, 1978), pp. 196-98, ne prononce pas de jugement sur le *Roman de Brut;* il déclare seulement que ce dernier l'emporte par sa valeur littéraire sur ses concurrents (p. 196).

[3]Paul Zumthor, *Essai de poétique médiévale* (Paris: Editions du Seuil, 1972), p. 348.

[4]Zumthor, *Essai,* p. 355.

[5]Toutes les citations du *Roman de Brut* proviennent de l'édition d'Ivor Arnold, 2 vol., Société des Anciens Textes Français (Paris: SATF, 1938-1940), tandis que celles de la *Historia regum Britanniae* sont tirées du vol. 3 (*Documents*) d'Edmond Faral, *La légende arthurienne. Etudes et documents,* première partie: *Les plus anciens textes,* Bibliothèque de l'Ecole des Hautes Etudes, Sciences Historiques et Philologiques, fasc. 257 (Paris: Honoré Champion, 1929), abrégé *HRB.*

[6]*HRB,* p. 94.

[7]Ce motif se trouve déjà chez Geoffroy.

[8]*HRB,* p. 124-25.

[9]*HRB,* p. 179.

[10]*HRB,* p. 253.

[11]*HRB,* p. 274: "Adveniente vero aestate, dum Romam petere affectaret et montes transcendere incipisset, nuntiatum est ei Modredum, nepotem suum, cujus tutelae commiserat Britanniam, ejusdem diademate per tyrannidem et proditionem insignitum esse reginamque Guenneveram, violato jure priorum nuptiarum, eidem nefanda venere copulatum fuisse." A cela, Geoffroy ajoute: "Ne hoc quidem, consul auguste, Galfridus Monemutensis tacebit"! Il est donc intéressant de noter que, pour Geoffroy, le fait que Modred s'était emparé de la couronne d'Artur semblait plus important que les rapports sexuels de celui-ci avec la reine: se pourrait-il donc que Geoffroy considère la possession de la reine comme conséquence naturelle de la possession de la couronne britannique? Ou faut-il conclure qu'il était simplement trop embarrassé de parler de cette affaire?

[12]Il est possible que nous ayons ici affaire à une trace de l'ancien rôle primordial joué par la reine dans les civilisations primitives.

[13]Sur l'importance de Caerleon pour Geoffroy, cf. J[ohn] S. P. Tatlock, *A Legendary History of Britain. Geoffroy of Monmouth's "Historia Regum Britanniae" and Its Early Vernacular Versions* (Berkeley-Los Angeles: University of California Press, 1950), pp. 69-72.

[14]*HRB,* p. 124.

[15]*HRB*, p. 110.

[16]*HRB*, p. 221.

[17]Nous renvoyons ici à l'excellente définition succincte de l'amour trouba-
douresque chez Pierre Bec, *Nouvelle anthologie de la lyrique occitane du moyen âge*
(Avignon: Aubanel, 1970), pp. 16-17.

[18]Cf., p. ex., parmi les thèmes et motifs amoureux de Bernart de Ventadorn
réunis par Moshé Lazar, *Bernard de Ventadour, troubadour du XIIe siècle: Chansons
d'amour* (Paris: Klincksieck, 1966), p. 20: "VII. Mal d'amour et mort. 1. Le mal
d'amour est mort: a) mourir d'amour . . . ; b) mourir de désir . . . ; c) mourir en
comtemplant la dame . . . ; mourir à force de soupirer et de douleur."

[19]Anglo-Saxon *Myrcna Lage,* les lois de la Mercie, dont il existe toujours un
fragment, publié en dernier lieu par Felix Liebermann, *Die Gesetze der Angelsachsen,*
vol. 1 (Halle a. S.: Max Niemeyer, 1898), p. 462.

[20]Il faut souligner que, pour Wace, une belle femme noble n'appartient pas
nécessairement à cette catégorie: Igerne, par exemple, ne reçoit que le compliment qu'il
"Nen ot plus bele en tut le regne; / Curteise esteit e bele e sage / E mult esteit de grant
parage" (vv. 8574-76) et n'est vantée que pour sa beauté et sa noblesse, tout comme
Guenièvre, "une cuinte e noble meschine; / Bele esteit e curteise e gente, / E as nobles
Romains parente" (vv. 9646-48), et nous savons maintenant ce que Wace pensait de cette
dernière.

[21]Rappelons à ce propos encore une fois l'épisode de Locrin et de Hestrild
(vv. 1329-1432): l'armée de la femme de Locrin, Guendoliene, bat celle de Locrin, qui est
tué dans la bataille, et Hestrild et sa fille, née de l'union Locrin-Hestrild, sont jetées dans
la rivière Avon.

[22]De nouveau, nous devons penser ici à André le Chapelain qui, lui aussi,
relègue, dans le second livre de son traité, les règles d'amour courtois au monde arthurien.

[23]Vv. 9787-94.

Description and Narrative in Romance:
The Contextual Coordinates of
Meraugis de Portlesguez and the *Bel Inconnu*

Douglas Kelly

The art of description has left its mark, indeed its debris, scattered everywhere in medieval romance. Most obvious are stereotypical descriptions of persons and things: beautiful women, armed knights on horseback, abundant and varied meals, hospitality, combats of various kinds. Identified, classified, and filed away in various catalogues and monographs, they stand as forgotten monuments to by-gone tastes.[1]

Medieval romancers themselves were not so inclined to set aside and forget descriptions. Not content with recreating them, they even borrowed from one another, as if they could not hear them often enough. Chrétien de Troyes and others contemporary with and after him recreate and continue to recreate received stereotypes from the twelfth into the thirteenth century and beyond, after the *romans d'antiquité* had firmly implanted them in romance. Some even practice outright plagiarism: the commonplace portrait of Blancheflor in Chrétien's *Conte du graal* reappears virtually intact in *Fergus, Cristal et Clarie,* and other works.[2]

But such descriptions are not merely repetitive. For Blancheflor also reappears in Chrétien's romance, transformed but recognizable (to Perceval at least) in the snow stained by three drops of blood, before which Perceval stands enraptured, lost in amorous contemplation.[3] In other romances by Chrétien we may note the skill with which he displays beautiful ladies and handsome knights, notably, in the portrait of Soredamors assimilated to a golden arrow, in the conventional catalogue of Laudine's wondrous features showing through the tears and lacerations that inspire Yvain's pity and love, in Erec and Enide equal *de matere, de maniere e de mors*.[4]

Although stereotypes are not the only kind of description in medieval romances, virtually all of them seem to employ the same technique. *Descriptio* as an art permits the author to fashion a person, thing, or action in conformity with the character or type he or she intends to identify it with.[5] The romancer applies his or her *painne* and *antancion* to the realization of precisely this kind of description. If it is necessary to explain love for a man or woman, one justifies the love by enumerating and expanding upon features that make him or her loveable—physical beauty and gorgeous apparel, as well as the qualities that make up worth or *bonté*. More important than the fact of description or the recurrent features our modern catalogues identify are the appropriateness of a given description when it is drawn and the techniques by which it is fashioned, whether we today believe it to be stereotypical or original.[6]

Medieval descriptions tend to be enumerative. This is so because there is a certain order in the topoi—the *loci* or common places—from which one draws attributes appropriate to authorial intention. Edmond Faral summarized the topoi for the description of persons in Matthew of Vendôme, topoi which the latter borrowed from Cicero's *De inventione,* a standard treatise on rhetoric for the Middle Ages. There are extant a number of commentaries on it both anonymous and by major writers:[7] "le nom, la nature (c'est-à-dire le sexe, la patrie, la nation, les défauts ou les qualités de l'âme et du corps), le genre de vie (c'est-à-dire l'éducation, les amitiés, la profession, etc.), la condition, les habitudes, les affections (c'est-à-dire les sentiments de l'âme, joie, désir, crainte, etc., ou les épreuves du corps), les goûts, les desseins, les actes, les événements, les paroles."[8] One invents and displays features that express how one construes the person and his or her role in the plot: beauty, prowess, courtesy, noble mind, love. All these may explain conduct in achieving a marvelous adventure. The constituent qualities of such abstract ideas are disposed according to a graded scale that defines the person while fixing the context in which that person will act and the narrative that will report those acts.[9]

Let us examine several examples of this technique.

The anonymous lay *Guingamor* begins with a short description.

.I. sien neveu avoit li rois,
qui molt fu sages et cortois;
Guingamor estoit apelez,
chevalier ert, preuz et senez.
Por sa valor, por sa biauté
li rois le tint en grant chierté.[10]

Like the analogous lays *Lanval* and *Graelent, Guingamor* contains the motif of the man between two women, the one queen of this world, the other a fay or maiden with magic powers at her disposal who lives in another world—in the woods, beyond a river or the sea, in Avalon. The knight opts for the realm of the marvelous, even though his knighthood or courtliness gives him an affinity to the court. For in each case the queen is a villain prepared to violate the bed of the king, whom the knight she desires serves. The latter rejects her advances, a mark of his nobility, in favor of the mysterious woman of the woods. The knight described as exemplary for his noble mind, prowess, courtesy, and especially love is finally located by each lay in a marvelous adventure deep in the other world. The amorous success, the charm, and the justification of the knight's otherworld love are found in the abstract, conventional qualities which the lays set forth at the beginning, between prologue and plot. The same is true in lengthier romances.

Descriptions such as that of Guingamor establish a context defining what is laudable in the ensuing narrative. They permit one to understand the actions of heroes and heroines, to appreciate their exemplarity in representing social or moral superiority and worth. They serve the essentially rhetorical function of lauding the qualities attributed to those whom the text proposed for our admiration, approval, and, perhaps, emulation.

In lengthy, complex plots the romancer may elaborate on or refine descriptions, introducing variants that support, enhance, or contrast with the simple ideal combination of attributes invented for hero and heroine, complementing descriptions such as that of Guingamor quoted above by striking innovations such as Blancheflor seen in the snow.

Raoul de Houdenc's *Meraugis de Portlesguez* is a 'contes de cortoisie'[11] in which "nest amor de cortoisie" (v. 1006). Raoul exhibits these simple truths by the disagreement he invents between two friends and companions-in-arms as to the best kind of love; Meraugis loves Lidoine for her courtesy and *bonté,* of which her beauty is a merely superficial, even superfluous by-product. Gorvain Cadruz loves the same Lidoine for her beauty alone; even if she were a devil or a serpent or otherwise repellent—like the queen in *Guingamor,* perhaps—that would not matter to him (vv. 536-40, 559-71). The courteous Meraugis will finally win out precisely because love is born of courtesy rather than beauty (vv. 475-79, 598-613). The difference between the two knights who are otherwise good companions and exemplary is, in the last analysis, one of *sens,* a feature of the noble mentality and the aristocratic quality of their minds (see vv. 112, 4025).

But Raoul establishes other comparisons in his romance, in descriptions whose components contain variants on the qualities and defects of Meraugis and Gorvain. A dwarf and his *amie* are ugly but of royal blood; they are destined for one another by their birth, their courtesy, and their ugliness. The Outredoté is essentially corrupt from the moral and courtly point of view, despite his physical strength and beauty; still, he shows that love can give birth to an at least superficial courtesy. Belchis unites not only physical defects and wickedness, but also physical strength (like the Outredoté) and a concern for family and lineage.[12] Taken together, these examples illustrate a hierarchy in the context of courtesy and love, just as in the *Queste del saint graal* chastity and virginity permit the evaluation of chivalry in the context of divine grace, distinguishing species of knights on the basis of a moral hierarchy.

Not all descriptions occur at the beginning of romances. A different arrangement—artificial order in the identification of a major figure—is found in Renaut de Beaujeu's (or de Bagé's) *Bel inconnu.* Like the lays discussed above, this romance contains a knight, Guinglain, who becomes embroiled with two women. One, the Pucelle aux blanches mains, is a kind of fay possessing magic powers, whom he first encounters on his quest; the other, Blonde Esmeree, is the lady he set out to help, and whom he eventually marries at Arthur's court after having freed her from a magic spell by which she had been transformed into a *guivre* or serpent. Only the *fier baisier*—a kiss from a knight of extraordinary prowess and accomplishment—can break the spell and return the lady to human shape, that is, to the exceptional beauty and courtesy attributed to her.

Guinglain is described at the moment he achieves the adventure of the *fier baisier.*[13] A voice delivers the description at the same time it identifies the Fair Unknown as Guinglain, son of Gauvain and the fay Blancemal. One learns later that the voice belongs to the Pucelle aux blanches mains. Analogous to the fay in the woods of the lays, the Pucelle fell in love with Guinglain before the chronological beginning of the *Bel inconnu*. She took advantage of his arrival at Arthur's court, which she foresaw, to have the adventure of the Fier Baiser proclaimed as a challenge to all the knights of the Round Table (vv. 4948-5004). Her magic showed her that Guinglain would undertake the quest and achieve the adventure.

The description of Guinglain includes the revelation of his name and parents. Now, name and family are topoi, what Matthew terms *locus a nomine* and *locus a cognitione*.[14] Guinglain's name is thus indicative not only of his singularity, but also of the prowess with which he achieved the quest and its final adventure, and which he inherited from his father.

> El monde n'a un chevalier
> Tant preu, ne tant fort ne tant fier,
> Qui osast enprendre sor soi,
> Fors ton pere Gavain et toi.
>   (vv. 3223-26)

Guinglain's quest becomes therefore both the discovery and realization of himself as an exemplary, yet unique knight. By his accomplishments he reveals his prowess, his skill at arms, and his courtesy. Because of these qualities we accept his spectacular triumphs over the villainy, wickedness, and felony of his opponents. The voice's description notes and rehearses those qualities while defining Guinglain's exemplarity. Naming and describing him after the Fier Baiser honors those qualities in their fictional, but exemplary realization.

Renaut gives no fewer than eight descriptions of the two women in love with Guinglain. Blonde Esmeree, the serpent-lady, appears twice in the romance.[15] Her beauty is exceptional, she is dressed with great distinction, and would be an excellent match for Guinglain, whom she wants to marry and finally does marry with Arthur's approval. But she is not her husband-to-be's preference. Guinglain loves the Pucelle aux blanches mains, which explains his fascination with her before the five descriptions of the woman's marvelous attributes.[16] Now, in *Meraugis de Portlesguez* Lidoine's preference for Meraugis was founded on the superiority of courtesy over physical beauty. But what distinguishes the Pucelle in the *Bel inconnu* from Blonde Esmeree is her magic powers, which assimilate her to the mother fay of Guinglain as well as to the wood maidens in the lays. But

Guinglain must stay with her if she is to possess, as it were, the qualities that distinguish him as a knight and noble human being. By contrast, Blonde Esmeree passes from the realm of supernatural enchantment to that of the court and the marriage celebrated at the end of the romance. The Pucelle stays in her own domain, to which she drew—and could draw again— her *ami,* by her magic arts.[17] But at the end of the romance Guinglain has lost the woman he loves by leaving her and marrying the woman he does not love.

The return of Guinglain to the Pucelle aux blanches mains depends on a will outside the plot: that of the lady whom the author, Renaut, claims to love, and about whom he speaks with the narrator's voice or addresses directly in several digressions scattered through the romance.[18] At the end of the single surviving manuscript version of this curious romance, Renaut leaves the plot in suspense. Or more precisely, he proposes two possible denouements. If the lady he professes to love is willing to show him a *beau semblant,* he will take up his story again and reunite Guinglain and the maiden he loves. If she does not, Guinglain will be condemned to remain with his wife whom he does not love. It appears that Renaut's lady did not accede to his request.

Let us look more closely at the relation between Renaut and his lady in the context of description.

The hierarchy, from the most courtly to the most felonious in *Meraugis,* becomes in the *Bel inconnu* a more complex assimilation of a gamut of analogous qualities. In fact, even the lady whom Renaut as author says he loves is attributed a role—a role not unlike Guinglain's within the romance plot in that she can make choices regarding conduct. Moreover, the Pucelle's is analogous to Renaut's as author, narrator, and lover because she, like Renaut, decides, and wishes to decide, which adventures her knight will encounter. But her actions, most notably her rejection of Guinglain's love, are influenced by the *sanblant* that he shows her. The same is true for Renaut himself. But his lady has never shown him any *sanblant* (v. 1269). Should she do so, he will complete the romance. Did he not already reconcile Guinglain and the Pucelle by means of Guinglain's own *sanblant* when he saw the Pucelle, as we perceive her in a description (vv. 4438-60)?

At the end of the extant romance Guinglain is married. Does Renaut's lady have a husband? If so, he might account for the contrast the narrator makes between true and false lovers. He says that the latter cause ladies to lose both good lovers and husbands who love them (vv. 1255-56). The hypothesis permits us to explain the otherwise surprising, unexplained marriage of Guinglain, and to assimilate the triangle Pucelle aux blanches mains - Guinglain - Blonde Esmeree to the implicit triangle Renaut - his lady - the latter's husband. By rewarding Renaut's love with a *beau sanblant,* his lady would make possible the reconciliation of the Pucelle and Guinglain in spite of the marriage. That much the author/narrator promises her. Despite the differences in the topos of sex, the qualities of the narrator and extradiegetic characters and their triangle are analogous to those of the narrative protagonists, which makes possible the assimilation. For apart from the sexual topos, the other topoi used, and therefore the attributes and total descriptions of the characters assimilated in the triangles, are the same. Does not Renaut exercise the same powers as the Pucelle? "Sacié," she explains,

> molt me sui entremisse,
> En tos sanblans, en tos servisse,
> Coment avoir je vos peüsse
> Ne coment vostre amie fuisse.
> (vv. 5005-08)

Guinglain's indecisive conduct causes the same uncertainty to the Pucelle as does his lady to Renaut watching for a *beau sanblant.* The love Guinglain could show to his *amie* depends on the *beau sanblant* Renaut's lady might grant him. The maid with magic powers, like the romancer Renaut, will perform in keeping with the will and deeds of the loved one. Renaut leaves everything to his lady. We may say that he leaves to her the choice of *matiere* and *sen,* much as Chrétien left to the Countess of Champagne those he received for the *Chevalier de la charrette.* Each romancer applies his *painne* and *antancion* to realizing the plot his lady wants to have written.

The use of description in the examples we have examined points to the multiplication of epithets enjoined by the arts of poetry and prose,[19] but multiplication of a particular kind. Not only are the principal figures displayed with a variety of epithets that define their unique excellence, they are also surrounded by secondary figures whose descriptions are comparable to theirs, or are distinguished from and even opposed to them. This produces an array of types, with diverse qualities and defects that focus on and narratively define a dominating context and intention. It is a variety of that "analogical composition" and "incremental recurrence" that have been identified in Chrétien's romances, and which his peers and epigones also practiced.[20]

Much has been made in recent years of the place of logic in Chrétien's art of romance.[21] The force of logical demonstration depends on the type of persons or things posited syllogistically. The positing of types and their narrative (the rhetorical hypothesis) is therefore fundamental to "plotting."[22] We must therefore take note of what kinds of persons we are shown in order to understand how to read a given romance. "Socrates is a man" like the herdsman in *Yvain*. What does this mean with regard to Calogrenant and his actions, or to Yvain and his? Guinglain is a lover. What does this mean, and how does it permit us to evaluate his acts? The simplicity of romance descriptions, the complexity of romance adventures, marvels, and narratives, are composite and integrated facets of the art of romance invention. Examining and comparing descriptions within a given work and among them, as the romancers themselves did, will facilitate our appreciation of their art, the narrative logic of their works, and their reception. They can appeal not only to abstract notions of good and evil (thesis), but also to personal instances of good or bad, desirable or undesirable actions or feelings. We have seen this in the illustrations selected from medieval descriptive theory and its application in representative French romances.

Notes

[1]See my chapter on "The Art of Description" in Norris J. Lacy, Douglas Kelly, and Keith Busby, eds., *The Legacy of Chrétien de Troyes* (Amsterdam: Rodopi, 1987), I, 191-221.

[2]See Alfons Hilka, ed., *Der Percevalroman von Christian von Troyes* (Halle: Niemeyer, 1932), pp. 657-58, esp. vv. 1805-09 note.

[3]Martín de Riquer, "Perceval y las gotas de sangre en la nieve," *Revista de filología española*, 39 (1955), 186-219; Don A. Monson, "La 'surenchère' chez Chrétien de Troyes," *Poétique*, 70 (1987), 232; Douglas Kelly, "Le lieu du temps. le temps du lieu," *Le nombre du temps: Mélanges Paul Zumthor* (Paris: Champion, 1988), pp. 123-26.

[4]See especially Karl-Heinz Bender's studies: "L'essor des motifs du plus beau chevalier et de la plus belle dame dans le premier roman courtois," in *Lebendige Romania: Festschrift für Hans-Wilhelm Klein*, Göppinger Akademische Beiträge, 88 (Göppingen: Kümmerle, 1976), pp. 35-46; "Beauté et mariage selon Chrétien de Troyes: un défi lancé à la tradition," in *Mittelalterstudien: Erich Köhler zum Gedenken*, Studia Romanica, 55 (Heidelberg: Carl Winter, 1984), pp. 31-42; and "Beauté, mariage, amour: la genèse du premier roman courtois," in *Amour, mariage et transgressions au moyen âge*, eds. Danielle Buschinger and André Crépin, Göppinger Arbeiten zur Germanistik (Göppingen: Kümmerle, 1984), pp. 173-83.

[5]See my *The Arts of Poetry and Prose*, forthcoming in the series "La Typologie des sources du moyen âge occidental" published by the Centre d'Etudes Médiévales at the Université de Louvain-la-Neuve, Belgium.

[6]Note Matthew of Vendôme's counsel: "Plerumque descriptio personae est tempestiva, plerumque superflua," in his *Ars versificatoria*, 1.38, in Edmond Faral, *Les arts poétiques du XIIe et du XIIIe siècle: recherches et documents sur la technique littéraire du moyen âge* (Paris: Champion, 1924); and the incisive observations by Don A. Monson, "La 'surenchère'," on catalogues and the use of rhetorical devices for stylistic and narrative invention.

[7]John O. Ward, "The Commentator's Rhetoric. From Antiquity to the Renaissance: Glosses and Commentaries on Cicero's *Rhetorica*," in James J. Murphy, ed., *Medieval Eloquence: Studies in the Theory and Practice of Medieval Rhetoric* (Berkeley, Los Angeles, London: Univ. of California Press, 1978), pp. 25-67, which rehearses material collected in far more complete form in his Univ. of Toronto doctoral dissertation: "*Artificiosa eloquentia* in the Middle Ages," 1972.

[8]E. Faral, *Arts poétiques*, pp. 77-78; cf. Matthew of Vendôme, *Ars*, 1.74-92. I have identified these topoi in the representation of Lancelot in Chrétien's *Charrette;* see "Les fées et les arts dans la représentation du Chevalier de la charrette," in *Lancelot: Actes du Colloque des 14 et 15 janvier 1984, Université de Picardie, Centre d'Etudes Médiévales*, ed. Danielle Buschinger, Göppinger Arbeiten zur Germanistik, 415

(Göppingen: Kümmerle, 1984), pp. 85-97. Eugene Vance has studied them in the *Erec* and *Yvain* in *From Topic to Tale: Logic and Narrativity in the Middle Ages*, Theory and History of Literature, 47 (Minneapolis: Univ. of Minnesota Press, 1987). On the critical problems of modern *Toposforschung*, see Walter Haug, *Literaturtheorie im deutschen Mittelalter: von den Anfängen bis zum Ende des 13. Jahrhunderts. Eine Einführung* (Darmstadt: Wissenschaftliche Buchgesellschaft, 1985), pp. 11-15.

[9]Cf. Rupprecht Rohr, "Zur Skala der ritterlichen Tugenden in der altprovenzalischen und altfranzösischen höfischen Dichtung," *Zeitschrift für romanische Philologie*, 78 (1962), 292-325.

[10]*Guingamor* vv. 9-14, in *Les lais anonymes des XIIe et XIIIe siècles*, ed. Prudence Mary O'Hara Tobin (Geneva: Droz, 1976).

[11]Ed. Mathias Friedwagner (Halle: Niemeyer, 1897), v. 28. See Ronald M. Spensley, "The Theme of *Meraugis de Portlesguez*," *French Studies*, 27 (1973), 129-33.

[12]For descriptions of the dwarfs, see vv. 1274-80, 2434-39, 2472-84; of the Outredoté, vv. 1860-943; of Belchis, vv. 3761-831.

[13]Renaut de Beaujeu, *Le Bel inconnu*, ed. G. Perrie Williams, CFMA (Paris: Champion, 1929), vv. 3212-44, 4998-5000.

[14]See my "Fées," p. 89.

[15]Vv. 3261-300, 5143-77; there is also the stereotypical description of her as serpent, vv. 3128-48.

[16]Of her magic powers, vv. 1931-43; her conventional beauty and *bonté*, vv. 2218-58, 3943-94; her physical beauty, vv. 2395-414, 4227-46; her beautiful garments in a springtime orchard, vv. 4291-355.

[17]Vv. 4552-88, 4634-58.

[18]Vv. 1-10, 1237-71, 4828-61, 6247-66. See as well Jeri S. Guthrie, "The *Je(u)* in *Le Bel Inconnu:* Auto-Referentiality and Pseudo-Auto-Biography," *Romanic Review*, 75 (1984), 147-61. John L. Grigsby, to whose memory this paper is dedicated, has written a number of studies on the author, narrator, and other inventors, voices, and performers in medieval verse romance: "The Narrator in *Partonopeu de Blois, Le Bel inconnu*, and *Joufroi de Poitiers*," *Romance Philology*, 21 (1967-68), 536-43; "Narrative Voices in Chrétien de Troyes: A Prolegomenon to Dissection," *Romance Philology*, 32 (1978-79), 261-73; and "The Ontology of the Narrator in Medieval French Romance," in *The Nature of Medieval Narrative*, eds. Minnette Grunmann-Gaudet and Robin F. Jones, French Forum Monographs, 22 (Lexington, KY: French Forum, 1980), pp. 159-71.

[19]See Matthew's *Ars*, 1.63 and 1.114.

[20]On these terms, see Norris J. Lacy, *The Craft of Chrétien de Troyes: An Essay on Narrative Art*, Davis Medieval Texts and Studies, 3 (Leiden: Brill, 1980), and Rainer Warning, "Formen narrativer Identitätskonstitution im höfischen Roman," in the *Grundriß der romanischen Literaturen des Mittelalters* (Heidelberg: Carl Winter, 1978), vol. IV/1: *Le roman jusqu'à la fin du XIIIe siècle*, pp. 25-59; repr. in *Identität*, eds. O. Marquard and K. Stierle, Poetik und Hermeneutik, 8 (Munich: Fink, 1979), pp. 553-89.

For the use of exemplary figures for this purpose, as in the relation between Pyrame and Thisbé's love and that of Lancelot and Guenevere in the *Charrette*, see D. A. Monson, " 'Surenchère'," p. 238.

[21]Tony Hunt, "The Dialectic of *Yvain*," *Modern Language Review*, 78 (1977), 285-99; ibid., "Aristotle, Dialectic, and Courtly Literature," *Viator*, 10 (1979), 95-129; ibid., *Chrétien de Troyes: Yvain (Le Chevalier au lion)*, Critical Guides to French Texts, 55 (London: Grant & Cutler, 1986); E. Vance, *Topic*.

[22]W. Trimpi, "The Ancient Hypothesis of Fiction: An Essay on the Origins of Literary Theory," *Traditio* 27 (1971), 55.

The Design of the *Didot-Perceval*

Norris J. Lacy

The *Didot-Perceval* is not, according to traditional views, what
Chrétien de Troyes would have called a *molt bele conjointure*. Of some
interest as a reworked version, presumably, of Robert de Boron's lost
Perceval romance,[1] it is generally seen as virtually formless,[2] a random
assemblage of material taken from Chrétien and the Second Continuation, as
well as from Robert. Furthermore, narrative interest in Perceval's initial
naïveté and in his gradual awakening and growth is largely lacking. What
remains, according to most assessments, is in other words a conglomeration
of disparate events, some of which do not fit the presumed design of the
work (or its model), and all of which are narrated rather perfunctorily, with
little concern for the development and elucidation of character.

Such assumptions about the work merit reexamination, although it is
clear from the outset that even the most obstinately revisionist of readings
will not let us pronounce the *Didot-Perceval* a masterpiece. On the other
hand, I am by no means persuaded that the work is devoid of merit, certainly not so much so that critical concerns should be limited to such questions
as authorship and sources. In particular, the design and form of the romance are in my view undeserving of neglect. Furthermore, we will see
that the author does depict Perceval's psychological and moral development—but not by commenting explicitly or by tracing it in detail (for the
evolution of his character is not his most pressing artistic concern). Rather,
he simply constructs scenes in which the hero progressively offers different
reactions to similar events, enabling the reader to evaluate the incremental
variations and draw appropriate conclusions about character development.

If we exclude the final four episodes, which constitute a *Mort Artu*
pendant, the romance takes us from the scene in which the fame of Arthur's

court makes Alain le Gros decide to send his son Perceval there, to the episode in which the healed Fisher King dies and is replaced by Perceval, the split Perilous Seat is joined together, and Merlin withdraws from the world. In the intervening material, scenes of standard chivalric endeavor alternate with quest episodes, and it is thus essential from the beginning to understand clearly the role and importance of chivalry in this work. Perceval's mission is to find the Fisher King's castle and ask about the Grail, and he announces his determination to do so, resolving never to remain two nights in the same place until his quest is complete (p. 151). What we might easily overlook is the fact that, while we may see traditional chivalry in some romances (e.g., Chrétien's *Perceval*) as a needless distraction that is finally incompatible with the moral development required of the successful Grail knight,[3] the *Didot-Perceval* implies no such incompatibility. On the contrary, Merlin specifically informs Arthur early in the work (in a kind of prologue, printed by Roach as an appendix) that the chosen knight must have done "tant . . . d'armes et de cevalerie, en tournois et par querre aventures, que il sera li plus alosés del monde" (p. 306). Soon after, the voice that rebukes Arthur for allowing Perceval to sit in the Perilous Seat repeats that the chosen knight must have ". . . tant fait d'armes et de bontés et de proueces . . ." and must have won "le pris de la chevalerie del siecle" (p. 151).

Perceval's task will thus be to achieve chivalric distinction in the most traditional sense, but to resist all the distractions from his quest that conventional chivalry may be expected to provide. Thus, whereas Chrétien's Perceval will presumably have to deny or transcend his chivalric ambitions in order to achieve the Grail quest, the hero of the *Didot-Perceval* must retain his and pursue them to their conclusion. Here, chivalric accomplishment is a prerequisite for success in the Grail Castle, and a realization of this fact will easily resolve some of the apparent structural and thematic problems of the *Didot-Perceval*.

These dual imperatives—the dogged pursuit of chivalric distinction, the resolute refusal to be distracted from his goal—are supplemented and complicated by a third: love. For Arthur, love appears to justify and permit all; when Perceval tells the king that he fought in disguise for the sake of love, the latter laughs and forgives him, remarking that "çou que on faisoit por amor devoit on legierement pardouner" (p. 148). But if love justifies all, love and women nonetheless provide the most serious threats of distraction from one's higher calling, and in at least one case, Perceval's preoccupation with a lady will cause him to commit an offense against proper conduct by inadvertently killing a knight.

To facilitate a detailed discussion of the romance's design,[4] it may be useful to offer first a schematic summary of the episodic organization of the work:

1.   Fame of Arthur's court leads Alain to send his son Perceval there.
2.   Joust at Court; Perceval abstains first day, then fights in a disguise provided by Gauvain's sister. Perceval sits in Perilous Seat. Grail quest is initiated.
3.   Orguelleus de la Lande episode (Perceval redresses an offense committed by a dwarf).
4.   Chessboard castle scene; Perceval undertakes a hunt for the white stag in order to win a lady's love.
5.   Perceval meets his sister; they visit their hermit uncle, who instructs him about the Grail and the quest.
6.   Episode of Ugly Damsel who later becomes beautiful at Arthur's court.
7.   Gué Perilleus: Perceval first defeats Urbain, then is attacked by birds, who are Urbain's lady and her damsels transformed in order to defend him against Perceval.
8.   Perceval is instructed in his quest by two children in a tree, then by Merlin in the form of a great shadow.
9.   Perceval's failure in the castle of the Fisher King. He is then reproached for his failure by a damsel in the forest.
10. Chessboard castle episode concluded successfully, but Perceval now refuses to remain with the lady of the castle.
11. Perceval's second visit to his uncle; additional instruction.
12. Tournament at the White Castle; Perceval abstains on the first day, then participates in unrecognized armor provided by the daughter of his host.
13. Merlin appears as a reaper to rebuke and instruct Perceval.
14. Second visit to the Fisher King. Perceval asks the Grail question and breaks the spell. The Perilous Seat is rejoined; Bron dies three days later, and Perceval becomes lord of the Grail.

Even a perfunctory reading of the text reveals an effort to organize the work according to a system of doubled or interrupted episodes.[5] Simple logic dictates, of course, the rejoining of the Perilous Seat, split during the second episode when an unworthy Perceval sits in it, and the doubling of the Grail Castle scene, as Perceval's failure during his first visit is redressed during a later return to the Castle. During the course of the work, Perceval twice visits his hermit uncle to receive instruction, and twice he encounters Merlin, who (once in the form of a dark shadow, once as a reaper) provides similar instruction and occasional rebukes for his failures.

One other episode (no. 3) is doubled in a way that is common in medieval romance:[6] Perceval hears from a maiden the detailed account of a failed adventure and immediately repeats it successfully, avenging the injustice of the original events. Some parts of the romance are divided rather than actually doubled. One of the major episodes, the visit to the Chessboard Castle (taken from the Second Continuation), is split into two parts; the strange events that occur when Perceval comes to the castle early in the work are suspended, to be completed and explained only much later, when Perceval returns to it.

There are two other doubled scenes, where the thematic and structural similarity is just short of identity. Episode 2, at the beginning of Perceval's chivalric career, consists of a tourney; the hero, whose hand is slightly wounded, abstains from participating the first day; the second day he agrees to fight, but in a disguise provided by Gauvain's sister. This episode very clearly foreshadows the third to last episode (the White Castle scene), the structure of which largely duplicates that of the earlier one. In that scene, inserted between Perceval's second visit to his uncle and his second encounter with Merlin, he again abstains (this time by choice, rather than because of a wound) on the first day; the next day he participates, once again fighting in disguise, and this time wearing the sleeve provided by his host's daughter.

We can best dramatize the separation and overlapping of doublets by a brief recapitulation with reference to the schema offered above. The Chessboard Castle scenes occupy episodes 4 and 10; the two tourneys are numbers 2 and 12. Episode 5, the visit to the hermit uncle, is reflected in the second visit, which is episode 11. No. 8 is Merlin appearing as a shadow, a scene recalled by Merlin as a reaper in No. 13, while the Grail Castle and Fisher King episodes are 9 and 14 (and the Perilous Seat is part of 2 and 14).

Thus, even without the episode that is divided into two reflecting halves (no. 3, the Orguelleus de la Lande), but counting the two scenes involving the Perilous Seat, there are six clear sets of doubled or divided episodes, arranged in overlapping or interlaced order:

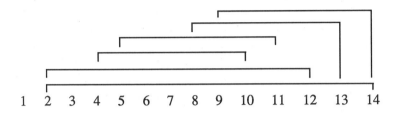

    The point in identifying such pairs of episodes is not merely to suggest that the poet is not indifferent to the construction of his work, although that is certainly one conclusion, but also to trace and analyze the thematic implications of form.[7] Logically, of course, the use of doublets invites us to compare and contrast the two components, and differences between them will often enable us to clarify thematic matters (such as the relationship of Perceval's love interest to the Grail quest), as well as to define the compositional skill of the *Didot-Perceval*'s author. There is generally a progression from the first to the second part of each set; such a progression is of course the entire point of the two visits to the Grail Castle, but in other cases we may detect only a small (but not insignificant) shift of fact or focus.

    The Chessboard Castle episode provides the first serious test of Perceval's character and resolve.[8] When he meets the lady of the castle, he falls in love with her and is immediately ready to undertake an adventure for her sake. The author's compositional method is effectively illustrated by the relationship of the two widely separated segments of this episode, and in particular by Perceval's reactions in each. Now, the Chessboard Castle is a scene that, in Roach's view, has "nothing to do with his [Perceval's] quest for the Grail" (p. 52). Roach is indeed correct, in a literal sense, for the two segments of Chessboard Castle scene contain no reference to the Grail quest until the very end of the second part, after Perceval has successfully accomplished his goal. Yet, in another sense, it has everything to do—at least by contrast— with his Grail quest, to which it forms an unmistakable counterpoise. In addition, it clearly illustrates the evolution of the hero toward the state he must attain as a prerequisite for success in his quest.

In the episode in question, he undertakes a task (hunting the white stag) for a lady who promises to love him and make him lord of her castle, a promise he receives with pleasure and anticipation. Moreover, when he first fails, he vows, in an obvious parallel to his vow concerning the Grail quest, that he will never rest until he recovers the stag's head and the lady's dog.[9] Much later, after numerous complications and adventures, he succeeds, only to decline the reward for which he had worked, for (we are told) he now had no desire to remain there, and ". . . jou ai un afaire en le cort le rice roi Artu . . . et sor vos le metrai tout" (p. 218). Here, as elsewhere, his maturation is indicated by the juxtaposition or dramatization of stages in his growth, without authorial commentary.

The fundamental tension and crisis of the work grow out of the presence of these two alternating forces and quests: desire to find the Grail Castle, and desire to serve the lady. Only in the conclusion of the Chessboard Castle scene does Perceval reject the second in favor of the first. Whereas he had responded to the lady's earlier promise by agreeing enthusiastically to do whatever she asked in exchange for the anticipated amorous and political reward, he responds now to her offer by refusing his reward and reaffirming his dedication to the Grail quest, insisting (pp. 218-19) that his quest precludes his even staying the night, since he had sworn never to spend two nights in one place and had already slept there once. Thus, the contrast between Perceval's initial aspiration and his eventual demurral provides the principal justification for the Chessboard Castle episode, which does indeed have a great deal to do, at least as counterpoint, with the Grail quest: love triumphs initially, but ultimately it is superseded by a nobler quest. The hero will perform the tasks he has agreed to undertake, but he will accept no reward that delays his pursuit of his paramount goal.

In some episodes, the contrast or gradation between doubled events is far more obvious than here. The two visits to Perceval's hermit uncle are related not only in their general subject matter, but also by the particular content of the scenes. In the first, Perceval learns that his mother has died; in the second, that his sister has died. The parallelism of these revelations is disrupted by his reaction—virtual indifference in the former, sincere grief in the latter—indicating something of his progressive maturation.

The hermit scenes are also revealing in a more specific way. The first visit includes his uncle's admonition that he not kill knights, but spare them and ". . . soufrés en maintes manieres por l'ame a la vostre mere" (p. 182); upon his departure, though, as if to underline his failing immediately, the poet has him mortally wound a knight who attacks him. Although brief, this is a complex and important scene, problematical because Perceval inflicts the wound only in self-defense and thus might be considered innocent of willful disobedience. Indeed, until the last instant, Perceval is entirely unaware of the attacking knight, and after the fight, he feels remorse, because "it is a great sin to kill a knight." Yet, Perceval's motivation is as important as the death itself: he ignores his uncle's advice because he is thinking not of his proper quest, but of other matters, specifically of the lady: "tant pensoit a sen afaire et a le demisele qui son braket li avoit baillié" (p. 184).

The two tournaments in which Perceval abstains the first day and fights thereafter offer a special case. Women play an important role in both, and the author tells us that Perceval undertakes the first simply for love. Motivation is less clear in the second, and it is never announced by the character or by the author. Perceval does agree to wear a lady's sleeve "out of love,"[10] but he had already planned to participate, and for want of another motive, we must ascribe to him a knight's most basic desire: to display and prove his chivalric excellence. Because this episode appears to be completely unconnected to Perceval's quest to find the Grail Castle, it is here in particular that a perception of the relative structural coherence of the romance is dependent on our understanding of the relation of chivalry to moral worth.

The similarities between the two episodes extend to the consequences of the events, for each is followed by important errors committed by Perceval and then by a marvelous occurrence in which he is rebuked for his failings. The first time, he is as impressed as others with his prowess, and he sits in the Perilous Seat (with unfortunate results[11]). That error is then followed by the appearance of a miraculous voice that upbraids Arthur and Perceval (for ignoring Merlin's instructions) and speaks of the Grail; immediately, Perceval vows to seek the Grail, never staying two nights in the same place. It is precisely this oath that he violates after the second tourney, when he wishes to return to his host's castle, where he has already spent two nights. Immediately, Merlin appears to him (as had the earlier mysterious voice) and rebukes him for his offense. Thus, the two tournament episodes appear to have been constructed in nearly identical fashion in order that the second, followed by Perceval's violation of his oath, might recall both the scene in which he made that oath and the reason for it.

To demonstrate that the poet has made an effort to tie up loose ends and to bring his work to a thematically effective conclusion, we need only review the events following Perceval's first, abortive, visit to the Grail Castle. That episode is followed by the return to the Chessboard Castle, where, as I have noted, he demonstrates his moral progress by declining the lady's love. Next is the return to his hermit uncle, where Perceval's reactions and renewed resolve (p. 222: ". . . je jamais n'aresterai si arai trovee le maison mon taion . . . ," the Fisher King) indicate his additional growth. The final episode before his successful return to the Fisher King's castle is the tournament at the White Castle, which confirms that he possesses the chivalric stature required of the Grail knight. Now he is ready to succeed where he had earlier failed. Thus, in the Grail Castle, he asks the question that repairs the Perilous Seat and allows the Fisher King to die after instructing Perceval, who will now succeed him as lord of the Grail.

To this point we have been dealing with pairs of episodes (or with halves of divided episodes) that mirror each other prominently. Yet, in addition to such evident systems of doubling, of foreshadowing and recall, the romance includes scenes that, without duplicating each other, contain identical or analogous elements. The result is a system of correspondences or echoes that resonate back and forth through the work. Obviously, the first half of the suspended Chessboard Castle episode (no. 4) leads us to anticipate its conclusion (no. 10), and that conclusion explains a number of remarkable phenomena, including the ability of an old woman to become beautiful at will. The latter motif inevitably recalls an earlier scene (no. 6), in which a hideously ugly damsel, ridiculed by Perceval and then by Kay, eventually does become beautiful. But no. 10, the concluding portion of the Chessboard Castle scene, also includes the story of a knight who, while agreeing to remain with a woman and serve her, asks to be allowed to continue practicing chivalry. That sequence very nearly duplicates an earlier one, at the Gué périlleux (no. 7), in which Urbain, in love with a fairy maiden, agrees to abandon errantry at her request but, reluctant to cease performing deeds of chivalry, is permitted to guard the ford and joust with all passing knights.[12]

The Gué périlleux episode in turn includes a sequence in which Perceval breaks a spell, killing a woman who had been transformed into a bird; at the bird's death she resumes her human form—but as a dead woman. Lest Perceval (or we) lament her death, he is quickly assured that she is now safe and comfortable in Avalon. The killing is thus an obviously salutary act, and the event is clearly related to the climactic episode (no. 14) when Perceval, now through verbal rather than martial means, breaks the final spell and offers a long-awaited release, also through death, to the Fisher King.

In some cases, the sharing of motifs in such a way is important for thematic reasons; elsewhere, it may contribute simply to the cohesiveness of the work, as it links one episode to another, itself connected to a third and perhaps to a fourth as well, and so on. Such a sharing of motifs, setting off a series of resonances throughout the work, is by no means uncommon in romances, and in some instances it is considerably more elaborate and more effective than here. In Chrétien's *Perceval,* for example, Perceval witnesses Arthur's reverie occasioned by the loss of his gold cup. That reverie foreshadows Perceval's own, in the scene of the blood on the snow, which itself connects with the bleeding lance, with Blanchefleur, and perhaps with Perceval's departure from home and his mother's death. Furthermore, Arthur's gold cup presents a clear analogy to the Grail, and various elements of the Grail Castle scene draw other episodes into the extensive web of analogical relationships that so effectively hold Chrétien's work together. Of course, Chrétien's superior talent is the primary reason for the structural superiority of his work, but it is also true that, at less than half the length of the Perceval plot of Chrétien's romance, the *Didot-Perceval* has no need for elaborate formal procedures; and the doubling of episodes and the sharing of motifs are clearly sufficient to exert a cohesive force within the romance. In fact, the selectiveness and over-simplification required for a brief analysis, such as this is, doubtless give the impression not of formlessness but of *over*-organization to the point of narrative predictability. Yet, many of the episodes abound in accounts of battles, encounters, and marvelous occurrences that I have not mentioned. Such detail provides a texture of open, unpredictable narrative elaboration counterbalancing the somewhat mechanistic compositional method that relies on structural and thematic doubling.

It is not my intention to offer an unreserved defense of the *Didot-Perceval* author. He is no Chrétien de Troyes. The mystery of the Grail Castle events is lacking, since they and the proper Grail question are explained to us at the very beginning (p. 151). Perceval is moreover severely lacking in the anguish that Chrétien's hero feels at his failure; throughout, he is a flat, unengaging character. Further, the author's method itself reduces many dramatic moments in the narrative to bland understatement that borders on the comical. When Merlin rebukes Perceval for breaking his vow, the young man says, in effect, "I just forgot about it," and Merlin replies: "In that case, it is easier to forgive you" (p. 238). Thus, the failure that jeopardizes the quest is simply forgotten.[13]

Yet, the author has not, as some critical treatments may have implied, succeeded only in bringing chaos out of order. Admittedly, he has taken episodes from several sources and has reordered and transformed some of them. But few are the medieval authors who do not do as much. The proper question is not whether he has followed a single source faithfully; in fact, if his source is pertinent at all, the question is whether his modifications of that source or sources have been made in the interest of effective elaboration of his design and expression of his themes. In the case of the *Didot-Perceval,* the answer, with only modest qualification, is yes.

Notes

[1]There is, however, less than unanimous agreement about the origin of this text, since the evidence is largely circumstantial. The authorship of the work is of no great consequence for this essay, and for the sake of convenience I refer to the *Didot-Perceval* as Robert's work.

[2]One early exception, involving at least a half-hearted defense of Robert's compositional skill, is offered by Pierre Le Gentil, in his chapter "The Work of Robert de Boron," in Roger Sherman Loomis, ed., *Arthurian Literature in the Middle Ages* (Oxford: Clarendon, 1959), pp. 251-62. Le Gentil contends that Perceval's exploits in the *Didot-Perceval* ". . . are not as haphazard and inconsequential as at first sight they seem to be" (p. 261) and that ". . . there is in the fortunes of Perceval a noble design" (p. 262). More recently, Rupert T. Pickens has expressed considerably greater enthusiasm for the composition, praising the author's "consciousness of his narrative artistry" and pronouncing the work "a minor masterpiece"; see his " 'Mais de çou ne parole pas Crestiens de Troies . . .': A Re-Examination of the Didot-*Perceval*," *Romania*, 105 (1984), 510.

[3]See, for example, my *The Craft of Chrétien de Troyes* (Leiden: Brill, 1980), pp. 2-6. Pierre Gallais makes the same point categorically in *Perceval ou l'initiation* (Paris: Les Editions du Sirac, 1972), p. 43.

[4]For a summary of the work and the division into episodes, see William Roach, ed., *The Didot "Perceval" According to the Manuscripts of Modena and Paris* (Philadelphia: University of Pennsylvania Press, 1941, p. xx. Roach follows the outline offered by Ernst Brugger but, as the first episode included by Brugger belongs, he says, to the *Merlin*, he omits it and begins his enumeration of episodes with "B," the passage concerning the fame of Arthur's court. Roach's summary of the narrative is divided into twenty episodes. He considers the "children in the tree" and "Merlin as shadow" passages as two distinct episodes, identified as "J" and "K" in his outline; I take them as one, but the distinction does not materially affect an analysis of the poem.

[5]My references to the *Didot-Perceval*, given parenthetically in the text, are to Roach's edition, and specifically to MS. *E,* the Modena manuscript. However, see also Bernard Cerquiglini, ed., *Perceval en prose, éd. d'après le MS. E. 39 de la Bibliothèque Estense de Modène* (Paris: U.G.E., 1981).

[6]As witness the story, in Chrétien's *Yvain,* of Calogrenant's exploit, which inspires the hero and gives him the opportunity to repeat the adventure and succeed where the former had failed.

[7]In fact, except for the initial scenes (the "prologue") and the first visit to the hermit uncle, the work is divided rather evenly into two halves, the first tracing Perceval's worldly adventures, the second his moral progress.

[8]The first adventure he encounters on his quest (the Orguelleus de la Lande episode) offers a test, but hardly an arduous one, of his resolve. The conclusion of the

episode notes, in passing, that a woman would like to remain with Perceval, but that that is impossible: he is eager to depart because he "pensoit molt a autre cose" (p. 164). Yet, he is obviously not seriously tempted by her, and his attention to his duty, although proper and admirable, is thus something less than a moral victory. As a result, the impression is that the association with the woman offers primarily a prefiguration, albeit an inverted one, of the scene to follow.

[9]The two episodes have other points in common, although some are small and subtle. For example, when he seeks directions to the Chessboard Castle, he is told to take the road to the left (p. 217); it is doubtless not coincidence that, by contrast (p. 203), he was directed to take the road to the right in order to reach the Grail Castle.

[10]Despite his statement, there is no evidence that he has any love for this lady (or perhaps even for the lady in the earlier tournament scene). The expression is clearly a formula required by courtesy; it means little, if anything, more than "out of respect." A particularly revealing use of the formula occurs in the *Mort Artu,* when a blind promise obligates Lancelot, passionately in love with the Queen, to participate in a tourney as the champion of a young woman who means nothing to him. In fact, he is vexed by her request (*l'en pesa moult*), for if the Queen knew of it, she would surely be angry with him. Having promised, he is of course required to do as the woman asks but despite his resentment, he says that it is *por l'amor de li* that he will fight. See Jean Frappier, ed., *La Mort le Roi Artu* (Geneva: Droz, 1936; 3rd ed. 1959), pp. 10-11.

[11]Specifically, the stone splits, and we soon learn that Perceval would have perished had it not been for the merit of his father Alain and his grandfather Bron, the Fisher King.

[12]Both of these episodes, and particularly the Gué périlleux scene, recall the opening of the Chessboard Castle scene, when the lady imposes a condition Perceval must meet; that episode is, however, an inverted prefiguration of the others, since her condition imposes on him not slavery or inactivity, but a specific chivalric quest that will require his departure.

[13]Of course, this technique is explained and implicitly defended within the text. The author notes that the work is the account dictated by Merlin to Blaise, and he insists that he is telling neither more nor less than was included in his source: ". . . nos n'en disons fors tant com au conte en monte et que Merlins en fist escrire a Blayse son maistre . . ." (p. 220). Nonetheless, this pretext, while offering an ostensible justification, does not obscure the author's stylistic and technical deficiencies.

The Quest for Significance in *La Queste Del Saint Graal* and Malory's *Tale of the Sankgreal*

John F. Plummer

Thomas Malory reduced by two-thirds the length of *La Queste del Saint Graal* in creating his *Tale of the Sankgreal,* and in particular he reduced the interpretations of dreams and visions offered by monks and hermits in the story. This reduction has been interpreted in a variety of ways. Because the excisions come so often at the expense of the elaboration of religious doctrine, it has often been argued, most prominently by Eugène Vinaver, that Malory sought to secularize the Grail adventure. Malory, in this understanding, "regarded the intrusion of the Grail upon Arthur's kingdom not as a means of contrasting earthly and divine chivalry and condemning the former, but as an opportunity offered to the knights of the Round Table to achieve still greater glory in *this* world. . . . [T]hroughout the story Malory is primarily concerned with 'erthly worship', not with any higher purpose, and his one desire seems to be to secularize the Grail theme as much as the story will allow."[1] Sandra Ihle, in a particularly sensitive reading, sees in Malory's reduction of the length as well as the figural and doctrinal qualities of the hermits' interpretations a "consistent effort to confine his work to the literal plane,"[2] and concludes that in the *Sankgreal* "the quest serves as a vehicle to test the knightliness—in the sense of Christian chivalry constantly set forth by Malory—of the members of the Round Table. The adventures encountered by the knights are not shadows of transcendent reality but are real adventures that prove their mettle."[3] Mary Hynes-Berry similarly argues that Malory "probably did not even see the invitation to read allegorically. . . . He reproduces the plot—stripped of its discursive presentation; the allegorical level of the romance is

subtracted."[4] Charles Whitworth, by contrast, feels that Malory understood
the spiritual quality of the *Queste* better than he is often given credit for:
"Malory dispenses with pages of homiletics, but retains just enough for us
to see that he was not out to ride roughshod over the religious legend. . . .
The spiritual message—not the same thing as doctrine—remains, as well as
a certain reverence."[5]

What follows is not intended to dispute any of these readings as
much as to attack the problem from another perspective. I agree that the
values of Camelot may still be taken earnestly in Malory's work after the
Grail has come and gone. But I think Malory's method, his strategy for
ensuring that Camelot's values would survive the comparison with those of
the Grail, has less to do with a simple reduction in the spiritual than a sharp-
ening of the contrast between secular and spiritual, the literal and figural. In
another context, Vinaver once noted that "it has never been properly
explained how it comes about that while in Malory there are fewer marvels
and more realistic detail, the feeling of the marvelous is not lessened, but
intensified."[6] In his *Sankgreal,* I believe, Malory's strategy was precisely
to accomplish that feeling of the marvelous, and far from secularizing the
Grail, rather to place it and keep it beyond any adequate comprehension of
the questing knights or his readers. Far from confining himself to a literal
plane, I would argue, Malory points to a gulf between two planes, one
occupied by his readers and Arthur's knights, and the other by the Grail.

An important feature of *La Queste del Saint Graal* is a concern for
the semiotics of the chivalric life. Horses, shields, ships, spears, and armor
are all susceptible to being taken as what they are and also as signs, part of
the significance of the world as God orders it and we apprehend it. The
Queste author's handling of signs is highly didactic, designed to wean the
Arthurian knights from trust in their arms, alliances, and senses, and to
promote a sensitivity to a higher reality, perceivable only through a subtle
and grace-filled reading of signs that are otherwise opaque, and that seem
devoid of significance to most men. As Albert Pauphilet puts it, the *Queste*
"ne nous plonge dans l'incohérence que pour nous en tirer et pour substituer
aux apparitions séduisantes de la fable la réalité d'un enseignement
profitable."[7] The recluses of the tale consistently interpret textually not only
dreams and visions but even actual events. To readers of medieval
romance, this process is not necessarily disconcerting, though the *Queste*
certainly develops the device in surprising ways. Under the influence of
Romans 1:20, "Invisibilia enim ipsius, a creatura mundi, per ea quae facta

sunt, intellecta, conspiciuntur" such early writers as Ireneus had found "nihil vacuum neque sine signo apud Deum," while Alan of Lille wrote that "Omnis mundi creatura / Quasi liber et pictura / Nobis est et speculum," and Bonaventura later held that "totus mundus est umbra, via, vestigium et est liber scriptus forinsecus."[8] Nor is a semiotics of chivalric objects unique to the *Queste* author within the Arthurian romance world; it has been a feature of the romance since Chrétien, as one can see clearly in the comic attempts of Perceval in the *Conte du Graal* to appropriate to himself the signs of chivalry, including his ungrammatical attempts to wear armor over his bumpkinish Welsh homespun, or in the unceremonious removal of Yvain's spurs in the portcullis of Esclados le Ros in *Yvain*. The *Queste* might indeed be seen as the logical extensional limit of a process already some centuries old at the date of its composition, a quest for significance that claims nothing less than a complete and consistent reading of meaning in the universe: "Nihil vacuum neque sine signo," because everything is "apud Deum."

Such semiotic imperialism ran its course in time, and was sharply challenged, certainly, by late medieval nominalism, whose proponents were far less confident that man could read the face of God—with any accuracy—in the landscape. For whatever reasons, and several come to mind, I believe Malory attenuated the sense of the *lisibilité* of the providential design implied in the *Queste* as he reduced it into English. His compressions of the passages featuring spiritual interpretation of dreams, visions, and historical events are due, I believe, not so much to his impatience with them, and not at all to his mystification by them, as to his inability to feel the confidence of his presumably monastically trained thirteenth-century colleague.[9]

In Galahad's first adventure after receiving his miraculous shield at the abbey of white monks, he expels a fiend that has terrorized the abbey with its voice, and removes the body of a false knight lying in the abbey vault, after which he is told by a monk the significance of the adventure. In the *Queste del Saint Graal,* this adventure occupies some four pages, two and a half pages of which are given over to a monk's explanation of the adventure. In Malory, the entire episode occupies a bare thirty-three lines, of which only seven are monastic *explicatio*. Quite evidently, Malory has abridged the episode, and I want to try to seize something of the effect of the abridgement.

Perhaps because this is a first clear instance of a monk's "glossing" an event or object in the world—as opposed to a dream or vision—the

Queste author is quite explicit, careful that Galaad and the reader recognize the nature of the task: Galaad asks a monk if he knows "por quoi tantes merveilles en sont avenues" (p. 37),[10] to which the monk replies that he does, and will be happy to explain, for "vos le devez bien savoir come la chose ou il a grant senefiance" (p. 37). Galaad's question need only mean "Do you know how the body and evil spirit came to inhabit the tomb," but the monk's response addresses not the literal history of the adventure but its significance, its purport, an entirely different level of explanation. The *explicatio* is postponed for a moment, as Galaad tells his young squire to prepare for his knighting by keeping vigil in the chapel for the night, which allows the author to signal a second time his intentions: the monk begins his tale with "Sire vos me demandastes ore la senefiance de ceste aventure que vos avez menee a chief" (p. 37), which is not quite true. Galaad had asked for history, while the monk provides allegory. In the future, both Galaad and the reader will become accustomed to this procedure.

The monk breaks his gloss into several parts: "La tombe qui covroit le mort senefie la durté dou monde" (p. 37) he says, and explains that this obduracy may be understood historically to have occasioned the incarnation, "por cele durté amoloier" (p. 38). Galaad shows his comprehension of the monk's message and methods by saying, eventually, "Or me dites . . . que li cors senefie; car de la tombe m'avez vos bien fet certain" (p. 38). "Et je le vos dirai," the monk continues: "Li cors senefie le pueple qui desoz durté avoit tant demoré. . . ." (p. 38). After his elaboration of this argument, the monk turns to the internal consistency of his explanations: "Or devons veoir," he says, "coment ceste semblance et cele de lors s'entracordent" (p. 39). The scene ends with the monk once more calling attention to his actions, and Galaad's reply: " 'Si vos ai ore dite la verité de ceste chose.' Et Galaad dit que molt i a greignor senefiance que il ne cuidoit" (pp. 39-40). The (considerable) intricacies of the *explicatio* may not be considered here. My interest in the scene is focused on the self-consciousness, the explicitness of the procedure: the monk is careful that Galaad understand that actual, tangible, nonliterary, nonvisionary experience has *senefiance*,[11] and that it is possible to approach that *senefiance* intellectually, to read the signs of providential design and redemption in the tangible world. Galaad's responses suggest that the monk would be satisfied in this regard.

Malory's version of this episode retains, for all its condensation, the essential doctrinal points of the allegory he found in the *Queste,* but the episode, which I quote in its entirety, has become cryptic:

And anone as [Galahad] was unarmed a good man cam and set hym downe by hym and seyd, "Sir, I shall telle you what betokenyth of that ye saw in the tombe. Sir, that that coverde the body, hit betokenyth the duras of the worlde, and the grete synne that oure Lorde founde in the worlde. For there was suche wrecchydnesse that the fadir loved nat the sonne, nother the sonne loved nat the fadir. And that was one of the causys that oure Lorde toke fleyssh and bloode of a clene maydyn; for oure synnes were so grete at that tyme that well-nyghe all was wyckednesse."

"Truly," seyde sir Galahad, "I beleve you ryght well."

(pp. 882-83)[12]

Here there is no invitation to understand method as well as matter, no repetition of intentions, no calling of attention to procedure, and on Galahad's part only an expression of belief, no expression of wonder at the amount of meaning available in the adventure. The *Queste* author has made it as easy as possible for his audience to comprehend the monk's method. Like a good teacher explicating a short story for a class, the monk has taken care to show his method, to emphasize the logic of explication rather than merely pursuing a clever reading whose genesis is obscure. The monk of the *Queste* is educating Galaad in spiritual semiotics, and the *Queste* author is educating his readers. Malory, by contrast, leaves his reader to turn back a page or two to discover whether the adventure was in fact a dream, or at least a vision, for either of those kinds of "text" would be susceptible to such hermeneutics in a way that reality, to our normal way of thinking, is not. But, with Keats's Madeline, Malory's reader may say "No dream, alas! alas! and woe is mine!" and may well feel that the monk has usurped the reader's exclusive prerogative to interpret, symbolically or otherwise, the action of the text.

Malory's severe compression of the scene leaves the kernel of the monk's interpretation of the adventure intact, if not elaborated. According to Ihle, the effect of Malory's abridgement is that "his source's context and indeed the entire allegorical structure are lost, including the highly spiritual *senefiance* attached to the adventure in the *Queste*. Only the moral intent of Christ's coming remains."[13] I would say rather that the primary effect of Malory's condensation is to decrease our sense of the rationality of the process whereby the monk arrives at his "reading," and thus to reduce our access to the process. We can say with Galahad that we believe, but we cannot understand or duplicate the monk's feat of interpretation, for his methods, if any, remain hermetic.

The same process may be seen at work in the adventure that follows: Galahad and the newly knighted Melias ride forth from the abbey and encounter a fork in their road marked by a cross that bears the following inscription:

> Now ye knyghtes arraunte which goth to seke knyghtes adventurys, se here two wayes: that one way defendith the that thou ne go that way, for he shall not go oute of the way agayne but if he be a good man and a worthy knyght. And if thou go on the lyffte honde thou shall nat there lyghtly wynne prouesse, for thou shalt in thys way be sone assayde. (p. 883)

Melias chooses the left hand of the fork, and in his riding discovers a pavilion in which is a rich crown, which he takes. He is immediately confronted by a knight who wounds him severely. Galahad comes upon the scene and defeats first this knight and then another, and helps Melias back to the abbey. As with the adventure of the tomb, there is a monastic *explicatio* for the adventure. A "good man" tells Melias and Galahad that Melias was wounded for the sins of pride and presumption, and that the message on the cross referred to heavenly, not knightly deeds. The two knights defeated by Sir Galahad signify the two sins within Sir Melias, who (or which?) could not withstand the sinless Galahad (p. 886). Though again highly abridged, the essence of the episode comes across from the *Queste,* and again what is omitted is in large part the logicality of the process of interpreting life as a text. For example, in the *Queste* a monk overhears Galaad telling the wounded Mélyant that he must leave him behind now in his quest of the Grail. " 'Coment,' " says one of the brothers, " 'est ele donc comenciee?' " (p. 44). On being assured that the quest has indeed begun, and that Galaad and Mélyant are participants, he says "donc vos di je, sire chevaliers malades, que ceste meschance vos est avenue par vostre pechié. Et se vos me deissiez vostre errement puis que la Queste fu comenciee, je vos mosterroie par quel pechié ce vos avint" (p. 44). The passage is not found in Malory, and significantly so, for here the *Queste* author signals clearly that once the Quest for the Grail has begun, adventure, reality, takes on a textual significance of moral purport, and that its interpretation is a straightforward proposition.

It is precisely this confidence in the rationality of the visible, its clear semiotic relations with the invisible, that is missing in Malory, missing, I believe, deliberately, for the monks' "readings," the significance they find in earthly adventure, Malory consistently reproduces faithfully. It is the clarity of their methodology, the logic of *invisibilia . . . per ea quae facta sunt,* which Malory suppresses. As another example, in the *Queste* we are told of the two knights who signified Mélyant's two sins that Satan had entered into the bodies of two recreant knights, and attacked Mélyant himself, which information transforms what appeared to be real into something close to visionary, in any case something clearly supernatural. In Malory there is no such explanation, and his questing knights and readers alike may find it difficult to understand how two knights may be both real knights, independently pursuing their adventures, and equally signs of another knight's sinful state.[14] It is an intrepid reader who can share the self-confidence of Malory's monks in determining in which cases and under what circumstances an adventure is what it is and is also a text.

Malory's suppression of the logic of Grail textuality opens a gap between the knights and the Grail itself, and thereby reduces the ironic distance between knights and reader. Put another way, the growing self-evidence of the presence of the spiritual within the carnal in the *Queste* separates the sympathies of the readers from Mélyant, Perceval, Lancelot, and Bohort, whereas the cryptic quality of higher reality in Malory's *Tale of the Sankgreal* has the opposite effect.

One can see the effect in a slightly different way in the trying experiences of Perceval, stranded in a wasteland, threatened by wild beasts, and visited by dreams and temptation. In his desert isolation Perceval is visited by a man wearing priestly garb who comforts him, interprets his dreams, and offers him spiritual advice. The priest is succeeded by a beautiful woman, who assures Perceval that the "priest" was a falsifier and liar. She asks Perceval for his help in her struggle to regain possession of lands of which she has been dispossessed, to which Perceval agrees. She then offers herself to him sexually, after extorting another promise, to which Perceval also agrees, being saved from sin only by the accident of glancing at the pommel of his nearby sword and mechanically crossing himself. The sign of the cross destroys the enchantment, for such it was, and the lady, who flees, is revealed as a demon (later as the Enemy himself). The old man returns to comfort the penitent Perceval.

Perceval's problem is to withstand temptations of the flesh. His task is made more difficult by the succession of illusions to which he is subjected, for how does one choose good over evil when one's senses are not to be trusted? Further complication is added by the gentlewoman's asking for Perceval's help in the language of the court, the symbolic system of Camelot itself: it is precisely such "disinherited gentlewomen," as the lady quite accurately points out, that Perceval as Round Table knight has sworn an oath to protect. When the temptation is over, the priest asks Perceval if he knows who the woman was. Perceval replies that he does not, but now feels it must have been a demon sent by the Enemy to tempt him. In both Malory and the *Queste* the priest replies that Perceval is a fool, for the woman was Satan. Perceval may feel sufficiently the fool having failed to see through the "woman" in the first place; that he is made to feel even further the fool for failing to see now that she was no stand-in demon but Satan himself, a point many readers might find secondary if not absolutely beside the point, raises again the question of reader sympathy. Didactically and artistically, everything depends here upon a balance: Perceval and we must feel the temptation—the story could not stand the weight of a half-dozen Galahads—but the signs of warning must be sufficiently clear so that the priest may call Perceval a fool for having missed them without seeming arbitrary or capricious.

As in the episode of Melias and the crossroad, the symbolism of the *Queste* landscape is clearer than Malory's. We might hesitate at hearing the woman denounce the priest as a "sorcerer, a spawner of phrases," for how are we to know that the priest was genuine? In the *Queste* the clues are there: when the woman asks Perceval how he may live in this desert, he replies that he is sustained by a Lord who said that his door will open to those who knock. "Et quant cele ot qu'il li fet mencion de l'Evangile," the *Queste* says, "si ne respont pas a cele parole, ainz le met en autre matiere. . . ." (p. 105). In Malory, the subject is changed, but the narrator does not tell us why. In the *Queste,* the woman claims to have seen Galaad chasing two knights into a river with the intent to kill them, and says that Galaad escaped drowning only by turning back, which both readers and Perceval ought to recognize as patently false; in Malory she says that the knights fled *for fear* of death, and that Galahad escaped drowning through his great strength. In Malory, as she welcomes Perceval into the pavilion where she will lie with him, she "put of hys helme and hys shylde," whereas in the *Queste* she removes his helmet, hauberk, and sword, and then strips him naked, "en pur le cors" (p. 108). Even the ease with which Perceval becomes inebriated on the woman's wine is significant in the *Queste:* "Car a celui tens n'avoit en la Grant Bretaigne point de vin se ce n'ert en mout riche leu, ainz bevoient comunalment cervoise et autres bevrages que il fesoient" (p. 109). There are a number of reasons Malory might have excised such a statement, including its whiff of Gallic condescension, but the effect of its absence is again to remove a moral marker (wine as exotic), which in the *Queste* facilitated one's reading the landscape.

Perhaps the clearest illustration of Malory's derationalization of the hermeneutics of everyday reality is found in Bors's adventure with the false religious. Bors is at a certain point faced with the choice of rescuing his brother Lionel from death or rescuing a maiden from dishonor. He chooses, correctly, to rescue the maiden but then suffers the pain of seeing his brother dead on the ground. In the *Queste,* there are several clear if subtle hints that the monk who shows Bohort Lyonel's body, leads him to a chapel where Lyonel may be buried, and explicates Bohort's vision of the pelican, black bird and white bird, and flower and rotten tree, is an enchanter, and no true monk. For example, when Bohort first encounters him, the man is described as "vestu de robe de religion, et chevauchoit un cheval plus noir que meure" (p. 177). The black horse is of course reminiscent, to the reader though naturally not to Bohort, of the black horse-demon which earlier had almost carried off Perceval.

Malory translates this passage with precision, even down to the—to modern English ears—faulty parallelism, significant black horse and all: "he overtoke a man clothed in a religious wede, and rode on a stronge blacke horse, blacker than a byry. . . ." (p. 962). Next the *Queste* author tells us that the monk shows Bohort a body lying on the ground, which Bohort recognizes as Lyonel's, or so he thinks: "Il le resgarde et conoist, ce li est avis, que ce est son frere" (p. 178). Malory catches this subtlety as well: "Than shewed he hym a new-slayne body lyyng in a buyssh, and hit semed hym well that hyt was the body of sir Lyonell, hys brothir" (pp. 962-63). But "ce li est avis" as a separate adverbial phrase following the main verb is much more striking than Malory's "hit semed hym well that hyt was." Even if we excuse the French Bohort for not suspecting something is wrong here—it is, after all, his *avis*—the *Queste* reader would be a slow learner who did not notice the gratuitousness of the phrase. The next clue in the *Queste* that something is false is the weightlessness of Lyonel's body. After a speech lamenting Lyonel's death, Bohort lifts him up to the saddle:

"Quant il a ce dit, il prent le cors et le lieve en la sele *come cil qui riens ne li poise, ce li est avis . . .*" (p. 178 [emphasis mine]). The "come" is a clue; the "ce li est avis" is a large flag. Something, or everything, about Bohort's surroundings is misleading.

In Malory the "ce li est avis" is dropped; neither Malory's Bors nor Malory's reader is so abundantly warned, and Lionel's weightlessness has lost its significance, its status as clue, appearing as a naturalistic and even touching description of Bors's strength: "And whan he had seyde thus he *toke the body lyghtly in hys armys* and put hit upon the harson of hys sadyll" (p. 963 [emphasis mine]). Bohort asks to be led to a chapel, where the body may be buried, and the monk leads him, in the *Queste* to "une meson viez et gaste en semblance de chapele" (p. 178). Not only might the "semblance" and the desuetude of the building suggest to the French Bohort that this chapel is false, the *Queste* author almost comically shows him looking high and low for any sign of Christian practice in the building: "Boorz quiert amont et aval, mes il ne voit ne eve beneoite ne croiz ne nule veraie enseigne de Jhesucrist" (p. 178).

Malory's Bors, by contrast, would need an actively suspicious imagination to find reason for alarm in this description: ". . . they saw a fayre towre, and afore hit there semed an olde, fyeble chapell; and than they alyght bothe and put hym in the tombe of marble" (p. 963). To be sure, the word "semed" is strange enough to catch a (very) careful reader's eye;[15] Malory has indeed not lost sight of the fact that the chapel is false. But he has reduced the signs of falsity to a shadow of the weight they have in the *Queste,* and he omits the most obvious clue, the absence of sacred signs in the chapel, altogether.

Malory clearly understands the *Queste* author's intentions—to provide the reader with signs that will allow him and Bohort (the reader before Bohort) to read the landscape as a text, and to perceive that the monk, the chapel, the body, and by extension the tower with its temptresses, are part of a spiritual test, or failing that, to reread the scene with a sense of "I should have guessed." The evidence shows too that Malory translates very closely, phrase by phrase; there is no evidence of haste or impatience with the matter. There is ample evidence, however, of a deep sympathy with Bors, and a consistent reduction of the signs in the landscape that might alert him to his danger.

The landscape of the *Queste* identifies itself, if subtly, as significant, as text. "Subtle," interestingly, derives from *sub + tela* ("web") hence

"finely woven," and *tela* in turn is from *texere,* "to weave," as is "text."
The knights embarked upon the quest of the Holy Grail are indeed faced
with a series of subtle subtexts woven into the web of their kingdom itself.
Melias's inscribed cross and two aggressive knights, Galahad's demon-
ridden corpse, Launcelot's tournament of black and white knights, Perceval's priest and beautiful disinherited gentlewoman, Bors's brother Lionel,
Lionel's body, the priest, and the chapel, all of these commonplace elements
of the Arthurian landscape are shown eventually to contain significant spiritual patterns woven into their surface.

If a poem should not mean but be, how much more might Bors feel
that his landscape should be and not mean. For the author of the *Queste,*
the landscape *is* a poem, the knights readers, and the poem's moral the
accessibility of the spiritual. Malory recognized the essential strategy of the
Queste, and had too much integrity to falsify it; his landscape is also a
poem, a text, but, stripped of much of the glossary, all the footnotes, most
of the introduction, and interpreted by cryptic commentators, the text has
become difficult of access. In a well-known addition to his source, Malory
has Launcelot join the recently returned Bors in dictating to the royal clerks
"the adventures of the Sangreall that he had sene" (p. 1036). For Vinaver,
the scene shows Malory making of Launcelot "to the end the dominating
figure . . . [who] speaks like a man who knows the significance of the
mysteries which have been revealed to him."[16] Certainly the image of
Launcelot is being burnished here, but I think we might put this another
way: in Malory, *neither* Launcelot nor Bors "knows the significance of the
mysteries"; Bors has seen and understood more, but his experience remains
enigmatic. The Grail story is, finally, as the colophon states, "one of the
trewyst and of the holyest that ys in thys worlde"; Malory required his
knights to feel and believe the true and holy, but not necessarily to
understand it.

Notes

[1]*The Works of Sir Thomas Malory*. 3 Vols. (Oxford: Clarendon Press, 1967), p. 1535.

[2]*Malory's Grail Quest: Invention and Adaptation in Medieval Prose Romance.* (Madison: Univ. of Wisconsin Press, 1983), p. 121.

[3]*Malory's Grail Quest*, p. 163.

[4]"Malory's Translation of Meaning: *The Tale of the Sankgreal*," *Studies in Philology*, 74 (1977), 244.

[5]"The Sacred and the Secular in Malory's *Tale of the Sankgreal*," *Yale English Studies*, 5 (1975), 20.

[6]"Sir Thomas Malory," in R. S. Loomis, ed., *Arthurian Literature in the Middle Ages: A Collaborative History* (Oxford: Clarendon Press, 1959), p. 547.

[7]*Etudes sur la "Queste del Saint Graal" attribuée à Gautier Map* (Paris: Champion, 1921), p. 171.

[8]Ireneus, *Contra Haereses,* IV, 218, 3 (*PG* 7:1046). Alanus, *Rhythmus* (*PL* 210:579); Bonaventura, *Collationes in Hexaëmeron, Col.* 12, *par.* 14 (*Opera Omnia* [Florence: Quaracchi, 1891], V, 386) and similarly in his *Itinerarium Mentis* II, 11 (*Opera Omnia*, V, 302).

[9]Whitworth, "Sacred and the Secular," p. 25, also feels that the reduction of the length of doctrinal passages need not imply an effort to "secularize" the story. He suggests that the "cutting and condensing have the effect of rendering sharper and frequently more impressive the spiritual lessons delivered by the monks and hermits. . . ."

[10]Albert Pauphilet, ed., *La Queste Del Saint Graal: Roman du xiiie siècle* (Paris: Champion, 1975). All references to *La Queste* will be to this edition; page numbers will, as here, be given parenthetically in the text.

[11]In *L'Arbre et le pain: Essai sur "La Queste del saint graal"* (Paris: SEDES, 1981), pp. 73-74, n. 10, Emmanuèle Baumgartner also notes that "toutes les aventures sont . . . présentées comme ayant pour leur destinataire, en texte et hors texte, le même poids de réel (de fictionnel) sans qu'il y ait jamais de démarcation nette entre ce qui pourrait relever du monde sensible et ce qui est pour nous du domaine de l'imaginaire."

[12]All citations of Malory will be to *The Works;* page numbers will be given parenthetically in the text.

[13]*Malory's Grail Quest*, pp. 120-21.

[14]Malory is well aware that some of the "texts" explicated during the course of the quest are visions or dreams while others are literal events. In the *Queste,* the anchoress who glosses Lancelot's adventure of the tournament of black and white knights insists on the point: the tournament was a figuration of Jesus Christ, she says, "Et neporquant sanz faillance nule et sanz point de decevement estoit li tornoimenz de chevaliers terriens; car assez i avoit greignor senefiance qu'il meismes n'i entendoient"

(p. 143). Malory's version is equally firm: ". . . for that turnamente yestirday was but a tokenynge of oure Lorde. And natforethan *there was none enchauntemente,* for they at the turnemente were erthely knyghtes" (p. 933 [emphasis mine]).

[15]At the risk of belaboring the point, there is nothing intrinsically non-naturalistic about Malory's phrasing; his "seemed" governs an understood "to be," whereas in the *Queste* "en semblance de" modifies the building itself and implies that it is *not* as it seems.

[16]*The Works,* I, xcii.

Initial Readers of Chrétien de Troyes

Hans R. Runte

The study of medieval literature has been greatly enriched in recent years by renewed critical interest in the visual arts of the Middle Ages. Against the background of such encyclopedic works as the Loomises' *Arthurian Legends in Medieval Art,* Lejeune and Stiennon's *La Légende de Roland dans l'art du moyen âge,* Scherer's *The Legends of Troy in Art and Literature,* Buchthal's *Historia Troiana,* or Ross's *Alexander Historiatus,*[1] other literary historians have in theory and practice defined and explored in great detail the field of iconographic representations of medieval narrative (Andersen, Baumgartner, Bullock-Davies, Fleming, McMunn, Nichols).[2] Triggered perhaps by the realization that much of this research, while essentially comparative in nature, has nevertheless remained compartmentalized in studies of the evolution and conventions of visual narration on the one hand, or of textual narration as a mere font of artistic inspiration on the other, current work in the field is attempting to bridge the gap and reverse the methodological thrust by inquiring into the influence of the visual narrative on the genesis, development, and contemporaneous interpretation of medieval texts.[3] According to Lori Walters, for example, scribes and illustrators set out very deliberately to give each of MSS. Paris, B.N. f.fr. 1450 (*Troie, Eneas, Brut,* Chrétien's romances, *Dolopathos*) and 1433 (*Atre périlleux, Yvain*) the appearance of one unified and coherent romance, a new text different from the sum total of its constituent parts.[4] Sylvia Huot considers manuscript illumination as a fundamental aspect of thirteenth- and fourteenth-century poetics.[5] And I have shown myself how visual structuring underscores or contradicts obvious authorial intents, or uncovers latent ones.[6]

The presence of nonauthorial creative wills in medieval copies of literary texts was hinted at, without being critically exploited, as long ago at least as 1909, by Henry Martin:

> Le copiste réservait dans le manuscrit certaines pages ou certaines parties de pages pour recevoir des peintures. . . .[7]

Such visual markers, dividing, subdividing, and graphically structuring the text, were often placed not haphazardly, but according to explicit instructions by a workshop master or supervisor who may be assumed to have had of the *sen* and *conjointure* of the work to be copied a particular understanding. The artist, too, followed instructions congruous with the meaning and organization of the text to be illustrated:

> Le chef d'atelier a sur la table devant lui le volume à illustrer qu'on lui a livré tout écrit, en cahiers volants. Il regarde les places blanches destinées à recevoir les images. . . . Quand le chef d'atelier a bien compris ce qu'il a à faire, il exécute . . . au crayon sur la marge une légère ébauche du sujet.[8]

Regardless of whether these instructions have survived, as is the case, for example, in *La Somme le Roy*[9] or Jean Lebègue's *Histoires que l'on peut raisonnablement faire sur les livres de Salluste,*[10] or lie hidden between the lines of manuscripts as we know them today, they undeniably hold important clues to the manner in which medieval texts were perceived and interpreted by that very early medieval reader, the professional conceptualizer who develops "un programme d'images qui [met] des accents dans le texte. . . ," and for whose existence and role Beat Brenk has recently adduced textual evidence from as early as the sixth century: according to Gregory of Tours, the wife of the bishop of Clermont

> tenebat librum in sinum suum, legens historias actionis antiquae, pictoribus indicans quae in parietibus fingere deberent [pictores].[11]

The manuscripts of Chrétien de Troyes's romances are not devoid of vestiges of interpretative medieval readings. In *Cligés,* MS. Paris, B.N. f.fr. 375 by Perot de Nesle and Jehan Madot, most of the initials are prescribed in the margins, including erroneous ones (on fol. 273e a prescribed

C has been executed as an E). In two lines of *Erec et Enide* (4088 and 5319)[12] and one line of *Yvain* (6143),[13] blank spaces for an *initiale ornée* and two *lettres montantes* clearly indicate that Guiot copied around these prescribed textual markers. In MSS. Paris, B.N. f.fr. 1374, and Turin, Bibl. naz. 1626 (L.1.13) of *Cligés,* blank spaces indicate where miniatures were planned but not carried out (Paris, fol. 21[c] and 21[d]; Turin, *passim*), and in MS. Paris, B.N. f.fr. 1453 of *Perceval,* fol. 44, the customary rubric is not as usual accompanied by a miniature.

Diffuse indices like these do little more than confirm the presence of a conceptualizer; they do not permit reconstructing his concept of the romances. Nor are the miniatures, whether executed or left undone, of great assistance here: in more than two dozen manuscripts, there are no more than three of them for *Erec et Enide* (Paris, B.N. f.fr. 24403), ten for *Yvain* (Paris, B.N. f.fr. 1433), sixty-two for *Perceval* (Paris, B.N. 1453, 12576, 12577, Nouv. Acq. 6614; Montpellier 249, Mons 4568), and that is all. Fortunately, this dearth of the richest of all visual structuring devices, the historical reasons for which are summarized by Gloria Torrini-Roblin (with references to Stones, Diringer, and Rouse),[14] is amply compensated by a great abundance of prominently displayed initials.

Nothing more than a cursory scan of this wealth of markers establishes that they were not so liberally sprinkled throughout the romances for reasons unrelated to the narrative: there emerges no nonliterary pattern, no purely mechanical initials-per-folio ratio, nor any other simple organizing principle in their physical distribution. Nevertheless, even when serving the narrative, could they not have been designated more or less at random? Alexandre Micha and Mario Roques, who alluded to their extra-esthetic function, did not think so, suggesting that there are "lettres . . . historiées au début de chaque division" of *Yvain,*[15] and that

> lettres ornées ou lettres montantes peuvent indiquer comment un scribe (ou un éditeur) comprenait les articulations du texte à une époque encore peu éloignée de l'auteur.[16]

Indeed, in the *premier vers* of *Erec et Enide,* for example, only 27 initials out of 145 in five manuscripts (Paris, B.N. f.fr. 375, 1376, 1420, 1450, 24403) do not serve any textual purpose. Furthermore, although none of the manuscripts under review here is a direct copy of any of the others, there is a far from coincidental number of common initials, as if the narrative left those anonymous conceptualizers only a limited choice in placing their markers. In *Erec et Enide,* MSS. Paris, B.N. 375, 1376, and 24403, representing the bulk of the right-hand branch in Foerster's and Micha's stemmas,[17] share initials more often than does any other manuscript grouping. Mario Roques estimated[18] that about half of the initials in the Guiot copy of *Erec et Enide* have corresponding initials in MS. Paris, B.N. f.fr. 1450. Foerster even toyed with the idea of using the evidence constituted by initials in the elaboration of stemmas.[19]

Authentic and legitimate, the initials in the manuscripts of Chrétien's romances are an immediate echo of the earliest recoverable readings of his texts, readings, essentially, of the thirteenth century. Studying their deployment and use makes it possible to understand today how Guiot and his fellow scribes, or rather their supervisors, understood Chrétien then, how they dealt with Chrétien's *premier vers* in *Eric et Enide,* or with his complicated technique of *enchevêtrement* in *Yvain,* or with bipartite vs. tripartite *conjointure,* to name only those aspects of his work to the elucidation of which this study of initials in selected manuscripts must be limited.

In six manuscripts of *Erec et Enide* (Paris, B.N. f.fr. 375, 794, 1376, 1420, 1450, 24403) there is a total of 560 initials which, when collated, mark the text in 297 places. Four manuscripts of *Yvain* (Paris, B.N. f.fr. 794, 1433, 12560, 12603) produce 256 initials marking the text in 154 places. On the average, there is an initial every 77 lines in *Erec et Enide,* and every 106 lines in *Yvain,* although in the actual case of Guiot's *Erec et Enide,* for example, as Mario Roques has pointed out, the initials obviously

> découpent à des intervalles très inégaux la copie du texte . . . elles sont
> plus nombreuses dans la première moitié . . . que dans la seconde . . .
> où l'on peut trouver des suites de 500 vers sans aucune coupure.[20]

Guiot's copy distinguishes itself furthermore not only by having the lowest number of initials (59), but also by placing no more than 18 of them at certain textually strategic points where they are meant to mark "le début d'épisodes ou de développements nouveaux"[21] and punctuate the narrative flow.

The grid of initials is traced more finely and more regularly in MSS. Paris, B.N. f.fr. 1420 and 1450 of *Erec et Enide:* Ms. 1420 contains the greatest number of initials (140, of which 24 or 17.1% are placed strategically), and in MS. 1450 a maximum of initials (28 out of 101, or 27.7%)

has a structuring function. How did the designers of the *Erec et Enide* copies, and in particular the conceptualizers of MSS. 1420 and 1450, use the initials they prescribed?

In all six manuscripts they place an initial in line 27 in order to separate clearly the prologue from the main text. In all copies except Guiot's, they comply with Chrétien's wish and provide an initial after the *premier vers* in line 1797. In MSS. 1420 and 1450 they then mark the beginning of the couple's adventures in line 2791; in MSS. Paris, B.N. f.fr. 375 and 1376 this section of the narrative starts with an initial in line 2762. Surprisingly perhaps, only in MSS. 1420 and 1376 is the beginning of the *Joie de la cour* episode recognized and duly initialized.

We have thus, in MS. 1420 at least, a clear division of *Erec et Enide* into four parts. The subdivisions of parts I, II, and IV fall into relatively neat, initialized packages: I.1 hunt, 2. sparrow-hawk, 3. Yder at Arthur's and the couple's departure, 4. Erec and Enide at court; II.1. wedding and gifts, 2. guest list, 3. festivities, bliss, and crisis; IV.1 arrival at Brandigan, 2. magic garden, 3. Evrain's explanations, 4. Maboagrain's defeat, 5. joy and departure, 6. at Arthur's, 7. coronation. Only part III subdivides in an unexpected way. Erec's fight with the two groups of three and five knights is clearly understood and initialized as one adventure (2791-3112), and what we may consider the aftermath or conclusion of one test is usually taken and marked as the introduction to the next in MS. 1420: the *courtois écuyer* (3113-3192) leads into the second adventure (3113-3652), Erec's altercation with Keu at Arthur's court (3911-4252) precedes the adventure with the two giants (3911-4446), Cadoc and Erec's fainting spell (4447-4635) introduces the Count of Limors (4447-4878), and Erec's reconciliation with Enide (4879-4900) is part and parcel of the sixth and last adventure with Guivret (4879-5318).

The conceptualizer of MS. 1450 subdivides the text more in parts I and II and less toward the end. More importantly, his adventure count differs significantly from the arrangements in MS. 1420: encounters with the knights, with Galoain, with Guivret and with the giants are clearly indicated (2791, 3193, 3653, 4253), after which we find, from the middle of the giants adventure onward, an off-beat echeloning of initials which intertwines the actual fight against the giants with the Count of Limors adventure (4353-4878), the actual fight against Limors with the final Guivret episode (4815-5130), and the recuperation at Pointurie with the reception by Evrain (5131-5620). Not only are the last three adventures seen to run together, but in the process the narrative caesura of the *Joie de la cour* (5319) has been missed; Maboagrain becomes just another giant, and the number of Erec's tests is reduced from seven in our reading, or from six in MS. 1420, to five or possibly four.

Table 1 lists 24 initials out of 140 for MS. 1420, and 28 out of 101 for MS. 1450. What functions, if any, do the remaining 116 or 73 intra-paragraphal initials have? "Il apparaît dans l'ensemble," says Mario Roques, "que [les] initiales annoncent moins les moments successifs de l'action" (which is true only quantitatively speaking) "que des épisodes mettant en relief les acteurs et leurs attitudes diverses."[22] Indeed, proper names (Erec, Yder, Gauvain) and titles (reine, roi, pucelle, barons, comte, sire, vavasseur) are readily targeted for initialization, but only under what seem to be carefully defined and consistently observed conditions. One of these is a change of narrative voice (MS. 1450, lines 125, 148, 397, 1337, to mention only examples from the *premier vers*); another a verbal or non-verbal response to direct discourse (MS. 1420, lines 59, 159, 601, 837, 1009, 1124, 1199, 1383, 1785; MS. 1450, lines 175, 311, 601, 639, 1733, 1785); a third an instance of plot progression with or without a capsule summary of preceding story events (MS. 1420, lines 115, 205, 299, 397, 501, 707, 747, 801, 863, 1085, 1337, 1707; MS. 1450, lines 747, 801, 863, 1167, 1227, 1287, 1411, 1497, 1611, 1707). Mario Roques gives a very sensitive interpretation of four changes of tone marked by initials in the middle of ongoing speeches (MS. B.N., f.fr. 794, lines 63, 533, 3395, 4599).[23]

The text of *Yvain,* studied here in four manuscripts (B.N., f.fr. 794, 1433, 12560, 12603), permits the same kind of observations (see Table 2). As far as visual structuring is concerned, MS. 12603 and Guiot's copy, which seems to have received a much better medieval reading for *Yvain* than for *Erec et Enide,* contain, respectively, the greatest number of initials (21 out of 71). Both manuscripts seem to divide the narrative into three parts, paragraphing the text after Calogrenant's story (line 722) and after Yvain's departure with Gauvain (2640). The internal packaging of narrative units holds few surprises in parts I and II; it might be pointed out that MS. 12603 lends special prominence to Yvain's picturesque and dramatic entrance into Laudine's castle (907), and that all four manuscripts single out the invisible Yvain's visible bleeding (1173).

The complexity of part III, for which I have proposed an interpretation elsewhere,[24] has largely escaped the visual structurer. How indeed

Table 1

Erec et Enide

MS. B.N., f.fr. 1450	MS. B.N., f.fr. 1420	
27- 68		
69- 274		
275- 492	27- 546	
493- 546		
547- 580		
581- 1078	547-1078	
1079-1458	1079-1458	
1459-1566		
1567-1796	1459-1796	
* * * * * * * * * * * * * * *		
1797-1864	1797-1864	
1865-1972	1865-1972	
1973-2761		
2762-2790	1973-2790	
* * * * * * * * * * * * * * *		

3 & 5 knights ⎰ 2791-3112 — 2791-3112 } 3 & 5 Knights
⎱ 3113-3192

Galoain ⎰ 3193-3430 — 3113-3430 ⎱ Galoain
⎱ 3431-3652 — 3431-3652 ⎰

Guivret { 3653-4252 — 3653-3910 } Guivret
2 giants { 4253-4352 — 3911-4446 } 2 giants
↓ ⎰ 4353-4740 — 4447-4514 ⎱
2 giants & Limors ⎱ 4741-4814 — 4515-4541 ⎰ Limors
4542-4814

Limors & Guivret { 4815-5130 — 4815-4878 ⎰ Guivret
4879-5318 }
Pointurie & Maboagrain 5131-5620 — * * * * * *
5319-5620

| 5621-5688 | 5621-5688 | |
| 5689-5776 | 5689-5776 | |

Maboagrain { 5777-6358 — 5777-6274 } Maboagrain
6275-6358

| 6359-6484 | 6359-6484 | |
| 6485-6878 | 6485-6878 | |

Table 2

Yvain

MS. B.N., f.fr. 794	MS. B.N., f.fr. 12603	Miniatures in MS. B.N., f.fr. 1433
	1- 172	1
1- 266	173- 266	
267- 482		
483- 560	267- 580	517
561- 722	581- 722	
* *		
723- 906	723- 906	791
907-1172	907- 961	
	962-1172	993
1173-1242	1173-1242	
	1243-1544	1301
1243-1592	1545-1592	
1593-1728	1593-1728	
1729-1944	1729-1944	
1945-2050	1945-2040	
2051-2640	2051-2640	2279
* *		
2641-3336	2641-3336	2785
3337-3478	3337-3556	3361
3479-3556		
3557-4250	3557-4250	
4251-5100	4251-4628	
5101-5983		
5984-6206	4629-6516	5069
6207-6516		
6517-6808	6517-6808	[6809]

would one render Chrétien's intricate *enchevêtrements?* MS. 12603 throws together Lunete's predicament and Harpin de la Montagne (3557-4250; also in Guiot's copy), Lunete's trial and Yvain's encounter with Laudine (4251-4628), as well as Yvain's recuperation, the Noire Epine sisters, Pême Aventure and the Yvain-Gauvain duel (4629-6516). Guiot's copy applies an only slightly finer comb by separating out Pême Aventure (5101) and the duel (5984) and recognition scenes (6207).

As mentioned earlier, *Yvain* is illustrated by ten miniatures in MS. 1433 (see note 3). They occur with consistent irregularity in unforeseeable places inside paragraphs and clearly serve narrative rather than structural functions. Six of them are in fact multiple-scene pictorials recalling and anticipating story material not contained in the unit in which they are placed, such as the fourth miniature (fol. 69ᵛ; line 993), which depicts Yvain fighting Esclados, Yvain in discussion with Lunete, and Esclados lying in state. Even less can be said about the illustrations in *Erec et Enide,* except that the two intra-textual miniatures occur in combat scenes (three knights at 2827, two giants at 4353).

We no longer question *Erec et Enide*'s readability as those named by Frappier or Dragonetti have done.[25] We continue, however, to disagree on Chrétien's *conjointure.* On the whole, the partisans of tripartition seem to represent the majority view.[26] For most of them, *Eric et Enide*'s *premier vers* poses a serious problem, which is solved by ignoring the author as well as the scribes. Both the *premier vers* and scribal structuring in general are best respected by Donald Maddox,[27] at least in the early stages of his analysis: there is visual justification for subdividing parts II (MS. 1376 at 2215 [not 2248] and IV (MSS. 375, 794, 1420, 1450, 24403 at 6359) to obtain two groups of three segments before and after line 2791 (not 2762).

While medieval readings of *Erec et Enide* point toward bipartition, such an arrangement cannot be defended for *Yvain* on the basis of scribal evidence. Even if part III is chapterized in a disorganized way, Yvain's rehabilitation (2641-6808) forms an organic whole mirroring his fall (723-2480), which began at the fountain and was foretold in Calogrenant's story (1-722).

It is not my intention to claim for the medieval readings a greater authority than we may wish to attribute to our own understanding of Chrétien's *conjointure.* However, if we are serious about optimal "recuperation of medieval texts as cultural phenomena,"[28] we cannot afford, given the dearth of direct testimony from the Middle Ages, to neglect even the humblest piece of evidence. Visual structuring offers such testimony.

Notes

[1]Roger Sherman Loomis, and L. H. Loomis, *Arthurian Legends in Medieval Art*, MLA Monograph Series 9 (New York: MLA, 1938); Rita Lejeune, and Jacques Stiennon, *La Légende de Roland dans l'art du moyen âge*, 2nd ed. (Brussels: Arcade, 1967); Margaret R. Scherer, *The Legends of Troy in Art and Literature* (New York and London: Phaidon Press, 1964); H. Buchthal, *Historia Troiana*, Studies of the Warburg Institute 32 (London: the Warburg Institute, 1971); David John Athole Ross, *Alexander Historiatus* (London: The Warburg Institute, 1963).

[2]Flemming G. Andersen, et al., eds., *Medieval Iconography and Narrative: A Symposium* (Odense: Odense University Press, 1980); Emmanuèle Baumgartner, "La Couronne et le cercle: Arthur et la Table Ronde dans les manuscrits du *Lancelot-Graal*," *Texte et image: Actes du Colloque international de Chantilly (13 au 15 octobre 1982)* (Paris: Les Belles Lettres, 1984): 191-200; Constance Bullock-Davies, "The Visual Image of Arthur," *Reading Medieval Studies* 4 (1983): 98-116; John V. Fleming, *The Roman de la rose: A Study in Allegory and Iconography* (Princeton: Princeton University Press, 1969); Meradith T. McMunn, "The Miniatures of the *Roman de Kanor* and the Illustration of Medieval Romance," *Manuscripta* 21 (1977): 18-19; Stephen G. Nichols, *Romanesque Signs: Early Medieval Narrative and Iconography* (New Haven: Yale University Press, 1983). I am grateful to Lori Walters, Meradith T. McMunn, and Gloria A. Torrini-Roblin for their kindness in giving me access to unpublished or forthcoming studies of visual structuring in medieval romances: Lori Walters, "Le Rôle du scribe dans l'organisation des manuscrits des romans de Chrétien de Troyes," *Romania;* ead., "Connections between *Yvain* and the *Atre Périlleux* in Paris, Bibliothèque Nationale, fonds français, MS. 1433"; Meradith T. McMunn, "The Interrelation of Text and Illustration in the Courtly Romance," Fifth Triennial Congress of the International Courtly Literature Society (De Bron, Netherlands, 1986); Gloria Ann Torrini-Roblin, "Semiotics of the Roman Courtois, A Model and its Replica: The Hypertextual Relationship between the *Conte du Graal* and the *First Continuation*," Diss. Washington University, 1987. I remain indebted to Professor Grigsby who had received very kindly a draft version of this article.

[3]A session on "The Illustrated Chrétien," organized by Professor M. Alison Stones, was held at the 23rd International Congress on Medieval Studies, Western Michigan University, on May 5, 1988: Keith Busby, "Text, Miniature, and Rubric in the Manuscripts of Chrétien de Troyes' *Perceval* and its Continuations"; Terry Nixon, "Romance Collections and the Manuscripts of Chrétien de Troyes"; Lori Walters, "The Use of Multi-Compartment Initial Miniatures in the Illustrated Manuscripts of the Romances of Chrétien de Troyes." See also Claudia Rabel-Jullien, "L'Image de tout le monde? Aperçu des recherches actuelles sur l'enluminure en France," *Gazette du livre médiéval*, 11 (1987), 1-4.

[4]See note 2.

[5]Sylvia Huot, *From Song to Book: The Poetics of Writing in Early French Lyric and Lyrical Narrative Poetry* (Ithaca: Cornell University Press, 1987).

[6]Hans R. Runte, "The Scribe and Miniaturist as Reader," *Essays in Early French Literature Presented to Barbara M. Craig,* eds. Norris J. Lacy and Jerry C. Nash (York, S.C.: French Literature Publications Company, 1982), 53-64. See also Torrini-Roblin, pp. 83-87, 158-92.

[7]Henry Martin, *Les Peintres de manuscrits et la miniature en France* (Paris: H. Laurens, 1909), p. 13.

[8]Martin, pp. 23-24.

[9]Eric George Millar, *An Iluminated Manuscript of "La Somme le Roy"* (Oxford: Roxburghe Club, 1953).

[10]Jean Louis Victor Porcher, *Jean Lebègue, Les Histoires que l'on peut raisonnablement faire sur les livres de Salluste* (Paris: Société des bibliophiles français, 1962).

[11]Beat Brenk, "Le Texte et l'image dans la *Vie des saints* au moyen âge: Rôle du concepteur et rôle du peintre," *Texte et image: Actes du Colloque international de Chantilly (13 au 15 octobre 1982)* (Paris: Les Belles Lettres, 1984), pp. 32, 31.

[12]Mario Roques, ed., *Erec et Enide,* vol. 1 of *Les Romans de Chrétien de Troyes,* Classiques Français du Moyen Age (Paris: Honoré Champion, 1968).

[13]Mario Roques, ed., *Le Chevalier au lion (Yvain),* vol. 4 of *Les Romans de Chrétien de Troyes,* Classiques Français du Moyen Age (Paris: Honoré Champion, 1980).

[14]Torrini-Roblin, pp. 85-86; M. Alison Stones, "Secular Manuscript Illumination in France," *Medieval Manuscripts and Textual Criticism,* ed. Christopher Kleinhenz (Chapel Hill: University of North Carolina Press, 1976): 83-102; ead., "Manuscripts, Arthurian Illuminated," *The Arthurian Encyclopedia,* ed. Norris J. Lacy (New York: Garland, 1986), pp. 359-74; David Diringer, *The Illuminated Book* (London: Faber and Faber, 1958); Richard H. Rouse, "Manuscript Books, Production of," *Dictionary of the Middle Ages,* ed. Joseph R. Strayer (New York: Scribner, 1982-), vol. 8, pp. 100-05.

[15]Alexandre Micha, *La Tradition manuscrite des romans de Chrétien de Troyes,* Publications romanes et françaises (Geneva: Droz, 1966), p. 44.

[16]Roques, *Erec,* p. xliii; my emphasis.

[17]Wendelin Foerster, *Kristian von Troyes: Erec und Enide,* 2nd ed., Romanische Bibliothek 13 (Halle: Max Niemeyer, 1909), p. xxxi; Micha, p. 154.

[18]Roques, *Erec,* pp. xlii-xliii.

[19]Foerster, p. xxi.

[20]Roques, *Erec,* p. xlii.

[21]Roques, *Erec,* p. xlii.

[22]Roques, *Erec,* p. xlii.

[23]Roques, *Erec,* p. xlii.

[24]Hans R. Runte, "Yvain: 'Li chevaliers qui s'an fuioit,' " *Incidences* NS 5,1 (January-April 1981), 17-25.

[25]Jean Frappier, *Chrétien de Troyes* (Paris: Hatier-Boivin, 1957), pp. 92-94; Roger Dragonetti, *La Vie de la lettre au moyen âge* (Paris: Seuil, 1980), p. 13.

[26]See summaries of the controversy in Robert G. Cook, "The Structure of Romance in Chrétien's *Erec* and *Yvain*," *Modern Philology*, 71, 2 (November 1973), 128-43; Z. P. Zaddy, *Chrétien Studies* (Glasgow: University of Glasgow Press, 1973); Donald Maddox, "Trois sur deux: Théories de bipartition et de tripartition des œuvres de Chrétien de Troyes," *Œuvres et Critiques*, 5, 2 (Winter 1980-81), pp. 91-102.

[27]Donald Maddox, *Structure and Sacring: The Systematic Kingdom in Chrétien's "Eric et Enide"*, French Forum Monographs 8 (Lexington: French Forum, 1978).

[28]Maddox, *Structure and Sacring*, p. 188.

"Avis li fu": Vision and Cognition in the *Conte du Graal*

Barbara Nelson Sargent-Baur

> Si com l'iaue aloit a regort,
> Torna li vallés a senestre
> Et vit les tors de[l] chastel nestre,
> Qu'avis li fu qu'eles naissoient
> Et que fors de la roche issoient.[1]

In all of his narrative works, Chrétien de Troyes demonstrates a keen interest in the interior states of his characters. That this is so is evident even in his "bit parts": Guinevere in *Cligés,* alert to the nascent love between Alexandre and Soredamors and active in furthering it; the vavasor in *Erec,* impoverished and yet the proud possessor of a new and expensive set of arms and armor (proud, too, of his daughter); the nameless *dameisele* who heals and clothes Yvain, found unconscious and naked, and then tactfully pretends to know nothing of the matter. On his protagonists, naturally the poet lavishes even more affectionate care; his romances in large part are comprised of what the heroes and heroines think, feel, speak aloud, and turn over in their minds.

Much of the psychological insight in the first four of Chrétien's romances stems from a particular approach to the problem of characterization. Whatever their differences (and they are many), the men and women who play the leading roles therein have two traits in common: they are articulate (at least occasionally, and in interior monologue if not in dialogue), and they are self-conscious. This is very far from asserting that they are invariably correct in their assessment of other people's motives, or even of their own; they are not noticeably intellectual, but they are very much alive and highly sensitive to what goes on around them in the social sphere.

In the *Conte du Graal* the techniques of characterization are markedly different. Here Chrétien presents a protagonist not greatly given to speech, even before Gornemant cautions him against garrulity, whose mental processes are directly reported only seldom and briefly, who exhibits no curiosity about people and little interest in them, except as they appear to be in some way useful to himself, and is nearly as devoid of conscious inner life as the beasts of those forests in which he feels most at home. An unpromising subject for psychological analysis, one would think; but then in this last romance Chrétien's interests clearly lie in the moral rather than the psychological sphere. Along with creating a perceptive yet unreflective hero he has embraced a narrative technique stressing observation and "fact." On the whole, the *Conte* gives prominence to external reality and to action, while still involving a character around whom the action turns. One way to achieve this sort of effect is to enhance the role of the narrator, increasing the quantity of "objective" information-giving with regard to events and other characters; a plentiful use of this technique is common with Chrétien's near-contemporaries and successors, and of course Chrétien uses it too in all five of his romances. But as John Grigsby has shown, his "last romance is recounted by the least intrusive narrator."[2] The *Conte du Graal* repeatedly demonstrates another and arguably more interesting approach. A considerable part of both the narration and the description in this work is provided not by the narrator but by the main character. Hearers or readers, we see what he sees, as he sees it; simultaneously we learn what—rightly or wrongly—he makes of it. At times he is simply mistaken, misconstruing the data that reach his senses. At others he does not react, or not in ways that would be appropriate under the circumstances; he sees, he hears, but he draws from these sensations only what is immediately relevant to himself and his needs of the moment. Yet the sensations themselves are conveyed to us with an abundance of highly nuanced detail, owing largely to a remarkable attention to point-of-view localized in the consciousness of the hero.[3]

This aspect of the poet's narrative technique might be illustrated by a number of passages in the Perceval segment of this unfinished romance. I propose to concentrate on three episodes in which the control of point-of-view is particularly marked, while observing that this is not an exhaustive

study of the matter.[4] The passages for examination are the approach to
Gornemant's castle, the encounter with the Fisherman, and the search for
and eventual sighting of the Fisherman's dwelling-place.

To begin, let us follow the young Welshman, who has just acquired
by unorthodox combat his military equipment and thinks himself thereby to
be a knight, as he rides off at top speed through a landscape unfamiliar to
him:

> Vers la grant riviere qui bruit
> S'en va toute une praerie,
> Mais en l'iaue n'entra il mie,
> Qu'il le vit molt corant et noire,
> Assez plus parfonde que Loire;
> Si s'en va tot selonc la rive
> Lez une grant roche naïve,
> Qui d'autre part de l'iaue estoit,
> Si que l'iaue al pié li batoit.
> Sor cele roche en un pendant,
> Qui vers mer aloit descendant,
> Ot un chastel molt riche et fort.
> (vv. 1312-23)

Here there is an abundance of descriptive detail, much of it presented objec-
tively by the narrator and yet not without connection with the psychological
state of the character: the traveler did not enter the water because of the way
it looked to him (dark, deep, and fast-flowing), hence he turned aside from
his course and went along the river bank, moving parallel to a great rock on
the other side. The narration moves also, from motivation back to action
and thence to a temporary abandonment of both the character's thoughts and
his movements in favor of a direct communication to us of information that
Perceval does not possess: there was a *chastel* there on the side of the rock
where it sloped toward the sea: a castle strong and rich, but invisible to the
character at this point in his progress. Now it is to him that the point of
view suddenly shifts, and the ensuing scene is presented just as he sees it:

> Si com l'iaue aloit a regort,
> Torna li vallés a senestre
> Et vit les tors de[l] chastel nestre,

Qu'avis li fu qu'eles naissoient
Et que fors de la roche issoient.
Enmi le chastel en estant
Ot une tor et fort et grant;
Une barbacane molt fort
Avoit tornee vers le gort,
Qui a la mer se combatoit,
Et la mers au pié li batoit.
A quatre parties del mur,
Dont li quarrel estoient dur,
Avoit quatre basses torneles
Qui molt estoient fors et beles.
Li chastiax fu molt bien seans
Et bien aesiez par dedans.
Devant le chastelet roont
Ot sor l'iaue drecié un pont
De pierre, d'araine, de caus;
Li pons estoit et fors et haus,
A batailles estoit entor.
Enmi le pont [ot] une tour,
Et devant un pont torneïs
Qui estoit fais et establis
A che que sa droiture aporte:
Le jor ert pons et la nuit porte.
                              (vv. 1324-50)

The striking feature of this description is that it not only is given as seen through the hero's eyes, but that we are simultaneously informed of what he sees and how he interprets it. Furthermore, all this is being imparted at the same time as the character observes it, that is, from a moving perspective. As he rides along, Perceval has no suspicion of the proximity of a *chastel,* indeed of a construction of any kind. What come into his field of vision are the towers of a hidden castle—or rather, by implication, the tops of the towers. The rest is at first concealed by the great rock; but as the traveler continues to move downhill and toward the sea, the towers appear to detach themselves from the rock or, as Chrétien puts it, to be growing up, being "born" from the rock, in a sort of inorganic parturition, as the first five lines of the above quotation attest. So, at least, it seems to Perceval: "Avis li fu." Although the expression is not used again, the description that follows is clearly from the same shifting perspective. From among the plural *tors* the narrative eye singles out one *tor*, strong and high, then a strong barbican dominating the river mouth, and so on. The attentive young man makes his way toward the drawbridge; and now a new element is introduced into the scene:

> Li vallés vers le pont chemine.
> Vestus d'une robe porprine
> S'aloit uns preudom esbatant
> Par sus le pont. Es vos atant[5]
> Celui qui vers le pont venoit.
> Li preudom en sa main tenoit
> Par contenance un bastonet,
> Et aprés lui furent vallet
> Doi, tot desaffublé, venu.
> Li vallés a bien retenu
> Ce que sa mere li aprist,
> Car il le salua et dist:
> "Sire, . . ."
>
> (vv. 1351-63)

The first impression recorded is that of the costume: civilian as opposed to military and of a color distinguishable at a distance;[6] the second is that of the wearer. This is a man, a *preudom*, that is, a respectable-looking person rather than a servant or a peasant. It transpires that he is doing something: taking a stroll, and then waiting for the approaching horseman. Now as the observer draws even closer, two more elements are supplied: the *preudom* is holding a stick (not a weapon, but an elegant accessory), and he is accompanied in his promenade by two coatless followers. By now the rider and the stroller are within speaking distance; they greet each other, and the scene of Perceval's approach is at an end.

This short passage (of some 60 lines) serves to illustrate the poet's highly developed sense of the way distant objects are first perceived and how perception is modified by continuous movement on the part of an observer. At the same time the mental processes of the observer are being kept firmly before us. The control of point-of-view is particularly impressive considering the fact that the description involves two kinds of

movement recorded by the seeing eye: a lateral one, which brings about that
a distant object is first glimpsed in part and is subsequently grasped as a
whole, intervening barriers being passed by; and also a direct one enabling
the observer, proceeding straight towards an object, to become progressively aware of more and more details until he can come no closer.

Fascinating in itself as an exercise in presenting fictitious *visibilia*
through the eyes and mind of a fictitious person, this scene of Perceval's
approach to the castle of Gornemant also serves as anticipation of another
scene, one that has attracted far more attention among students of this romance: Perceval's first sight of the Grail Castle. In terms of the information
supplied and of how it is ordered, the narration in the two scenes is strikingly similar; yet there are noteworthy differences. The Grail episode begins, once again, with the hero riding across an unfamiliar landscape. (This
time, he is attempting to return home, but does not know the way.) Here
too he chances upon a river, sees that the water is swift and deep, does not
venture to enter it, and journeys along the bank. As before, he encounters a
great rock; in this instance the rock, being on the near side of the stream,
bars his path. (It also, we might note, blocks his view of the man-made
feature that lies beyond.)

> Et tote jor sa voie tint,
> Qu'il n'encontra rien teriene
> Ne crestïen ne crestïene
> Qui li seüst voie ensaignier.
> Et il ne finoit de proier
> Damedieu le soverain pere
> Qu'il li donast trover sa mere
> Plaine de vie et de santé,
> Se il li vient a volenté.
> Et tant dura cele priiere
> Qu'il esgarda une riviere
> En l'avalee d'une angarde.
> L'eve rade et parfonde esgarde,
> Si ne s'ose metre dedans,
> Et dist: "Ha! Sire toz puissans,
> Se ceste eve passer pooie,
> Dela ma mere troveroie,
> Mien escïent, se ele est vive."

Ensi s'en va selonc la rive
Tant que a une roche aproce,
Si que l'eve a la roche touche
Si qu'il ne puet avant aler.
Atant vit aval l'eve aler
Une nef qui d'amont venoit;
Deus homes en la nef avoit.
Et il s'areste, si atent,
Qu'il quida qu'il najassent tant
Que il venissent jusqu'a lui.
Et il s'aresterent andui,
Enmi l'eve tot coi s'esturent,
Que molt bien aancré se furent.
Et cil qui fu devant peschoit
A la ligne et si aeschoit
Son ameçon d'un poissonet
Un poi greignor d'un vaironnet.
Cil qui ne set que faire puisse
Ne en quel liu passage truisse,
Les salue . . .

                    (vv. 2976-3013)

Here, too, the object of scrutiny is presented through the eyes of the
character. Now it is he who is stationary; his attention is fixed on something moving towards him. Again, in this contracting perspective, the
ordering of the elements is from the general to the specific: Perceval sees a
boat descending from up-stream, then notes that there are two men in it.
When their progress is arrested, they are at a level with Perceval, anchored
in midstream, the man in the bow fishing with a line and baiting his hook
with a fish scarcely larger than a minnow. They are close enough, in other
words, for the spectator to notice quite small details, and to engage the boat-
men in conversation; this he proceeds to do. He makes no distinction between them, nor does the narrator intervene; hence no distinction is relayed
to the hearers or readers of the romance; Perceval addresses them together
as *seignor,* gets speech of only one of them concerning lodging for the
night, and promptly loses interest in them. It is only after having spent the
night and having departed from the place that he learns his host's identity.
Whether the fisherman, who as it transpires is a king, was on that first

encounter distinguishable from his companion (who disappears from the story), we shall never know, for we generally obtain only so much information as is available to the protagonist at a given moment.

This conversation, in its context of at best partial understanding on Perceval's part, serves as a bridge to the third and last passage to be considered here. This episode, again involving an object and its perception, is one of the most often studied and warmly debated in all of the *Conte du Graal*. In the course of the exchange between river bank and midstream, the angler informs the benighted traveler that the river cannot be crossed,[7] offers him hospitality, and gives directions. Perceval is to ride up through a cleft in the rock; once up on the heights he will see before him, in a valley close to river and forest, a *maison* where the fisherman dwells.

> "Je vos heberjerai anuit:
> Montez vos ent par cele fraite
> Qui est en cele roche faite,
> Et quant vos la amont venrez,
> Devant vos en un val verrez
> Une maison ou je estois,
> Pres de riviere et pres de bois."
> Maintenant cil s'en vait amont
> Tant que il vint enson le mont,
> Et quant il fu enson le pui,
> Si esgarda tot entor lui,
> Si ne vit rien fors ciel et terre
> Et dist: "Chi que sui venus querre?
> Le musardie et le bricoigne.
> Diex li doinst hui male vergoigne
> Celui qui cha m'a envoié;
> Si m'a il or bien avoié
> Qui me dist que je troveroie
> Maison quant cha amont venroie.
> Peschieres qui ce me deïs,
> Trop grant desloiauté feïs,
> Se tu le me deïs por mal."
> Lors vit pres de lui en [un] val[8]
> Le chief d'une tor qui parut.
> L'en ne trovast jusqu'a Barut

Si bele ne si bien assise;
Quarree fu, de roche bise,
S'avoit deus torneles entor.
La sale fu devant la tor,
Et les loges devant la sale.
Li vallés cele part avale . . .
                    (vv. 3028-58)

The debate over the scene centers on the nature of this construction,
which as it later transpires is the dwelling of the *Roi Pescheor*. Is it, as has
been claimed, an enchanted castle, sometimes visible and sometimes not,
appearing and disappearing according to a mysterious law of its own, a
castle that at this moment manifests itself to the awaited hero so that he can
perform his role as healer and liberator? Or is it to be understood as the
work of human hands, an artifact endowed with the same degree of "reality"
that the poet bestows on the other numerous constructions introduced into
this romance?[9] There are a number of reasons why I am persuaded that the
latter view is the more probable, and I cannot go into all of them here. One
reason (and I believe it carries some weight) is the technique already employed in this romance: a gradual presentation of an object as the observer's
perspective is modified by angle, motion, and decreasing distance. As we
have seen, the presentation of Gornemant's castle unambiguously incorpor-
ates these factors; the observer, moving along, had the initial impression of
change in the landscape: that the towers of a *chastel* were themselves in
upward motion (whereas we readers knew, thanks to the narrative voice,
that there was a castle there *en permanence*). In the later scene there are
some differences of importance. Here Perceval fully expects to see a construction and is actively seeking it with his eyes. Furthermore, following
the information provided in the conversation just ended, he is looking for
what the fisherman mentioned: a *maison* (3033). This is a portmanteau
word, here and elsewhere in Chrétien's *œuvre*;[10] it designates structures
ranging from Arthur's habitation at Caradigan and that of the count, Enide's
uncle, both in *Erec* (286, 1256), to the hermit's hut ("molt basse et molt
petite") and the giant's stronghold, both in *Yvain* (2831, 3867). In the
Conte du Graal it is applied by Perceval to his mother's house (727), by
both him and his mother to a church (578, 655), and by his cousin to the
regal seat of the Roi Pescheor (3532).[11] Clearly implied in the passage that
occupies us (yet it seems to have escaped scholarly attention) is that the

expectation engendered in the hero by this broad term *maison* is that of a private dwelling and moreover one of rather modest proportions, such as would be appropriate to a man who engages in the unaristocratic activity of fishing.[12] (That the edifice turns out to be far more imposing is immaterial at this point in the tale.) Such a house he does not find, nor indeed any house on top of the great rock, where he thinks to find it.

Rather less clear is the modality by which the real structure meets his eyes. As is his frequent habit, Chrétien is less than precise here, and his vagueness has furnished fertile soil for a luxuriance of interpretations. There is, though, no compelling reason to suppose that in this scene he has entirely abandoned his characteristic preoccupation with the interior states of his human creations, nor more specifically with description as conveyed through the eyes and mind of a beholder. During the over three thousand lines that precede the hero's encounter with the Pescheor, Chrétien had been teaching the original audience of the *Conte* how to hear it, and subsequent readers how to read it. He does not again tell us (why should he?) that the traveler keeps moving on his way, that the point of view moves with him, and that as a result there is a successive perception of an object: inchoative, partial, and at last total. Nevertheless there is enough similarity between this passage and the ones already examined to infer that here, too, the poet is guiding us toward finding a subjective treatment of description: objects seen from a single, yet mobile, viewpoint. An edifice, which later turns out to be the Grail Castle (although it is never called that), appeared (*parut*) to the hero, and was by him perceived not immediately nor all at once, but after an unspecified yet short lapse of time and successively.[13] Absent any indication in the text of a supernatural manifestation, the safest course, in my opinion, is to assume that Chrétien meant us to understand a natural (albeit man-made) object becoming visible to a human observer through natural means. When Perceval scans the landscape in the diminishing light of evening (the late hour is repeatedly mentioned in subsequent references), he at first finds no house; nothing but sky and earth is to be seen on top of the rock (but then the fisherman had not affirmed that his house was on the heights but "en un val"). As the disappointed traveler continues to ride forward (a detail that admittedly the text does not specify, but that I think it strongly suggests), he catches sight of the top (*chief*) of a tower, which is visible, which "showed" (*parut*), which he apprehends with subsequent refinement of detail as his moving viewpoint permits him to grasp the edifice in its entirety. First the upper part of the tower, then the shape and color of the whole, its two flanking turrets, the (lower) *sale* forward of the tower, and the *loges* in front of the *sale*. Once Perceval has identified this construction with the *maison* he has mistakenly been seeking at the summit of the great rock, he rides downhill towards it and towards his greatest adventure.

A modern reader must be careful to avoid exaggeration, and to be particularly aware of the danger of anachronism. It would not be out of place, at the end of this study, to remind ourselves that after all Chrétien de Troyes was not only a romancer but a psychologist and (increasingly) a moralist. He is at very many removes from the preromantic and romantic novelists who, enthusiastic about landscape, loaded a corresponding enthusiasm on the shoulders of their characters. With such writers as Gustave Flaubert and Henry James, intensely preoccupied with point-of-view as a major technique of characterization, he has somewhat more in common; yet for him literary technique is very far from being a *summum bonum*. In his last romance, the experience of sense impressions and the individual's response to them are still subordinated to a concern with that individual's progress: from *l'homme moyen sensuel,* wrapped up in his own immediate gratification, to a mature human being involved with others and answerable to God for his deeds of omission and commission. The gradual illumination of a soul is paramount in the *Conte de Graal*. Yet the soul of Perceval is attached to a body that, *inter alia,* perceives reality through sensory organs. Vision, with plentiful help from a whole series of personages who supply interpretation and commentary, is a first step toward that cognition that was, I am sure, Chrétien's basic theme in this last romance of his. Nevertheless, and perhaps incidentally, he devotes to the element of who-sees-what-and-how an attention quite remarkable within the whole corpus of twelfth-century narrative.

Notes

[1]Chrétien de Troyes, *Le Roman de Perceval ou le Conte du Graal*, ed. William Roach, T. L. F. (Genève: Droz/Paris: Minard, 1959), vv. 1324-28. Unless noted, this edition will provide all the quotations from the *Conte*.

[2]"Narrative Voices in Chrétien de Troyes: A Prolegomenon to Dissection," *RPh* 32 (1979), 272.

[3]This element has been pointed out briefly by Jean Frappier in *Chrétien de Troyes: l'homme et l'œuvre* (Paris: Hatier, 1957), p. 174, and in *Chrétien de Troyes et le mythe du Graal: Etude sur Perceval ou le Conte du Graal* (Paris: S.E.D.E.S., 1972), p. 76. D. H. Green has taken a slightly longer look at it (though *en passant*) in *The Art of Recognition in Wolfram's "Parzival"* (Cambridge University Press, 1982), pp. 4-5.

[4]The Gawain portion, as well, furnishes examples; see, e.g., Gauvain's progress to and through the *chastel* of Guingambresil, vv. 5754 ff.

[5]The variant of ms. A, "et si atant," makes better sense.

[6]According to Hilka's variants, all the mss. except T. give *d'hermine* instead of *porprine*. See *Der Percevalroman von Christian von Troyes*, hgg. von Alfons Hilka (Halle: Niemeyer, 1932), p. 59.

[7]That is, not by a man and a horse.

[8]Var.: *devant lui*.

[9]These divergent interpretations have been proposed by, respectively, Jean Frappier, "Féerie du château du Roi Pêcheur dans le Conte du Graal," in *Mélanges Jean Fourquet*, ed. P. Valentin and G. Zink (Paris: Klincksieck/Munchen: Hueber, 1969), 101-17, rpt. in *Autour du Graal* (Genève: Droz, 1977), 307-22; and by Maurice Delbouille, "Réalité du château du Roi-Pêcheur dans le Conte du Graal," in *Mélanges René Crozet*, ed. P. Gallais and Y. J. Riou (Poitiers: Société d'Etudes Médiévales, 1966), 903-13.

[10]For its appearances in ms. A, see Marie-Louise Ollier, *Lexique et concordance de Chrétien de Troyes d'après la copie de Guiot* (Montréal: Institut d'Etudes Médiévales/ Paris: Vrin, 1986).

[11]"Et si a fait teus maisons faire / Come il covient a riche roi" (3532-33). Ms. A reads "tel meison."

[12]This uncertainty as to the status of the person so encountered is confirmed later, when Perceval discusses the episode with his cousin: he still does not know (until she enlightens him) "s'il est peschiere ou rois" (3497).

[13]There is, of course, some kinship between this gradualistic approach to the art of narration and a favorite technique of Chrétien's, the building of suspense, hence the retention of the listening public's interest, through the retention of information. Of this, John L. Grigsby has reminded us in "Remnants of Chrétien's Aesthetics in the Early *Perceval* Continuations and the Incipient Triumph of Writing," *RPh*, 41 (1988), 380.

Oral or Written Model?: Description, Length, and Unity in the *First Continuation*

Gloria Torrini-Roblin

> Chascun de vos cuide savoir
> Du grant conte trestot le voir,
> Mes nu set pas, se Diex me gart.[1]

Most readers of medieval literature will recognize such an apostrophe, this from the pen of the *M* redactor of the *First Continuation* of Chrétien de Troyes's *Conte du Graal,* as a narrative cliché, a formulaic attempt at legitimizing the discourse of a writer not yet possessed of authorial credibility.[2] Yet, whether deployed merely as a standard narrative technique or not, this remark's presence in the *Perceval* tradition gives particular pause. If indeed all the redactors who set out to continue Chrétien's unfinished work believed they could replicate the "whole truth" of the master's text, the diversity of their resulting continuations poses serious questions about both the nature of their knowing and the complexity of the object to be known.

The eleven extant Old French MSS containing the *First Continuation* offer four distinct versions of "the" text. Each has been called a continuation, just one of a variety of textual relationships that, according to Gérard Genette, are characterized by the "grafting" of one text (the *hypertexte*) onto another (the *hypotexte*) in a manner other than that of commentary.[3] Genette claims that in literature continuations arise when one or more authors capable of imitating the "manière" of an incomplete text use this stylistic competence to imitate their model as faithfully and earnestly as possible (p. 182). Thus, behind every continuation is a good imitator, and in semiotic terms, to imitate, or copy, is to borrow the code of another and make it one's own. The more successful the imitation, the fewer the differences between the codes regulating the copy and the model.

Of course any text is the product of many subcodes, narrative, poetic, pragmatic, each of which is divisible into ever smaller units. Here I will focus my attention on somewhat less than "trestot le voir," limiting the discussion to the poetic code that embraces the issues of description, length, and unity. If the different redactors of the *First Continuation* are to be judged knowledgeable on aesthetic grounds, it must then be in terms of their fidelity to the aesthetics of their model. For the writers of the *First Continuation,* the text to be imitated was none other than the *Conte du Graal,* whose poetic code is an admixture of different generic codes and text-personal codes specific to Chrétien's unfinished work. For its imitators, such a textual hybrid must have constituted a puzzle. The multiple subcodes that contribute to the overall poetic code are not necessarily subject to a global interpretation. Indeed, the full-blown presence of both oral and written models for "literature" in the twelfth and early thirteenth centuries enabled a single signifying surface to be interpreted in more than one way.

What in the model constituted by the *Conte du Graal* would give rise to such a great diversity of imitations? Most obviously, two different poetic codes appear active at different points: the bipartite and interlace models. The former implies a structure with a clearly marked beginning and end that confine the narrative, limiting it in length and lending it a measure of unity. The latter is open-ended, the narrative consequently unbound, and length increases while unity collapses under the sheer mass of the narrative material. The switch from one structure to the other marked a major point in the evolution of the *roman courtois,* and Chrétien is clearly sitting on the fence when it comes to choosing between the earlier and later versions of the genre. He remains more traditional, however, when it comes to his use of suspense and description. A generic outlaw when it comes to structure, a generic paradigm in other issues embraced by the poetic code; such is the hypotext constituted by the *Conte du Graal.*

The redactors of the *First Continuation* all opted for the open-ended structural model based on narrative interlacing. Their rejection *en masse* of the bipartite model necessarily follows certain changes in the narrative: Perceval's disappearance as the protagonist as well as Gauvain's purposeless errings preclude a tidy ending based on the alienation-reintegration scheme described by Erich Köhler.[4] Given Chrétien's model, the open-ended text *par excellence,* the basic interlace structure of the *Continuation* is a logical, correct reading of the hypotext's code. The way in which each redactor implements this structure varies greatly, however, and these differences are reflected in the length and unity of each redaction, as well as in the relative importance description assumes in each text.

In any discussion of the *First Continuation,* length is ostensibly the most obvious area for comparison, as witnessed by the only labels up until now found suitable to designate the texts: Long, Short, and Mixed.[5] The introduction of the open-ended model extended Chrétien's grail poem well beyond the 6600-7000 lines characteristic of his other romances. Its abrupt ending at the line 8960 (Lecoy's edition) suggests, if anything, an even greater "final" total. The redactors, though, go much further: the "Short" version is about three hundred lines longer (*L* ends at 9509, *A* at 9457), the "Mixed" version one and a half times as long (*T* goes to 15322), and the "Long" version is more than twice as long as Chrétien's text (*E* concludes at 19606). These enormous differences raise a number of questions concerning the nature of the poetic code of the *First Continuation* in particular, and the interlace model in general: first, what is the source of these wildly differing lengths if all of the redactions tell approximately the same story? Can increased narrative content alone explain the added length of a MS such as *E,* or do descriptive passages play a greater role in his text? Second, once the bipartite model with its closed universe is abandoned, does it remain meaningful to discuss the length of an open-ended text as if it were a totality? Does not the interlace structure imply poetic units whose length and unity must be measured on a different scale than that employed for the conventional *roman courtois?* If so, how is one to interpret *L*'s enigmatic "pauses du conteur" (the term is Gallais's) in terms of the structure of the text as a whole?[6] Finally, given these differences, how faithful are the individual redactors to the poetic code of Chrétien's hypotext?

In an attempt to answer these questions, I will examine in detail one section of the text where the question of length is particularly hard to ignore: the Carados narrative. The hero is the son of King Carados and Ysave de Carahés, but his natural father is the magician Elïavrés. When the young man learns of the treachery of his mother, he denounces her to the King, who encloses her in a tower. Elïavrés continues their liaison and, when discovered, is punished. To avenge her lover, Ysave causes an enchanted serpent to attach itself to her son's arm. Carados goes into hiding, ashamed of the withering effects of the snake, but his friend Cador finds him. With the help of his beloved, Guignier, he is delivered of the serpent, and they are wedded. The Long and Mixed redactions take more than four times as many verses to tell the story as the Short redaction as represented by *L*. *E*, 6671-12506, is 5835 lines long, *T*, 3083-8734, is 5671 lines long, and *L*, 2047-3271, is 1224 lines long.[7] When the four different MSS are compared, it is immediately apparent that the differing lengths of the redactions are in part attributable to the addition of narrative material to the story common to all eleven MSS: of the sixteen episodes described by Roach (I, li-liv), three (7-9) are completely lacking in *L*, and yet appear in *E* and *T*, as well as in *P*. Episode 13, relating Cador's search for Carados, takes up some 570 lines in the Long and Mixed redactions; *L* expedites the affair in a single sentence: "Par maint païs le va querant, / Tant qu'il vint a un avesprant / Herbergier a une abeïe / Qui sist sor une praerie; / La dedens Caradué trova, / De joie et de pitié plora" (III, vv. 2687-92). Additional material is to be found not only in the story, but in the narrative discourse as well, that is, the Long redactor inserts often lengthy moralizing asides. Among his commentaries are a critique of Elïavrés, an exposé on courtly qualities, a dissertation on the meaning of true love, and a diatribe against women, to name just a few. These didactic passages are largely absent in the Short redaction, which not only condenses more, but analyzes less.

It is not only a matter of quantity, however, but of quality too. While these additions represent a large number of verses, a closer comparison of the redactions suggests that *E* is also consistently longer in those episodes it shares with the Short redaction, and the reasons are many. First, *E* tends to repeat himself, whereas *L* says things only once, and then moves on. More significant than his redundancies, however, is the fact that *E*'s redactor gives us much more detail. Whether relating a ceremony, reporting a conversation, or painting a portrait, he always uses description to give a close-up view. The very first episode furnishes a prime example of the process: the account of the marriage of King Carados and Ysave. From *L* we learn only that there was a wedding:

> Li rois remest an grant sejor,
> Et en grant pais fu puis maint jor.
> Entretant fist un marïage
> D'une niece qu'il ot molt sage;
> Ysaive ot non de Carahés,
> Plus gente n'ot tresc'a Rahés.
> Au roi Caradoé la douna

De Venes, qui grant joie en a,
Si l'esposa sans atargier.
(III, pt. 1, vv. 2047-55)

L's terse "and he married her without delay" contrasts sharply with *E*'s sixty-line account of the festivities. *E* tells us who was in attendance ("Vienent i dames et pucelles, / Et des chambres les damoiselles, / Roi, duc, princë et aumaçor, / Baron, chastelain, vavasor." II, vv. 6695-98), mentions the precise date of the ceremony ("Ce fu a un m[a]rdi matin / Que Damediex par bon destin / Ot telle joië ajornee;" II, vv. 6709-11), and describes the religious protocol:

Li bons rois par la main l'a prise,
Et lors san nule autre devise
Se sont tuit a l'eglise tret
Tant que le marïaige ont fet,
Dont mainte gent fu puis haitiee.
Ez vos la messe conmanciee.
Et quant l'ofrandre fu alee
Et la messe dite et chantee,
Li rois est issus dou mostier
Et il et tuit si chevalier,
Et la roïne an a menee
An ses chambres la marïee.
(II, vv. 6719-30)

and sketches the magnificence of the feast and ensuing jousting:

Messires Kex a fait soner
Un graille por l'eve doner,
Et quant l'eve ot [eü] li rois,
Si s'est asis au mestre dois.
Ja des mes parler ne vos quier,
Car assez orent a mangier.
Qant beü orent et mangié,
Parmi ces prez se sont loigié.
Lors conmancent a behorder, . . .
(II, vv. 6731-39)

L's expeditious "sans atargier" seems to apply as much to his story-telling style as to the story itself. *E* on the other hand appears to luxuriate in relating the smallest particles of a rich reality. The contrasting diegetic and mimetic tendencies of the Short and Long redactors respectively also manifest themselves in the treatment of reported speech, or conversation: whereas *L* tends to summarize exchanges between characters using indirect discourse, *E* gives us dialogues in abundance. An example from Episode 11, in which Ysave tricks her son into opening the chest containing the deadly serpent, illustrates the two techniques. *L* relates the exchange thus:

> Ne demora mie granment
> Que Caradués en la tor vint
> Veoir sa mere qui lors tint
> Un pigne et sist desus un lit.
> Si tos con la dame le vit,
> Li dist que a l'armaire alast,
> Son mireoir li aportast;
> Et il i vait grant aleüre.
> (III, pt. 1, vv. 2630-37)

Although one would imagine mother and son greeting one another and perhaps exchanging a bit of nervous small talk after a long separation, not unmarked by a certain amount of resentment, *L* passes over these details, which would seem to have little or no significance for the plot. He even claims that the mother herself got right to the point ("*Si tos* con la dame le vit . . ."), and rather than wasting his time on her exact words, he gives us the gist of the exchange. *E*'s approach to the scene is clearly different:

> Ne demora pas longuement
> Qu'a Caradoc vint a talant
> Qu'i[l] viaut sa dame aler veoir.
> He, las! c'or ne le set por voir,
> La cruauté et la mervoille
> Que sa mere li aparoille,
> Mais il ne s'an [re]gardoit pas.
> An la tor tot le petit pas
> An vient devant sa dame amont.
> "Dame, li Crïator dou mont,

Qui le bien dou mal anestie,
Vos saut et gart et beneïe."
Et la reïne li respont
Tot el que ses cuers ne despont:
"Biaux filz, et Damediex vos gart.
Je ne me donnoie regart
Que vos ore venissiez ça,
Que je ne vos vi mes pieç'a;
Venuz estes [ça] a celee.
Trové m'avez eschevelee,
Car un po pignier me voloie
D'un pigne, c'ou chief me doloie,
Qu'aportez me fu de Cesaire.
Vez le vos la an celle aumere;
Or alez, si le m'aportez.
Ansamble o moi vos deportez
Ça sus mes hui trestote jor,
Car molt desir vostre sejor
Et molt me torne a grant annui
Que je ça sus si seules sui."
                    (II, vv. 9885-914)

He is, in short, an eavesdropper, a truly omniscient narrator with the capa-city to abstract himself from the action to make editorial comments, as well as to disappear completely while the characters speak for themselves. Their exchange of greetings, six lines long, adds little to the overall progression of the narrative; the author of *E* uses it to enhance the illusion of reality, and/or to promote the overall religious tenor of his work. Ysave's lengthy monologue serves to refine the portrait of what in *L* appears only as an "evil" woman: here she is a liar, a coquettish flirt, and even a snob (hers is no ordinary comb, but a comb from "Cesaire").

   Portraiture is yet another field for comparison. In his abbreviated version of Cador's wedding to Guignier ("Guignier s'amie prist a fame," III, pt. 1, v. 2865), *L* describes the bride as "la suer Cador, la gentis dame," (III, pt. 1, v. 2866), and her name is mentioned but this once in the entire account. This monolithic representation stands in sharp contrast to *E*'s multi-layered description in which the heroine's name, or epithets such as "la belle Guignier," "la meschine," and "la pucelle gente," appear some

seven times in over forty lines (II, vv. 11763-801). *E* is particularly attentive to clothing, not only detailing her vestments, but also describing the
fabric and jewels and fur of which they were made. Her crown is the object
of a long description that sparkles with the jewels that stud the coif:

> Il est rois et elle roïne,
> Et li rois mist a la meschine
> El chief une corone riche.
> Une pierre c'on clainme oniche,
> Molt precïeuse et de grant pris,
> Qui vint dou flun de paradis,
> Avoit anz ou cercle devant.
> Et desoz un sarfir molt grant
> Ravoit an molt petit espace,
> Et apres ravoit un topace,
> Safers et jafes et onix,
> Unes pierres molt tres gentis,
> Esmeraudes et ometites
> Et jagonces et crissonites
> Et escharbocles et bericles;
> Et si avoit molt de reliques
> Dignes et de molt grant saintaige.
> Onques nus hom de nul aaige
> Ne vit a roi ne a persone
> Nules si tres riche corone
> Que celle estoit . . . .
>   (II, vv. 11826-45)

The narrator announces "He (Carados) is king and she queen," and then
focuses on the symbol of their royalty, the crown. It tells the audience what
it means to be a queen (the splendor and bounty) and what kind of queen
Guignier is (like the relics, "worthy and of great holiness"). This visually
rich description ("Onques nus hom de nul aaige / Ne *vit* a roi . . . ," my
emphasis) brings the audience right up to the surface of the crown, multi-
plying and enriching the signifiers of the jewel and in turn of the queen.[8]
Conversely, in *L,* the total absence of visual data has a distancing effect; in
fact there is no mention of the crown itself, only of the coronation ("A
Venes se fist coroner / Et la roïne o lui sacrer," III, pt. 1, vv. 2867-68).

The consecration is an abstract concept unsupported by material references to the reality of the event.

Clearly the Short redactor distills reality down to its narrative residue, retaining only the results with significance for the action. He wants to answer the question posed by the narrative as fast as possible. In fact, he may have no choice in the matter, if indeed he is (or, more accurately, models himself after) a storyteller before a live audience, for there may be more at stake than a good story. Oral cultures cannot generate abstract categories for "managing" knowledge, reports Walter Ong, so they "use stories of human action to store, organize, and communicate much of what they know."[9] As the sole repository for the cultural history and tradition, the narrative must remain intact, that is, compact enough to sustain many repetitions. In addition to this general feeling of haste with which the Short redactor conducts his task, other signs point in the direction of an oral poetic model.

1) First, it is surely no accident that, whereas the narrators of the Long redaction express their refusals in terms that depict their task as a leisurely diversion (e.g., je ne veux pas "gaster ma paine," "me lasser," "metre ma cure," "trop seroie debatus," "por quoi m'an travailleroie?" etc.), L's narrator is alone responsible for the refusal of the form "ne me loist" (see Gallais, "Formules," pp. 216-19). He cannot indulge in descriptive digressions because he does not have the time, constrained apparently by the real limits of the performance situation.

2) The Short redactor labels signifiers with one-dimensional tags (e.g., "la gentis dame") more often than he evokes them with multiple signifiers. Characters are good or bad, beautiful or ugly, "heavy (or flat) figures" in the words of Ong, who described this mode of characterization as the result of the mnemonic demands of oral poetic processes (p. 70).

3) Finally, the Short redactor analyzes, indeed comments very little at all, presenting the facts in as simple a version as possible. Oral cultures are characterized by the absence of "such items as geometrical figures, abstract categorization, formally logical reasoning processes, definitions, *or even comprehensive descriptions* [my emphasis], or articulated self-analysis, all of which derive not simply from thought itself but from text-formed thought" (Ong, p. 55). Moreover, when called upon to represent the world, they tend to depict concrete actions as opposed to static abstractions referring to visual appearance (p. 49). A man is not how he looks or what he wears, but what he does.

If in his use of description the Short redactor exhibits a more oral poetic code, the Long redactor to the contrary shows the influence of a written model. Consider the contrasting portrayals of Ysave in light of Ong's observation that the "flat" characters typical of primary orality become more "round" under the influence of the written word (pp. 151-52). Consider too the visually rich descriptions of persons and objects in the Long redaction. These are products of the "analytic, dissecting tendencies," which "come with the inscribed, visualized word . . ." (Ong, pp. 73-74). The colorful portraits and detailed visual, analytic descriptions are just a few signs that the Long redactor envisioned a written poetic code as his model. They make his version of the *First Continuation* longer, interrupting the narrative line and undermining the narrative momentum.

If it is now apparent that more narrative material and detailed descriptions account for the increasing length of the Mixed and Long redactions, the aesthetic consequences of this increase remain to be seen. John L. Grigsby argued that in the early *Perceval* Continuations, increased length tended to be accompanied by crumbling unity and decreased suspense.[10] With respect to the *First Continuation* in its various forms, any discussion of unity would do well to begin by questioning the meaning and scope of the term itself. To be perceived as something separate from and other than the continuous flow of everyday discourse, any artistic text must constitute itself as an autonomous unit. For this, boundaries are established setting the artistic apart from nonartistic. Jurij Lotman states simply that "[demarcation] is inherent to the artistic text."[11] This constitution of limits precedes any thought of internal organization, for it defines at once that which the text is not and that which it can be. "La fonction de l'œuvre artistique—modèle fini d'un 'texte verbal' de faits réels infinis par nature—fait du moment de la *délimitation,* du cadrage, une condition indispensable à l'existence de tout texte artistique dans ses formes primitives . . . ."[12] "Interior" structure, coherence, "unity," can only be discussed once the limits between interiority and exteriority have been drawn.

Unity, or a sense of wholeness, self-sufficiency, integrity, etc., is a concept that may be applied on all levels of the generic code. On the narrative level, the sentence constitutes the model unit for the story; it is the basis for the narrative syntaxes of Roland Barthes and others. Unite a subject and a predicate, and a narrative unit has been formed. This is true of all forms of narrative. Units of narrative discourse are not so simply defined, for they are dependent on the pragmatics of the speech act. In oral cultures, the narrative discourse is bound by the constraints of the performance situation: the physical limits of performer and audience, that is, fatigue may determine where a narration will begin and especially end. In "literate" cultures where texts are written, space, and not time, constitutes the field of narrative discourse. Consequently, the limits are different: a line, a paragraph, a page, a chapter, a book. The question is no longer "how long can you listen," but "how much can you read?"

Within the poetic code, stylistic markers for beginnings and endings appear in a variety of forms: frames (e.g., prologues and epilogues), *topoi* such as the "ouverture printannière" referring to the concept of boundary itself (usually temporal; cf. "Once upon a time" and "they lived happily ever after"), and often references to harmony, reflected in the happy ending of the narrative story. Pragmatic units are closely bound to the unity of narrative discourse in oral cultures, but this is not the case in literate ones. Practical concerns governing the production of early manuscripts dictated that signs of some sort be introduced to allow the reader to find his place in the otherwise continuous flow of the text. As Ong reminds us, the paragraph sign, which we now take as a unit of discourse, was originally used simply for the "visual location of materials in a manuscript text" (Ong, p. 124). Initials, "lettrines," rubrics, miniatures could all be taken as signs of units. But so could folios, tomes, collections, etc.

Thus, when we speak of unity, we are referring to a number of issues of a narrative, aesthetic, and pragmatic nature. Given that these codes, which for practical reasons we consider as separate entities, in reality interact, the concept of "unity" as applied to a work is elusive at best. Units from different coded levels may correspond, but they do not necessarily do so. In a discussion of twelfth-century romances, Peter Haidu commented that "the narrative structure is imbedded in the medium of language, whose stylistic functioning may *support, shade, or contradict* the implications of linear action."[13] Since the narrative story forms the baseline for all higher levels of the generic code of the *roman courtois,* its unity is usually deemed essential, a *sine qua non,* to that of a work on the whole; aesthetic and pragmatic units are at best secondary considerations presumed, sometimes erroneously, to follow the lead of the narrative story. In the case of the *roman courtois,* those works displaying the bipartite narrative structure with a marked beginning and end are thus found to be unified. But in the "unbound" interlace model, where the notions of ending and even beginning are sometimes undermined, an overriding narrative unity is absent.

Although a global narrative unit lacks in these texts, they abound in a variety of intersecting boundary markers, signifiers of diverse sorts for the signifieds "beginning" and "end." Perhaps they can furnish clues to the poetic code of the interlace model. The Long redactor encoded beginnings and endings in: 1) the narrative discourse: e.g., "A mon conte voil revenir" (*E*, II, v. 9613) and "N'an voil pas ci endroit conter" (*E*, II, v. 9610); 2) the poetic discourse: there is a special "vocabulary" of beginnings of the type "Once upon a time. . . ." Compare "En icel tans que je vos di" (*E*, II, v. 6671), "Ce fu a un m[a]rdi matin" (*E*, II, v. 6709), "Ce fu an mai el tans d'esté" (*E*, II, v. 7037), "Ce fu le jor de Pantecoste" (*E*, II, v. 7273), to name just a few examples. Likewise, endings are signaled by the medieval version of "and they lived happily ever after"; when the verb "deduire" appears, the end of a unit is not far behind (e.g., "Et se deduient par la terre" and "Sejorna tot l'iver antier / Por soi deduire et aisier" in *E*, II, vv. 11936 and 12505-06).

For the Short redactor, boundaries were determined apparently by the demands, real or imaginary, of an oral performance. The poetic discourse is broken up into units corresponding in length to a hypothetical recitation time.[14] Gallais discovered that *L* was the only MS containing all three major "pauses du conteur" to be found in the various redactions of the poem (*L*, III, pt. 1, vv. 5171-78, 7035-44, 8299-310); moreover, *L*'s redactor appears responsible for the minor, but unusual formula "Ici recomencent noveles" (*L*, III, pt. 1, vv. 1520 and 3375) ("Formules," pp. 185-89). Significantly, these pauses break the poem up into three major units, each of which is divided almost exactly in the middle. Their lengths—approximately 3300, 3500, and 2400 verses—would allow them to be recited aloud in one sitting.

Of course it is absurd to claim that the Short redactor followed a strictly oral code any more than the Long redactor adopted a purely literate one. The evidence to the contrary—and in favor of code switching—is simply too great to ignore. First, several of the "storyteller's pauses"— presumably a sign of orality—are present in the Long redaction as well as in the Short. Then, in one of these pauses occurs a reference to the structure of the text that testifies to a *shared* concept of the evolving poetic code. The narrator, in both the Long and Short redactions, claims that he must change subjects and begin a new episode, because the main story is branching off into some unrelated material:

Signeur, la brance se depart
Del grant conte, se Dex me gart;
Des or orois coment il fu
De ce c'avés tant atendu;
    (*L*, III, pt. 1, vv. 7039-42)

The appearance of the word "branche" in *L, M, Q,* and *U* to refer to the structure of the tale is a first in the Perceval tradition, according to Grigsby ("Remnants," p. 384).[15] Pickford's study of the evolution of Arthurian romance revealed that from an early date, the term designated a section of a larger work, but that it remained otherwise undefined until the end of the medieval period.[16] "Mais ce qui est frappant, c'est que ces répartitions en branches . . . deviennent systématiques vers la fin du Moyen Age. Les copistes du XIVe et du XVe siècles . . . s'efforcèrent de présenter au lecteur une histoire disposée selon un plan méthodique au lieu d'un vaste ensemble ininterrompu de matière romanesque" (p. 153). "Branching out" appears to have been the result of the rise of the expansive interlace pattern, and neither the Long nor the Short redactor, be their codes primarily of oral or literate inspiration, could ignore this nascent poetic division.

The disappearance of the bipartite narrative model has long been considered a sign of decline in the artistic value of the genre, owing to the unerring focus on an idea of narrative integrity that excludes the interlace model. The presence of non-narrative signs signaling different types of textual units challenges us to reconsider this prevalent conception. In fact, Lotman's work has shown that there are two ways of viewing narrative unity, which depend on the types of syntagmatic conjunctions present in the text. The closed narrative is composed of diverse structural elements strung together in the manner of a phrase or sentence. The open narrative, however, is made up of identical or structurally equivalent elements arranged in a geometrical design. For Lotman, "The essential difference between [these] constructions . . . consists in the presence or absence of a structurally marked end and beginning" (*Artistic Text,* p. 85).

Whereas the "closed" text is demarcated at two points, the "open" text displays a series of beginnings and endings, whose repetition results in the semantization of the boundaries themselves. Lotman argues that the pronounced character of segment borders "creates the illusion of a structure that seems to reproduce a text of speech (infinite) activity . . . and therefore can be broken off or continued at any point, like a design or an endless story" (*Artistic Text,* p. 86). The Long redactor is particularly aware of the "speech-infinite" nature of his discourse as a poet, and he is the most generous of the continuators with refusals. He is always self-conscious when beginning and ending, and the internal boundaries of his text are loaded with reflections on the process of composition itself. Perhaps the best example of this "semantization" of the boundary occurs at the end of the "branche" relating Gauvain's Grail Visit, where the narrator/redactor addresses the audience in these terms:

> Li contes faut ci entreset,
> A une autre branche revet
> Que vos m'orroiz sanz demorer
> Tout mot a mot dire et conter.
> Chascun de vos cuide savoir
> Du grant conte trestot le voir,
> Mes nu set pas, se Diex me gart.
> Tot en ordre, par grant esgart,
> Covient la chose deviser;
> Ja ne m'en orroiz ainz parler
> S'en ordre non et a droit point,
> Einsi con li contes se joint.
> (*M,* II, vv. 18363-74)

The narrator distinguishes between the "grant conte" and its "branches," emphasizing the importance of telling "la chose" "tot en ordre" out of respect for what is presumably his source. We can guess that his defensive tone betrays his uneasiness with the length of his tale, and this is confirmed when, to justify his poetic technique, he inserts what appears to be an oblique reference to Chrétien's "conjointure." His voiced concern with respecting the way in which "li contes *se joint*" echoes the master's instructions on the making of a good poem and points once again to an emerging poetic code in which the text is composed of distinct units strung together, joined at the edges in an aesthetically satisfying manner.

Given that these "segments" are constituted by boundaries, demarcated from the flow of the textual discourse itself, they must be considered as integral units. It is thus the "integrity" of these segments that becomes the standard for unity within the open narrative model. Episodes may be unrelated, but this is not the point; what happens within each episode, and the way in which the beginnings and endings of all the episodes compare, is. The increasing length of the Short, Mixed, and Long redactions is thus not necessarily an aesthetic weakness, if the text is to be viewed not as a totality, but as the repetition of many small textual units.

Were the redactors of the *First Continuation* faithful to the aesthetics of the *Conte du Graal?* The answer is a matter of degree. Chrétien's text showed clear signs of departing from the closed, bipartite model in favor of the open, interlace structure: its length, its incompletion cannot be refuted. His use of description stands somewhere between that of the Short and the Long redactor, however. The former refuses most all opportunities to give a visual account of the people or events in his story; Chrétien on the other hand does not hesitate to paint the portrait of a beautiful heroine or an enchanted castle when it serves his purposes. Neither does he "waste" his effort when he deems it unnecessary, though; the Long redactor by contrast appears a compulsive, indiscriminate describer.

With respect to unity, both redactors carried the incipient interlace model much further than Chrétien. Although we can now speak of the "Perceval" and "Gauvain" branches of the *Conte du Graal,* its author does not articulate the division to the same extent as the continuators. In the two places where there is a major change in subject matter—in hero, in fact— Chrétien simply says that the story says no more of Gauvain/Perceval at this point ("De mon seignor Gauvain se test / li contes ici a estal, / si parlerons de Perceval," 6006-08; and "De Perceval plus longuemant / ne parole li contes ci, / einçois avroiz asez oï / de mon seignor Gauvain parler / que plus m'oiez de lui conter," 6288-92). Nowhere does Chrétien make mention of the "branches" of his tale. This is clearly the continuators' contribution, and their ability to recognize and name this new textual division shows that the poetic code of the hypertext had already separated itself in an irrevocable way from that of Chrétien's hypotext.

Notes

[1]*Continuations of the Old French* Perceval *of Chrétien de Troyes,* 5 vols., ed. William Roach (Philadelphia: U. of Pennsylvania P. and The American Philosophical Society, 1949-1985), II, vv. 18367-69).

[2]*Le Conte du Graal (Perceval),* 2 vols., ed. Félix Lecoy (Paris: Champion, 1975); following Roach we will use the following sigla to represent the MSS of the *First Continuation:*

A, Paris, Bibliothèque Nationale, fr. 794

E, Edimbourg, National Library of Scotland, 19.1.5

L, London, British Museum, Additional 36614

M, Montpellier, Faculté de Médicine, H. 249

P, Mons, Bibliothèque publique, 331/206

Q, Paris, Bibliothèque Nationale, fr. 1429

R, Paris, Bibliothèque Nationale, fr. 1450

S, Paris, Bibliothèque Nationale, fr. 1453

T, Paris, Bibliothèque Nationale, fr. 12576

U, Paris, Bibliothèque Nationale, fr. 12577

V, Paris, Bibliothèque Nationale, nouv. acq. fr. 6614

[3]*Palimpsestes: La littérature au second degré* (Paris: Seuil, 1982), p. 10.

[4]*L'aventure chevaleresque: Idéal et réalité dans le roman courtois,* trans. Elaine Kaufholz (Paris: Gallimard, 1974).

[5]Roach has classified MSS *EMOU* as belonging to the Long redaction, *TV* to the Mixed, and *ALSPR* to the Short. For the purposes of this discussion, I will concentrate primarily on the contrast between the Long and Short redactions.

[6]"Formules du conteur et interventions d'auteur dans les manuscrits de la *Continuation-Gauvain," Romania,* 85 (1964), 181-229.

[7]Note that one MS belonging to the Short redaction, *P,* oscillates between the Short and Long models, as represented by *L* and *E.* While it basically belongs to the family of Short redactions, *P* inserts, *tel quel,* an entire chunk of narrative material from the Long redaction without regard for blatant aesthetic differences. It thus falls somewhere in the middle on the question of length, lasting a total of 3341 lines (III, pt. 1, vv. 12451-15792).

[8]Cf. Michelle A. Freeman, *The Poetics of* translatio studii *and Conjointure: Chrétien de Troyes's* Cligés (Lexington, Ky.: French Forum, 1979), p. 141 ff., particularly the analysis of the description of Enide's saddle.

[9]*Orality and Literacy: the Technologizing of the Word* (New York: Methuen, 1982), p. 140.

[10]"Remnants of Chrétien's Aesthetics in the Early *Perceval* Continuations and the Incipient Triumph of Writing," *Romance Philology,* 41 (1988), 392.

[11]*The Structure of the Artistic Text*, trans. Gail Lenhoff and Ronald Vroon (Ann Arbor: U. of Michigan, 1977), p. 52.

[12]J. M. Lotman, "La Signification modélisante des concepts de 'fin' et de 'début' dans les textes artistiques," *Travaux sur les systèmes de signes: Ecole de Tartu,* eds. J. M. Lotman and B. A. Ouspenski, trans. Anne Zouboff (Bruxelles: Editions Complexe, 1976), p. 200.

[13]"Narrativity and Language in Some XIIth Century Romances," *Yale French Studies* 70 (1986), 139, our emphasis.

[14]Within these units, the secondary boundaries (narrative interventions, the happy end, and the "ouverture printannière") typical of the Long redaction can be found, though they are used more sparingly (e.g., *L*, III, pt. 1, vv. 3106, 3265, and 3272).

[15]*E,* alone of the MSS of the Long redaction, is excluded from the list because there is no extant text for vv. 16579-19006, owing to two missing quaternions (see *Cont.* II, p. 498). For the comparable passage in the Long redaction, cf. *M,* II, vv. 17115-18.

[16]Cedric E. Pickford, *L'Evolution du roman arthurien en prose* (Paris: Nizet, 1959), p. 144 ff.

La Poupée d'Evalac ou la conversion tardive du Roi Mordrain

Colette-Anne Van Coolput

Pour décrire les origines du Graal, raconter l'implantation progressive du christianisme et développer l'histoire de la famille des Rois Pêcheurs, seigneurs de Corbenic, et celle du lignage privilégié dont serait issu Galaad, le narrateur de l'*Estoire del saint Graal* a puisé dans les données éparpillées dans la *Quête del saint Graal*.[1] La ville de Sarras, épicentre à partir duquel Joseph d'Arimacie et son fils Joséphé entreprennent la conversion du monde, siège du Palais Spirituel où Joséphé fut sacré évêque et destination ultime du Graal après son périple en Occident, semblait désigner tout naturellement son roi, Evalac, comme la première cible des évangélisateurs. Sans aucun doute, dans la *Quête,* c'est bien Evalac, baptisé sous le nom de Mordrain, qui est le protagoniste du récit touchant à la période du christianisme naissant: c'est à lui qu'est confié l'écu destiné à Galaad; c'est lui qui prend l'initiative de voler au secours de Joséphé, emprisonné en Grande-Bretagne par un roi félon et cruel; c'est encore lui qui reçoit la révélation des générations de son lignage dans une vision où neuf fleuves sortent d'un lac; c'est lui, toujours, qui contemple le mystère du Graal, audace qui le condamne à terminer ses jours aveugle et sans forces, mais qui lui vaudra le privilège de vivre jusqu'à la venue du Bon Chevalier afin d'être guéri par lui.

Ce héros attendu, Mordrain lui-même le nomme, comme le rapporte un prudhomme s'adressant à Perceval, "li noviemes de mon lignage" (Q, p. 85, v. 26). Le roi, cependant, est sans héritier direct dans la *Quête*[2] et c'est en réalité de son beau-frère Nascien que le Bon Chevalier descend en droite ligne. "Neuvième du lignage de Mordrain" alterne, dans cette œuvre, avec "neuvième du lignage de Nascien." Or si ces deux personnages semblent, d'un point de vue fonctionnel, interchangeables, cela ne se justifie évidemment qu'à condition que le terme *serorge* appliqué à Nascien le désigne comme mari de la sœur du roi Mordrain. Dans ce cas seulement, Célidoine se trouve dans la position de "neveu privilégié" ou quasi-fils, et de toute manière héritier naturel de son oncle maternel, comme le sont Roland par rapport à Charlemagne ou Gauvain et Mordred par rapport à Arthur.

Mais le prosateur de l'*Estoire* ne l'entend pas ainsi. En effet la structure familiale attendue se trouve inversée dans la mesure où Mordrain a épousé Sarracinte, la sœur *de Nascien,* celui-ci ayant de son côté contracté un mariage exogamique avec Flégétine, fille du roi des Médiens. Célidoine est bien, le texte est formel sur ce point, le fils de Nascien et de Flégétine. Les liens entre Mordrain et Célidoine sont donc bien moins intimes ici, puisque le neveu du roi n'est que le fils du frère de sa femme. Et l'*Estoire* se démarque effectivement de la *Quête,* car le roi de Sarras n'y revendique jamais le héros parfait à venir comme sa descendance propre. Après avoir été châtié pour avoir approché le Graal, Mordrain adressait à Dieu cette prière dans la *Quête:*

> einsi m'otroiez vos par vostre plaisir, en guerredon de mon servise, que
> je ne muire jusqu'a cele hore que li Bons Chevaliers, li noviemes de
> mon lignage, cil qui doit les merveilles dou Saint Graal veoir aperte-
> ment, me viegne visiter. (Q, p. 85, vv. 24-28)

Les manuscrits de l'*Estoire del saint Graal* s'accordent à reproduire littérale-ment ce passage, sauf précisément sur un point:

> si motroies vous par uostre saint plaisir que ie ne mure deuant ce que li
> boins cheualiers noefismes del lignage nascien me viegne uisiter. (ES,
> p. 242, vv. 5-7)

Par ailleurs, si la révélation des neuf fleuves à Mordrain reste maintenue dans cette œuvre, les générations à venir sont encore évoquées dans un épi-sode beaucoup plus élaboré. Cette fois-ci c'est à Nascien qu'est communi-quée la liste de ses descendants, consignée sur un rouleau de parchemin. L'accent, manifestement, se déplace, et Mordrain paraît dans une large mesure évincé par son beau-frère.

Avant de hasarder une hypothèse sur le pourquoi d'une telle disgrâce, voyons comment le prosateur s'y est pris pour la justifier lui-même. En fait, il a tout d'abord exploité adroitement un passage de la *Quête-Vulgate* portant sur la conversion d'Evalac. Ce texte dit en substance qu'après la victoire du roi de Sarras sur Tholomer, Nascien reçoit le baptême aussitôt après avoir compris l'impact de Joséphé et de son écu sur l'issue de la bataille:

> Et quant il fu venuz a sa cité de Sarras, si dist a tout le pueple la verité
> que il ot trovee en Josephe et manifesta tant l'estre del Crucefié que
> Nasciens reçut baptesme. (Q, p. 33, vv. 5-7)

Suit la guérison de l'homme au poing coupé, à qui Joséphé a fait toucher la croix de l'écu. Après quoi nous assistons à une autre merveille:

> Car la croiz qui en l'escu estoit s'en parti et s'aerdi au braz de celui en
> tel maniere que puis ne fut veue en l'escu. Lors reçut Ewalach
> baptesme et devint serjanz Jhesucrist. (Q, p. 33, vv. 13-17)

De cette petite scène l'auteur de l'*Estoire* a déduit de façon toute personnelle qu'il a fallu plusieurs miracles avant qu'Evalac ne se décide à adhérer au christianisme. Son nom de baptême est du reste interprété dans le même sens: "mordrains & ce uaut autretant comme tardif en creance" (ES, p. 75, v. 12). Tout au long du récit de cette conversion laborieuse, qui occupe approximativement un cinquième de l'œuvre (ES, pp. 21-83), l'empressement et l'ardeur dans la foi de Nascien seront opposés aux doutes théologiques du souverain, à ses hésitations et à ses tourments intérieurs, à son besoin de preuves tangibles. Réticence qui place ainsi Mordrain dans un jour défavorable.

D'autre part, l'*Estoire* fait planer sur le roi d'autres soupçons, qui motivent à plus d'un titre son surnom péjoratif de "mesconneu." Celui-ci est mis tout d'abord en relation avec ses origines, ignorées de tous y compris de lui-même: "onques ne sot ou il auoit este nes" (ES, p. 21, v. 32). Mais il convient aussi à quelqu'un dont la biographie a des replis secrets—et rien, dans la *Quête,* ne laissait présager une telle orientation du personnage: Mordrain est fils d'un humble cordonnier de Meaux, qui s'est élevé grâce à ses qualités personnelles; mais il a un meurtre sur la conscience. Toutes ces révélations sont apportées par Joséphé et contribueront à vaincre la résistance au christianisme opposée par le roi.

Mais un secret autrement plus compromettant encombre le présent d'Evalac. En entendant Joseph d'Arimacie exposer la doctrine chrétienne, le souverain butait sur deux difficultés: le mystère de la Trinité et la virginité de Marie, intacte malgré la conception et la naissance du Messie. Le roi reçoit alors deux visions pour l'aider à comprendre et à accepter ces points délicats. C'est la seconde qui nous occupera. Evalac voit un enfant pénétrer dans une chambre attenant à la sienne et en ressortir tandis que la porte reste parfaitement close. Comme on sait, cette image est tirée d'Ezéchiel 44, 1-4 et l'*Estoire* puise ici dans une tradition théologique et iconographique bien attestée au Moyen Age pour illustrer la virginité de la mère du Christ.[3] Le roi de Sarras est d'autant plus troublé par l'apparition qu'il croyait cette chambre inconnue de tous:

> li huis estoit de marbre séelés dedens le mur si soutivment que à paines
> péust iestre connéus ne apiercéus que il i eust wis ne feniestre, tant il
> éust esgarder ententivement; ne il meismes ne quidoit mie que nus de sa
> maison le séust fors que il seulement. (EH, II, p. 160)

Le texte rentre ainsi dans le jeu du personnage en préservant le secret de ce lieu. Le lecteur, en effet, n'apprendra que plus tard l'utilisation qu'en fait Mordrain, lors d'une scène qui se déroule bien après son baptême mais que l'œuvre semble cependant considérer comme la dernière étape de sa conversion, puisqu'elle la fait suivre de ces mots: "Ensi amena iosephe le roy a la loy ihesu crist & tous chaus de la terre ausi" (ES, p. 83, vv. 27-28). L'originalité de l'épisode réside dans le fait que l'auteur suggère une analogie entre le Christ passant par la porte close et Dieu sondant l'intimité de l'âme humaine[4] pour que soit dénoncé ce qui fait obstacle à l'adhésion parfaite de Mordrain aux principes chrétiens. Le piquant est en outre que se superposent ici une démonstration de la virginité et la révélation d'un lieu où Evalac s'adonne aux plaisirs de la chair en toute discrétion. Déjà la *Vie de sainte Thaïs*, du XIIe siècle, évoque une chambre retirée où seul pénètre le regard divin. L'abbé Panuncius insiste pour que la protagoniste, encore prostituée à ce moment, l'introduise

> "En plus privee liu (. . .)
> U plus a aise puisse feire mun desir,

Ke hunte me semble," dist il, "ici gesir
U autres nus purreient mult tost survenir."
—"Plus avant," diseit ele, "vus puis je mener,
U nul ne nus purra, fors sul Deu, veer;
Mès li oil al Creatur est si granment cler
Que de lui ne se porra unkes nul mucier."[5]

La même crainte d'être surpris, la même honte ont poussé Evalac à doter sa chambre d'un accès au mécanisme sophistiqué, sur lequel le manuscrit du Mans s'étend longuement:

Chil huis estoit si soutilement fais et séelés que si tost comme il clooit, si caoit par dedens uns engiens de fer en guise de barre et pour quoi li huis estoit si fermement apoiés que tousjours i péust-on bouter jà ne se méust, ançois le couvenit dépechier que on i entrast. Et qant li roys le voloit ouvrir, si avoit une claciele de fier à mierveilles tenue et sitost comme il boutoit par les jointures des coulours par quoi l'entrée de la claciele estoit plus désapiercéue, et tantost caoit uns engiens de quevre en samblance d'un mail sour la première bare el chief derière, et tantost souslevoit li chiés devant et saloit hors dou croqet ù la barre tenoit, et en ceste manière entroit ens li roys. . . . (EH, II, pp. 319-20)

Grâce à ces précautions, Evalac est parvenu à garder son entourage dans l'ignorance de ses pratiques sexuelles avec une statue de bois parée de somptueux vêtements comme une femme: "A ceste hymagène gisoit li roys carnelment et de si grant amour l'avoit amée bien quinze ans que nus hom ne péust avoir gregnour amour à nule femme mortel" (EH, II, p. 318). Poupée qui n'a sans doute plus rien de bien extraordinaire aux yeux de l'homme du XXe siècle, mais qui n'a certes pas dû être un objet de consommation courante au Moyen Age. Sur l'injonction de Joséphé elle sera jetée au feu par le roi lui-même, en présence de Nascien et de Sarracinte, qui ne sont pas peu ébahis en découvrant son existence.

S'il peut être tentant de rapprocher la statue de bois de certains textes littéraires tels que le *Tristan* de Thomas, le *Roman d'Alexandre,* le *Lancelot propre* ou *Hunbaut,* où une image donne également lieu à des rituels amoureux, il faut toutefois se souvenir que la représentation renvoie, dans tous ces cas, à une femme réelle dont on cherche à compenser l'absence. Or la "desloyal semblance" de Mordrain n'est pas le substitut d'un être aimé précis: c'est une vertigineuse apparence, sans référent et sans nom.

Heinzel avait cru pouvoir déceler sur l'*Estoire* une vague influence orientale.[6] Rejetant son hypothèse, J. D. Bruce a attiré l'attention sur un passage des *Amores* du pseudo-Lucien où un personnage rapporte l'histoire extraordinaire d'un jeune homme amoureux d'une statue d'Aphrodite, qu'il viole à la faveur de la nuit après s'être laissé enfermer dans son temple.[7] Mais l'anecdote sert ici à illustrer comment l'admiration suscitée par l'œuvre d'art peut être portée à son paroxysme. Préoccupations esthétiques qui ne sont pas le fait d'Evalac...

Le récit garde quelque chose d'insolite. Certes, que la destruction de la statue soit l'ultime étape de la conversion du roi suggère qu'il faille y voir un aspect de son idolâtrie. Le sous-titre donné par l'éditeur américain—"Mordrain burns his idol"—invitait déjà à cette interprétation. Ce passage serait ainsi l'expansion, par un auteur imaginatif, des paroles bibliques fustigeant le mécréant "forniquant avec les idoles."[8] Il est certain, en tout cas, que luxure et idolâtrie restent associées dans la pensée médiévale. Beryl Smalley rappelle par exemple que le franciscain anglais Ridevall dépeint l'idolâtrie sous les traits d'une prostituée.[9] Et dans la *Chanson d'Aspremont* et l'*Entrée d'Espagne* les idoles déchues ne sont-elles pas brisées, puis abandonnées aux filles de joie?[10]

L'explication, cependant, est un peu courte, d'autant plus que, contrairement aux divinités exposées et adorées dans le temple de Sarras, la statue privée n'est l'objet d'aucune croyance, d'aucune attente; le démon ne l'habite pas et elle n'est même pas dotée d'un pouvoir illusoire, comme le sont Apollin et Martys. A supposer d'ailleurs qu'elle soit chargée de connotations plus ou moins religieuses, pourquoi Evalac l'entoure-t-il de secret, alors même qu'elle ne se rattache à aucun rituel initiatique? Et la stupéfaction de Sarracinte et de Nascien, qui disent n'avoir jamais entendu parler d'une pratique aussi étrange, n'indique-t-elle pas que le comportement du roi est strictement individuel?

En réalité, si dans tout l'épisode le texte insiste tellement sur la volonté qu'a le roi de maintenir cachée la chambre à la femme de bois, c'est que son habitude a en elle-même toujours été vécue comme une transgression. La conscience d'un interdit violé, la honte qui l'accompagne sont bien antérieures à l'entreprise de conversion de Mordrain, même si c'est en définitive la percée du christianisme qui l'oblige à avouer sa faute et à brûler la poupée. Cette faute est tour à tour qualifiée de "péché"—terme qui n'a pas forcément des connotations chrétiennes—et "déloyauté"—action contraire à la loi.

Mais en quoi consiste l'infraction? Est-ce seulement la luxure qui est stigmatisée, comme en plusieurs autres passages de l'œuvre?[11] Est-ce plutôt l'union contre nature et nécessairement stérile avec une chose inerte, dans un espace verrouillé qui peut faire songer à une chambre mortuaire? Et faut-il dès lors opposer cette pulsion mortelle, ce néant où s'abîme le souverain, à un christianisme prometteur de Vie éternelle? Ou cette histoire doit-elle se lire comme un scénario complexe dans lequel le jeu avec la statue-simulacre dissimule un désir illicite et non prononcé?

Il est difficile de trancher. On sait cependant que dans les romans du Graal la transgression sexuelle par excellence est l'inceste, inscrit de manière voilée dans le "trouble généalogique"[12] qui affecte la famille du Graal, mais dénoncé explicitement ailleurs.[13] Or tout, dans la généalogie de Galaad selon l'*Estoire,* est transparent, élucidé, au-dessus de tout soupçon. En modifiant la structure familiale trouvée dans la *Quête,* comme nous l'avons montré plus haut, le prosateur a conjuré l'inceste et Célidoine échappe à une position potentiellement dangereuse.[14] Mais comme dans d'autres romans du Graal, l'amour coupable d'un frère pour sa sœur apparaît dans l'*Estoire,* à propos du passé du roi Labiel: Célidoine rappellera à ce souverain qu'il a coupé la tête à sa sœur qui se refusait à lui et qu'il a ensuite jeté son corps à la mer (ES, p. 147, vv. 18-24).

Dans la vie de Sarracinte elle-même, le lien fraternel n'est pas sans ambiguïté, même s'il reste somme toute assez innocent. La reine relate à Josephé les circonstances dans lesquelles elle a embrassé la foi chrétienne et fait alors allusion à un frère très beau, auquel elle semble très attachée. Amenée devant un ermite, la jeune Sarracinte promet de croire au Sauveur s'il est "plus beau que son frère" et exprime le désir de le voir. Son vœu sera exaucé mais l'ermite fait comprendre à la jeune fille que choisir le Christ signifie aussi renoncer à son frère: "tu verras celui tout maintenant que iou tai dit qui est tant biaus que puis que tu lauras ueu iamais lautre [= le frère] apres ne verras" (ES, p. 68, vv. 20-22). Le jeune homme disparaît effectivement peu après en chassant une Bête mystérieuse qui sème la terreur dans la campagne autour d'Orbérique. Mais le rôle fraternel est en quelque sorte récupéré en la personne de Seraphe, nommé Nascien après son baptême. Le début de l'œuvre pose le trio Evalac-Sarracinte-Seraphe, alors que Flégétine, la femme étrangère, ne sera introduite que tardivement dans l'intrigue. Tandis que le roi est aimé mais craint de son épouse,[15] la relation entre le frère et la sœur est toute de confiance et d'affection. Seraphe est celui qu'on appelle dans la nécessité—il portera secours à Evalac à la demande pressante de sa sœur—c'est le confident et le refuge:

> la roine fu moult esbahie de ce que ses sires estoit en si grant pense. si se leua & sen vint au lit nascien son frere tout plorant. & quant nascien le uit si en fu moult esbahis car il lamoit de mout grant amor. si la prinst entre ses bras & li demanda porcoi ele ploroit. (ES, p. 85, vv. 7-11)

Face à ce lien de parenté privilégié, quelle peut être l'attitude de l'époux? Le texte évoque plus d'une fois la haine sourde que les deux hommes nourrissent l'un envers l'autre:

> Et quant li rois vint a sarras si li fist la roine moult tres grant ioie & a son frere & moult fu lie de ce quele les vit ensamble car il auoient eu moult longement content ensamble & moult sestoient entrehai. & ne quidoient mie les gens du pais que iamais eust entreus pais ne acorde. (ES, p. 73, vv. 29-33)[16]

La rancune paraît émaner en premier lieu d'Evalac car, après l'aide de Seraphe dans la guerre contre Tholomer, il s'excuse d'avoir si mal traité son beau-frère et promet de s'amender. Si l'œuvre laisse son ressentiment sans motivation claire, n'est-il pas tentant cependant d'y lire une manifestation personnelle devant une structure affective dont il est doublement exclu: à la fois comme tiers face à Sarracinte et Seraphe, et comme individu sans famille, incapable de vivre à son tour la relation sororale? Dès lors, la poupée d'Evalac ne contribue-t-elle pas à mettre le doigt sur une frustration fondamentale, sur un manque qu'aucune femme *réelle* ne parvient à combler? Et si la sculpture n'était que l'expression d'une infinie nostalgie?

Notes

[1]Rappelons que l'*Estoire del saint Graal* se donne pour la première partie du *Lancelot-Graal* composé par ailleurs du *Merlin* et de sa *Suite-Vulgate,* du *Lancelot Propre,* de la *Queste del saint Graal* et de la *Mort Artu;* elle a toutefois été rédigée en dernier lieu. Pour la *Quête* nous utilisons le texte publié par Albert Pauphilet (Paris: Champion, 1923) [= Q]. L'*Estoire del saint Graal* sera citée tour à tour dans l'édition procurée par H. Oskar Sommer, *The Vulgate Version of Arthurian Romances,* vol. I (Washington: Carnegie Institution, 1909) [= ES] et dans la version, par moments plus développée, fournie par Eugène Hucher, *Le Saint-Graal ou Joseph d'Arimathie, première branche des romans de la Table Ronde,* tomes II et III (Le Mans, 1875-78) [EH].

[2]C'est également le cas dans l'*Estoire.* Deux manuscrits de Paris, Bibl. Nat. fr. 98 et 2455, ont cependant introduit un long développement connu sous la dénomination *Histoire de Grimaud* (éd. Hucher citée, tome III, pp. 311-738). Le héros éponyme est fils naturel de Mordrain et d'une jeune fille nommée d'abord Gratille (p. 326) puis Florée (p. 540). Par ailleurs, le roi a, sur le tard, un fils légitime de sa femme Sarracinte: Elyezer.

[3]On lira les pages qu'Emile Mâle a consacrées à l'explication du portail de la cathédrale de Laon, où sont regroupés différents sujets de l'Ancien Testament annonçant ou figurant la virginité de Marie, dont le prophète Ezéchiel (*L'Art religieux du XIIIe siècle en France. Etude sur l'iconographie du Moyen Age et ses sources d'inspiration* [Paris, 1898], pp. 197-202). Comme l'a établi ce savant, le programme iconographique de ce tympan suit exactement le sermon de l'Annonciation composé par Honoré d'Autun (*Speculum Ecclesiae,* éd. Migne, *Patrologie latine,* tome 172, col. 904 et suiv.). D'autres représentations d'Ezéchiel, auquel on a parfois joint, en guise d'attribut, un phylactère faisant allusion à la porte close, sont signalées par Louis Réau dans *Iconographie de l'art chrétien,* tome II *Iconographie de la Bible* I: *Ancien Testament* (Paris, 1956), p. 377.

[4]"or entent qui fu chil qui en samblance d'enfant entra en la cambre et issi, chou fu li (sains) esperis nostre segnour de la qui bouce, ceste parole issi; 'ne nule cose, n'est repuste qui ne soit séue, ne nule cose n'est couvierte qui ne soit descouvierte' " (EH, II, pp. 317-18).

[5]Paul Meyer, "Notice sur le manuscrit fr. 24862 de la Bibliothèque Nationale contenant divers ouvrages composés ou écrits en Angleterre," dans *Notices et extraits des manuscrits de la Bibliothèque Nationale et autres bibliothèques,* vol. 35 (1896), 1ère partie, p. 147, vv. 25-32.

[6]Richard Heinzel, "Uber die französischen Gralromane," dans *Denkschriften der kaiserlichen Akademie der Wissenschaften,* phil.-hist. Klasse XL (1892), pp. 139 et 194.

[7]"Human Automata in Classical Tradition and Mediaeval Romance," dans *Modern Philology,* 10 (1912-13), 12. Pour le pseudo-Lucien voir l'édition de M. D.

Macleod, *Lucian,* vol. VIII (Londres: Heinemann et Cambridge: Harvard U. P., 1968), pp. 173-77, chap. 15-16.

[8]Exode 34, 15-16, Ezéchiel 16, 15-17, Jérémie 2, 20-24, etc.

[9]Beryl Smalley, *English Friars and Antiquity in the Early Fourteenth Century* (Oxford, 1960), pp. 114-15.

[10]*Chanson d'Aspremont,* éd. Louis Brandin, 2e éd. revue, vol. II (Paris: Champion, 1924), vv. 7855-56; *L'Entrée d'Espagne, chanson de geste franco-italienne* publiée d'après le ms. de Venise par Antoine Thomas, vol. I (Paris: SATF, 1913), vv. 4411-14.

[11]Le prosateur fait l'éloge de la continence observée par Joseph d'Arimacie et sa femme Eliap, qui ne "gisoient pas comme gens luxuriose mais comme genz ploine de religion" (ES, p. 30, note 5). Joséphé reproche à certains de ses compagnons de n'avoir pas tenu leurs promesses: "chascuns de vous li vo[u]a de cuer & de bouche quil tenroit sa char castement & netement iusqua tant quil eussent congie de connoistre lor femes. Ceste promese feistes vous ce sachies vous bien. ore esgardes comment vous laues puis tenue. si bien que li plusor en sont puis enchoit en pechie de luxure uiel & orde" (ES, p. 210, vv. 5-9). Le châtelain de la Colombe est emporté par le Malin après avoir violé une femme qu'il croyait être Flégétine; c'était en réalité le démon qui avait pris son apparence (ES, p. 235, vv. 9-27).

[12]Nous empruntons l'expression à Jacques Roubaud, sans faire nôtres toutes ses idées, qu'il qualifie lui-même de "fiction théorique" et de "construction phantasmatique" ("Généalogie morale des rois-pêcheurs. Deuxième fiction théorique à partir des romans du Graal," dans *Change,* 16-17 [1973], pp. 228-47).

[13]Outre les matériaux rassemblés par Jacques Roubaud dans l'article mentionné ci-dessus, nous renvoyons aux travaux de Fanni Bogdanow, *The Romance of the Grail. A Study of the Structure and Genesis of a Thirteenth-Century Arthurian Prose Romance* (Manchester, 1966), pp. 148-52 et d'Emmanuèle Baumgartner, "Quelques réflexions sur le motif des *Enfances* dans les cycles en prose du XIIIe siècle," dans *Perspectives médiévales,* 3 (1977), pp. 60-61. Le motif de l'inceste est récurrent dans la *Demanda,* traduction portugaise de la *Quête* post-vulgate qui n'a été que partiellement conservée en français (cf. Colette-Anne Van Coolput, *Aventures querant et le sens du monde. Aspects de la réception productive des premiers romans du Graal cycliques dans le Tristan en prose* [Louvain: Presses Universitaires, 1986], p. 147, note 95).

[14]Rappelons que Mordred est, dans les cycles vulgate et post-vulgate, le fils incestueux d'Arthur, tout comme dans certaines œuvres épiques Roland est le fruit du péché de Charlemagne avec sa sœur (*Karlamagnus Saga, Tristan de Nanteuil,* le roman en prose de *Berthe aux grands pieds*).

[15]"Il [Evalac] est vns moult crueus hom si meust moult tost guerpie ou destruite se iou leusse mis en parole de cose que ne li pleust" (ES, p. 72, vv. 25-26) affirme Sarracinte. Par ailleurs le narrateur observe: "il [Mordrain] auoit este moult crueus & mout fiers si le doutoit mout" (p. 84, vv. 10-11).

[16]Cf. aussi p. 52, vv. 12-14 et 22-26; p. 55, vv. 7-8; p. 85, vv. 23-33.

II. THE OLD FRENCH EPIC

The Religious Content of the Chansons de Geste: Some Recent Studies

Gerard J. Brault

At the end of the nineteenth century, Léon Gautier underscored and extolled the Christian content of the *chansons de geste,* and many scholars, notably Adolphe J. Dickmann, Sister Marianna Gildea, and Brother J.-L. Roland Bélanger, have gone into all the details.[1] No one denies this influence. However, down through the years, specialists have often viewed the religious matter in the epics with a jaundiced eye.

In 1963, for instance, George Fenwick Jones claimed that the Christian content of the *Song of Roland* was very superficial and that in reality this work reflects a pagan ethos.[2] And, in 1978, Jean-Charles Payen affirmed that: "la chanson de geste fomente intentionnellement le plus surnois des racismes: le racisme religieux, celui qui excuse la honte du génocide au nom d'une foi confortablement impérialiste."[3]

Other scholars have tended to attach more importance to the feudal aspect than to the religious side of the *chansons de geste* or have emphasized the way the poets harmonized Christian and feudal values. For example, in the introduction to his *Chansons de geste du cycle de Guillaume d'Orange,* Jean Frappier wrote:

> Guillaume, Vivien, Bertrand, comme Charlemagne, Roland, Olivier, sont les soldats de Dieu, les guerriers d'une croisade toujours recommencée. . . . Donnée permanente et nécessaire; à cet égard le cycle de Guillaume ne diffère pas du cycle du Roi, tout en résumant le sens religieux du combat dans une formule qu'ignore la *Chanson de Roland:* "essaucier sainte crestienté", exalter la foi crétienne. . . . L'inspiration

religieuse de cette geste est autre chose qu'une manifestation de l'esprit clérical, et la morale chrétienne y compose, du reste sans beaucoup de difficulté, avec le sentiment féodal de l'honneur et avec le culte de la vaillance guerrière.[4]

As a result of these reactions on the part of literary critics and for other reasons, too, no doubt, including secularism, scholars have perhaps not been paying enough attention to religion in the *chansons de geste,* this in spite of the fact that there have been considerable advances in our knowledge of this important element in recent years. Although by no means an exhaustive survey, the present review is intended to alert readers to some new findings and to help them see the religious matter in the *chansons de geste* in its true perspective.

Religion pervades the *chansons de geste,* but this certainly does not mean that all is sweetness and light. Jones and Payen may have overstated the case, but there is no denying the fact that characters in the Old French epics often behave in an uncivilized fashion and in a way that runs counter to their Christian beliefs. Personally, I remain convinced that the *chansons de geste* are profoundly Christian,[5] but I have also suggested, for instance, that the distorted image of Islam in these works is based on prejudice, the conventional Muslim perhaps being a character on whom authors projected the worst instincts of their own nation.[6] I have pointed out, among other things, that François-Marc Gagnon has shown that the negative descriptions many early French explorers made of the American Indians, including their religious beliefs, were a similar projection of their own faults.[7]

Anticlericalism, too, is a familiar refrain in the epics. There is a whole category of poems called *moniages,* that is, *chansons de geste* in which an aging warrior decides to atone for his sins and to spend his declining years in a monastery. The baron immediately comes into conflict with the other monks and, bored to death, absents himself to give battle once again to the enemy.[8] Micheline de Combarieu has shown that the *jongleurs* condemned laxity in monastic life by contrasting the knight with the clerk, on the one hand, and the hermit with the monk, on the other.[9] Jean Batany has suggested that the satire on monasticism in these epics derives not so much from the diatribes of Abelard, Saint Bernard, or Peter the Venerable as from the Latin fable tradition.[10]

The Church in turn gave the *jongleurs* a hostile reception. "Les jongleurs s'attirèrent les foudres de l'Eglise," wrote Jean Rychner in his justly famous book on the *chansons de geste* published in 1955.[11] Rychner was no doubt alluding to the many prohibitions cited by Edmond Faral in his seminal work on the *jongleurs* (1910).[12] However, the hierarchy's position was far from consistent in this regard, and Faral made it clear in the chapter in question, entitled "L'Eglise contre les jongleurs," that many bishops, abbots, and other dignitaries, and, above all, clerks "ne craignaient pas d'afficher leur prédilection pour de pareilles gens," that is to say the jongleurs who "célèbrent la vertu des ancêtres [et qui] ont trouvé à leur talent un emploi honorable."[13] All too often, too, scholars overlook the fact that Faral devoted the following chapter, entitled "L'Eglise favorise certains jongleurs," to the other side of the issue.

For it was not what the *jongleurs* composed that antagonized the churchmen—after all, the *chansons de geste* present a more or less orthodox view of divine interventions, martyrdom, prayers, and the struggle against the Infidel—or even the anticlerical thrust of some of their poems. The Church thundered against the *jongleurs'* reputedly dissolute life and maintained that their presence was an invitation to carousing.[14]

Although it is certainly true that one should not take *trouvères* literally when they maintain—as they often do—that they have based their works on books preserved at Saint-Denis, nothing indicates, on the other hand, that this idea upset the monks of that abbey. In the prologue of the *Enfances Guillaume,* an epic dating from the first half of the thirteenth century, the *trouvère* goes so far as to claim that a monk of Saint-Denis composed the poem and that he bought it from him.[15]

It is important to note that religious and certain educated laymen enjoyed listening to the *chansons de geste* and interpreting them in their own way. If proof is needed, one has only to consult the *Pseudo-Turpin Chronicle,* a Latin adaptation of the *Song of Roland,* and the *Rolandslied,* a German adaptation of the same work, the one dating from the beginning, the other from the latter part of the twelfth century.[16] I shall return to this below.

Religious feeling underwent evolutionary change in the *chansons de geste.* In his study of the fifteenth-century prose *Guillaume d'Orange,* François Suard has noted, for example, "la disparition du climat de ferveur religieuse dans lequel se déroulait le combat Guillaume-Corsolt" and a diminution of joy when the hero has death in prospect. The author has substituted "une piété réelle, que manifeste l'observation régulière de certaines pratiques, l'assistance à la messe et l'oraison, et une confiance

évidente en la bonté de Dieu." Suard has concluded that the writer pays
mere lip service to religion, which earlier had been an essential part of the
chansons de geste.[17]

Nevertheless, having studied the role of the supernatural in certain
thirteenth-century poems of the cycle of William of Orange, Bernard Guidot
has rejected "l'idée reçue selon laquelle la féerie a envahi le genre épique à
cette époque." On the contrary:

> Il est beaucoup plus frappant de constater que la religion chrétienne s'est
> infiltrée dans la féerie et d'assister à des scènes où des fées parlent et se
> comportent comme des anges ou des hommes d'Eglise. Les preux
> contemporains de Guillaume dans le *Couronnement de Louis* avaient
> l'âme pétrie d'un très sincère esprit religieux, ceux du treizième siècle
> n'ont souvent rien à leur envier sur ce plan, néanmoins le merveilleux
> folklorique et païen a perdu une partie de sa couleur primitive pour
> prendre une étrange teinte chrétienne.[18]

It is not surprising that the *jongleurs* sometimes combined Christian
and pagan supernaturalism or gave Christian meaning to profane matter.
After all, this is precisely what one finds in many contemporary works of
different genres: see, for example, the studies of Anne-Marie Cadot on the
motif of the *aître périlleux* in the twelfth-century romances, of Jean Larmat
on Béroul's *Tristan,* of Jeanne Lods on the *Perlesvaus,* of Guy Raynaud de
Lage on the *Eracle,* and of Jean Subrenat on the *Roman d'Aubéron.*[19]

In an article on the *Chanson d'Antioche,* Robert Deschaux has
shown that the poet routinely introduced Christian wonders even though
describing recent historical events. The reason is quite simple: the people
of the day were steeped in an atmosphere where pagan belief and the Christian faith were constantly mingled and where religious meanings were often
given to meteorological phenomena or to ordinary events.[20]

Anthropologists distinguish between institutional and popular religion but also point out that these two forms of beliefs and practices are often
symbiotic.[21] Studies of French Canada before the advent of the Quiet
Revolution—the situation in Quebec before 1940-60 is often compared to
the French Middle Ages[22]—have shed new light on this phenomenon.
According to Nive Voisine:

Ils croient fermement à Dieu, au petit Jésus, à la Vierge, aux Saints (sainte Anne, la patronne de la paroisse. . .), aux anges gardiens, au diable, aux âmes du purgatoire et aussi, parfois, aux feux follets. . . Soumis aux lois de la nature, à la merci des éléments, vivant au rythme des saisons, ils reconnaissent facilement l'existence des "puissances supérieures", qu'ils essaient d'ailleurs de mettre de leur côté par des prières éprouvées. Ce culte et ces dévotions de toutes sortes viennent du lointain des âges et, dans beaucoup de cas, ont été sanctionnés par l'Eglise officielle. Qu'il s'y glisse parfois des pratiques moins ortho- doxes ou carrément superstitieuses ne devrait pas nous surprendre ou nous scandaliser.[23]

Jean Larmat used this distinction between the religion preached from the pulpit and that of actual experience in a recent article on the miracles of Gautier de Coincy[24] and the concept, I believe, has a significant bearing on the matter at hand. It suggests an approach, for example, to the *prière du plus grand péril,* a petition to God at times containing unorthodox elements.[25]

Turning now to the cult of the saints in the *chansons de geste,* Jean Subrenat has observed that, contrary to all expectations, most epics seem unaware of Saint James and the pilgrimage to Compostela. The only excep- tion is *Garin le Lorrain* where the saint's name figures several times. Subrenat, who noted in passing an isolated instance of the saint's name in *La Mort de Garin* and a single mention of the pilgrimage in *Gerbert de Metz,* concluded that "le chemin de Compostelle n'est pas une grande axe épique et l'apôtre de Galice est sans doute trop spiritualisé ou cléricalisé pour intervenir trop directement aux côtés des chevaliers."[26]

Saint James figures in the *Pseudo-Turpin Chronicle* and, according to a widely diffused legend in Spain, routed the Moors at the battle of Clavijo in the year 930.[27] This saint may not play an important role in the *chansons de geste* in general, but the convergence of allusions to him in three epics of the same cycle, the *Geste des Lorrains,* may not be entirely coincidental. The situation here bears a striking resemblance to that found in the *Couronnement de Louis* and in the other poems in the cycle of William of Orange, where there are a large number of references to Saint Peter.[28] The cult of universal as opposed to local saints made great strides in Europe about this time, but the devotion to Saint Peter and to Saint James was largely the work of the Cluniac Order.[29] There is reason to believe, then, that these two cycles each had their own patron saint, as it were, and to infer the indirect influence of Cluny here.

Everyone agrees that religion plays a key role in the *Song of Roland,* and certain Biblical allusions are obvious.[30] There can be no doubt, for instance, that the storm and the earthquake that announce the hero's death are modeled on the disturbances that preceded the passing of Christ according to the gospels, and when God stops the sun so that Charlemagne may pursue and destroy the fleeing Saracens, it is in all likelihood an allusion to the miracle God performed for Joshua.[31]

On the other hand, not all critics subscribe to the view that the *Song of Roland* as a whole and many of its apparently profane elements have religious meaning. Moreover, because the poet sometimes proceeds allusively and with subtlety, those who do accept this theory are not always in agreement about every detail and even, at times, about essential points.

Turoldus makes it clear that the Francs are motivated by two "laws" in particular, the *lei des chrestïens,* that is, the Christian faith, and the *lei de chevaler(s),* a synonym for *chevalerie,* in other words the conduct that is expected of an ideal knight.[32] But it is clear, too, that the principal characters—and even at times the hero—are impelled by motives or feelings we generally consider to be base or unworthy. The fact that the author of the *Song of Roland* reconciles such reprehensible thoughts or behavior with the acts of supposedly civilized men and, above all, with the Christian faith gives us pause.[33]

There are five basic religious ideas in the *Song of Roland:* (1) Christianity transcends all other faiths; (2) God chose the Franks and especially Charlemagne to establish His rule throughout the world; (3) true wisdom consists in having blind faith in God and in believing in the inevitability of Christian victory; (4) Roland dies a martyr and his sacrifice edifies and fortifies the Christians; and (5) the hero, like Christ, provokes dissension because he counsels following the hard road. This Christian dimension may also be seen in such major themes as good versus evil, betrayal, conversion, and victory, and in the related metaphors of the struggle, the road, the ascent, the two cities, and Roncevaux. The landscape—for example, the mountains, valleys, stream, trees, and four marble objects—are also replete with Christian symbolism. I have developed this interpretation in a series of papers and articles dating from 1967 and culminating in a two-volume edition of the *Song of Roland* (1978).[34]

Working independently, Jacques Ribard has drawn up a similar list of Christian elements in the poem that he interpreted in nearly identical fashion, though emphasizing the more general notion of Salvation and using the principle of the macrocosm and the microcosm.[35] Ribard later established unsuspected points of similarity in the *Song of Roland* and the *Quête du saint Graal,* noting a striking convergence of tone and situation but important differences in accent and form.[36]

In her doctoral dissertation (1970), which, except for a few extracts, remains unpublished, Marianne Cramer Vos has studied several characters in the *Song of Roland* from a medieval typological perspective.[37] The same year, Larry S. Crist maintained that: "La *Chanson de Roland* que nous possédons dans le manuscrit d'Oxford est bien d'un seul tenant et est bien une allégorie de la vie chrétienne telle que l'on sait que l'homme médiéval la concevait."[38]

Vos and Crist have perhaps confused modern critics who are not aware that they used the term allegory in the broad sense found, for example, in Isidore of Seville, namely *alieniloquium,* that is, roughly, representing one thing by another. Because allegory usually conjures up the *Roman de la Rose* or *Everyman,* it is probably a good idea to avoid using this word when writing about the *Song of Roland,* which belongs to a different genre. On the other hand, it is also true that the Latin *Pseudo-Turpin Chronicle* and the German *Rolandslied,* glossed versions of the *Song of Roland*—and, consequently, valuable guides for anyone today wishing to understand how the poem was interpreted by contemporary exegetes—are not epics either.[39]

Familiarity with Romanesque iconographic formulas, which are practically all based on religious art, enables one to grasp more readily the way Turoldus imagined certain scenes or conceived of certain characters.[40] In an interesting book published in 1983, Stephen G. Nichols has underlined a host of other advantages afforded by a knowledge of art when interpreting the *Song of Roland.*[41]

The single most important finding of recent scholarship on the religious content of the *chansons de geste* is that critics went astray when they began to dwell on the opposition between Roland and Oliver and to assert that the hero incarnates bravery, but his companion-in-arms wisdom. In two famous passages, Joseph Bédier declared:

Turold a obtenu que l'intérêt ne sera point dans les épisodes extérieurs, dans les grands coups d'épées; l'intérêt sera tout entier dans le conflit d'Olivier et de Roland, dans la curiosité passionnée qui désormais nous porte à observer Roland.

Pour que, des éléments légendaires, vagues et amorphes, qui végétaient dans les églises de Roncevaux ou dans les églises de la route de Ronce-vaux, naquît la *Chanson de Roland,* il est inutile et vain de supposer qu'il y ait fallu des siècles, et que des "chanteurs" sans nombre se soient succédé. Une minute a suffi, la minute sacrée où le poète, exploitant peut-être quelque frustre roman, ébauche grossière du sujet, a conçu l'idée du conflit de Roland et d'Olivier.[42]

Which of the two companions was right in the Horn debate? According to Bédier, the poet never provides the answer: "il semble les approuver tous les deux."[43] Later critics, however, decided that in bringing about the catastrophe Roland was guilty of *desmesure* or—and this was the position adopted by Pierre Le Gentil—he committed the sin of pride but, because he sacrificed himself to save Charlemagne, he was absolved by God.[44] In any event, guilt, sacrifice, and absolution are plainly religious concepts.

There is a growing tendency today to reject the view that Roland committed a tactical error or, even worse, the sin of pride. Normand R. Cartier, Robert F. Cook, Larry S. Crist, Alfred Foulet, William W. Kibler, Jean Misrahi and William L. Hendrickson, and the present writer, among others, have marshalled facts intended to exonerate the hero.[45] What emerges in the end is the view that Roland's apparently insane decision not to sound the oliphant is a metaphor of the Folly of the Cross or, if one prefers, of Sapientia.[46]

It would be a mistake to characterize the *chansons de geste* as purely devotional literature. On the other hand, recent studies have clearly shown that religious sentiment in these works is far more complex and varied than earlier suspected. It is also manifest that religious symbolism currently constitutes one of the most active and promising areas of research in the Old French epic field.

Notes

[1]Léon Gautier, *Les Epopées françaises*, 3 vols. (Paris: Palmé, 1865-68); Adolphe J. Dickmann, *Le Rôle du surnaturel dans les chansons de geste* (Paris: Champion, 1926); Sister Marianna Gildea, *Expressions of Religious Thought and Feeling in the Chansons de Geste* (Washington, D.C.: Catholic University of America Press, 1943); Brother J.-L. Roland Bélanger, *Damedieus: The Religious Context of the French Epic. The Loherain Cycle Viewed Against Other Early French Epics* (Geneva: Droz, 1975).

[2]George Fenwick Jones, *The Ethos of the Song of Roland* (Baltimore: Johns Hopkins Press, 1963).

[3]Jean-Charles Payen, "Une poétique du génocide joyeux: devoir de violence et plaisir de tuer dans la *Chanson de Roland*," *Olifant*, 6, Nos. 3 & 4 (1979), 233 (Roncevaux 778-1978: Proceedings of the Pennsylvania State University Conference).

[4]Jean Frappier, *Les Chansons de geste du cycle de Guillaume d'Orange. I. La Chanson de Guillaume, Aliscans, La Chevalerie Vivien* (Paris: Société d'Edition d'Enseignement Supérieur, 1955), pp. 106-08.

[5]My views in this respect have been set forth in *The Song of Roland: An Analytical Edition* (University Park, Pa., and London: Pennsylvania State University Press, 1978), 2 vols.; see also "The *Song of Roland* 778-1978," *Olifant*, 6, Nos. 3 & 4, pp. 207-08, and the introduction to *La Chanson de Roland: Student Edition* (University Park, Pa., and London: Pennsylvania State University Press, 1984), pp. xxiii-xxvi ("The Ethos of the *Song of Roland* and Its Ideology").

[6]Gerard J. Brault, "Le portrait des Sarrasins dans les chansons de geste, image projective?" in *Au Carrefour des routes d'Europe: la chanson de geste (Xe Congrès international de la Société Rencesvals pour l'étude des épopées romanes, Strasbourg 1985)* (Aix-en-Provence: C.U.E.R. M.A., 1987), I, 301-11. Paul Bancourt, "Les chansons de geste sont-elles 'racistes'?" forthcoming in the proceedings of the Eleventh International Congress of the Société Rencesvals (pour l'étude des épopées romanes) held at Barcelona, Spain, 22-27 August 1988, is a discussion of Payen's article and my paper.

[7]François-Marc Gagnon, *Ces Hommes dits sauvages: l'histoire fascinante d'un préjugé qui remonte aux premiers découvreurs du Canada* (Montreal: Libre Expression, 1984), pp. 72-82, 169-76.

[8]*Les Chansons de geste du cycle de Guillaume d'Orange. III. Les Moniages, Guibourc (Hommage à Jean Frappier)*, eds. Philippe Ménard and Jean-Charles Payen (Paris: Société d'Edition d'Enseignement Supérieur, 1983).

[9]Micheline de Combarieu, " 'Ermitages' epiques (de Guillaume et de quelques autres)," in *Les Chansons de geste du cycle de Guillaume d'Orange*, III, 143-80.

[10]Jean Batany, "Les 'Moniages' et la satire des moines aux XIe et XIIe siècles," in *Les Chansons de geste du cycle de Guillaume d'Orange*, III, 209-37.

[11]Jean Rychner, *La Chanson de geste: Essai sur l'art épique des jongleurs* (Geneva: Droz, and Lille: Giard, 1955), p. 12.

[12]Edmond Faral, *Les Jongleurs en France au Moyen Age* (1910; 2nd ed. Paris: Champion, 1964), Chap. 2.

[13]Faral, pp. 29 and 25, respectively.

[14]Faral, Chap. 2.

[15]Faral, p. 195.

[16]*The Song of Roland: An Analytical Edition*, I, 32.

[17]François Suard, *Guillaume d'Orange: Etude du roman en prose* (Paris: Champion, 1979), pp. 403, 415, 423, 451.

[18]Bernard Guidot, *Recherches sur la chanson de geste au XIIIe siècle d'après certaines œuvres du cycle de Guillaume d'Orange* (Aix-en-Provence: Université de Provence, 1986), II, 635, 636.

[19]Anne-Marie Cadot, "Le motif de l'*aître périlleux:* la christianisation du surnaturel dans quelques romans du XIIIe siècle," in *Mélanges de langue et de littérature françaises du Moyen Age et de la Renaissance offerts à Charles Foulon* (Liège: Marche Romane, 1980), II, 27-35; Jean Larmat, "La religion et les passions dans le *Tristan* de Béroul," in *Mélanges de philologie et de littératures romanes offerts à Jeanne Wathelet-Willem* (Liège: Marche Romane, 1978), pp. 327-45; Jeanne Lods, "Symbolisme chrétien: tradition celtique et vérité psychologique dans les personnages féminins de *Perlesvaus*," in *Mélanges de langue et de littératures médiévales offerts à Pierre Le Gentil* (Paris: Société d'Edition d'Enseignement Supérieur, 1973), pp. 505-22; Guy Raynaud de Lage, "La religion d'*Eracle*," in *Mélanges . . . Le Gentil*, pp. 707-13; Jean Subrenat, "Merveilleux chrétien et merveilleux païen dans le prologue d'*Huon de Bordeaux*," in *Société Rencesvals: Proceedings of the Fifth International Conference, Oxford 1970* (Salford: University of Salford, 1977), pp. 177-87.

[20]Robert Deschaux, "Le merveilleux dans la *Chanson d'Antioche*," in *Au Carrefour des routes d'Europe*, I, 431-43.

[21]Pierre Boglioni, "Pèlerinages et religion populaire: notes d'anthropologie et d'histoire," in *Les Pèlerinages au Québec*, eds. Pierre Boglioni and Benoît Lacroix (Quebec City: Les Presses de l'Université Laval, 1981), pp. 5-6.

[22]Benoît Lacroix, "Histoire et religion traditionnelle des Québécois (1534-1980)," in *Culture populaire et littératures au Québec*, ed. René Bouchard (Saratoga, Cal.: Anma Libri, 1980), p. 21.

[23]Nive Voisine, "Les valeurs religieuses de l'émigrant québécois (1850-1920)," in *L'Emigrant québécois vers les Etats-Unis, 1850-1920*, ed. Claire Quintal (Quebec City: Conseil de la vie française en Amérique, 1982), p. 32.

[24]Jean Larmat, "La religion populaire chez Gautier de Coinci," in *Mélanges . . . Foulon*, I, 167-75.

[25]The bibliography on the epic prayer in the hour of greatest need is extensive; see *Song of Roland: An Analytical Edition*, I, 460, n. 1.

[26]Jean Subrenat, "Saint Jacques, ses pèlerins, son chemin dans les chansons de geste françaises," in *VIII Congreso de la Société Rencesvals* (Pamplona: Institución Príncipe de Viana, 1981), pp. 505-11.

[27]Louis Réau, *Iconographie de l'art chrétien*, III, 2 (Paris: Presses Universitaires de France, 1958), 693, 700; Barton Sholod, *Charlemagne in Spain: The Cultural Legacy of Roncesvalles* (Geneva: Droz, 1966), pp. 69, 110-15.

[28]Gerard J. Brault, "The Cult of St. Peter in the Cycle of William of Orange," *French Forum*, 6 (1981), 101-08.

[29]Réau, III, 2, 693; III, 3 (1959), 1081.

[30]Felix Busigny, *Das Verhältnis der Chansons de geste zur Bible*, Inaugural Dissertation (Basel: Reinhardt, 1917).

[31]*Song of Roland: An Analytical Edition*, I, 25-26.

[32]*La Chanson de Roland: Student Edition*, ed. Gerard J. Brault (University Park, PA., and London, 1984), pp. xxiv-xxv.

[33]*La Chanson de Roland*, ed. Brault, p. xxv.

[34]Gerard J. Brault, "Le Thème de la Mort dans la *Chanson de Roland*," in *Société Rencesvals: IVe Congrès international (Heidelberg, 18 août-2 septembre 1967). Actes et Mémoires* (Heidelberg: Winter, 1969), pp. 220-27; "Quelques nouvelles tendances de la critique et de l'interprétation des chansons de geste," in *Société Rencesvals pour l'étude des épopées romanes: VIe Congrès international (Aix-en-Provence, 29 août-4 septembre 1973). Actes* (Aix-en-Provence: Université de Provence, 1974), pp. 19-22 (other studies listed, p. 24, n. 28). For my edition, see above, n. 5.

[35]Jacques Ribard, "La *Chanson de Roland*: aspects symboliques," in *VIII Congreso de la Société Rencesvals*, pp. 405-12.

[36]Jacques Ribard, "La *Chanson de Roland* et la *Quête du saint Graal*," in *Essor et fortune de la chanson de geste dans l'Europe et l'Orient latin: Actes du IXe Congrès international de la Société Rencesvals pour l'étude des épopées romanes (Padoue-Venise, 19 août-4 septembre 1982)* (Modena: Mucchi, 1984), II, 553-63. See also Jaume Vallcorba, "Pour une perspective mythologico-religieuse de la *Chanson de Roland*," forthcoming in the proceedings of the 1988 Congress of the Société Rencesvals mentioned above in n. 6.

[37]Marianne Cramer Vos, "Aspects of Biblical Typology in *La Chanson de Roland*," Diss. University of Rochester 1970. See idem, "Projet pour un livre sur la signification de la *Chanson de Roland*," in *Essor et fortune de la chanson de geste*, II, 989-91.

[38]Larry S. Crist, "A propos de la *desmesure* dans la *Chanson de Roland*: quelques propos (démesurés?)," *Société Rencesvals: Proceedings of the Fifth International Conference*, p. 148.

[39]*Song of Roland: An Analytical Edition*, I, 30-39.

[40]*Song of Roland: An Analytical Edition*, I, 44-47.

[41]Stephen G. Nichols, *Romanesque Signs: Early Medieval Narrative and Iconography* (New Haven: Yale University Press, 1983).

[42]Joseph Bédier, *Les Légendes épiques: Recherches sur la formation des chansons de geste,* 2nd ed. (Paris: Champion, 1914-21), III, 333-34, 448.

[43]Bédier, III, 432; cf. III, 444; "le poète les approuve tous les deux. . . . Entre le 'preux' et le 'sage' il n'a pas choisi, trop humain pour choisir."

[44]Pierre Le Gentil, *La Chanson de Roland* (Paris: Hatier-Boivin, 1955), pp. 118-19. For a discussion of this and related views, see *Song of Roland,* ed. Brault, I, 10-15.

[45]Normand R. Cartier, "La sagesse de Roland," *Aquila: Chestnut Hill Studies in Modern Languages and Literatures,* I (1969), 33-63; Robert F. Cook, *The Sense of the Song of Roland* (Ithaca and London: Cornell University Press, 1987); Larry S. Crist, see above, n. 38; Alfred Foulet, "Is Roland Guilty of Desmesure?" *Romance Philology,* 10 (1957), 145-48; William W. Kibler, "Roland's Pride," *Symposium,* 26 (1972), 147-60; Jean Misrahi and William L. Hendrickson, "Roland and Oliver: Prowess and Wisdom: the Ideal of the Epic Hero," *Romance Philology,* 33 (1979-80), 357-72.

[46]Gerard J. Brault, "*Sapientia* dans la *Chanson de Roland,*" in *Société Rencesvals: Proceedings of the Fourth International Congress,* pp. 85-104.

Funerary Rituals in the *Chanson de Roland**

Peter Haidu

The Baligant episode interrupts, in its various segments, narrative developments whose coherence is defined by a common theme: not only do they come after Roland's death, these narrative syntagms are concerned with problems posed by that death. Death is a problem for the living, as is well known, not the dead. Anthropologically speaking, the crucial problem is the reintegration of the members of the social group into its unity after the disappearance of one of its crucial members. Vis-à-vis the fact of death, the social group performs its rituals, the means by which the absentification of the dead is acknowledged and the re-presentification of the living achieved. The values of the group define the individual who dies as a hero, and his actions as the idealized narrative representation of at least one ideological potential in the group's semiotic universe. Issues of responsibility and culpability, problems of the figuration of value in a mode transcendent of the quotidian, the radical incommensurability between the survivors and the human gap facing them, are social and ideological fissures obsessing the survivors, not those who are gone. The group's task is to knit again the web of its social unity, to reintegrate its members into the collectivity.

While portraying the generality of the surviving Frankish troops as grieving their losses, the narrative focuses on the figure of Charles as survivor. It is Charles who is cast into the textual figures of the consciousness of loss. The rhetorical charge of this aspect of the figure is not to be denied. It is perhaps that aspect of the Roland-text that remains the most accessible to the poetic taste and values of the typical reader of our time: an academic reader, haunted by the nostalgia for an imagined past of wholeness and integration. The continued effectivity of this emotional charge, however, must not be allowed to mask the fact that the poem is here performing an essential operation. The section in question changes things, it performs a transformation upon those materials that, at its beginning, are givens because they are the product of the earlier sections of the poem. In doing so, of course, it functions like any narrative syntagm: it constitutes a transformation of its narrative materials.

The essential Moments of this transformation are three: the lament for the dead, the revenge upon the retreating Saracens, and the discovery, collection, evisceration, and burial of the heroes' bodies. These three moments imply successive locative displacements: Roncevaux, the River Ibre, Roncevaux again. They also are constituted by different types of textualizations: as implied by the noun that designates it, the lament is a purely verbal textualization; the revenge, though it includes some dialogue, is primarily a narrative moment; the complex "burial" of the heroes is composed of a particular combination of the verbal and the narrative.

The lament takes the form, somewhat surprising, of a classical topos in an oral text: it is the first use of the *ubi-sunt* theme in vernacular French poetry. The appearance of this poetic theme from the classical and written tradition in the oral text of the *Chanson* presents clear evidence of the mixed character of the *Chanson de Roland*. It is "mixed" not only in its ontological status, but also in its socio-historical and ideological content. Its form as a rhetorical question—Where are the dead?—is "empty" in the sense that the question is not a real one: the answer is not open to question. In this case, the inevitable answer to the rhetorical question is, after each naming of a hero, that he is dead, dead on the field of battle [. . .][1]

Although "empty" in this sense, the lamentation in the form of *ubi sunt* does perform essential narrative structural roles. It presents itself as the expression of emotions, a theme textualized a number of times in this syntagm. This textualization is a necessary precondition of the following narrative program. It is only once the emotions of Charles and his men have been given socio-textual existence that they provide the content of a qualifying statement justifying the revenge obtained against the fleeing Saracens. Duke Naimes intervenes upon the expression of the emperor's great grief, pointing to the fleeing Saracens: "Look, two leagues ahead of us, See the great dusty roads, There is the mass of the pagans: Ride! Avenge this pain!" (vv. 2425-28). *Vengez ceste dulor!*[2] provides the link between the emotion and the succeeding action. The grief is experienced as an impermissible trespass upon the survivor, a damage done him for which legal reparation can be claimed. That reparation is the basic narrative stuff of the *chanson de geste* as a whole, in particular that which is known as the rebellious barons cycle: there, revenge is taken upon the feudal lord whose treatment of the vassal is unjust. Here, it is revenge against those who by definition have no moral or juridical status before a strictly Christian law, the nonbelievers. In any case, the survivor experiences his grief as an injury done him, for which the appropriate mode of treatment is the exaction of vengeance, conceived as a legal mode of compensation. The expression of grief here transforms what a twentieth-century consciousness would consider pure interiority into a social and semiotic fact that is the basis for narrative action.

That narrative action is collective: *"tuit en sunt cummunel"* (v. 2446). In fact, it is so collective that it requires the intervention of God in a new mode. In the Roland-text, God intervenes by saintly interposition, either cognitively (as in the dreams brought to Charles by the angel Gabriel) or pragmatically (to collect Roland's soul as his ultimate Destinator). Here, however, God is presented as directly interfering with the operations of Nature: at Charles's prayer, God stops the flow of time to allow the Franks to catch up with the Saracens. It is thus a miracle, a type of grant of a magic Adjuvant that had not been awarded Roland. Charles is endowed by the text with the power not only to receive privileged communication from God in the form of proleptic dreams—a power he already had in the Roland-section, and which he retains in this second major half of the *Chanson:* Charles will once again be visited by annunciatory dreams. His communicative competence with the divinity extends to the point of being able to request and obtain a change in the fundamental assumptions, not only of human life, but of narrative itself. The suspension of the flow of time, the ability to perform narrative actions that would otherwise be prevented by something as fundamental as the passage of time, changes the very conditions of possibility of narrative itself. What would be impossible for any normal /human/ actor becomes possible for Charles. The miraculous interference of the divinity in the workings of Nature foreshadows the perhaps equally miraculous solution that will be achieved in the final trial scene of the epic.

At this occasion, "religion" makes a striking entry into a text that is anything but religious or Christian in its fundamental content. In view of this limited import, the form this religiosity takes should be noted. It constitutes a direct grant of power to Charles as King and Emperor, utterly disregarding (as the poem does in general) the historical institutions of religion: the medieval Church in any of its forms. It may well be that the Pope and Emperor are mutually defining binary opposites in the historical, extra-textual domain: in this concrete text, the Pope and the institution he heads simply do not exist. All the ideological power associated with the Pope and the Church in contemporary cultural codes is attributed to the figure of the King of France who is also the Emperor of Christendom. Within the economy of the text, this "extra" ideological valorization is of the same order and function as the Baligant episode: the extraordinary investment of ideological value in this particular figure is functionalized by the need to enable him to perform certain narrative acts that might otherwise prove too difficult for an ordinary human agent. The character of these acts, the specific isotopy on which they will occur is indicated by the third Moment.

Having despatched the fleeing Saracens by drowning and by the sword, Charles and his men return to Roncevaux. This a/b/a structure marks the revenge wrought upon the Saracens as necessary on the one hand, but as a necessary interruption of the basic business of this section, namely the enactment of the rituals of the dead. Before their performance, however, the weary Franks take their rest and sleep for the night. Charles lies down as well, but does not sleep immediately:

> Carles se gist, mais doel ad de Rollant
> E d'Oliver li peseit mult forment,
> Des .XII. pers e de la franceise gent
> Qu'en Rencesvals ad laiset morz sanglenz.
> Ne poet muer n'en plurt e nes dement
> E priet Deu qu'as anmes seit guarent.
> (vv. 2513-18)

As at the moment of Roland's death, when he surrenders his glove to God as a sign of final and ultimate fealty, so here as well the relation of the individual to his God is figured by the feudal Metaphor, the divine assumption of dead souls and hope for their salvation being figured by the relationship of feudal protection [. . .]

When Charles, wearied by grief, does fall asleep, it is to encounter annunciatory dreams that parallel those of the first part. In terms of the twentieth-century reader, these proleptic dreams "make sense," that is, carry specific meaning, only on the basis of a retrospective reading: one must have read the *Chanson* to the end at least once before in order to understand that these two successive dreams refer first to the impending battle with Baligant, and secondly to the trial scene at Aix, with an allegorical representation or pro-presentation of Ganelon, his thirty relatives, and both Thierry and Pinabel. Reading, for us, is a punctual, datable event, whose cognitive function is clearly delimitable. But the cognitive conditions of the medieval audience were quite different from ours. For the medieval audience, there is likely never to have been a "first" time: the *Chanson de Roland,* from what we know of it, was a popular text, and is likely to have been performed by *jongleurs* repeatedly, albeit in different forms. As a result, the events of the poem have an identity under the specific variations characteristic of any individual performance: they exist in some field of permanence external to the particular performance. Functionally speaking, they exist in a sphere that is analogous to the neo-Platonism typical of medieval aesthetics descending from Philo and St. Augustine. As a result, the meaning of these proleptic dreams, definable for the modern reader only on a linear dimension of temporality, are extra-temporal for the medieval audience of the oral performance *and* immediately accessible. That audience, even illiterate, will always already have known the story and its outcome: even though this was obviously not true in any one particular case (even a medieval individual biography had to contain a "first" time hearing of the text), it is nevertheless an ontological condition of the oral medieval text that its basic narrative pattern has to be construed as always already known.

Thus it is that the proleptic dreams that come to Charles, ambiguous as they are if taken in a unidirectional successive temporal sequence that permits them to be semantically informed only by a retrospective look upon the narrative, must be considered as endowed with the semantic content that, for the modern interpretant, devolves from a forward look to the later narrative events. The first dream sets Charles in a battle accompanied by multiple "natural" signs of terror—thunder, winds, and ice, storms and tempests, fires and flames falling upon his army; lances and shield take fire, weapons and armor twist, and the army is in great distress. It is attacked by bears, leopards, serpents, vipers, dragons, and demons—a plethora of the supernatural, to which are added thirty million griffins! The battle is general, until Charles himself is attacked by a great lion filled with rage, pride, and courage. There is little reason to hesitate in identifying the proleptic narrative referent of this laisse as the later battle between the Frankish army, led by Charles, and the troops of Baligant, a battle that will find its conclusion in the individual combat between the two emperors. The second dream, localized at Aix, sets into the dream scene one chained bear, thirty more claiming to be his relatives and demanding that he be returned to them. At this point, a hunting dog arrives, a greyhound to be exact, who attacks the largest of the thirty bears. The emperor witnesses a miraculous combat, but, as in the preceding dream, does not know in his dream who wins. Again, there is little reason to hesitate in juxtaposing this dream with the combat between Pinabel, representing the thirty relatives of Ganelon at his trial who are also his hostages, and Thierry, the lean and unheroic knight who will, in fact, win against Pinabel.

The structural import of these dream syntagms is not their allegorical significance, which is so patent as not to require "interpretation" in any serious sense at all, but rather their function within a narrative structure. They occur at the hinge point between two larger syntagms: the narrative of the funereal rituals of the survivors, and the beginning of the Baligant episode. Whether they are to be considered a part of the former or of the latter is not an issue for the present reading, which accepts the presence of the Baligant material in spite of a conviction of its later and additive nature. For these proleptic dreams, and the meaning they bear and which is demonstrated to Charles by the angel Gabriel who brings him the dreams themselves (*senefiance l'en demustrat mult gref*, v. 2531), those dreams rejoin a general semantic level of the text. They demonstrate the connection of the present narrative moment with a later one, by "re-telling" the later and narratively "real" event ahead of time, before its actual place in the outplay of the narrative. The establishment of the semantic connection produces the meaning that both the funereal rituals and the Baligant episode have to be seen in relation to the later syntagms they announce. In particular, the funereal rituals and the reintegration they operate, lead to the ultimate narrative sequence of Ganelon's trial. They lead to it, in that they perform a function that is prerequisite to the later narrative syntagm. The reintegration of the living must be performed before the final judgment of the cause and responsibility for the dead can be passed. Ganelon's trial could not occur unless its actors retrieve their full standing as Subjects within the social group.

After the Baligant episode stages the encounter of Baligant's messengers and Marsile, and then between Baligant himself and his vassal, the text shifts back to Charles at Roncevaux. The third Moment of the funereal syntagm is the essential one. It is constituted by a compound of verbal and narrative subsections. In a battlefield covered by the twenty thousand bodies of the rear-guard, the problem is that of finding the one body Charles wants above all, Roland's. He finds it by a speech that recalls and re-presentifies the extraordinarily moving moments of Roland's death. At a solemn festival observance at Aix, Roland had once boasted that he would not die in a foreign land unless he had gone farther forward than his men and his peers; he would have his head turned toward the foreigners' land, and the hero would end as a victor. In order to find his nephew, Charles restates that aspect of him that led to his death, the combination of heroic virtue and boastful supererogation of knightly prowess that we "mean" by the name "Roland." Charles recalls the traits that made the subordinate knightly group so problematical for their lords and for the society at large.

In other words, the mere recall of the actor's words, at a party sometime before the current war, also implies, because of the earlier narrative context, the political isotopy, which is doubled, here, by the identification of the familial bond between Charles and Roland (v. 2859, 2870, 2876). The political isotopy is reiterated. Finding the body of his nephew among the red flowers and green grass, under the two trees, near the marks of the blows Roland struck on the rocks in trying to destroy Durendal his sword before dying, Charles faints dead away. Coming to, he begins to "regret" Roland, that is, to mourn him in lamentation. At this level the verbal syntagm is identical with the earlier *plainte* in the *ubi sunt* form. But in looking more specifically at the content of this particular lament, a major difference is found. If the *ubi sunt* theme looks backward and stresses the absence of the dead, Charles's lamentation now does quite the opposite. The absence of the dead is presented in a proleptic framework, looking forward to a future point in time and presentifying the effects that Roland's death and absence will have then. Recommending Roland to God's mercy, Charles touches on his uniqueness as a warrior and concludes the first brief speech:

> "La meie honor est turnet en declin."
>
> (v. 2890)

Literally: my "Honor" is turned toward its decline. But "honor" is a strange word. What is restricted to the valorial field for us moderns— "honor" for us is strictly a matter of opinion, either internal or that which others hold of an individual—is simultaneously material in the medieval language. "Honor" can indeed have the same meaning it has for us, the credit or esteem in which a given individual is held by his fellows; but it also has the meaning of the complex of land and social organization that produces wealth and power and that often takes the specific form of a fief. Indeed, the ambiguity of the word (an ambiguity that is apparent only to us, since we—unlike the medievals—separate the material base from its ideological value) suggests the interdependence of the two semantic components: one is not "honorable" unless one has a certain material base of power and wealth; and possessing such a base produces the credit and esteem of one's fellows, unless one acts in such a way as to lose that respect. In certain ways, the Middle Ages were far more materialistic than we are; or perhaps their materialism was simply more self-evident. Charles's *honor* is then *both* his reputation and that complex of geographical territory and socio-political organization upon which that reputation is based: his fief, his kingdom, his empire. All three are profoundly weakened by Roland's death [. . .]

The necessary dualism of funereal ritual—"letting go" and reaffirming the unity of the social group, assertions of absence and presence as simulaneities—is thus laid over, by Charles's own complaint, with the specifically political form that is the ultimate isotopy of the *chanson de geste* in general. That dualism is restated in the most primitive moment of the ritual, in the burial of the great majority of the dead, the extraction of the hearts of the heroes—Roland, Oliver, and Turpin—and their enclosure in marble sarcophagi, well washed with spices and wine. The hearts are to retain for the survivors the strength of the dead, even as their (ultimate) burial is to recognize their departure. Presence and absence both, the anthropological ritual has a complexity that the political does not. Where the funereal ritualization of loss affirms a duality against the brutal fact of death, the political isotopy allies itself with that brutality. There is nothing in this *plainte* about the inspirational value of the legend and *chanson* to be told and sung about Roland and his peers. In Charles's political evaluation of the meaning of Roland's loss, there is room only for loss, for the resulting political and military weakness of his reign. His personal grief is doubled by a political issue that overrides the personal. Indeed, the personal must be expressed, indulged in perhaps, in order to allow for the movement toward the political. For the personal loss is not resolved, but met, by the funerary rituals of the text; the political loss, and its implications, must yet be met and resolved, more directly and more brutally.

Finally, the syntagm of funereal ritual has as narrative function the
(re)statement of this dual valorization of the loss of the hero, the personal
and the political. It does so with an internal organization of closure. I have
pointed out that the first Roncevaux syntagm is verbal, the Ebre syntagm is
narrative, and that the second Roncevaux syntagm is both verbal and narrative. That second Roncevaux syntagm, however, is internally organized in
a pattern that is recursive of the overall organization of the ritual syntagm.
Its first "move" is to discover Roland: as we have seen, that takes a predominantly verbal form as Charles recounts Roland's earlier boast at Aix.
That is followed by another verbal syntagm, Charles's long lamentation.
These two verbal syntagms are followed by the concluding syntagm,
narrative in nature, in which the dead are buried, the heroes have their hearts
extracted and are both shrouded and encased in sarcophagi. This recursiv-
ity, recapitulating in the final narrative subsection the pattern of the whole,
thereby gives closure to the whole. That sense of closure marks the fact that
one moment of the narrative has ended, another begins.

The major burden of most of the text after the conclusion of the
Baligant episode is to deal finally with the issue of culpability for Roland's
death, as well as the socio-political development of a way to prevent the
recurrence of what led to the disaster at Roncevaux. In the Oxford *Roland,*
the syntagm concerned with these issues—Ganelon's trial—is preceded by
a brief, two-laisse passage that returns to the isotopy of the funereal rituals.
It also initiates another isotopy, that of exchange: the brief episode is a
narrative isotopic connector between the funereal rites and the trial.

The emperor has returned to Aix. Aude, Roland's betrothed, comes
to the court to ask for her man. She asks, and the manner in which she
asks, and the manner in which her demand is received, indicate that what
she asks for is her right. Charles acknowledges Roland's death; he offers
instead his son Louis as substitute. The text asserts the advantageous character of this offer: Louis would inherit Charles's reign. Nevertheless,
Aude rejects the offer, and does so radically: she dies on the spot. Her
corpse is turned over to nuns in a convent, who bury her properly,
alongside an altar:

Mult grant honur i ad li reis dunee.
(v. 3733)

The syntax suggests what the text does not specify, that the "honor" is financial value.

The syntagm is framed by two lines that seem to announce something else. The two laisses of the Aude syntagm are laisses 268 and 269. The last line of laisse 267—preceding the Aude syntagm—announces a different topic:

> Des ore cumencet le plait de Guenelun.
>
> (v. 3704)

Then, in laisse 270, the theme of the return to Aix is restated (v. 3734) and developed, and in the following laisse, the beginning of Ganelon's trial is announced once again:

> Des ore cumencet le plait et les noveles
> De Guenelen, ki traïsun ad faite.
>
> (v. 3747 f.)

Thus, both before and after the Aude syntagm, Ganelon's trial is announced. On the one hand, it is patent that the Aude syntagm is not Ganelon's trial, or any part thereof. Nevertheless, the repeated assertion of the text suggests a connection between Aude's death and Ganelon's trial.

The likeliest explanation, for both the discrepancy between the topic announced in v. 3704 and the succeeding syntagm, and the isotopic continuity between the earlier section dealing with the funeral rituals of the dead of Roncevaux and the Aude scene at Aix, is fairly obvious. In an earlier stage of the *Chanson de Roland,* the episode of funereal ritual and the death of Aude were two subsidiary parts of the same narrative syntagm, whose topic was the collective and individual griefs, and the rituals of reintegration and exclusion that follow upon the death of the culture-hero, the icon of the warrior society. It is a syntagm whose topic is the reconstitution of the collectivity after a disaster that calls its very values into question. The present state of the evolution of the oral epic contains an additional syntagm, inserted between two subsidiary parts of the earlier stage, in which an outsider and his troops come and interrupt the collective ritual of grief and reconstitution. The Baligant episode, in other words, interrupts a narrative unit that had a unified production of meaning dealing with social emotions after a great disaster, intervening between the narration of the great defeat itself and the legal and political fall-out that succeeds it. The new episode interrupts the sequence: (loss) + (mourning) + (adjustment), each of these terms occurring on both the individual and the collective isotopies. The present syntagm adds new elements to the textual production of signification; it also introduces a new cultural and valorial logic of coherence into the world of textuality. Insofar as social contracts determine the exchange of social value, Charles does more than merely discharge his responsibility as a social agent: his offer contains a valorial supplement, a surplus value that might have been expected to determine, even to overdetermine, an acceptance by the Recipient of the communicative exchange. The surplus value here is the difference between the value of a great noble, even a culture hero, and the king's son. More determining than cultural values, the political value and the implicit territorial and financial values are expected to assuage the damage to her own value that Aude has undergone in her grief and the loss of her betrothed. Aude's refusal is all the more striking then, since it not only rejects the proposed exchange and the supplementary surplus value it contains: in her death, she also refuses any further social intercourse and verbal exchange with the Destinator.

To the modern reader, the notion of the substitution Charles proposes seems absurd: how shall one man be accepted as the substitute for another in a romantic relationship that consists precisely in the election of one individual as the unique cathexis of certain emotions? Here again, twentieth-century codes are inappropriate. Marriage, far from an expression of the romantic election of another person as the primary cathexis of the individual and the announcement to the collectivity of the couple's desire to make their union permanent (perhaps, at this point in 1989, already a somewhat old-fashioned view of marriage!), marriage in the Middle Ages, at the social level with which we are concerned, is a dynastic and diplomatic affair generally more concerned with the aggrandizement of dominion over lands and other forms of property than with tender emotions. Not that tender emotions do not exist in this text, or in the epic in general: they do, and this particular syntagm is only one example of such emotions in the *Chanson de Roland.* Others are the not infrequent references to wives and women who wait for the warriors in *dulce France,* to whom they are eager to return; the equivalent is stated of the Saracen warriors. The text recognizes such attachments as normative and refers to them without hesitation. But the text is a warrior epic, and such topics are not the topics that are developed within its frame; in this respect, the Old French epic is poorer than the Greek. On the other hand, while the Greek epic may be more inclusive, the French is both more intense, and perhaps accomplishes social transformations that remain unthought of in the *Iliad*. While the tender emotions do exist at the edges of the *Roland,* however, they are not the basis of the politics of marriage, nor are they a major concern of the text. The theme of individual fidelity is touchingly deployed, here, but it masks another operation that is of more moment to the achievement of this text.

The two laisses that deal with Aude are more than a romantic interlude (the way they have most frequently been taken by traditional criticism), and more than a textual supplement incorporated into the text itself. They have a function; they perform a transformation. First of all, the narrative syntagm provides an isotopic connector, incorporating the theme of death, and of Roland's death in particular, within a textual space that also places the action at Aix, where the trial takes place. It does more than merely state these two themes of death and the trial simultaneously, however. The funerary theme, as we saw, was meant to achieve the reintegration of society as a whole after a crucial loss, and in particular the reintegration of the primary grievant, Charles. That reintegration is not achieved yet, however. Charles's effort to set things right, as feudal overlord, as monarch, as uncle, is unsuccessful: the issue of compensation for Roland's death is still unsettled.

That issue is as foreign to the modern reader as that of the values actually involved in noble marriage. Whether because of a religious heritage that can be taken to assert the sanctity of human life, or because of a tradition of individual subjectivity that represents each person as a unique phenomenon, our ideology does not allow for the principle of compensation to be recognized overtly in cases of death. Both the Judaic tradition and the Germanic are more sensible. Acknowledging that perhaps there are emotional components in such a loss for which compensation is literally unimaginable, both traditions recognize that the dead person was also a social value, and that compensation for that aspect of the person can be arranged. That is to say that a system of exchange, in which the social being of the individual is recognized as a social value for which other forms of social value can be exchanged, is elaborated in both traditions. It is probably the Germanic tradition that was most determinative in shaping medieval attitudes. The tradition of a fixed tariff of equivalencies—the *wergeld*—of compensation even in the case of the unemendable *morth* (murder), was a characteristic of archaic German law that continued into the

period of the *Chanson de Roland*. Such legal compensation is an extension
of the principle of exchange into the domain of law, even as law governs the
most extreme disruptions of social relations. The principle of exchange is at
work, then, in Charles's offer, which is neither unfeeling nor crude: it is a
recognition both of the reality of loss and of the limited nature of the
compensation that society, as an entity, is capable of providing its members.
The offer is an entirely appropriate enactment of social and conventional
codes and bears with it a surplus of valorial supplementation that signifies
generosity or, in medieval terms, *largesse*.

Nevertheless, the offer is absurd, even in Charles's own terms.
Charles's offer refers to Roland as an *hume mort*. In a line already quoted,
he says:

> Jo t'en durai mult esforcet *eschange*.
> (v. 3714)

Aude's response, by its very rhyme within an assonanced text, stresses that
it is the notion of exchange she is rejecting:

> Alde respunt: "Cest mot mei est *estrange*"
> (v. 3717)

What is *estrange* (L. *extraneum;* foreign; the term belongs to the same
semantic family as the Greek *barbaroi*) is exchange. Aude takes the position
that no exchange is possible for Roland: it is an anomalous position in the
codes of her society. It is also a costly position to take: it costs her her life.
The beloved's death implies an absolute cathexis on one individual. What
may strike the post-romantic reader as a literary cliché is, in the textual and
cultural context of the end of the eleventh and the beginning of the twelfth
century, quite remarkable. That anomalous character, rather than the
romantic associations, is what is textually most functional.

Oddly enough, Aude's refusal of the principle of exchange in connection with Roland had been prefigured in our text, and prefigured by none
other than Charles himself. It was Charles who, speaking of Roland to
Naimes, said earlier:

> "Deus! se jol pert, ja n'en avrai escange."
> (v. 840)

It was Charles himself, then, who established the principle of nonsubstitutability in Roland's case, well before he offered a substitute for Roland to Aude. Aude's refusal is merely a reiteration to Charles of Charles's own understanding: it is his own cognition that comes back to haunt him. No man can be a substitute for Roland. Roland was unique, but as soon as that is said, it is crucial to specify what that adjective comports, lest our conceptions of the uniqueness of the individual flood into the receptacle of the waiting signifier.

Roland's uniqueness, at the actorial level, is specified so frequently that it is hardly necessary to cite those bits of the text in question. It is military, and hence political. Not only is there no trace of a unique interiority in Roland—one might make a better argument for Oliver, Charles, or Ganelon in this regard—his uniqueness is entirely constituted by the social qualities that are those of his social class carried to extremes: both his warring abilities, and their characterological implications, are those of the knight as a social type. Simply, he has a far greater allotment of the more specific traits than the ordinary knight. In terms of the inner-outer dichotomy, Roland's uniqueness, like his individualism, is entirely "external." What counts is not some hidden and unique subjectivity, but the fact that, as a Subject, Roland is capable of undertaking narrative programs—and carrying them out successfully—that no one else can.

Aude's refusal of Charles's offer and the implication of Roland's uniqueness that it bears have as their meaning a reassertion of the momentous loss that is Roland's death. It reasserts that the issues implicit in that death, and in the narrative syntagms that lead up to it, have not yet been resolved, especially as they attach themselves to Charles's person. Not only is the sequence of funerary rituals undergone ineffective in reintegrating Charles as survivor into the social group: insofar as Aude is in her rights in demanding of Charles her betrothed, his inability to produce Roland causes her death. [. . .]

Not only is the ideal hero of the society dead [. . .]: the basic principle of social organization—that of exchange—has been at least interrupted and suspended. This is the ultimate significance of Aude's refusal. If the normal pattern of exchanges encoded in the laws and conventions of the society no longer hold, if the damage to the social fabric is so grievous that its system of compensatory awards is refused by those whom it should benefit, then the very principle of sociality has been suspended. What is at stake is not a romantic attachment, nor even the justice to be accorded heroism, betrayal, and contractual responsibility: because of the character-istics of the textual actors involved, what is at stake is the continuation of society. [. . .] The stakes that are set into play by the *Chanson de Roland*—as by any great work, from the *Iliad* and the Greek tragedians to Samuel Beckett—are the ultimate values of the society in which it is embedded. That "setting into play" is also a "setting at risk": each time textuality "plays" with the values of its social structure, it not only takes the risks of an aesthetic adventure, it also risks the survival of the social text, the social fabric, the social body.

Notes

*The present text, excerpted from a longer discussion of the *Chanson de Roland*, seems apt in honoring the memory of a colleague who was unique in his particular combination of respect for the concrete text, attention to an inherited tradition of medievalism, and attentiveness to the paradigms of contemporary theory.

[1]Major excisions from my longer essay are indicated by ellipsis marks within square brackets.

[2]All citations are from Joseph Bédier's edition of the *Chanson de Roland* (Paris: Piazza, 1921).

Garin de Monglane and La Chanson de la croisade albigeoise: A Comparative Old French-Occitan Study

William L. Hendrickson

At first glance a comparative study of the Old French *Garin de Monglane* and the old Provençal, or more accurately, Old Occitan *Chanson de la croisade albigeoise* appears to be somewhat far-fetched. However, just as the *matières* in the Middle Ages were divided up into three, the *matière de France* was in turn divided up into three again by Bertrand de Bar-sur-Aube, author of *Girart de Vienne*. The same division is given in *Doon de Mayence*. Depending upon which of these enumerations is consulted, the "Geste de Garin de Monglane" is the second or the third of the three *gestes*. In 1975 Robert Sabatier reminded us in his *Poésie du Moyen Age,* the first volume of his *Histoire de la poésie française,* that in this particular *geste* of Garin de Monglane or of Guillaume d'Orange, his legendary great-grandson, "Il s'agit des héros du Sud restés fidèles à la royauté."[1] Thus the geographical boundaries are approximately the same for the Old French *chanson de geste* and the Occitan historical epic. Sabatier, of the Académie Goncourt and not a medievalist, continues: "*Garin de Monglane* qui a donné son nom au cycle en est une des branches. Monglane, c'est Glanum que conquit Guillaume sur son vassal rebelle avant d'épouser la fille du comte de Limoges."[2] Attempts to locate Sabatier's source were all in vain. It then became apparent that Sabatier must have confused Guillaume with Garin. Wolfgang van Emden, in the *Table des noms propres* of his critical edition of *Girart de Vienne,* gave a brief résumé of the hypotheses concerning the name "Monglane":[3]

pour les origines de ce toponyme, fort discutées, voir surtout H. Suchier, *Romania*, XXXII, 1903, pp. 356-61 (Glane, près de Fribourg, dont les seigneurs prétendaient être liés avec ceux de Vienne; Suchier lui-même n'attache guère de poids à cette hypothèse); R. Louis, *Girart*, pp. 59-65 (l'antique Glanum, près de Saint-Remy de Provence, dont les ruines imposantes subsistent même aujourd'hui, mais dont le nom n'était plus connu à l'époque de Bertrand); F. Lot, *Romania*, LXX, 1948-49, pp. 383-4 (rejette Glanum, parce qu'il conçoit mal que Bertrand ait pu avoir connaissance de ce nom, et croit plutôt que le poète a inventé Monglane de toutes pièces). Aubri de Trois-Fontaines (*M.G.H.*, *Scriptores*, XXIII, 716) place Montglane "versus Tolosam" (*cf.* Louis, *op. cit.*, p. 68, n. 2), mais cette expression pourrait avoir un sens très vague ("dans le Midi").

It should perhaps be stated that even before René Louis, Paulin Paris had proposed that Glanum be identified with Monglane. It appears to have been Bertrand de Bar-sur-Aube who created Garin and made him the founder of the epic cycle. Bertrand is also thought to have created the stronghold of Monglane, which in his poem *Girart de Vienne* he placed on the banks of the Rhone River. The anonymous author of *Garin de Monglane* who refers to Girart de Vienne has, however, a very different idea of Monglane's location. For him it is high on a cliff overlooking the ocean, and he sometimes refers to it as "Monglane-sor-Mer." The Glanum ruins, while interesting in themselves and surrounded by a beautiful countryside now identified with Van Gogh, reveal nothing from a geographical point of view that would suggest a commanding position for a fortress.[4] The geographical basis for a comparison of the two works does remain valid, however, in spite of the specific puzzle of Monglane.

The second reason for comparison is line 730 of *Garin de Monglane,* which states, concerning the inhabitants of Monglane, "Or sont tot Aubigois, felon et mescreant."[5] Léon Gautier in *Les Epopées françaises* had drawn attention to that line: "Le nom d'Aubigois, sous lequel on désigne les ennemis de Garin vient du souvenir encore tout récent sans doute, de la grande guerre religieuse qui a rempli une partie du règne de Philippe-Auguste."[6] Nevertheless, he insisted that "Les luttes entre le Nord et le Midi de la France ont pu tout au plus servir de donnée générale, d'une façon très vague, aux péripéties de ce Roman."[7] Gautier summed up his impressions with the statement "*Garin de Monglane* est une œuvre absolument

fabuleuse; elle n'a rien d'historique, ni même de traditionnel ou de légendaire."[8] Despite my great respect for Gautier's accomplishments, I have
always considered this absolute statement open to debate. In support of his
opinion is the fact, unknown to him, that the above quoted line is only in the
Paris manuscript (B.N., f.f. 24403), one of the three complete manuscripts,
and that the word does not occur again in the epic poem.

A comparison of the Old French work and the contemporary
thirteenth-century Occitan historical epic, *La Chanson de la croisade
albigeoise,* permits a closer examination of the question, looking at the Epic
as both History and Fiction and considering a variety of aspects such as
point of view, the role of the narrator as well as the *narrataire.*

The *Chanson de la croisade albigeoise* is a work of 7582 lines,
divided into 214 laisses. It is not the work of a single author, however, but
rather that of Guillaume de Tudèle, who wrote the first 131 laisses, in all
2172 lines, and of his anonymous continuator, who added 6810 lines in 83
laisses.[9] Therefore, it should be said that the aspects under consideration
provided a different set of answers for each of the parts of the *Chanson.*

All that is known of Guillaume (or Guilhelmes in Occitan) is what
he himself relates in the beginning laisses. He is from Tudela in Spanish
Navarre, where he studied, attaining the *maîtrise ès arts,* for he identifies
himself as "maestre" and "clercs."[10] We know that he went to Montauban,
where he spent eleven years, leaving there in 1211. Because he claimed to
possess the art of "géomancie," foretelling the future, he foresaw the
impending disaster that was to consume the South. He left for nearby
Bruniquel under the protection of Count Baudouin, brother of Raymond VI
of Toulouse, who saw to it that Guillaume was provided with a sinecure in
the city of Saint-Antonin, which Simon de Montfort had recently left in
Baudouin's keeping.[11]

[2] Senhors, esta canso es faita d'aital guia
Com sela d'Antiocha et ayssi.s versifia
E s'a tot aital so, qui diire lo sabia.
   Ben avet tug auzit coment la *eretgia*
Era tant fort monteia (*cui Domni-Dieus maldia!*)
Que trastot Albiges avia en sa bailia,
Carcasses, Lauragues tot la major partia.
De Bezers tro a Bordel, si co.l camis tenia,
A motz de lors crezens e de lor companhia;

Si de plus o diches ja non mentria mia.
Can lo rics apostolis e la autra clercia
Viron multiplicar *aicela gran folia*
Plus fort que no soloit, e que creichen tot dia,
Tramezon prezicar cascus de sa bailia.
E l'ordes de Cistel, que n'ac la senhoria,
I trames de sos homes tropa mota vegia;
Si que l'avesques d'Osma ne tenc cort aramia,
E li autre legat, ab *cels de Bolgaria,*
Lai dins e Carcassona, on mota gent avia,
Que.l reis d'Arago y era ab sa gran baronia,
E qu'en ichit adonc can ac la cauza auzia
Que *eretges* estavan e aperceubut o avia:
Et trames sos sagels a Roma en Lombardia.
   No sai que m'en diches, si Dieus me benaziga:
No prezan lo prezic une poma porria;
Cinc ans, o no sai cant, o tengon d'aital guia.
No.s volon covertir cela gent esbaya,
Qu'en son mant home mort, manta gent peria
E o seran encara, *tro la guerra er fenia,*
     Car als estre non pot.

[3]   En l'orde de Cistel una abaya ot
      Que fo pres de Leire, qu'om Poblet apelot;

As one can see from the second laisse, Guillaume was very much a literary *jongleur*. He found both his literary form and the music he used to accompany it in the Provençal *Chanson d'Antioche*. The form is rhymed dodecasyllabic laisses which end with a short line, or *vers orphelin* of six syllables. This line establishes the rhyme for the following laisse. Guillaume's attitude (as indicated by my emphasis) toward the Crusade is clear. It was no doubt also the attitude of his *narrataires*, who would include those associated with the individuals he praises—Baudouin, his benefactor and the brother of Raymond VI of Toulouse, but also a collaborator of Simon de Montfort; Eléonore of Aragon, the Countess of Toulouse; the Abbot of Cîteaux, one of the leaders of the Crusade; Simon de Montfort himself; the Papal Legate Tédise; Foulque, the Bishop of Toulouse; as well as Guillaume de Contres, who had protected St-Antonin. As a member of the Catholic clergy in the South, he favors and encourages the Crusade. He blames, however, only the guilty *few* and condemns the unnecessary massacres perpetrated by the Crusaders. He attempts to be impartial and performs the exceptional service of rendering a contemporary account of the Crusade and its battles nearly day by day.

For his relating of the Crusade, which he began in 1210 as he states in the third laisse, he first gives the background of the religious conflict. He then narrates the early Crusader conquests including Béziers, Carcassonne, Minerve, Lavaur, and Moissac. His narration abruptly ends in 1213. He has just finished a laisse telling of the preparation of Peter of Aragon, who is going to Toulouse to support his brother-in-law, Count Raymond VI, there in his fight against the Crusaders. Laisse 131 ends with a quotation from Peter, and the first laisse of the continuation picks up Guillaume's *vers orphelin* for its rhyme, while continuing to quote Peter.

In the continuation, however, there is a change in the language and the form. The *vers orphelin* at the end of each laisse no longer determines the rhyme for the following laisse. Beginning with its second laisse, 133 in the continuing sequence, the *vers orphelin* becomes rather a mnemonic device, which is repeated as the first hemistich of the first line of the following laisse. Moreover, the continuation's laisses are of more than double the previous length. Martin-Chabot's study of the language reveals that the anonymous author is from Toulouse.[12] From references within the text, it appears that the continuation began in 1228. The style is lively and the artistry of the author evident. What is lacking is the historical authenticity. The dialogues, which clarify so well the opposing positions and approaches, have rhetorical and didactic rather than historical importance.

In the place of the clerical observer originally from Spain, we have an insider from Toulouse who looks at the situations and gives his own opinion. The following is his summation of the Lateran Council deliberations in laisse 147:

> Aisi l'a autrejada al comte de Montfort;
> Puis per aquela terra l'an a Tholoza mort,
> Don totz le mons alumna e Paratge es estort;
> E, per la fe q'ieu.s dei, sap milhor a.n Pelfort
>   Que a.n Folquet l'avesque!

Here we have a foretelling of Simon de Montfort's death, and a celebration of it, as well as a bitterly ironic commentary concerning Foulque, the Bishop of Toulouse. Whereas Guillaume considered Foulque one of his heroes, the continuation paints him as a vile traitor. In laisses 159 and 160 both God and the anonymous author take distinctive moral stances:

> Oimais dins e deforas er lo setis pleniers,
> Cant Monfort e Belcaire se son fait frontalers.
> *Mas Dieus sab be conoicher cals es pus dreiturers*
> *Per qu' el ajut e valha als plus dreitz eretiers,*
> *Car Engans e Dreitura se son faitz cabalers*
> > *De tota aquesta guerra.*

> *De tota aquesta guerra es parvens e semblans*
> *Que Dieus renda la terra als seus fizels amans;*
> Car orgulhs e dreitura, l'ialtatz e engans
> Son vengut a la soma, car aprosma.l demans,
> Car una flors novela s'espandis per totz pans
> Per que Pretz et Paratges tornara en estans;

The continuation underlines its arguments with the use of Allegory: *Engans* versus *Dreitura, orgulhs* against *dreitura, l'ialtatz* as opposed to *engans* with the end result that *Pretz* and *Paratge* will be raised again. *Paratge,* according to Nelli and Lavaud in *Les Troubadours,* represents that unique combination of "noblesse chevalresque; l'ensemble des valeurs morales d'origine aristo-cratique, qui ont constitué en s'élargissant la civilisation occitane."[13] For our anonymous author there is very little mention of heresy; rather it is a battle of virtues and vices, or of the heroes (the followers of Raymond VI and particularly Raymond VII) against the villains from the North (all those who encouraged and aided the Crusade). Just as the narrator of the contin-uation interprets the Crusade differently, his *narrataires* have become God-loving legitimate inheritors of the land. The last two volumes of Martin-Chabot's edition are devoted to the anonymous continuation. One almost feels that the change in tone and attitude prompts the change in fortune of the Crusade. After the taking of Muret and Toulouse by Simon and his supporters and the decisions of the Lateran Council in Rome, the tide begins to turn. Young Raymond VII regains Beaucaire easily, while Simon, when he tries to retake it, is obliged to retreat. Simon makes the inhabitants of

Toulouse bear the weight of his defeat. As Simon goes out into the countryside to expand his authority, Raymond VII approaches Toulouse and is aided by the exasperated Toulousains themselves. After many an effort to regain this city, Simon is killed in a final attempt, June 25, 1218. His son Amaury is named to succeed him. At the end of the *Chanson de la croisade albigeoise,* in 1219 the city of Toulouse prepares for its defense against the French crown prince Louis and his considerable forces:

[214]   La vila es establida dels baros finamens
        E de lor de Tholoza ab els mescladamens
        E del glorios martir e dels autres cors sens.
        Car le Filhs de la Verge, qu'es clars e resplandens,
        E dec sanc preciosa per que la Merces vens,
        Gart Razo e Dreitura e.lh prenga cauzimens
        Que los tortz e las colpas sian dels mals mirens!
        Que.l filhs del rei de Fransa ve orgulhozamens,
        Ab trenta quatre comtes et ab aitantas gens
        Que non es en est setgle negus hom tant sabens
        Que puesca azesmar los milhers ni los cens.
        Que.l cardenal de Roma prezicans e ligens
        Que la mortz e lo glazis an tot primeiramens,
        Aissi que dins Tholoza ni.ls apertenemens
        Negus hom no i remanga ni nulha res vivens
        Ni dona ni donzela ni nulha femna prens
        Ni autra creatura ni nulhs efans laitens,
        Que tuit prengan martiri en las flamas ardens.
        Mas la Verges Maria lor en sira guirens,
        Que segon la dreitura repren los falhimens,
        Per que la sanc benigna no.s sia espandens.
        Car sent Cernis los guida, que no sian temens,
        Que Dieus e dreitz e forsa e.l coms joves e sens
            Lor defendra Tholoza!
                    Amen.

The continuator ends his tale on an optimistically reverent note, knowing that that particular outcome will match his prayerful prediction. He also indirectly forecasts the eventual slaughter and flaming extinction of the Cathars or Albigensian believers. Concerning Occitan literature and the period of repression, this extinction inspired Robert Lafont in *Les Cathares en Occitanie* to entitle his chapter "Catharisme et littérature occitane: La marque par l'absence."[14]

In order to complete the comparison, it is necessary to return to *Garin de Monglane,* a nearly 15,000-line epic poem written in *langue d'oïl* with distinctive Picard traits. Once more the form is the dodecasyllabic laisse with a final *vers orphelin.* The six-syllable *vers orphelin* in this case only provides a conclusion for the laisse. It is rare to find any concatenation from one laisse to the following one. The rhyme of the laisse is never determined by the preceding *petit vers,* which plays more a musical role, as it ends in a limited number of rhymes and/or assonances.[15]

[P1]   Oiés, seignor, por Dieu / le voir / omnipotent,
        Que damediex vos doinst honor et joie grant!
        Oï avés canter de Bernart de Braibant,
        Et d'Ernaut de Beaulande, d'Aimeri, son enfant,
        De Gerart de Viane a l'orgoillox samblant,
        Et de Renier de Genvez que Dex parama tant,
        Ki fut pere Olivier le compaignon Rolant,
        De Guillame, de Fouke et du preu Viviant
        Et de la fiere geste dont cantent li auquant
        Ki tant soffri de paine sor sarrasine gent.
        Mais tot en ont laisié le grant commencement
        De Garin de Monglane, le chevalier vaillant,
        Dont issi cele gent dont on parole tant.
        Ja sarés qui il fu et dont et de quel gent,
        Et comment il conquist Monglane et Montirant
        Et la tere environ une jornee grant
        Qu'en ice tans tenoient felon et souduiant,
        Et qui fu cele dame dont furent li enfant
        Que on apele geste tres le commencement
        El roiaume de France.

[P2]   Segnor, vos savés bien, quant Pepin fu fenis,
        Karlemaines, sez fiex, fu cachiez de Paris.

It is obvious that this epic poem is directed to those who are already familiar with the long "French" tradition and its series of three *gestes,* in particular the one concerned with Garin's children and grandchildren. The time has finally come for the narrator/*jongleur* to fill in the initial gap of the origins of the *geste*. Garin, the son of the Duke of Aquitaine, as we are told, was visited in a dream by an angel who described for him Monglane, a city held by infidels. The angel set him on his distinct course, which will exalt Christianity. Garin thus requested from Charlemagne the right to conquer Monglane on his own:

[P25] "Sire, ce dist Garins, oiés que je demant!
        Je ne quier vostre tere, vo or ne vo argent.
        Ja tere n'en arai a jor de mon vivant,
        Se je ne le conquier a mon acerin brant.
        Se tenir me volés et foi et convenant,
        Un castel me donés que tienent mescreant.
        Il n'i a crucefis ne autel en estant;
        La mere gist au fil et au pere ensement;
        Li freres prent sa suer, se li vient a talent;
        Et s [e] il en a fille, si i gist ensement,
        Ja n'en sera blasmés por nul home vivant.
        Ançois croient Jupin, Mahon et Tervagant,
        Si furent baptisié, quant il furent enfant;
        Or sont tot Aubigois, felon et mescreant.
        Ne croient rien qui soit en cest siecle vivant
        Fors le duc lor segnor Gaufroi de Montirant.
        N'a si mal traitor, tant com la tere est grant.
        Por ce que on le set felon et soduiant.
        Le doutent Sarrasin, amiral et soudant
        [Et] li Hongre et li Bougre et tot cil d'Oriant,
        Et Raos de Caors et Butors d'Agimant
        Car Huges de Tolouse le tient a son parent
        Et li sires d'Orenge et de Nimes le grant;
        Trestot cil Sarrasin li sont apartenant.

It is his description that is important. Here we have an evocation of the traditional pagan nonbelievers, the Saracens, including the Saracen trinity created by the uninformed Christian mind. But even if we discount line 730 with its mention of *Aubigois,* there are certain fascinating elements—the statement that the Monglane inhabitants had been baptized when they were

children. Now there is neither crucifix nor altar in the castle. Incest
abounds and is never criticized. The mention of "li Hongre et li Bougre et
tot cil d'Oriant" is particularly interesting. Reference was made in the first
excerpt by Guillaume de Tudèle to "cels de Bolgaria." The Bulgars (or
Bougres in Old French) are considered to have been the origin of the
Manichean heresy in France, best represented by the Cathars or the Albigen-
sians. The statement concerning incest could be linked to the Cathar attitude
toward carnal relations, here described by René Nelli in his *La Vie
quotidienne des Cathares*.[16]

> Les cathares enseignaient que les péchés charnels étaient tous égaux et
> que, par conséquent, il n'était pas plus grave, en bonne logique, d'avoir
> des relations sexuelles avec sa mère ou sa sœur, qu'avec n'importe
> quelle femme. Cela était une conséquence de la doctrine des réincarna-
> tions qui supprime tout degré de parenté entre les âmes. Mais cette
> théorie—que l'on affecte souvent de prendre à contresens—n'autorisait
> pas davantage les Croyants à commettre l'inceste que la théorie
> stoïcienne—selon laquelle il était aussi criminel de tuer un coq que de
> tuer son père.

Later in *Garin de Monglane* it is stated that a male relative of Gaufroi de
Monglane prefers to sleep only with boys. This sexual preference was
associated very early with the word *bougre:*

> Le 'bougre' est cloué dans les pages des glossaires moyenâgeux et aussi
> dans les références des dictionnaires contemporains non seulement
> comme 'hérétique'. 'Bougre' équivaut à un personnage ignoble, impur,
> méprisable. On lui attribue des attitudes et des comportements outra-
> geants. Il est un sodomiste, un pendard. Le cathare-bogomile—ce
> puritain absolu, ce bonhomme qui fuit le luxe somptueux des églises,
> qui cherche la pureté du corps et de l'âme, étranger aux débauches—est
> poursuivi par la débauche linguistique. Le slavisant français Louis
> Léger note dans *La Grande Encyclopédie:* "Le mépris que l'hérésie
> inspire aux catholiques explique sans doute le sens injurieux qu'a pris,
> au Moyen Age, le nom de BOUGRES ou BULGARES."[17]

As is so often the case in the "geste de Monglane," the hero's quest
for a city becomes identified with a woman, Mabille or Mabillette. When

she reaches the castle of Monglane, we are told that no mass has been sung there for over thirty years (P28). Later Garin is befriended by Berart de Valcomblée, who explains that Gaufroi de Monglane had disinherited Berart and his family because they believed in God.

If we look again at the geographical area related to the conquest of Monglane, we see that there are specific references that place it in the locality of the Albigensian heresy—Agenais (Agenois), Bigorre, Foix, Montégut (Montaigu), Toulouse, and the Garonne River. The Counts of Foix and Agenais are specifically mentioned. Cahors is found only in the laisse cited above, as are Nîmes and Orange (with the exception of a later reference to Garin's great-grandson, Guillaume d'Orange). What is striking is the fact that *Garin de Monglane* does not take place in the localities connected with the *geste* of his great-grandson Guillaume, even though a conscious effort has been made by the narrator/*jongleur* to tie this epic work directly to the others mentioned in the opening laisse. Here "mescreant" refers to a people who have rejected the true religion.

Perhaps then, Garin de Monglane is a Simon de Montfort. Just as Garin was granted by Charlemagne a Monglane yet to be won and for which there was already a duke, so Simon de Montfort, a Northerner of minor nobility, became Viscount of Béziers and Carcassonne through a decision of the Roman Catholic Church while the legitimate viscount, Raymond-Roger Trencavel, was still alive. Simon de Montfort had to try to win the people's acceptance even after the presumed-heretical viscount died in prison. He later proclaimed himself Count of Toulouse under similar circumstances. The area of Béziers and Carcassonne, or even of Montségur, would generally fit our poet's geographical description, as these fortified castles would Monglane. It should be noted that mass destruction and burnings are missing in *Garin de Monglane*. There does exist a Montgraner, a castle near Montgaillard that was attacked and won by Simon de Montfort. None, however, is high on a cliff overlooking the ocean.

It is interesting to note that the viscount was the vassal of Peter II of Aragon who also protected the Cathars and died in the Crusade supporting Raymond VII of Toulouse. Among *Garin de Monglane*'s cast of characters is the evil Salatrez who arrives with his men from Balaguer. Robastre battles the giant Turnigeant who is said to be from Aragon. Perdigon tricks his way into the castle of Monglane by claiming that he, Garin, and the disguised Mabille are messengers from Aragon.

In conclusion, consideration of these specific aspects of *Garin de Monglane* suggests that this Old French epic is a somewhat better reflection of the Albigensian Crusade than Gautier had supposed and that Garin's battle cry "Monglane le fort" is a distorted echo of "Montfort," the one used by Simon. The Song of the Patriarch of one of the three major epic *gestes* could then be seen as a manifestation of popular expression in the service of the idea of Northern French imperialistic expansion, as supported and encouraged by the Roman Catholic Church.

Notes

[1]Robert Sabatier, *La Poésie du moyen âge* (Paris: Hachette, 1969), p. 60.

[2]Sabatier, p. 61.

[3]Bertrand de Bar-sur-Aube, *Girart de Vienne*, ed. Wolfgang van Emden (Paris: SATF, 1977), p. 358.

[4]These geographical conclusions are based upon an on-site visit in 1983.

[5]The excerpts cited from *Garin de Monglane* are taken from my critical edition now in progress. The project of an edition of *Garin de Monglane* was begun at the Univerity of Greifswald in Germany in the first part of this century by three students of Edmund Stengel: E. Schuppe, E. Mueller, and H. Menn. Each student edited a few thousand lines for his doctoral dissertation, with the last of the group taking the edition up to line 4693 of the approximately 15,048 lines. For my doctoral dissertation at Princeton University, I did a critical edition of a fragment found in the Garrett 125 manuscript at Princeton University, which went up to line 5010 of the complete work, cf. my "Un nouveau fragment de *Garin de Monglane*," *Romania*, 96, No. 2 (1975), 163-92.

[6]Léon Gautier, *Les Epopées françaises*, 2nd ed., vol. 4 (1888; Osnabruck: Otto Zeller, 1966), p. 128.

[7]Gautier, p. 128.

[8]Gautier, p. 128.

[9]The statements and excerpts are drawn from the critical edition of Eugène Martin-Chabot, *La Chanson de la croisade albigeoise*, 3 vols. (Paris: Société d'Edition "Les Belles Lettres," 1957-61).

[10]Martin-Chabot, vol. 1, 8-10.

[11]Martin-Chabot, vol. 1, viii.

[12]Martin-Chabot, vol. 2, ix-xiii.

[13]René Nelli et René Lavaud, eds., *Les Troubadours II. Le Trésor poétique de l'Occitanie* (Bruxelles: Desclée de Brouwer, 1966), p. 546.

[14]Robert Lafont et al., *Les Cathares en Occitanie* (Paris: Fayard, 1982), p. 339.

[15][P—] refers to the laisse number in the Paris MS, the most authoritative of the *Garin de Monglane* manuscripts.

[16]René Nelli, *La Vie quotidienne des Cathares* (Paris: Hachette, 1969), p. 60.

[17]Vladimir Topentcharov, *Boulgres et Cathares: Deux brasiers une même flamme* (Paris: Seghers, 1971), p. 173. *Webster's Third New International Dictionary* gives *bougre* as the origin of the English "bugger," noun and verb.

The Prologue to the Lyon Manuscript
of the *Chanson de Roland*

William W. Kibler

Among John L. Grigsby's most significant contributions will surely be counted his editions of the Middle French *Liber Fortunae* (Berkeley,
1967) and *Joufroi de Poitiers* (Geneva, 1972). As I undertook my own
edition of *Lion de Bourges,* a fourteenth-century *chanson de geste,*[1] these
texts were signaled out to me as models for the edition of late-medieval
manuscripts, and I began at that time a correspondence with their author that
led to a friendship of nearly twenty years. It is a pleasure, now tinged with
sadness, to acknowledge again the advice and encouragement he offered me
at the time.

Owing to the rapidly evolving state of the language, editing a later
medieval manuscript involves different principles from those commonly
employed in editing twelfth- and thirteenth-century texts. As Professor
Grigsby stated in the introduction to the *Liber Fortunae,* one must seek "to
offer a readable, understandable text and, at the same time, to reproduce the
base MS as closely as critical sense will allow."[2] Although the versification
and orthography may appear aberrant or downright incorrect by "classical"
standards, it would give a false picture of the state of the language to attempt
to "correct" every perceived error. One should intervene only in evident
cases of scribal error, preferring otherwise to attempt to understand, explain, and present clearly the MS as written.

The Lyon MS of the *Chanson de Roland* (Lyon, Bibl. mun. 743),
written down in the late thirteenth or early fourteenth century, offers a case
in point. Not only is its orthography frequently capricious, but the state of
the poem itself is open to question, since at 2931 lines in the standard

editions[3] it is considerably abbreviated by comparison with other versions of the epic. *Ly* opens as the great battle of Roncevaux is about to begin, omitting the council scenes, Charles's dreams, the designation of Roland to the rear guard, the selection of the Christian and pagan forces, and the first horn scene. Then, following the battle, the so-called Baligant episode is likewise omitted from *Ly*. Moreover, the text proper actually begins with a dozen lines that are not included in the two standard editions of this redaction:

> Li bons rois artus de bretaigne
> La sien proesce nos enseigne
> Que nos seons prou et cortois
> Tient cort si riche come rois
> A cele feste qui tant coste
> *Con* doit conter la pentecoste
> La corz fu la ou dist en gales
> Apres mengier parmi ces sales
> Li chivalier se desportoient
> Lai ou dames les apeloient
> Et les *com*paignes de sarrazins sont granz
> De la grant traison q*ue* i fist agolanz

These twelve lines, which pose an unusual problem, have been dismissed by prior editors of the poem. Foerster[4] includes them in the introduction to his transcription (p. vii), and wonders in print: "Wie der sonderbare Angang zu erklären, ist nicht sicher zu ermitteln. Hat der Schreiber den Löwenritter Christians kopiren [sic] wollen und sich dann eines andern besonnen? Was sollen dann die Zeilen 11.12 (Agolant)?" (p. viii). His edition consequently commences (p. 22) with

> Bel fu li iors et li soleouz luisanz
> et la paroi des uers hyaumes luisanz

which he labels laisse L[yon] 1.

Raoul Mortier, in his comprehensive edition of the *Roland* manuscripts (vol. 8),[5] does not even transcribe the initial twelve lines, being content to note in his brief *avant-propos* (p. i) that the manuscript

débute par un couplet de douze vers, qui semble annoncer la guerre de
Grifonel l'enfant, du *Chevalier au lion* de Chrestien de Troyes; puis,
sans transition, du douzième vers:

De la grant traïson que i fist Agolanz

nous voici aux préludes de la bataille qui va mettre aux prises Français
et Sarrazins, trente vers avant les reproches adressés par Olivier à
Roland pour n'avoir pas voulu sonner de l'olifant.

Thus, neither editor considers these lines an integral part of the poem, and
for neither do they count among the numbered lines of the text.

Similarly, the typewritten "Notice du ms. LYON, Bibl. mun. 743
(649)" furnished by the Lyon municipal library, characterizes this anomalous beginning as follows: "1 dizain qui, par hasard ou intentionnellement,
précède le poème du Roland. Texte incohérent en raison de deux vers qui
suivent ce dizain, sans rapport avec ce qui précède ni avec ce qui suit."

But should these initial lines, in the same hand as the rest of the MS,
be so summarily dismissed? It is absurd on the surface of it to suggest that
the poet/scribe began copying Chrétien's *Yvain* on precious parchment,
wearied of it or changed his mind after only ten lines, sought his bearings
with two lines of uncertain provenance, then launched into the *Roland* in
mid-stream. The principle evoked above, that one must strive to make
sense of the MS as it comes down to us before seeking to emend it, makes it
imperative that we study these lines closely, and evidence, both codico-
logical and literary, suggests that they may have been conceived as a
prologue to the *Roland* material proper.

The MS is a small parchment volume from the late thirteenth or early
fourteenth century, probably from the Burgundian or even the immediate
Lyon region. It contains 73 folios in eight gatherings, of which the 73rd is
a *folio de garde,* originally blank, but now with Latin text in a different hand
from that of the rest of the MS, added in the fourteenth century after the MS
had been assembled. A 74th folio is glued to the back cover. The first
gathering measures 158 x 107 mm, while the last seven measure 158 x 103
mm. The size of the writing block is 131 x 80 mm throughout, and appears
(with the above-mentioned exception of the 73rd folio) all to have been
written by the same hand in an ink now faded to brown. The catchwords to
the fourth, fifth, and seventh gatherings were cut off when the originally

larger margins were cut down to accommodate the current leather binding, which is of a yellowish-brown vellum like the MS pages themselves.

Gatherings and catchwords are as follows:

gathering	folios	catchword	location of catchword	no. of leaves in gathering
1	1-10	sil ne deffendent	10v	5
2	11-20	apres ocist	20v	5
3	21-30	[lost]	30v	5
4	31-40	[lost]	40v	5
5	41-48	or ge iray	48v	4
6	49-58	[lost]	58v	5
7	59-66	Qui tot ne vont	66v	4
8	67-74			4

The contents of the Lyon MS are:

fol. 1-60:	*Chanson de Roland*
fol. 60-65:	*Vie de Ste. Marguerite* (in verse)
fol. 65-68v:	*La Chantepleure*
fol. 69-70:	Latin litanies
fol. 70-72:	Latin prayers (in prose)
fol. 73:	*Recordate Domine* (Latin prayer, later hand)

The Lyon *Roland* thus begins on the first page of the first gathering, and there is no evidence that the volume has been mutilated or that any material has been lost from it. On opening the MS, one is confronted on the first line of the first folio by a large initial "L" beginning the line "Li bons rois artus de bretaigne" and measuring 12 x 21 mm (the equivalent of three lines of text). Such three-line initials are only found in this MS to mark the beginnings of discrete texts: the *Vie de Ste. Marguerite* (f. 60), the *Chantepleure* (f. 65), and several short prayers in Latin (f. 70). Elsewhere two-line initials are employed consistently, and this is the case with the line heretofore reckoned as the beginning of the *Roland*, "Bel fu li iors et li soleouz luisanz."

Thus, evidence from the layout of the MS shows beyond any doubt that the first work in Lyon MS 743, the *Roland*, begins with the twelve lines discounted by previous editors. There is no break indicated or intended between these lines and the laisse that has previously been reckoned to constitute the beginning of the poem. Had the poet/scribe changed his mind at this point, or lost his exemplar of *Yvain,* surely he would have effaced or expunctuated the lines from *Yvain,* begun a new folio, or at the very least recommenced his copying with a large capital. In the absence of any of these indications, I believe we are compelled to accept these lines as germane and seek to understand their function within the economy of the *Roland* text that has come down to us in this MS.

As previously noted, the Lyon *Roland* is unique in being much more compressed than any other medieval redaction of this legend. Not only does it omit much of the traditional beginning of the story and the Baligant episode, but as I have shown elsewhere, it systematically shortens and focuses the laisses it does reproduce.[6] Previous editors have considered it acephelous and sought to explain its state by alleging that the exemplar from which it was copied was already missing major portions,[7] or by claiming that the copyist was simply inattentive or incompetent.[8] The first page of the municipal library's description simply indicates "Chanson de Roland, incomplète du début." Such explanations, however, are the products of desperation and indicate a refusal to recognize the originality and uniqueness of the *Ly* text.

It is more likely that the omissions, as well as certain additions to the text by the *Ly* redactor (among them, most notably the opening lines), are thematic and programmatic rather than accidental. To Foerster's argument that the exemplar from which the *Ly* redactor copied was acephelous, one need only note that the cuts are practiced throughout the text, not merely at the beginning, and that, as we shall see, they have a deliberate focusing effect. Such a view has already been outlined by Jules Horrent in his masterful study of the medieval manuscript tradition of the *Song of Roland, La Chanson de Roland dans les littératures française et espagnole au moyen âge.*[9] He insists particularly upon the systematic reductions practiced by the *Ly* redactor, finding that "le remanieur bourguignon a été constamment dominé par cette intention [de réduire le poème] et s'est donné à sa tâche avec une audace originale" (p. 371). Though this allows him to concentrate upon the central character of Roland and his heroic achievements at Roncevaux, for Horrent this constitutes an essentially negative accomplishment:

La refaçon du *Roland* rimé qu'offre le MS de *Lyon* est la plus personnelle de toutes celles qui nous sont parvenues en bon état. Mais elle est fondée, si je puis dire, sur une conception négative: elle extrait de l'œuvre existante un poème plus court. *Lyon* n'enrichit pas à proprement parler la tradition rolandienne, il met en relief un aspect du poème qui, heureusement, est son aspect principal. (p. 373)

His explanation of the initial twelve lines is more helpful and merits citation in full, since his interpretation is one I would like to expand upon here:

W. Foerster qui reproduit les douze premiers vers ne sait comment expliquer ce début singulier. Je crois pour ma part que le copiste n'a nullement eu l'intention de copier un roman arthurien; je ne crois pas qu'il ait changé d'avis après dix vers. Singulier caprice! Son propos a été de transcrire l'histoire de la bataille de Roncevaux, débarrassée de ses scènes préliminaires. S'il a introduit dans ses premiers vers Artus et ses chevaliers, s'il y associe Agolant, ses armées et sa « traïson », c'est-à-dire le défi solennel que celui-ci lança à Charlemagne, c'est que ces deux événements ont en commun leur date: la Pentecôte. L'autre événement que le remanieur y associe, la bataille de Roncevaux, s'est donc, dans son esprit, déroulé également à la Pentecôte. Mais je vois dans l'étrange début de *Ly* autre chose encore qu'un simple moyen de situer chronologiquement la fameuse bataille: tandis qu'à la cour bretonne, les preux chevaliers d'Arthur célèbrent la grande fête qu'est la Pentecôte en festoyant, en se divertissant, en courtisant les dames, bref dans une atmosphère de repos et de gaieté, à l'armée de Charlemagne, armée de croisade, on est en butte, même en ce jour de fête, à la trahison (Agolant) et à la mort (Roland). Le scribe, utilisant ses connaissances littéraires, veut faire ressortir, par cette association, par cette opposition, tout ce que l'épisode de Roncevaux a de grave, de terrible, de tragique. C'est aussi la raison pour laquelle notre scribe ne reprend le récit qu'au moment pathétique où va s'engager le cruel combat. C'est volontairement, et selon une intention littéraire précise, que sa version est « acéphale ».

Horrent's attempt to associate all of these poems with Pentecost is not supported by the text, but he is on target in insisting that the *Ly* redactor has his own special conception of the Roland matter and develops his poem in accord with his vision of the whole. However, whereas Horrent sees the focal point as the tragic battle of Roncevaux, I believe the poem is intended rather to underscore the human drama of Roland against Ganelon. For the *Ly* redactor, the battle is the culmination of a human struggle of hero (Roland) against villain (Ganelon), rather than the more grandiose epic conception epitomized by the Oxford MS, focusing as it does on the struggle of the forces of Good (Christians, led by Charlemagne) against the forces of Evil (Saracens, led by Baligant).

Our first view of Roland in *Ly* is of him sitting confidently astride his charger, and the poet spends some eighteen lines describing his physical splendor—lines that have no real parallel in *O*. And, as he views the Saracens rushing to their deaths, Roland makes the first reference in the poem to Ganelon's treason:

> "Chivalier Dieu," ce dist li cuens Rollanz,
> "traï nos a Gaines li soduanz,
> mais Dieus de gloire nos puet estre garanz,
> et nos meïsme as espees tranchanz."

These lines, like most of the subsequent references to Ganelon's treachery, have no equivalent in *O* or in the other poems of the rhymed tradition. Or, if there is a reference to Ganelon's treason already in his source, the *Ly* redactor expands it to underscore the perfidy. In what is currently numbered the third laisse, for example, the *Ly* redactor expands a single line of *O*,

> Traït vos ad ki a guarder vos out
> (v. 1192)

into

> Tra[ï] a Gaynes, tuit i perdrez la vie!
> Gaynes en ot de par luy la balie,
> qui en a l'or et la grant manantie.
> Vos morrez tuit, je n'i avre[z] aïe;
> chiers fu venduz li ors d'Esclavonie!

Ganelon is now mentioned by name twice, and his motive is clearly understood to have been avarice. At the end of the laisse describing the death of Gautier del Hum, the *Ly* poet adds, in his own voice, a curse of Ganelon:

> E! lere Gaynes! Dieus te doint encombrier;
> per toy morront maint vaillant chivalier!
> > (vv. 1264-65)

Roland, as he laments Oliver, thinks of both Aude and Ganelon in lines unique to *Ly:*

> "Aÿ, bele Aude! Or m'estuet esloignier,
> de vostre amor n'avrai mais recovrier.
> Aÿ, fauz Gaines," dist Rollanz au vis fier,
> "por quoi nos fis si mortel encombrier?"
> > (vv. 1401-04)

And after he has recovered from his swoon, Roland prays God to damn the traitor:

> e li requist qu'il pregne vangison
> del traïtour, le conte Ganelon,
> qui les vendi per male traïson.
> > (vv. 1428-30)

Here again, as earlier, the emphasis is on the materialistic nature of the betrayal, as it is once more when Charlemagne returns to the field of battle:

> por son nevou fu mauz e garmentanz . . .
> ensamble ou lui .xx. mile combatant,
> que li fauz Gaines vendi as mescreanz;
> toz les vendi as cuvers soduianz.
> > (vv. 1709, 1713-15)

While there is clearly an echo in these passages of the "traïson que i fist Agolanz" of the initial lines, there also appears to be one of the "feste qui tant coste" of Arthurian splendor. The complex and little-understood motivations of Ganelon in the Oxford version have been reduced here to one that everyone can comprehend in the mercantile world of late thirteenth-century Lyon: avarice.

And just as Ganelon is given human motivation, so too Roland is given a human heart and human stature. Though as a warrior he is still writ larger than life, as a person he is more believable. Early in the battle he suffers from thirst: "Li cuenz Rollanz a la char tressuee; / la soif l'argüe, si a la boche crevee" (233-34), and the scenes of battle in the Lyon redaction are even bloodier and more pathetic than in *O*. But it is in the final scenes of his poem, where the *Ly* poet follows the rhymed tradition in according a much larger role to the love between Roland and Aude and to the choice of punishment for Ganelon, that we see in its greatest clarity the human interest of the poem. For Aude, the rhymed tradition as represented in *Ly* expands the two laisses of *O* [267-68] to thirty-seven [122-25, 139-70], and the judgment of Ganelon, which is efficiently handled in *O* in a little over 200 lines (3742-974), becomes some 500 lines in *Ly* (2017-165, 2577-926), which include an escape by Ganelon from his guards, the combat of Thieri and Pinabel, and a detailed debate on the best way to put Ganelon to death.

Thus I believe there is real justification in contending that both the omission of the standard opening episodes of the *Roland* matter and the addition of the anomalous initial lines are deliberate modifications to the traditional matter by the *Ly* poet/scribe. They accord with his overall conception of his material, which is not the grandiose epic *soufflé* of the Oxford poet, but rather a conception grounded in human emotions and pathos. Two further arguments can be adduced in favor of accepting the initial lines of the manuscript as germane rather than a false start, one bearing on subject matter and the other on versification.

We find similar seemingly unrelated beginnings in other medieval works. Such unusual material foils audience expectations and alerts it to new meanings. For example, in the *K* redaction of the *Roman des Sept Sages,* there is a unique account of the baptism of the child whose youthful adventures constitute the romance. Mary B. Speer has recently studied this episode in detail, and from a comparison of it with other baptism episodes concludes that "the irregular material that *K* added was no doubt intended to dramatize character and emphasize the elaborate frame narrative, perhaps in imitation of the elaborate frame of the Dolopathos."[10] Similarly, in the much more well-known *Sir Gawain and the Green Knight,* the opening stanza traces the foundings of Rome and Britain back to the fall of Troy, which has nothing immediately to do with Arthur's Britain, but does set the story in a much vaster historical frame.

The initial lines of *Ly* differ from those of the *Roman des Sept Sages* and *Sir Gawain and the Green Knight,* of course, in having not only a different subject matter but also a different versification from that of the rest of the poem. The initial ten lines are octosyllabic rhymed couplets, associated with the romance tradition, while lines 11-12 are eleven[11] and twelve syllables respectively, providing something of a segue into the rhymed *Roland.* However, as I have argued above, the octosyllabic couplets announce, as it were, a poem whose spirit is in many respects that of romance, while its body is in the form of a *chanson de geste.* They provide what might be termed a thematic prologue to the entire text, forcing by their unexpected presence the auditor/reader of the text to adjust his or her generic expectations. It is well established that while the interest of epic is nationalistic, with heroes fighting essentially for God and country, the interest of romance is primarily individualistic. We have already seen that the *Ly* redactor concentrates his attention on the individual human struggle between Roland and Ganelon, rather than the epic struggle between nations. The initial lines of *Ly* could therefore have signaled to its audience that the poem it is about to hear should be "read" on the human level, on the level of the individuals in play; that they are of more interest than the clash of religions. In essence, although it is a poem treating the "matière de Charlemagne," it should be understood as one treating the "matière de Bretagne."

The late medieval epic is in its very conception quite different from the traditional *chanson de geste*—so much so in fact that I have suggested providing it with a generically distinctive name, the *chanson d'aventures.*[12] By this late period of epic production, poets were freely mixing romance and traditional motifs and themes. Even the versification, which to critics today is often crucial in providing generic distinctions, is not definitive, as the case of *Lion de Bourges* makes clear. This *chanson de geste* is extant in two forms: a fourteenth-century alexandrine version, and a fifteenth-century octosyllabic rendering. Indeed, our *Ly* text itself begins with decasyllables, mixing in occasional alexandrines before shifting to the latter versification for most of the final 200 lines. In a genre closely akin to the *chanson de geste,* we find a similar mixing of versification as early as the twelfth century in Jordan Fantosme's *Chronicle,* where laisses 70 to 81 are decasyllabic in a poem composed essentially in alexandrines. By the fourteenth century such mixtures of verse forms had become commonplace, as the example of the *dit amoureux* makes clear. Thus we may conclude that while the beginning lines of the Lyon *Roland* are indeed unusual, their presentation of contrasting versification and subject matter is not unique, and therefore they merit study rather than dismissal.

The suggestion that the *Ly* redactor is proposing a romance frame for an originally epic narrative might explain as well the curious final lines of *Ly:*

> Puis en ot il en France moult doleirous tormant,
> e de ce muit la guerre de Grifonel l'enfant.

This war of Grifonel l'enfant is otherwise unknown, and there is no corresponding Grif(f)onel to be found in the *chansons de geste,*[13] though the name is clearly a diminuitive of the more common Griffon, of which the most well known is Griffon d'Hautefeuille, the father of Ganelon. However, since this war occurs after Roncevaux, it could not concern Ganelon's father, and we must look elsewhere to identify our Griffonel. Raoul Mortier, in the passage cited earlier, apparently believed that the war alluded to occurs in Chrétien de Troyes's *Chevalier au Lion*. It is hard to imagine to what he could be alluding in Chrétien, but his insight might possibly be explained by references to a Griffon del Mal Pas, who occurs prominently in the *Charrette* portion of the *Prose Lancelot*.[14] It is possible, though admittedly only tenuously so, that our poet had in mind some such romance villain, and that in closing his poem in this fashion he was completing the frame introduced in his initial strophe.

In keeping with the principle underscored by John Grigsby in his edition of the *Liber Fortunae,* I have sought here to justify including in any subsequent edition of the *Ly* redaction of the *Chanson de Roland* the opening lines of the MS in exactly the form they have come down to us. There is no suitable explanation for this twelve-line segment other than as a deliberate act of redaction on the part of the poet/scribe who produced the Lyon MS. I have attempted to show that the lines are integral to the MS and cannot be explained as scribal error. It is inconceivable that a scribe would copy ten lines from *Yvain,* then suddenly shift to write an incomplete *Roland*. It is more accurate, I believe, to see the initial lines as a thematic prologue to the rest of the poem, a prologue that loudly proclaims the author's intention to treat his material in a personal and independent manner.

Notes

[1]With Jean-Louis Picherit and Thelma S. Fenster (Geneva: Droz, 1980).

[2]John L. Grigsby, ed., *The Middle French* Liber Fortunae: *A Critical Edition* (Berkeley and Los Angeles: U. of Calif. Press, 1967), p. 52.

[3]The poem actually contains 2932 lines, since Mortier followed Foerster in conflating lines 1328-29, or even 2944 if the initial twelve are added to the official line count.

[4]*Das Altfranzösische Rolandslied. Text von Paris, Cambridge, Lyon und den sog. Lothringischen Fragmenten.* Altfranzösische Bibliothek 7. (Heilbronn: Henninger, 1886).

[5]*Les textes de la Chanson de Roland,* tome VIII, *Le Texte de Lyon* (Paris: La Geste Francor, 1944).

[6]"The *Roland* after Oxford: The French Tradition," *Olifant* 6 (1979), 275-92.

[7]"Wie man sieht, fehlt unsrer Hds. der Anfang des Rolandstextes, der aber auch seiner Vorlage gefehlt haben muss" (p. viii).

[8]Mortier attributes the omission of the beginning as well as the Baligant episode to a "fantaisie de copiste" (p. i).

[9]Paris: Les Belles Lettres, 1951, esp. pp. 369-73.

[10]"The Prince's Baptism in the *Roman des Sept Sages:* Formal and Doctrinal Intertexts," *Medievalia et Humanistica,* New Series, Number 14 (Paul Clogan, ed.), 59-80; passage cited, p. 75.

[11]Or ten, if counted as an epic decasyllable with lyric cæsura.

[12]"La « chanson d'aventures », " in *Essor et Fortune de la chanson de geste dans l'Europe et l'Orient latin. Actes du IXe congrès de la Société Rencesvals.* 2 vols. (Modena: Mucchi Editore, 1984), 2, pp. 509-15.

[13]See André Moisan, *Répertoire des noms propres de personnes et de lieux cités dans les chansons de geste françaises et les œuvres étrangères dérivées.* 5 vols. Publications romanes et françaises 173 (Geneva: Droz, 1986).

[14]See G. D. West, *An Index of Proper Names in French Arthurian Prose Romances,* Univ. of Toronto Romance Series 35. (Toronto: Univ. of Toronto Press, 1978).

III. MISCELLANEOUS

The Arthurian Fabliau
and the Poetics of Virginity

R. Howard Bloch

Like the commingling of species on medieval versions of the robe of Nature, the Arthurian fabliau is a generic perversion whose scandalous indeterminacy has always disturbed medievalists. Specialists, anxious above all to maintain sharp distinctions between the species (that is, between literary genres), are embarrassed by the promiscuity of a work belonging properly neither to high nor low, learned nor popular tradition, one that seems to mix the idealistic with the lewd. Indeed, having written a 400-page book whose thesis is the popular origin of the comic tale, Joseph Bédier invents the category of "fabliau aristocratique," to describe what happens when the antifeminism of popular literature permeates the courtly ideology of the Arthurian world. Per Nykrog, who wrote another 400 pages to prove the fabliau's aristocratic origin, opts instead for the "lai burlesque." R. Dubuis describes the Arthurian fabliau as "une œuvre hybride," just as Emmanuèle Baumgartner saw in them signs of "an unclassifiable Arthurian counterculture."[1]

If the hybrid scabrous Arthurian tale represents a scandalous excess, that excess is both thematized and pushed to its logical limit in a series of works involving an ordeal of feminine chastity. I am thinking of the chastity testing motif contained in the *First Continuation of Perceval*, the *Livre de Caradoc*, the *Vengeance Raguidel*, the *Prose Tristan*, and, more specifically, of the ordeal of the mantle and horn of "Du Mantel mautaillié" and the "Lai du corn."

"Du Mantel mautaillié" is the story of a knight who arrives at King Arthur's court carrying an adventure and a magic coat designed to fit only the woman who has been faithful to her husband or lover:

> La fée fist el drap une oevre
> Qui les fausses dames descuevre;
> Ja feme qui l'ait afublé,
> Se ele a de rien meserré
> Vers son seignor, se ele l'a,
> Ja puis à droit ne li serra,
> Ne aus puceles autressi,
> Se ele vers son bon ami
> Avoit mespris en nul endroit
> Ja plus ne li serroit à droit
> Que ne soit trop lonc ou trop cort.[2]

As becomes painfully obvious in the course of more than one hundred public fittings in "Du Mantel mautaillié," the tailoring of the coat is assimilated to a certain monotonous misogynistic tailoring of the tale. One right fit and the tale is too short; too many wrong fits and it never ends. More important, beneath the magic garment, which is as potent a paradigm of what it is to make fiction (or of representation) as the Middle Ages produced, beneath the cloak lies the indiscretion of marital and courtly infidelity. And this at the highest level, since the anonymous author singles out Guenevere as the incarnation of unfaithfulness, the archetypal adulterer; and her clever defense proves the deceitfulness of all women:

> La Roïne se porpenssa
> S'ele fesoit d'ire samblant
> Tant seroit la honte plus grant;
> Chascune l'aura afublé;
> Si l'a en jenglois atorné.
> (*Recueil*, III: 12)

The tale and the coat are linked in the assimilation of deceit—trickery, infidelity, lies, hiding—to poetic invention, a link to which we shall return shortly.

An even more virulent form of the chastity-testing motif is to be found in Robert Biket's "Lai du corn." Here the disclosing instrument of feminine transgression is a drinking horn that spills its contents upon the man whose wife has been unfaithful, has ever contemplated infidelity, or who himself has experienced jealousy:

> cest corn fist une fee
> ramponeuse, iree,
> e le corn destina
> que ja houm(e) n'i bev(e)ra,
> tant soit sages ne fous,
> s'il est cous ne gelous.[3]

Here, too, as in the "Mantel mautaillié," Guenevere is designated as the archetypal unfaithful wife, the scandal of her conduct made manifest in the spiced wine that spills all over Arthur:

> Li rois Arzurs le prist
> a sa bouche le mist
> kar beivre le quida,
> mes sour lui le versa
> cuntreval desk'as pez:
> en fu li rois irrez.
> *(Corn, v. 291)*

The "Lai du corn" turns around a play on the word "cors," the drinking horn, which reveals betrayal or jealousy; the woman's body, which is at stake; and the horns, which are the emblem of the cuckold. Beyond word play, however, the magic vessel becomes the defining principle of an all-pervasive guilt; for, again, there is no one at court who has not experienced jealousy, whose wife has not been unfaithful, or, according to the medieval equation of concupiscence with adultery, who has not betrayed her husband in thought: "kar n'i est femme nee, / qui soit espousee, / qui ne eyt pensé folie" (*Corn*, v. 309). Like a totemic secret that unites Arthur's court, the complicity of cuckolds transforms the desire of woman into a scandalous excess that stains all who try to drink; or, as in the "Mantel mautaillié," all whose wives try to make the garment fit. This suggests that Guenevere, far from an exception, is the figure of every-woman. Both motifs imply an inadequation of container and contained, which comes to constitute a paradigm of exorbitance inherent to medieval articulations of the question of woman. Further, I think it can be shown

that the Arthurian fabliau, far from a generic oddity, is evidence of a certain
enmeshed thinking of the questions of language, of narrative, and of
woman as a problem of scandalous surplus. More precisely, the unclassifiable lewd lai participates in the topos of the *molestiae nuptiarum,* the
"tribulations of marriage" that loom so large within the medieval discourse
of misogyny—from the early Church Fathers to the Latin satirists and
vernacular poets of the twelfth and thirteenth centuries to the works grouped
for want of a better term under the rubric of "les genres du réalisme
bourgeois" (the animal fable, comic theatre, fabliaux, as well as Jean de
Meun's portion of the *Roman de la rose*), and, of course, the *XV. Joies de
mariage,* Boccaccio, and Chaucer.

    According to the discourse of medieval misogyny, which still, I
maintain, plays a large role in how we think the question of gender, woman
is conceived, as the Arthurian fabliau asserts, as an inadequate vessel with
respect to which there can be no position of innocence whatsoever. A wife
represents a perpetually overdetermined signifier never adequate to her man.
To wit: if she is poor, claims Jean de Meun, one must nourish, clothe, and
shoe her: "Et qui vuet povre fame prendre, / A norrir la convient entendre /
Et a vestir et a chaucier."[4] But if she is rich, she is uncontrollable:

> Et se tant se cuide essaucier
> Qu'il la prengne riche forment,
> A soffrir la ra grant torment,
> Tant la trueve orguilleuse et fiere
> Outrecuidie et bobanciere.
>   (*Rose,* v. 8582)

If a woman is beautiful, all desire her (*Rose,* vv. 8587-96), and she will in
the end be unfaithful; yet if she is ugly, she will need all the more to please
and, again, will eventually betray: "Maintes neïs par eus se baillent, / Quant
li requerreor defaillent" (*Rose,* v. 8658). If she is reasonable, she is subject
to seduction ("Penelope neïz prendroit / Qui bien au prendre entenderoit; / Si
n'ot il meillor fame en Grece" [*Rose,* v. 8605]); yet if she is irrational, she
becomes the victim, as in the example of Lucretia, of madness and suicide
(*Rose,* v. 8607). Nor is such a view restricted to the Romance vernacular.
John of Salisbury is just as precise: "A beautiful woman is quick to inspire
love; an ugly one's passions are easily stirred. What many love is hard to
protect; what no one desires to have is a humility to possess." Chaucer

echoes virtually the same motif in the Wife of Bath's reproach of all such reproaches: "Thou seist to me it is a greet meschief / To wedde a povre womman, for costage; / And if that she be rich, of heigh parage, / Thanne seistow that it is a tormentrie / To soffre hire pride and hire malencolie." Woman by definition finds herself in a position of constant overdetermination, movement. She is, as Jean contends, "contenz et riotes"; and, as Jehan Le Fèvre, author of the fourteenth-century translation of the *Lamentations de Matheolus,* adds, of "tençon rioteuse."[5]

Woman as riot is a topos in medieval literature and has a special sense in Old French. The word itself, meaning chaos or upset, also refers to a kind of poetic discourse belonging to the rich tradition of nonsense poetry—the *fatras, fatrasie, dervie, sotie,* and *farce* as well as to the more specific type known as the *Riote del monde,* of which one example is the prose *Dit de l'herberie* and another the fabliau entitled "La Rencontre du roi d'Angleterre et du jongleur d'Ely." Here, however, the crafty jongleur works a curious and revealing reversal. He substitutes for the cliché of woman's trickery, associated with that of poets, the impossibility of speaking to women:

> "Veiez cesti mavois holer,
> Come il siet son mester
> De son affere bien mostrer".
> Si vus ne les volez regarder
> Ne volenters ou eux parler,
> Si averount mensounge trové
> Que vus estes descoillé! . . .
> (*Recueil,* II: 252-53)

The examples with which we began are, then, complicated by the fabliau's positing of the problem of overdetermination in terms of speech itself. There is, the anonymous poet asserts, no possibility of an objective regard upon the opposite sex and, therefore, no innocent place of speech. The mere fact of speaking to women makes one a pimp; a refusal to speak or even to look is the sign of a castrato. The unreliability of what is said about those who speak to women shifts the focus of recrimination away from woman per se and towards language in general; for, the poet maintains, there can be no discourse about woman that is not as treacherous as women themselves are assumed to be.

This changes somewhat our paradigm, since the inadequacy of women to Being, expressed as an everpresent overdetermination, becomes, in the passage cited, indissociable from the inadequacy of words; or, as the anonymous author of *La Ruihote del monde* suggests, of speech itself:

> S'il se taist, il ne set parler;
> S'il parole, vés quel anpallier,
> Il ne cese onques de plaidier. . . .
> S'il cante bien, c'est uns jougleres;
> S'il dist biaus dis, c'est uns trouveres.[6]

The riotousness of woman is linked to that of speech and indeed seems to be a condition of poetry itself. And if the reproach against woman, repeated monotonously by the vernacular writers of the High Middle Ages, is that she is a bundle of verbal abuse—contradictory, argumentative, garrulous, indiscreet, gossipy, a liar and seducer with words, such annoyances make her at least the fellow-traveller of the *trouvère*. What I propose to show is the extent to which the popular tradition with which we began participates in so-called high culture of the Middle Ages and, more generally, the extent to which the Arthurian fabliau, whose recriminatory bile is concentrated upon Guenevere, exemplifies the way the Middle Ages conceived the relation of woman to symbolic activity. I say "more generally" not to posit unconsciously a relation of these terms to nature, and thus to become trapped in the movement of that which I seek to undo, but because the assumptions attached to this relation are so deeply rooted in the West's manner of conceiving gender that it is necessary to begin almost at the beginning, that is, with the story of Creation.

Genesis II 7. And the Lord God formed man of the slime of the earth, and breathed into his face the breath of life; and man became a living soul. . . .

18. And the Lord God said: It is not good for man to be alone; let us make him a help like unto himself.

19. And the Lord God having formed out of the ground all the beasts of the earth, and all the fowls of the air, brought them to Adam to see what he would call them: for whatsoever Adam called a living creature the same is its name.

20. And Adam called all the beasts by their names, and all the fowls of the air, and all the cattle of the field: but for Adam there was not found a helper like himself.

21. Then the Lord God cast a deep sleep upon Adam: and when he was fast asleep, he took one of his ribs, and filled up flesh for it.

22. And the Lord God built the rib which he took from Adam into a woman: and brought her to Adam.

23. And Adam said: "This now is bone of my bones and flesh of my flesh; she shall be called woman, because she was taken out of man."

What often passes unnoticed in the Genesis story is the degree to which the creation of woman is linked to a founding, or original, linguistic act. Adam is said to be the first to speak, the namer of things: woman, or the necessity of woman, her cause, seems to emanate, in turn, from the imposition of names. The designation of things, or a primal instance of man's exertion of power over them, and the creation of woman are coterminous. Further, in this account of the *ad seriatim* creation of the genders, woman is by definition a derivation of man who, as the direct creation of God, remains both chronologically antecedent and ontologically prior. This at least is how early commentators on *Genesis*—Augustine, Jerome, Philo Judaeus—understood things. "It is not good that *any* man should be alone," writes Philo, "For there are *two* races of men, the one made after the (Divine) Image, and the one moulded out of the earth. . . . With the second man a helper is associated. To begin with, the helper is a created one, for it says 'Let us make a helper for him'; and in the next place, is subsequent to him who is to be helped, for He had formed the mind before and is about to form its helper."[7] Thus, woman, created from man, is conceived from the beginning to be secondary, a supplement. Here the act of naming takes on added significance. For the imposition of names and the creation of woman are not only simultaneous, but analogous gestures thoroughly implicated in each other. Just as words are the supplements of things, which are supposedly brought nameless to Adam, so woman is the supplement to, the "helper" of, man. She comes into being metonymically as a part of a body more sufficient to itself because created directly by God and to whose wholeness she, as part (and this from the beginning), can only refer—that is, defer.

Woman's supervenient nature is thus imagined to be indistinguish-able from that of all signs in relation to the signified, of all representations. As Philo Judaeus maintains, her coming into being is synonymous not only with the naming of things, but with a loss—within language—of the literal:

> "And God brought a trance upon Adam, and he fell asleep; and He took one of his sides" and what follows (Gen. ii, 21). These words in their literal sense are of the nature of a myth. For how could anyone admit that a woman, or a human being at all, came into existence out of a man's side? (*Creation,* p. 237)

Since the creation of woman is synonymous with the creation of metaphor, the relation between Adam and Eve is the relation of the proper to the fig-ural, which implies always derivation, deflection, denaturing, a tropological turning away. The perversity of Eve is that of the lateral: as the outgrowth of Adam's flank, his *latus,* she retains the status of *translatio,* of translation, transfer, metaphor, trope. She is side-issue.

This link between the derivative nature of the female and that of figural representation itself explains why the great misogynistic writers of the first centuries of Christianity—Paul, Tertullian, John Chrysostom, Philo, Jerome—were so obsessed by the relation of women to decoration, why they themselves were so fascinated by veils, jewels, makeup, hair style and color—in short, by anything having to do with the cosmetic. Such an obsession is evident even in the titles of the essays of, say, Tertullian: "On the Veiling of Virgins," "On the Pallium," "On the Apparel of Women." For the third-century apologist, woman is a creature who above all else and by nature covets ornamentation:

> *You* are the devil's gateway: *you* are the unsealer of that (forbidden) tree: *you* are the first deserter of the divine law: *you* are she who per-suaded him whom the devil was not valiant enough to attack. *You* des-troyed so easily God's image man. On account of *your* desert—that is, death—even the Son of God had to die. And do you think about adorn-ing yourself over and above your tunic of skins? Come, now; if from the beginning of the world the Milesians sheared sheep, and the Serians spun trees, and the Tyrians dyed, and the Phrygians embroidered with the needle, and the Babylonians with the loom, and pearls gleamed, and onyx stones flashed; if gold itself also had already issued, with the

cupidity (which accompanies it), from the ground; if the mirror too, already had licence to lie so largely, Eve, expelled from paradise (Eve) already dead, would also have coveted *these* things, I imagine! No more, then, ought she *now* to crave, or be acquainted with (if she desire to live again), what, when she *was* living, she had neither had nor known. Accordingly, these things are the baggage of woman in her condemned and dead state, instituted as if to swell the pomp of her funeral.[8]

If man's desire for ornament, or for that which is secondary, is analogous to man's desire for woman, it is because woman is conceived as ornament. She is, by her secondary nature, automatically associated with artifice, decoration. The mildest version of such a paradigm is found in the often repeated licence for men to pray with head bare while women are enjoined to be veiled—and in its corollary, that woman is covering or veil: "But if a woman nourish her hair, it is a glory to her," writes Paul, "for her hair is given to her as a covering" (I Corinthians 11: 15). Woman naturally decorates herself; and, according to Tertullian, is by nature decoration:

> Female habit carries with it a twofold idea—dress and ornament. By "dress" we mean what they call "womanly gracing"; by "ornament," what is suitable should be called "womanly *dis*gracing." The former is accounted (to consist) in gold, and silver, and gems, and garments; the latter in care of the skin, and of those parts of the body which attract the eye. Against the one we lay the charge of ambition, against the other prostitution. ("Apparel," p. 16)

It is tempting, in connection with this passage, to equate a certain hostility towards women with a more generalized horror of the flesh. And yet, it is not the flesh which Tertullian denounces. On the contrary, it is the draping of the flesh with "dress and ornament" which is the equivalent of seduction:

> The only edifice which they know how to raise is this silly pride of women: because they require slow rubbing that they may shine, and artful underlaying that they may show to advantage, and careful piercing that they may hang; and (because they) render to gold a mutual assistance in meretricious allurement. ("Apparel," p. 16)

To decorate oneself is to be guilty of "meretricious allurement," since embellishment of the body, a prideful attempt "to show to advantage," recreates an original act of pride that is the source of potential concupiscence. This is why Tertullian is able to move so quickly and naturally from the idea of dress to a whole range of seemingly unapparent associations—e.g., between transvestism and the monstrous, or between the toga and lust, adultery, cannibalism, intemperance, and greed. It is as if each and every act of clothing an original nakedness associated with the sanctity of the body, and not the weakness of the flesh, were a corrupting recapitulation of the Fall entailing all other perversions.

If clothes are at once the sign, the effect, and a cause of the Fall, it is because, as artifice, they, like woman, are conceived to be secondary, collateral, supplemental. Dress is unnatural since, like all artifice, it seeks to add to, to perfect, the body of nature or God's creation:

> That which He Himself has not produced is not pleasing to God, unless He was *unable* to order sheep to be born with purple and sky-blue fleeces! If He was *able,* then plainly He was *unwilling:* what God willed not, of course, ought not to be fashioned. Those things, then, are not the best by *nature* which are not from God, the *Author* of nature. Thus they are understood to be from *the devil,* from *the corrupter* of nature: for there is no other whose they *can* be, if they are not God's; because what are not God's must necessarily be His rival's. ("Apparel," p. 17)

A recreation, the artificial implies a pleasurable surplus that is simply inessential:

> Thus (a thing) which, from whatever point you look at it, is in *your* case superfluous, you may justly disdain if you have it not, and neglect it if you have. Let a holy woman, if naturally beautiful, give none so great occasion (for carnal appetite). ("Apparel," p. 20).

Tertullian does not, of course, seek to determine how something can be "naturally beautiful," much less to wrestle with the supervenient status of his own thought upon the superficial. His indictment of the artificial condemns not only what we think of as the realm of the esthetic, "adulteration with illegitimate colours," but extends to any investment of nature with human intention. Thus the constant comparison of iron, the use-value par excellence, with gold, which is perverse because its worth is extrinsic. The affinity between gold, the product of excess labor, "the arts," and women constitutes an economic nexus taken as a given; their natures, by definition inessential and antinatural, attract each other because they partake coevally in a scandalous excess that offends.

Here we arrive at an idea that runs deep throughout medieval thought and that indeed can be considered to constitute the essence of a certain theologizing of the esthetic. To wit, the artificial participates in a supervenient and extraneous rival creation that can only distract man's attention from God's original "plastic skill": Whatever is *born* is the work of God," Tertullian concludes, "Whatever is *plastered* on is the devil's work. . . . To superinduce on a divine work Satan's ingenuities, how criminal it is!" ("Apparel," p. 21). The decorative not only constitutes, as in the case of gold, an artificial investment of value, with all that such intention implies by way of potential concupiscence, but is a literal adding to the "weight" of creation:

> The wonder is, that there is no (open) contending against the Lord's prescripts! It has been pronounced that no one can add to his own stature. *You,* however, *do* add to your *weight* some kind of rolls, or shield-bosses, to be piled upon your necks! . . . Nay, rather banish quite away from your "free" head all this slavery of ornamentation.
> ("Apparel," p. 21)

From the always scandalous dressing of the naked body of nature emanates the entire range of perverse terms associated with "meretricious garbs and garments." In particular, the Church Fathers move quickly, by association, from the symbolic—artifice, idolatry—to the erotic—concupiscence, fornication, adultery, as if representation itself were, always and already, an offense. Verbal signs, in particular, stand as a constant reminder of the secondary and supplemental nature of all "the arts." "With the word the garment entered," Tertullian asserts, implying that language is a covering that, by definition and from the start, is so wrapped up in the decorative as to be essentially perverse.[9]

This nexus of ideas suggests that the representation of woman as ornamentation is an integral part of a broader paradigm, or that her perverse secondariness is the secondariness of the symbolic. The deep mistrust of the body and of the materiality of signs defined by their accessibility to the sense constitutes, in fact, a commonplace of what we know about the Middle Ages. Where it becomes interesting for our purpose is in the explicit analogy between woman and the sensible; for, as Philo reminds us, the relation between the mind and the senses is that of man to woman:

> To begin with, the helper is a created one, for it says, 'Let us make a helper for him'; and in the next place, is subsequent to him who is to be helped, for He had formed the mind before and is about to form its helper. In these particulars again, while using the terms "Outward nature," he is conveying a deeper meaning. For sense and the passions are helpers of the soul and come after the soul. (*Creation*, p. 227)

The ontological status of woman is, then, analogous to that of the sense within the cognitive realm. Man as mind and woman as sensory perception are, as Philo explains, mutually exclusive: ". . . it is when the mind (Adam) has gone to sleep that perception begins, for conversely when the mind wakes up perception is quenched." Woman, formed of flesh from the rib, remains bound by the corporeal. " 'He built it to be a woman (Gen. ii, 22)'," Philo continues, "proving by this that the most proper and exact name for sense-perception is 'woman' " (*Creation*, pp. 237, 249). Woman as sensitive soul is allied with the sensual; to perceive her, John Chrysostom maintains, is no less dangerous to men in general than the faculty of perception is to the soul of every man:

> Hence how often do we, from beholding a woman, suffer a thousand evils; returning home, and entertaining an inordinate desire, and experiencing anguish for many days; yet nevertheless, we are not made discreet; but when we have scarcely cured one wound, we again fall into the same mischief, and are caught by the same means; and for the sake of the brief pleasure of a glance, we sustain a kind of lengthened and continual torment. . . . The beauty of a woman is the greatest snare. Or rather, not the beauty of woman, but unchastened gazing![10]

It may seem that we have come a long way from the mantle and horn chastity-testing motif. In fact, we have arrived at a series of paradoxes that deserve to bring the very idea of chastity into a relation with the feminine, with the senses, and with the material nature of representations, that allows us to read the expressed impossibility of female chastity as a contradiction within not only the Arthurian fabliau, but within the medieval discourse on women. To wit, if woman is conceived to be synonymous with the sense or perception, then any look upon a woman's beauty must be the look of a woman upon a woman; for there can be no such thing as a male gaze or desire. This is why any answer to Saint Chrysostom's question "How is it possible to be freed from desire?" must be to be free of perception, or from the feminine altogether.[11] In this sense misogyny is bound to the will to escape the senses, perception, the corporeal, or consciousness itself, and, as a desire for totality becomes the site of another contradiction—that between the keenness of the awareness of woman as flaw and the desire for absolute wholeness expressed in the persistent exhortation to chastity, which is the unmistakable symptom of a death wish. "While in the flesh let her be without the flesh," urges Jerome; "The virgin . . . both yearns for her death and is oppressed by life, anxious as she is to see her groom face to face and enjoy that glory," John Chrysostom assures us. And, in fact, a certain inescapable logic of virginity, most evident in medieval hagiography, leads syllogistically to the conclusion that the only good virgin—that is, the only true virgin—is a dead virgin. Martyrdom is practically synonymous with virginity, as Ambrose insists in his tale of St. Agnes's beheading: "Why are you delaying?" the soon to be perfected virgin taunts her executioner. "Let this body perish which can be loved by eyes which I would not."[12]

The mutual exclusion of life and chastity serves as measure of the degree to which virginity is of necessity defined in terms of negative potential. The mere thought of losing it is sufficient to its loss. "For a *virgin* ceases to be a virgin from the time it becomes possible for her *not* to be one," Tertullian warns.[13] This means, to return to our beginning examples, that the desire to locate the chaste woman is a sexualized version of the wish for transcendance, an embodiment of the desire to escape embodiment altogether. And if the chastity of the women of Camelot seems, according to the horn and mantle motif, an impossibility, it is because the very notion of betrayal, consisting in a woman's infidelity, in her desire to be unfaithful, and, finally, in her husband's imagining her desire, is a category without substance. The very category of virginity, which so obsessed medieval theologians, is, through a process of reduction analogous to that of the Arthurian fabliau, relegated to the realm of pure idea. That is, the Patristics, in their desire for the absolute (which, as absolute, is synonymous with virginity), are not satisfied until the concept of virginity, like woman, is also emptied of sense.

The definition of virginity within the Patristic corpus is even more elusive than a chaste woman at Arthur's court. To be more precise, virginity contains a historical reference to Adam and Eve and to a theological state of man, as in Augustine's notion of technical virgins who reproduce in Paradise without desire or pleasure; this implies within the writings on virginity the corollary that with the end of human time everyone will again be a virgin because sexual difference will no longer be necessary. Virginity carries with it always a doctrinal reference to Mary, the Virgin, who redeems Eve; and it implies, on the individual level, a lack of personal sexuality. It is here that the concept of virginity becomes more interesting, since the more one seeks to fill the category, the more evasive it becomes. One begins, of course, with the assumption that a virgin is a woman who has not slept with a man. Yet, as the Fathers make abundantly clear, it is not enough merely to be chaste. The distinction between virgins in mind and chastity of the body is emphasized throughout: a virgin is a woman who not only has never slept with a man, but who has never desired to do so. Thus Jerome: "There are virgins in the flesh, not in the spirit, whose body is intact, their soul corrupt. But that virgin is a sacrifice to Christ whose mind has not been defiled by thought, nor her flesh by lust." To think, then, of not being a virgin is not to be one. "There must be spiritual chastity," John Chrysostom insists, "and I mean by chastity not only the absence of wicked and shameful desire, the absence of ornaments and superfluous cares, but also being unsoiled by life's cares."[14] One might well ask how the absence of "superfluous cares" can be anything but the very superfluity it renounces, but that is one of the defining paradoxes of virginity that must await the conclusion of our paradoxical escalation.

To continue: since the desire of a virgin is sufficient to make her no longer a virgin, and since, according to the Patristic totalizing scheme of desire, there can be no difference between the state of desiring and of being desired, a virgin is a woman who has never been desired by a man. St. Cyprian:

> But if you . . . enkindle the fire of hope, so that, without perhaps losing your own soul, you nevertheless ruin others who behold you, you cannot be excused on the ground that your mind is chaste and pure.

> Your shameless apparel and your immodest attire belie you, and you
> can no longer be numbered among the maidens and virgins of Christ,
> you who so live as to become the object of sensual love.[15]

Or Tertullian: "For that other, as soon as he has felt concupiscence after your beauty, and has mentally already committed (the deed) which his concupiscence pointed to, perishes. . . ." ("Apparel," p. 19).

What's more, the Fathers argue, since desire is engendered by, and indeed consists in, a look, a virgin, seen, is no longer a virgin. Almost to a man they quote the dictum from Mathew 5: 28—"Whosoever looketh on a woman to lust after her hath committed adultery"—and are obsessed by public baths. It seems, Cyprian argues, that no amount of soap and water can cleanse the body sullied by being seen: "You gaze upon no one immodestly, but you yourself are gazed upon immodestly. You do not corrupt your eyes with foul delight, but in delighting others you are corrupted. . . . Virginity is unveiled to be marked out and contaminated" ("Dress," p. 47). "Seeing and being seen," Tertullian states, "belong to the self-same lust" ("Veiling," p. 28). And, finally, in what is perhaps the most violent expression of the deflowerment of the look, Tertullian insists that "every public exposure of a virgin is (to her) a suffering of rape" ("Veiling," p. 29). There is in the founding thinking of the problem of desire in the first four centuries of the Christian era a profound link, which will surface occulted to dominate the Western love tradition, between the distortion implicit to the gaze and erotic desire. Ambrose speaks of the "guilt even in a look"; Chrysostom of "unchastened gazing"; Cyprian of the "concupiscence of the eyes"; and Novatian of "the adultery of the eyes." A virgin, in short, is a woman who has never been *seen* by a man. But not exactly, since, in condemning public baths, the locus par excellence of the gaze of the other, Jerome wonders if it is licit for virgins to bathe at all since, in seeing their own bodies, there is always the potential for desire: "For myself, I wholly disapprove of baths for a virgin of full age. Such a one should blush and feel overcome at the idea of seeing herself undressed."[16] Nor do things end here really: since desire resides in sight, and since it makes no difference whether one sees or is seen, either by the other or oneself, and, finally, since sight does not reside entirely in the faculty of perception but is also a faculty of the intellect, a virgin is a woman who is not thought not to be one in the thought of another. The virgin is above suspicion: "Even though they (men and women) may be separated by walls, what good is that?" John

Chrysostom asks. "This does not suffice to shelter them from all suspicion." And Clement of Rome, supposedly the disciple of Peter, warns
against sitting next to a married woman, "lest anyone should make insinua-
tions against us. . . ."[17] Thus, the only true virgin is the one who has never
sat next to or been in the presence of the opposite sex, or, finally, one who
has not entered the thought of another. "For," to quote Tertullian again, "a
virgin ceases to be a virgin from the time it becomes possible for her *not* to
be one."

The time has come to wrap a few of the myriad of paradoxes attendant upon the concept of virginity, which lies at the center of one important
strain of the medieval discourse on women. First, and here the theologians
are fully aware of the contradiction, if virginity were general, then there
would be no human race. Virginity as absolute cannot, in other words, be
absolute, but depends upon the difference it excludes. This is one of the
persistent justifications for sexual intercourse—that, in losing one's
virginity one can give birth to a virgin. Second, though virginity may
represent the antithesis of the cosmetic, it remains, because of its very
typical status, an adornment in its own right. And despite the fact that
Cyprian, for example, maintains that "virgins, in desiring to be adorned . . .
cease to be virgins" and that the only proper adornment of the virgin are the
wounds of the martyr, Jerome speaks of continence as the "ornament of the
inner man"; and Methodius, of Christ as "arming the flesh with the ornament of virginity." There is, again, no way of dissuading the reader from
ornamentation without becoming complicit with that from which one
pretends to dissuade. Third, to the extent that virginity is conceived as a
quietude of the senses, an escape from desire, it itself becomes a source of
desire: ". . . true and absolute and pure *virginity* fears nothing more than
itself," Tertullian observes. "Even *female* eyes it shrinks from encounter-
ing. Other eyes itself has. It takes itself in refuge to the veil of the head as
to a helmet, as to a shield, to protect its glory against the blows of tempta-
ions, against the darts of scandals, against suspicions and whispers and
emulations; (against) envy also itself" ("Veiling," p. 36). Though virginity
may hold the fantasy of an escape from desire, it cannot escape the logic of
the desire to escape desire, which remains internal to desire itself. Nonetheless, this passage from Tertullian's "On the Veiling of Virgins" brings us
closer to a conclusion, according to which there can be only two possibilities: 1) either virginity, as absolute, has no substance, does not exist; or, 2)
the abstraction that virginity implies is destroyed by its articulation. This is

another way of saying, again, that the loss of virginity implied in its exposure is analogous to the loss of universality of an Idea implicit to its expression; or, more simply, that there is no way of talking about virginity that does not entail its loss since the universal is always veiled by the defiling garment of words. For if, as Tertullian maintains, the veil is the *sign* of the virgin, protecting her from both the gaze of others and her own gaze, then virginity itself can be nothing else but a veil; and, as veil, it falls within the material pale implicit to all embodied signs. There can be no difference between Tertullian's "veil of virginity," Jerome's "veil of chastity," and Methodius's "veil of letters." "With the word the garment entered," Tertullian assures us elsewhere. Which can only be read: language is the ornament, the veil, that defiles the virgin by exposure, since the senses, equated with the body, have no direct access to the Idea, allied with the soul. "No one," John Chrysostom writes, "has anywhere seen a soul by itself stripped of the body,"[18] which might be turned upon the Arthurian fabliau to read: "The reason no one has seen a chaste woman is that to be seen is to be deflowered. If no woman is chaste, it is because embodiment itself is defilement." No narrative account even of such an attempt can be other than the very act of despoiling that which fiction presents as the possibility of virginal perfection. "Who could describe the pleasure?" Chrysostom asks. "What expression could suggest the joy of a soul so disposed? It does not exist" (*Virginity,* p. 104).

Notes

[1]J. Bédier, *Les Fabliaux* (Paris: Champion, 1925); P. Nykrog, *Les Fabliaux* (Copenhagen: Munksgaard, 1957); R. Dubuis, *Les Cent nouvelles nouvelles et la tradition de la nouvelle en France au Moyen Age* (Grenoble: Presses Universitaires de Grenoble, 1973); E. Baumgartner, "A Propos du Mantel mautaillié," *Romania*, 96 (1975), 315-32.

[2]A. de Montaiglon, *Receuil général et complet des fabliaux* (Paris: Librairie des Bibliophiles, 1872), III: 8. For a discussion of this tale see R. Howard Bloch, *The Scandal of the Fabliaux* (Chicago: University of Chicago Press, 1986).

[3]*Le lai du corn*, ed. P. Bennett (Exeter: University of Exeter Press, 1975), v. 229.

[4]Jean de Meun, *Le Roman de la rose*, ed. Daniel Poirion (Paris: Flammarion, 1974), v. 8579. See R. Howard Bloch, "Medieval Misogyny" in *Representations*, special issue *Misogyny, Misandry, Misanthropy* 21 (1987): 1- 24.

[5]John of Salisbury, *Frivolities of Courtiers and Footprints of Philosophers*, ed. J. B. Pike (Minneapolis: University of Minnesota Press, 1938), p. 357; Chaucer, "The Wife of Bath's Prologue" in *Canterbury Tales*, ed. F. N. Robinson (Cambridge: Houghton Mifflin, 1957), v. 248; Jehan Le Fèvre, *Les Lamentations de Matheolus*, ed. A. -G. Hamel (Paris: Emile Bouillon, 1872), v. 829.

[6]V. Le Clerc, *Histoire littéraire de la France*, 23 (Paris: H. Welter, 1895), p. 98.

[7]Philo, *On the Creation* (London: Heinemann, 1929), p. 227.

[8]Tertullian, "On the Apparel of Women" in *Ante-Nicene Fathers*, eds. A. Roberts and J. Donaldson (Buffalo: The Christian Literature Publishing Company, 1885), IV: 14.

[9]"On the Pallium," in *Ante-Nicene Fathers*, IV: 8.

[10]John Chrysostom, Homily XV in *Nicene and Post-Nicene Fathers*, ed. P. Schaff (Grand Rapids: Wm. B. Erdmans Publishing Company, 1956), IX: 441.

[11]Homily XVII in *Nicene and Post-Nicene Fathers*, X: 116.

[12]St. Jerome, Letters in *Nicene and Post-Nicene Fathers*, VI: 194; John Chrysostom, *On Virginity, Against Remarriage*, tr. Sally Rieger Shore (New York: Edwin Mellen Press, 1983), p. 96; Ambrose, *Three Books of St. Ambrose, Bishop of Milan, Concerning Virgins, to Marcellina, his Sister*, eds. P. Schaff and H. Wace (New York: Christian Literature Company, 1896), X: 364.

[13]Tertullian, "On the Veiling of Virgins" in *Ante-Nicene Fathers*, IV: 34.

[14]St. Jerome, *Against Jovinianus* in *Nicene and Post-Nicene Fathers*, VI: 357; Chrysostom, *On Virginity*, p. 115.

[15]St. Cyprian, "The Dress of Virgins" in *Treatises*, ed. and tr. R. J. Defarrari (New York: Fathers of the Church, 1958), p. 39.

[16]*Nicene and Post-Nicene Fathers*, VI: 194.

[17]Saint Jean Chrysostom, *Les Cohabitations suspectes, comment observer la virginité*, ed. and tr. J. Dumortier (Paris: Les Belles Lettres, 1955), p. 130; Clement of Rome, "Two Epistles Concerning Virginity," in *Ante-Nicene Fathers*, VIII: 64.

[18]John Chrysostom, "Letters to the Fallen Theodore" in *Nicene and Post-Nicene Fathers*, IX: 104.

Gastrographie et pornographie dans les fabliaux

Larry S. Crist

Appelé piéça à me pencher sur la question de "gastronomie et littérature" dans la littérature française du moyen âge, le souvenir des nombreux repas dans le fabliau me vint immédiatement à l'esprit. Hélas, je dus rapidement constater l'absence de ce que l'on peut appeler "gastronomie" dans ce genre particulier de ladite littérature. Par contre, ma recherche sur cette question m'a permis d'y déceler un lien certain entre l'univers sémantique de la /nourriture/ et celui de la /sexualité/, ce dernier thème étant, tout le monde l'admettra, l'un des plus importants dans le fabliau. C'est donc par le thème—ou plutôt le motif—moins étudié, de la nourriture que cette enquête commencera.

Qui ne se souvient pas que, d'une certaine façon, toute la *Recherche,* "Longtemps, je me suis couché de bonne heure. . . ," découle autant des asperges interdites que des baisers refusés? Qui donc dit "gastronomie et littérature" ne veut pas se cantonner au seul sous-domaine de la mode descriptive que serait la seule description des repas, de leur ordonnance, de leur préparation (toutes deux "externes") ou ses sensations "internes" que sont l'odeur et le goût. Il doit s'agir plutôt d'examiner la place, la fonction des repas dans l'œuvre littéraire.

La gastronomie, c'est les lois du manger en amont (la préparation, les recettes) et en aval (les plaisirs du nez et du goût) de l'acte de manducation ou de simple ingestion de nourriture tant liquide que solide. La gastrographie, si on me permet ce terme, c'est la mise en discours de ces lois, leur narrativisation hétéro-isotopique. J'explique ce barbarisme: le livre de cuisine, en tant que manuel technique, n'a—pour l'utilisateur moyen—qu'une seule isotopie, celle, précisément, de la /cuisine[1]/.[1] La mise en discours hétéro-isotopique branche cette isotopie[2] sur d'autres isotopies plus ordinairement littéraires. C'est dire que la description culinaire, mise en littérature, prend une autre dimension isotopique et parle maintenant de /classe sociale/, de /luxe/, de /loisir/, bref, se complique. (Il y a, bien entendu, la philogastrie,[3] mais elle dépasse le sujet que je me suis donné ici.)

Pour ne pas m'embourber dans la question de "qu'est-ce que la littérature," je prends une autre sorte d'exemple: l'ami qui nous raconte, un regard lointain dans les yeux, son repas de l'année dernière chez les frères Troisgros ou chez maître Tuillier aux Baux,[4] avec force détails, ne nous parle pas en tant que cuisinier nous baillant tout simplement un autre morceau de "logiciel" pour notre travail. Non, il s'appesantit sur les détails pour insister sur le sème[5] de /la bonne vie/ ou, si c'est un m'as-tu-vu, de la /meine Mittel erlauben mir das/[6] (mes moyens me le permettent). Cette personne parle autant d'elle que de cuisine.

Tout cela est bien théorique, l'on dira. Aux faits.

Je pars d'un constat plutôt global. C'est que *gula et luxuria pari passu ambulant* (la luxure et la gourmandise marchent d'un même pas),[7] et que cela se manifeste bien dans les fabliaux.

Or, quand on fait l'analyse, on n'est pas étonné d'apprendre qu'il s'agit souvent de sexe dans les fabliaux. Je prends, sans la discuter pour le moment, la liste des 160 fabliaux donnée par Per Nykrog.[8] En regardant de près et la liste des fabliaux à sujet érotique qu'a dressée Nykrog (pp. 59-66) et les fabliaux eux-mêmes, on en trouve 115 à sujets érotiques (115/160 = 23/32, soit un peu plus que les deux tiers). Mais, par contre, dans les fabliaux, d'après mon analyse, on ne trouve que 24 fabliaux où il s'agit de manger.[9] Pourtant, 21 de ceux-ci appartiennent à la classe "à sujets érotiques." On peut donc faire une petite constatation de travail: dans le monde des fabliaux, le sexe peut se passer de manger, mais la nourriture se sert rarement non accompagnée de sexe; autrement dit, dans 7/8 (= 21/24) des fabliaux à motif "gastrographique" il s'agit de sexe.

Deuxième constatation, qui formera une petite digression: il y a un seul cas (dans deux fabliaux étroitement apparentés) de jonction immédiate—par la métaphore— des deux activités, *manducare + copulare;* il s'agit des numéros 39, "Le débat du c. et du c." et 40, "Le dit des c.". Le cul dit au con: "Ersoir menjas tu une andouille. . ."[10] Il faut remarquer qu'il s'agit aussi d'un peu plus de détails sur ce "repas," car il y a eu "du brouet" (de la sauce) aussi; mais la modestie m'empêche d'appuyer sur la comparaison, de spécifier cette isotopie non-culinaire (ou métaphore plus ou moins filée).

Troisième constatation, de détail: c'est que, de détails, il y en a fort peu. Et c'est là que je reviens à ma pornographie. Dans la littérature littérante, canonique, il s'agit souvent de sexe, mais jusqu'à récemment, seulement sous la forme de suggestions et de déclarations; on rencontre très peu souvent des modes d'emploi ou de faire, peu de ce que l'on pourrait appeler des recettes. La description précise sera le domaine du bricoleur sexuel (manuels anciennement dits "de mariage")[11] ou, avec la mise en récit de ces descriptions, de la franche pornographie—et même, quand un Henry Miller écrira: "Elle avait un petit con juteux qui m'allait comme un gant,"[12] on remarque plutôt la métaphore que la description.

Je le note tout de suite: il n'y a pas de description de l'acte sexuel dans les fabliaux. Il y a les mots: "Il la fouta," "Il la baisa," mais ce ne sont que des mots, pas des descriptions. Il en est ainsi de la gastrographie, qui restera au niveau de la "gastronomie."

Examinons les faits de plus près. La liste des composantes du repas est assez restreinte:

/manger/ pas de détails	8, 18, 28, 61
viande	91
char	51, 84, 131, 136
(oison	34)
chapon	2, 31, 34, 89, 109, 110
poucin	77
oie	31, 77, 139, 143
(geline	34)
perdrix	17
malar	31
plunjon	31
("oisiaus nouviaus"	34)
porc	34, 110, 132
(connin	34)
poisson	33, 34, 134
œufs	119
pasté	32, 34, 119, 136
tarte [de viande]	32, 33, 89
pois au lard	2

pain		33, 34, 51, 100
gasteau		31, 34, 109, 132, 143
fromage		119
(amandes		34)
(noix		34)
ailliée [= aioli]		143
(kaniele		34)
(gyngembras		34)
(ricolisse		34)
("bonnes herbes"		34)
(espice		34)
lait		119
vin		33, 51, 84, 91, 100, 109, 132, 136, 143
(vermeil et blanc		34)
blanc		100
blanc de Soissons		31
pers		100
d'Auxerre et de Soissons		131
Détails		
chapons	en rost	110
char	cuite en pot	51
perdrix	rotis	17
porc	roti	132
poucin	au poivre	77
pastez	au poivre	51
tarte	doré à l'œuf	89

Quatre fabliaux parlent de /manger/, sans autres détails. Un fabliau fait référence à la /viande/ sans plus, et cinq mentionnent la /chair/, sans dire quelle sorte. Ensuite, il n'y a que 26 références à des choses comestibles particulières. Et si l'on soustrait les cas de *hapax legomenon* du fabliaux 34—que nous examinerons tout à l'heure—il ne reste que quinze références spécifiques.

Le boire est encore plus limité. Il y a du /lait/ une fois, et la sorte, même générale, de vin n'est spécifié que dans 2/7 (4/14) des cas, auxquels il faut ajouter une référence au vin d'Auxerre et de Soissons.

Dans cette liste, six mets ont une spécification, soit à propos de leur préparation, soit de leur accompagnement. Finalement, il y a deux sauces avec certains de leurs ingrédients, mais bien malin celui/celle qui pourrait en refaire une d'après la description donnée.[13]

Il n'y a que deux cas, me semble-t-il, qui sortent un peu de l'ordinaire:

Dans le premier cas, il s'agit d'une notation quant aux classes sociales. Dans le n° 119, "Le meunier et les .ii. clers," le meunier offre aux clercs un repas simple: "Pain et lait, et eues, et fromage," avec la notation du narrateur/énonciateur: "c'est la viande del bochage. . ." (V: 89; vv. 200-01). C'est-à-dire: ne vous attendez pas à de la chair d'animal ou de poisson; nous sommes trop pauvres/simples pour vous offrir ce luxe-là.

La syntagmatique des repas est restreinte dans les fabliaux. D'ordinaire, il n'y a que de deux à quatre éléments de repas nommés dans un fabliau. Il y a, pourtant, une grande exception, et c'est notre deuxième cas extra-ordinaire. Il s'agit ici de ce que l'on peut appeler, avec un peu de bonne volonté, de la gastrographie/-ronomie. Milon d'Amiens, dans "Du prestre et du chevalier" (n° 34), nous montre un membre de la classe militaire qui triomphe sur un membre de la classe cléricalo-ecclésiastique, classe orgueilleuse et avare dans les fabliaux.[14]

Le chevalier, qui demande l'hospitalité chez un prêtre pour lui et pour son écuyer, se fait rebuter d'abord. Mais quand le chevalier promet au prêtre de bien payer son logement, celui-ci le reçoit et lui promet de faire ce qu'il lui demandera, ayant toutefois fait monter le prix des 85 sous offerts à 100 sous. L'accord fait, voici le prêtre qui fait faire un vrai festin—le seul dans notre collection—par son queux; les servantes, la femme du prêtre et le prêtre lui-même, tel un patron de grand restaurant, mettent la main à la pâte. Et nous entendons le récit, non seulement des préparatifs du banquet, mais aussi, une seconde fois, du banquet lui-même.

> Li keus faisoit peler les aus,
> Comin broier et poivre ensanle,
> Et jà cuisoient, ce me sanle,
> .Iiii. capon et .ii. gelines.
> Molt èrent beles les cuisines,
> Car li connin et li oison
> Erent jà cuit et li poison.
> Gille, au cors avenant et biel,
> Fist .ii. pastés et un gastel;
> Dame Avinée eslut le fruit,

C'on dut mangier par grant deduit,
Et en après autres viandes.
Li Prestres poile les amandes;
Cius bat les aus, l'autre le poivre,
Et si ont fait un moult boin soivre;
Li tierch levent les escuielles,
Li quart met les bans et les seles
Et les tables pour asséoir.
Là péuissies manger veoir
Bien atorné et sans faitis (*sic pour* faitise).

                    (II: 56; vv. 298-315)

Sans contredit et sans dangier
Les servi on .i. à un mès.
Et, devant tous les autres mès,
Fu premiers li pains et li vins.
Li chars de porc et li connins
Aporta on, pour .ii. mès faire;
Celle viande doit bien plaire.
Après orent oisiaus nouviaus;
Puis fu aportés li gastiaus,
Et li capon furent au soivre,
Et li poisson à le fort poivre,
Et les pastés à déerains
Fait aporter li Capelains,
Por ce qu'il èrent bien et chier.
Por mieus séoir le Chevalier,
Et à toute l'autre maisnie
Dame Avinée, qui fu lie,
Aporta nois et autre fruit,
Et kanièle, si com je cuit,
Et gyngembras et ricolisse;
Mainte boine herbe et mainte espise
Lors aporta Dame Avinée.
Ains que la table fust ostée,
S'en mengèrent, toutes et tuit,
Tout par loissir et par deduit,
Et burent vin, vermeil et blanc,

Cler comme larme, et pur, et franc,
Assés et as grans alenées.
(II: 56-57; vv. 340-366)

Un bon banquet pour un bon prix, ce n'est que justice. Mais—revigoré par l'excellent et copieux repas—le chevalier doit rétablir le juste ordre des choses. Car il faut donner l'hébergement gratis aux chevaliers, errants ou non.

Puisque le prêtre a eu l'imprudence de promettre au chevalier non seulement repas et gîte, mais aussi de lui donner contre son argent tout ce qu'il voudrait, le chevalier demande maintenant la nièce du prêtre, moyennant paiement de 5 sous de plus. L'homme de Dieu offre 40 sous au chevalier pour qu'il renonce à elle, mais celui-ci reste intraitable, obtient ce qu'il exige et la possède cinq fois.

Le chevalier demande maintenant la femme du prêtre. On comprend que le prêtre offre de rendre tout ce que le chevalier a payé (moins 40 sous); qui plus est, il lui offrira un autre repas. Le chevalier, à son tour, offre 10 l. 5 s. pour la femme; le prêtre cède. Heureuse de ce que le chevalier se soit montré plus fort que le prêtre, la femme ne se fait pas prier et vient, apportant avec elle bon vin et fruits (restauration intermédiaire).

Le tour de la femme fini, le chevalier envoie son écuyer mander le prêtre enfin. L'ecclésiastique, voulant éviter le péché mignon de la classe cléricale, offre de ne pas prendre les 10 l. pour sa femme si le chevalier renonce à lui; l'écuyer est renvoyé chercher le prêtre néanmoins. Cette fois, monseigneur offre 10 l. en plus d'une quittance complète, et il jure de recevoir, désormais, gratuit sous son toit, tout voyageur. Le chevalier accepte ces termes.

J'ai peut-être trop insisté sur ce fabliau, exceptionnel dans son emploi du motif de /manger/. Mais les exceptions aident souvent à mieux percevoir la norme.

Le /manger/ est codé comme préliminaire au sexe, même si l'intention n'en est pas explicitée chez le pourvoyeur du repas. Dans deux des trois cas que j'ai indiqués comme étant des exceptions, s'il n'y a pas sexe, il y a au moins sème de l'isotopie sexuelle. Dans "Les trois boçus," le mari avare et jaloux qui reçoit et nourrit les ménestrels, bossus comme lui, leur interdit ensuite sa maison. Que sa femme, ayant été exclue du concert, les fasse revenir pour entendre leur musique n'a rien de sexuel. Mais quand revient son mari, elle les cache immédiatement, et ils meurent d'étouffement (souffrent donc un dommage) comme n'importe quel amant dans la situation de "Ciel! mon mari!"

Dans le "Dit des perdrix," la femme, gourmande, mange toute seule les deux perdrix que son mari lui faisait rôtir pour lui-même et pour le prêtre. Elle dira au prêtre que le mari a menacé de lui "couper les couilles," ce qui le fait s'enfuir pendant que le mari aiguise son couteau pour les volailles; la fuite montre donc, aux yeux du mari qu'il s'en va avec les perdrix, qu'il a très évidemment volés. Codage double donc: prêtre = *gula* + *luxuria*.

Le motif des "plaisirs de la table" ou du /manger/ tout court n'est donc pas innocemment décoratif; il sert à quelque chose. Les repas dans la *Recherche* seront, entre autres choses, occasions pour un luxe de descriptions[15] et connoteront, d'autre part, /la bonne vie/, /la haute société/. Il en a été de même chez Balzac. Dans le monde des fabliaux—comme dans celui de *Tom Jones* (qui ne se souvient pas, dans le film de Tony Richardson, de la scène du repas entre Tom et cette femme mystérieuse. . .)—la gastrographie n'a qu'une connotation: si l'on se met à table, le lit n'en est pas loin.

Notes

[1]= nourriture (/cuisine[2]/ = fabrication; /cuisine[3]/ = lieu).

[2]Dans le sens "élargi," où l'isotopie "se définit comme la récurrence de catégories sémantiques, que celles-ci soient thématiques (ou abstraites) ou figuratives. . . ," *s.v.* ISOTOPIE dans Algirdas Julien Greimas et Joseph Courtès, *Sémiotique: Dictionnaire raisonné de la théorie du langage* (Paris: Hachette, 1979), pp. 197-98; comme exemple d'isotopie figurative les auteurs donnent, par hasard, celui d'isotopie *culinaire* (p. 198). V. aussi Bernard Pottier, *Linguistique générale* (Paris: Klincksieck, 1974): "[C]ontinuité sémantique à travers une séquence (redondance reflétant une cohérence)," p. 326.

[3]Dont le texte maître est celui de Jean-Anthelme Brillat-Savarin, *Physiologie du goût;* nouvelle édition publiée d'après l'édition originale (Belley: Gustave Adam, 1948); citons également, comme très à-propos de notre sujet, Curnonsky (Maurice-Ed. Sailland), *Souvenirs littéraires et gastronomiques* (Paris: Albin Michel, 1958).

[4]V. dans le vademecum des gourmets, *Le Guide rouge Michelin France;* ici l'édition 1983 (Paris: Service de Tourisme Michelin), pp. 939 (Roanne) et 181 (Les Baux-de-Provence).

[5]V. Greimas et Courtès, *Sémiotique, s.v.* SEME: "[D]ésigne communément l'unité minimale . . . de la signification. . ." (p. 332) et plus précisément: "[L]es sèmes figuratifs . . . sont des grandeurs du plan du contenu des langues naturelles, qui correspondent aux éléments du plan de l'expression de la sémiotique du monde naturel . . ." (p. 333); et la discussion dans Pottier, pp. 29-31.

[6]Que l'on m'excuse ce langage; c'est le refrain d'un *Kummerslied*, "Besitz und Bildung," qui commence: "Ich hab' eine Loge in Theater. . ."; dans *Erich Kunz Sings German University Songs* (disque Vanguard VRS-477, 2: 7); cela exprime assez bien une certaine attitude bourgeoise.

[7]Proverbe de notre cru; nous n'avons pas vérifié dans les recueils de proverbes latins du moyen âge; si cela n'a pas existé, il l'aurait dû.

[8]*Les Fabliaux,* nouvelle édition; PRF, 123 (Genève: Droz, 1973), pp. 311-24.

[9]La seule collection "complète" des fabliaux est le *Recueil général et complet des fabliaux des XIIIe et XIVe siècles . . .* pub. par Anatole de Montaiglon et Gaston Raynaud; 6 vols. (Paris, 1872-90; réimpr. New York: Burt Franklin, n. d.); *Le Nouveau Recueil complet des fabliaux,* pub. par Willem Noomen et Nico Van der Boogard (†), destiné à remplacer le *RGCF*, en est à son quatrième (sur 10) volume (Assen: Van Gorcum, 1983 -); j'ajoute entre parenthèses les numéros donnés dans cette édition et entre crochets les numéros dans les volumes à paraître. Voici donc ma liste des fabliaux à motif gastronomique: 2 [47] Les trois boçus (pas de sexe directement); 8 [19] La bourgoise d'Orléans; 17 [21] Le dit des perdrix (pas de sexe directement); 18 [27] Du prestre crucefié; 88 [59] Du foteor; 31 [91] Du prestre et d'Alison; 32 [-] Du prestre qui fu mis au lardier;

33 [110] Du meunier d'Arleux; 34 [103] Du prestre et du chevalier; 51 [95] Du prestre et de la dame; 61 [98] Du prestre qui abevete; 77 [68] De l'evesque qui beneï le con; 84 [18] Du boucher d'Abbeville; 89 [102] Du prestre qu'on porte ou de la longue nuit; 91 [119] Du clerc qui fu repus deriere l'escrin; 100 [19] De la dame qui fist batre son mari; 109 [49] Du vilain de Bailluel; 110 [4] D'Auberee la vieille maquerelle; 119 [35] Le meunier et les .ii. clers; 131 [70] Li sohaiz desvez; 132 [79] Le povre clerc; 136 [74] Du segretain moine; 139 [81] Du prestre teint; 143 [86] De l'oue au chapelein (pas de sexe).

[10]II: 134; vv. 65-66.

[11]Si l'on voulait donner libre suite à la création de termes, on pourrait proposer ici: "pornonomie."

[12]*La Crucifixion en rose;* traduit de l'anglais par Jean-Claude Lefaure; Livre premier: *Sexus;* 2 vols. (Paris: Editions de la Terre de Feu, 1949), I, 271; *The Rosy Crucifixion,* vol. 1: *Sexus* (New York: Grove Press, 1965), p. 180: "She had a small juicy cunt, which fitted me like a glove."

[13]N° 34, v. plus bas, deuxième citation; n° 136: "Pain et char achata assez / . . . / Et Ydoine apele .I. garçon, / Qu'iluec ele envoia au vin, / Et si au poivre et au coumin; / El meïsmes fist la savor . . . (V: 222; vv. 248, 250-53).

[14]Par contraste avec la classe clérico-vagante ou non-bénéficiée, donnée comme fûtée et traitée avec sympathie.

[15]De ce qui entoure le repas—habits, parures et surtout conversations—mais pas de l'ordonnance même du repas, de la suite, sorte, couleur, odeur et goût des mets. V., dans l'éd. par Pierre Clarac et André Ferré (Bibliothèque de la Pléiade; Editions Gallimard, 1954), *Du côté de chez Swann,* v. I, pp. 251- ; *A l'ombre des jeunes filles en fleurs,* v. I, pp. 768- , 810- ; *Le Côté de Guermantes,* v. II, 165- .

Martin Le Franc, Fortune, Virtue, and Fifteenth-Century France

Peter F. Dembowski

Martin Le Franc[1] was born in Normandy in about 1410. Although he studied in Paris where he became a priest, most of his life he was closely connected with the house of Savoy. We know that he participated in the long Council of Basel convoked in 1431 by Pope Eugene IV (Gabriele Condulmer) in order to reform the Church. In 1439, the pope transferred the Council to Ferrara and later to Florence, but a certain number of disgruntled bishops stayed in Basel. They were excommunicated by Eugene IV. As a result, they deposed him and elected in his stead Amadeo VIII, Duke of Savoy, a widower and a religious since 1434. This antipope, Felix V, took Martin Le Franc under his patronage making him his secretary and conferring upon him the title of Apostolic Protonotary. Martin was thus associated with the "Basel party," that is, the party of schismatic Basel Fathers, throughout its existence. In 1443, he received the dignities of Canon and Provost of Lausanne. Four years later he was appointed as an Apostolic Legate to Philippe le Bon, Duke of Burgundy, and spent some time in his court. In 1447, Pope Eugene IV died. The Council, transferred to Lausanne and accompanied by the full College of Cardinals, elected Thomas Parentucelli as the new pope, under the name of Nicholas V. By then, only parts of Switzerland and Savoy recognized the antipope Felix V. He abdicated, therefore, in favor of Nicholas V in April 1449. The new pope, a man of patience and conciliation, not only permitted Amadeo to keep the title of Cardinal until his death, in January 1451, but also lifted the excommunication and confirmed the honors and titles of all the prelates who participated in the later stages of the Council of Basel. Martin's titles of

Papal Secretary, Apostolic Protonotary, as well as Provost and Canon of Lausanne were reconfirmed by Nicholas V on June 18, 1449. He remained in the service of Amadeo and later of his son, Louis I of Savoy. We know that in 1453 he participated in the conflict between the Canons and the Bishop of Lausanne, and in 1459 he received the administration of the Abbey of Novelesa (Val di Susa, west of Turin). He died in Rome in 1461.

Martin Le Franc as a writer is chiefly remembered for his long poem (24,000 octosyllables in eight-line stanzas), *Le Champion des Dames,* a kind of *défense et illustration* of courtly love and of ladies, which is, in a sense, a continuation of the *Querelle du Roman de la Rose.* He wrote it sometime between 1440 and 1442. Judging from a short "Complainte du livre du *Champion des Dames* a maistre Martin Le Franc," the work did not receive as much attention as the poet apparently had expected. His other long work might have been influenced by the lack of success of the *Champion.*

The later work—the subject of this paper—is a long and serious treatise written in prose with twenty-three inserted poems. It was received more favorably, at least if we judge its popularity by some thirty extant manuscripts. *L'Estrif de Fortune et Vertu* was composed between 1447 and 1448.[2] The composition of it began in all probability during the author's stay at the court of Philippe le Bon, Duke of Burgundy. The subject, the perennial discussion of the relationship of fortune (= determinism) and virtue (= free will),[3] was apparently suggested and ordered by the Duke himself: "Je n'ay jugié," says the author in his preface, "prince tres redoubté, tant pour accomplir vostre commandement de toute ma poyssance, que remonstrer sommairement combien Vertu sur Fortune doibt avoir de honneur, de loenge et de pris" (fol. 1v°).[4]

This sentence offers *in nuce* the subject of the *Estrif.* In order to demonstrate once and for all the precedence of virtue over fortune in the affairs of men, Martin Le Franc sets a series of debates between Lady Virtue and Lady Fortune. They argue in front of Lady Reason, who, as the debate progresses, herself participates more and more in the presentation of the arguments. She is of course on the side of *Dame Vertu,* especially in combatting all sorts of deterministic explanations of the sense of history constantly put forth by Lady Fortune.

Martin Le Franc's work is a *prosimetrum.* The text contains twenty-three inserted poems. I am convinced that the judgment of Harry F. Williams concerning them is right:

Ces poèmes de mètres très variés, bien encadrés dans la discussion en prose, ont une grande portée philosophique; l'auteur y fait preuve de virtuosité et d'élans lyriques. Martin eut peu de succès auprès de ses contemporains, bien qu'il fût un des meilleurs poètes du XVe siècle. . . . Parmi les écrivains du XVe siècle, il mérite de se classer, après Villon, à côté d'Alain Chartier et de Charles d'Orléans.[5]

But Martin Le Franc's work has remained virtually unknown. We have no accessible text. Scant literary judgments concerning the *Estrif* are usually based on the summary of it made by Piaget.[6] There is no doubt in my mind that Lady Fortune played some of her most celebrated tricks with the text of his serious and influential *Estrif*. Arthur Piaget[7] not only judged this treatise severely, but also expressed a strong conviction that there was no need for a modern edition of it:

L'*Estrif de Fortune et de Vertu*[8] mériterait-il une réimpression?[9] Non, certainement. Le sujet a perdu tout intérêt pour nous. Mais cet ouvrage n'en place pas moins son auteur au nombre des bons prosateurs du XVe siècle. Et certes, il faut savoir gré à Martin Le Franc, l'ami des humanistes italiens, imbu des classiques latins, d'avoir su écrire une prose claire et bien française, dans ce XVe siècle si souvent lourd et pédant. (p. 195)

These words written exactly one hundred years ago could now be considered prophetic. The modern edition of the entire text of the *Estrif* has not materialized and, as far as I could ascertain, has not even been attempted. But it was precisely Martin Le Franc's relationship with the Italian humanists and, to a lesser extent, with the classical *auctores,* that chiefly attracted the interest of Oskar Roth (see above, n. 2). As we have seen, he has studied the manuscripts and put forth convincing arguments in favor of the "best" manuscript.[10] Most of his exhaustive (648 pp.) and insightful study is, however, devoted to the analysis of the ideology of Martin's work and to placing it in the current of thought of the times. The study includes an edition of eleven of the poems. Since, as in its prototype *De Consolatione Philosophiae,* the poems in the *Estrif* often restate and reemphasize the main points of the prose texts, Roth comments extensively on the poems that he has edited. His commentaries stress above all Martin's role in introducing into France the early humanist ideas from Italy.[11]

As I said, Fortune did play her tricks in the editorial domain. We have seen that Arthur Piaget did not believe that any interest in the *Estrif* would justify a modern edition. His views were certainly proven wrong by Oskar Roth's *Studien*. But on a purely practical, editorial level, other factors also intervened. In 1928, Alphonse Bayot published his *Martin Le Franc, l'Estrif de Fortune et de Vertu*.[12] The content of this study was clearly indicated by its subtitle: *Etude du manuscrit 9510 de la Bibliothèque royale de Belgique, provenant de l'ancienne « librairie » des Croy de Chimay*,[13] but since the subtitles are often omitted from bibliographies, and since Bayot was an important textual critic and editor in his own right, the entry in Cabeen's *Bibliography* stated erroneously: "critical edition with notice . . ."[14] Bibliographies are apparently made from other bibliographies, for Bossuat's entry #4794 is preceded by an unambiguous: "Un seul de ses [= Martin Le Franc's] ouvrages, l'*Estrif de Fortune,* en prose mêlé de vers, a fait l'objet d'une édition moderne," and then translated *verbatim* Cabeen's entry: "Edition critique précédée d'une notice."[15]

Thus despite the fact that Martin Le Franc and his works have been known to the academic public for some hundred years now, his works are still inaccessible to that public. Apart from the poems edited and analyzed by Roth, the *Estrif de Fortune et Vertu* remains unpublished.[16] His other long verse work, the *Champion de Dames,* seems also to have been persecuted by Fortune: Arthur Piaget, encouraged by his master, Gaston Paris,[17] announced in his dissertation an intention to give a critical edition of the poem, and worked on this task intermittently until his death in 1952. In 1968 two former students of Piaget, Eugénie Droz and Jean Rychner, as well as Charles Roth, published the first two books (containing 8,144 verses out of some 24,000) of his edition.[18] We can see that to date only one shorter poem of Martin Le Franc has seen a complete critical edition.[19]

Apart from the undeniable influence of unfriendly Fortune (*habent fata libelli!*), I believe that it is possible to advance some intellectual reasons for the relative lack of interest in the *Estrif*. Arthur Piaget, in his *Martin Le Franc prévôt de Lausanne* (see n. 1), was quite persuasive in arguing the irrelevent character of this work: "De Goujet[20] à nos jours, l'*Estrif de Fortune et de Vertu* a été regardé comme une œuvre lourde, ennuyeuse et indigeste, dans laquelle on retrouve pêle-mêle toute l'antiquité classique" (p. 188). But what really displeased Piaget about the treatise is the fact that this interest in antiquity supposedly lead to the neglect of contemporary history. Evoking the authority of Paulin Paris, Piaget describes the treatise as

[u]n ouvrage vide de faits historiques et indications littéraires et morales. Vide de faits historiques qui nous intéressent, c'est vrai. Rarement Martin Le Franc, laissant de côté l'histoire ancienne, grecque, latine ou juive, a choisi ses exemples dans celle de son temps. (p. 188)

Piaget tries to be fair and even to exculpate our author by pointing out that his approach and method were inevitable in the fifteenth century and that even Christine de Pizan in her *Livre de Mutacion de Fortune* speaks only at the end of her work about contemporary history. Finally, and somewhat reluctantly, he adds: "Relevons dans l'*Estrif* tout un chapitre,—Martin Le Franc, il est vrai, y reste dans les généralités,—sur l'état déplorable de la France" (p. 189). Piaget does not attempt to explain Martin's reluctance to treat his own epoch. What could have been the reasons for it? Ultimately we do not know, but it is reasonable to believe that Martin was mindful while composing his *Estrif* of the cool reception given his *Champion des Dames*. Léon Barbey (p. 31) believes that Martin's sympathies to the Council of Basel, his hostility to the English cause, his admiration of Joan of Arc, his unveiled attacks on French aristocracy and on higher clergy in the *Champion* were the chief causes of the poor reception in 1440-42. Martin Le Franc's still ambiguous position in the Basel party in 1447-48 could doubtless have made him more careful, that is, more abstract in discussing contemporary France in the *Estrif*. But whatever the causes of Martin's caution, Piaget's insistence on the "dullness" and "irrelevance" of the *Estrif* certainly played an important role in discouraging critics and editors from working on the text.[21]

* * *

The passage concerning the social and political situation of France is placed in the first part of the Second Book of the *Estrif*, the subject of which is summed up in the *incipit* as follows:

Commence le second livre sur l'*Estrif de Fortune et Vertu* ou est demonstré que de la prosperité et adversité des empires, royaumes, seignouriez, gloire, estat, meschance ['misfortune'] et mutation d'empereurs, roys et aultres personnes Fortune principale cause n'est. (fol. 33r°)

The short excursus on France follows the passage in which Lady Virtue, having discussed the happy or unhappy outcomes of the governments of man, goes on to speak about natural disasters, such as deluges, fires, landslides, and epidemics, which can profoundly affect a state. In her typical fashion, she cites the destruction by water of the five cities of the Old Testament, as well as of ancient Achaea and Thessalia. Lady Virtue states her main point with usual forcefulness: "On voit tous les jours par ces naturelles causes mille mutations au monde venir; des quelles qui maistresse vous clame, il n'entend le cours de Nature, ne puissance divine honnoure" (fol. 45r°). It is impossible, says she, that her opponent, Fortune be responsible for natural or providential causes. So important is this point that Lady Virtue reiterates it in poem X:

> Ne jectéz la vostre plainte
> Contre fortuneuse empainte ['shock'].
> Se Romme est orez[22] despainte ['destroyed'],
> 4   Jadis du monde lumiere,
> Ou se Venise est enchainte [Mod. Fr. *enceinte*]
> D'orgueil, d'or et d'argent painte. . . .
> 9   Fortune n'est la premiere
> Cause, ne la derreniere,
> Que l'une luyt, l'autre estainte.
>   (fol. 45v°)

The second strophe of this twenty-two verse poem exposes the real cause of the "prosperity or adversity" of states: divine Providence. Man can also influence the change for better or worse either by accepting God's will or following worldly glory.

Lady Fortune is astonished that her opponent who has the perfect memory of historical facts lacks so obviously the knowledge of current events: "C'est bien ce que tousjours dit avons, il semble que vous songiéz, ou ne saichéz que une chanson" (fol. 45v°). Precisely, in order to force Lady Virtue to consider not only the time of *jadis,* but of *orez,* Lady Fortune asks the question:

> Combien y a que ne fustes en France? Dictes nous les derraines nou-
> velles que receu en avéz. De ce royaume debvéz parler, car on le voit a
> l'oeul, non pas des aultres pieça fondus, dont n'est aultre chose

demoeuré, comme dictes, que les fresles et les legieres plumes ont
escript en poy de papier. (fol. 45r⁰-46v⁰)

Bringing the subject of the debate back to the "real world" from the
universe of historical writing is particularly advantageous for Lady Fortune's argument, because, she says, in France everybody believes in the
efficacy of her power: "Interroguéz le premier François fuitif ['refugee']
qui par cy passera.[23] Se de moy tantost ne vous parle, je voeul avoir perdu
la cause" (fol. 46r⁰). Here, as Lady Fortune waxes eloquent, she delivers
her most important (and only) argument. The very devastation of France is
intimately tied with the universal belief in the power of fate, that is, the
power in her hands:

> Est il en France aultre bruit ['renown'] que de nous? Non seulement les
> hommes, maiz tout ce qui a royaume heureux poeut appartenir, a sentu
> et apperceu en France les cops de ceste main. Va par citéz, villes,
> bourgs et villages, champs, forests et rivieres, que verras tu fors la trace
> d'un grand et espouventable arsin, ou relief d'un grand disner?
> Commence aux reaulx ['those belonging to King's court'], jusques a cil
> qui grate la terre. Visite tous les places et lieux qu'il te plaira.
> Demande non aux sages et anciens, maiz aux petis enffans, combien a
> duré ceste male meschance. Tes yeulx et oreilles empliront du hault
> nom de Fortune. Les pierres nous y scevent nommer, tant longement y
> avons nostre povoir monstré. Ha! Vertu, bien pert que n'estes pas
> françoise et que en France guerez d'amys n'avéz, puis que tant mal estez
> des besognes aprise. De Babilloine, de Troye, de Carthage, de Thebes,
> d'Athenes, de Romme destruictes ne faictez extimation ['do not attach
> importance']. Cestuy royaume [France] poeut en tout jugement
> tesmoignage porter, que soubz nos piéz est toute vaine gloire, et n'y a
> fleur de lys tant richement doree que ne ruons au loing. (fol. 46r⁰)

Let us note that Fortune explicitly refuses, at least temporarily, the historical
method followed by Lady Virtue. She wishes to argue by using examples
based not on books, but on common knowledge, that is to say, taken from
contemporary French life. But neither Lady Virtue nor Lady Reason are
willing to accept such a line of argument. Only the long view supported by
historical examples can demonstrate the futility of determinism and the
efficacy of free and virtuous action.

Lady Reason then suggests to Lady Virtue to demonstrate "contre qui Françoys doibvent leurs cris et complaintes jecter" (fol. 46rº). With her usual humility, the latter hesitates a little, but delivers her main argument. The French kingdom was made noble above all other kingdoms by God Himself. Like ancient Rome,[24] France deserved her fame because of the noble actions of her past princes. They labored for the sake of God's love and became famous in all corners of the earth by following her advice. Here, Lady Virtue presents most eloquently a picture of a past utopia, in fact an earthly paradise founded on high moral principles. Let me cite here but one phrase: "Es roys, princes, seigneurs et gouverneurs du royaume luisoit ung soleil de justice, dont les bons estoient enluminéz et regardéz en honneur et en gloire, et les maulvaiz monstréz au doy de reprouche et de honte" (fol. 46vº).

Lady Virtue goes on contrasting this idealized past with the real present: "Or est la chose au rebours retournee, comme se de toute gent estrange France fust habitee. Tout y est nouvel et different du temps passé" (fol. 46vº). There is now both poverty and vice, just as in the past there was plentifulness and virtue. Indeed, Lady Virtue knows that she was banished from France. But worse still, the French, corrupted by their errors and misfortunes, have lost all hope and believe that God is asleep, wishing thus "leurs oultrages et pechiéz . . . par le Createur excuser" (fol. 47rº).

Lady Virtue preaches an eloquent sermon, addressed directly to the French, against this loss of hope. In it, she insists that the past glories of France were based on the homage that the French of yore paid to her: "Se Charlemaine et aultres pluseurs, dont veéz encores les ymages, resuscitoient et veoient vostre laache gouvernement, que feroient se non en souspirant nous reclamer?" (fol. 47rº). In most bitter but always non-specific terms, she chastises the great men of France for the sins of selfishness and self-seeking: "Rien ne vouléz ouir se cueur ne le desire. Ce qui vous plait est licite et louable. Que convient il mectre les livres de vos consciences devant voz yeulx?" (fol. 47rº). She continues her castigations in such sonorous lines as: "Peséz vos meurs justement en balance et verréz se plus y a de vaine ambition que de divine devocion, plus de paresse que de proesse, plus d'amer ['bitterness'] que d'amour" (fol. 47rº).

Such phrases as this help us to grasp the rhetorical method of Martin Le Franc,[25] not only here, but throughout this work. He juxtaposes "then" to "now," "vice" to "virtue," "ambition" to "devotion," "laziness" to "prowess," "hate" to "love," etc. Such a rhetoric of juxtaposition naturally leads on the one hand to a certain abstraction (for the sake of the "symmetry" of opposition, he cannot be too specific and concrete) and, on the other, to a constant retreat into historical examples (which precisely because of their well-mythicized qualities of *exempla* permit him to maintain this rhetoric of opposition and juxtaposition).

It is only natural, therefore, that Martin let Lady Virtue interrupt her analysis of the French situation to offer the perfect example of civic virtue found among the ancients, Scipio the African, and cites then (from Terence, according to him) the story of a young Roman scandalized by the sexual license of Jupiter, who visited the imprisoned Danae in the form of a shower of gold. This *exemplum* (followed by a citation from Cicero) proves that, by their personal conduct, the great of this world corrupt the people whose morality they are supposed to safeguard. This brings him back to his own times: "[N]'est grande merveille se entour vous gueres de Rolands ne voiéz, sans doubte car nul ne voeult Charlemaine, c'est a dire, grandement vertueux et de haulte vaillance apparoir. En vostre court n'est Roland ne Olivier!" (fol. 47v°).

Having established the parity of princely virtue and princely valor,[26] Martin, through his Lady Virtue, exhorts the princes to abandon the vain pleasures of this world and to face their duties, because they are the backbone and the heart of *la chose publique*. "Pestilential" Fortune assails France precisely because the virtues of the French ancestors are dormant. The princes of "now" have lost the sense of duty and honor through their sloth, and nothing will change in the terrible situation of France unless they become active:

> Paix demandéz, paix souspiréz, paix criéz vers les cieulx, et semble que
> a grand tort Dieu vous delaisse en ceste affliction, ou que Fortune
> desmesureement vous traveille et desface. Mais doubtance ay se vos
> estranges conditions ne changeriéz en mieulx par paisible repos. (fol.
> 48r°).

So corrupted are the princes that Martin puts in the mouth of Lady Virtue a truly desperate idea. If not for the foreign wars, which keep them partially occupied, the princes would spend their time inventing new ways of sinning and destroying each other:

> Je me doute que nouvelles façons de courroussier Dieu et l'un l'autre
> destruire ne trouvissiéz, et a troubler les aultres ne fussiéz trop fretillans
> ['eager'], car il n'est vray semblable se en extreme adversité complaisiéz
> de legier a vos premiers vouloirs, que prosperité ne vous empulenist
> ['would have not infected'], corrumpit et amortist le vice. (fol. 48v°).

Here *Dame Vertu* reaches the highest point of her "sermon." This
situation in which France now finds herself must be considered as a "transi-
toire et asséz doulce adversité" sent by Divine Mercy to "charitablement
amonester" the sinners in order to reclaim them. Only through the return to
former virtues and through repentence can the situation change:

> Soubz Dieu vivéz, qui en sa main tient la paix et la guerre, qui vos
> entencions, vos consaulx, vos traictiéz, vos faitz regardant de son oeul
> eternel, pourvoit ce que vous est et sera convenable en commun et en
> particulier; qui voeult que de vous soye ['that I be'] amee et prisee en
> ceste tribulation. (fol. 48v°).

The only way to be free from the perceived oppression of Fortune,
concludes Lady Virtue, is to trust God: "Tout temps prendréz en gre, au
plaisir et honneur de cil qui ne fait rien sans juste occasion. Plus ne feréz
vos huees et cris contre Fortune disants que contre vous elle est trop
forsenee" (fol. 49r°). You, yourself, rather than Fortune, are the cause of
your miseries: "Et tres longement dure ceste indignation [against Fortune],
car elle n'est cause de vostre desolation, mais vous mesmes . . . (fol. 49r°).
    Here follows poem XI. Like all the inserted poems in the *Estrif,* it
reemphasizes in its seventy-five lines the main arguments presented in Lady
Virtue's long discourse: Unhappy is he who "unlooses the misfortune"[27]
and through his own deeds hurts himself:

8   Certainement,
         Telx estes vous, Françoys, communement,
         Qui de vos maulx cause estes seulement.
         Entendéz moy, je monstrerai comment:
12   N'avéz vous pas
         Contre rayson, sans regle et sans compas ['mesure']
         A tous vices habandonné le pas,
         Dont de vie est France alee a trespas?

16   Vous par pechié
            Avéz malheur des liens destachié . . .
            (fol. 49r°-49v°)

After having chastised the French for blaming God for their misfortunes and
saying that He is asleep, Martin Le Franc allows Lady Virtue to make the
strongest attack on the vices of his contemporaries. It seems as if the rhetoric of poetry gives him greater oratorical freedom than the reasonableness
of his prose:[28]

            [God] . . . pechié vous a tant exposé
44   A grand malheur
            Que sens n'avéz, proesse ne valeur
            Par qui France languissant en douleur
            Puist recouvrer sa premiere couleur.
48   Tant est au bas
            Par vos haine, divisons, debas
            Que d'elle on fait comme d'un viel cabas ['prostitute']
            Et est subgecte au gorrel ['harness,' 'halter'] et au bas ['burden'].
52   Champs et villages,
            Villes, citéz, bourgs, monstiers, ports, passages,
            Dix mille maulx, plus de cent mille oultrages
            Monstrent asséz que tous ne sont pas sages.
56   Ce ne fait Dieu . . .
            (fol. 49v°-50r°)

God is good and wishes no harm to anybody or anything. He only
punishes "doulcement et par jeu" those who oppose him. Do not give Him
new occasions to punish you, for the old sins are not yet expiated. Most
importantly, turn your hearts to God, shun vice, and protect the common-
weal with acts of charity and then do not worry about Fortune, she is as
unstable and changeable as the moon.

    Since not only in this passage, but in the whole *Estrif,* the debate
between Lady Virtue and Lady Fortune is largely a *dialogue de sourds,* a
standoff between two irreconcilable positions, Lady Fortune is not convinced by the arguments presented by her opponent. She repeats her previous arguments, but this time making an appeal to truth: "la ou vous cuidéz
de nostre estat mesdire, verité vous fait le nom de Fortune de la bouche

sallir" (fol. 50°). She reiterates her ability to turn her Wheel anytime she wishes, for the French certainly deserve to be mistreated. Babilonians, Assyrians, Trojans, Persians, Greeks, Africans, Romans, Germans, and Spaniards had their glory turned into nothing by her, why should the French be exempt from the effects of the movement of her Wheel? Notice that Lady Fortune herself takes up the same method as Lady Virtue. Sooner or later she too returns to the use of the precedents, to the boundless store of exemplary history.

The discussion between Lady Virtue and Lady Fortune on the fate of fifteenth-century France is almost finished. Lady Virtue agrees with her opponent that the French merit what they got, but she insists, of course, that Fortune is not the cause of it: "Ores est flectrie la gloire du royaume qui jadis flourissoit. Ores y est le hault en bas, le blanc en noir, le tout en nient converty et mué. Ilz [the French] ont leur tour, c'est jeu party ['alternative'], je le confesse, mais ce ne vien de vous" (fol. 51r°). Providence has always been ultimately responsible for punishing them for their vices and their misgovernment. Lady Virtue concludes by restating the indictments against the French, as well as the three main points of her discourse: 1. The French have been making efforts to "unmake" their kingdom rather than to construct it. 2. Those who do not believe that God is indifferent ("que Dieu dorme") should accept the just punishment from His hands, for it reclaims the sinners. 3. The law and use of Nature demands that neither persons, nor things, nor times rest unchanged: "Est il rien par-durable? Comme tout a commencement, ainsy tout a fin cueurt ['runs'], et a nient retourne tout ce qui est de nient venu" (fol. 51r°). And this declaration leads Lady Virtue quite naturally back to history, which teaches us again and again that nothing lasts forever. And in all the innumerable examples that Virtue cites here and throughout the *Estrif,* we are told that God granted Fortune many things, some more durable than others, although in all of them not Fortune but He himself decides.

Thus ends this short excursus into contemporary history. The rest of the Second Book is occupied with the discussion of the role of Providence. This excursus certainly indicates that Martin was not unaware of what was going on in France in the late 1440s. If he was not writing like a nineteenth- or twentieth-century journalist, he certainly did not hide his head in the sand. Neither did he write like a twentieth-century *engagé* ideologist defending a tyranny. His insistence on past history is a fundamental part of his method, which is basically composed of exempla "speaking for themselves." Like so many in his time, he understood political problems chiefly if not exclusively in their moral dimensions and certainly *sub specie aeternitatis*.

Our brief analysis of this passage thus gives us a good picture of the problems Martin wishes to present and of the kind of rhetoric he uses in the rest of the *Estrif*. He deserves to be better known, for he certainly is a fine example of a serious writer of his age. And if we criticize Martin Le Franc and his age for being abstract and concentrating on biblical, Greek, and Roman historical examples, let us remind ourselves that when a Boccaccio or a Petrarch argues chiefly by means of *exempla* we praise them, and justly so, for being not only great medieval writers, but also harbingers of the Renaissance and of Humanism. So, too, was Martin Le Franc.

Notes

[1]The life and works of Martin Le Franc have been studied by Arthur Piaget in his University of Geneva dissertation: *Martin Le Franc: prévôt de Lausanne* (Lausanne: Payot, 1888).

[2]Oskar Roth is the only scholar, as far as I know, who has studied in detail Martin's treatise, in his *Studien zum "Estrif de Fortune et Vertu" des Martin Le Franc* (Bern: Herbert Lang, 1970). The problems (thoroughly examined by Roth) of the exact date of the composition, as well as the question of the determination of the best manuscript—Bruxelles, Bibliothèque royale 9573 (Roth's siglum *Bd.* ours *B*)—need not occupy us here. Suffice it to say that Martin names "Phil[i]ppe Marie, duc de Milan nagueres trespassé, comme nous avons entendu. . ." (fol. 93 r°). And we know that Filippo Maria Visconti died on August 14, 1447. There is yet another textual indication of the date of composition. As Roth (p. 625) points out, the phrase "des sa [= du monde] creation jusques a cestuy an, nous contons six mille .iiij^c. .xlviij." (fol. 60v°) means that this sentence was written in the year of 1448 of our era, since Martin traditionally counted 5000 years from the Creation to Jesus's birth.

[3]Howard Rollin Patch studied this general theme in his 1915 Harvard dissertation, published as *The Goddess Fortuna in Mediaeval Literature* (Cambridge, Mass: Harvard University Press, 1927), as well as in his shorter monographs. The more specifically medieval French figure of Fortune has been finely analyzed by John Grigsby in his critical edition of *The Middle French "Liber Fortunae,"* University of California Publications in Modern Philology, 81 (Berkeley and Los Angeles: University of California Press, 1967), 9-16. For Grigsby's judgment concerning the close resemblance between the *Liber Fortunae,* Alain Chartier's *L'Esperance ou la Consolation des trois vertus,* and the *Estrif* in the treatment of the theme of Fortune see p. 15, n. 35. A major part of Oskar Roth's study (pp. 77-340) deals with Fortune seen in the Western theological, philosophical, and astrological tradition.

[4]Henceforth all citations will be taken from the Brussels manuscript (*B*) mentioned in n. 2.

[5]Georges Grente, et al., *Dictionnaire des lettres françaises: Le moyen âge* (Paris: Fayard, 1964), p. 502.

[6]Thus Howard Rollin Patch in his *Goddess Fortuna* (see above, n. 3), see p. 43, n. 4; p. 44, n. 4; p. 71, n. 3; and 154, n. 1, as well as in his more specifically French "catalogue" (*Fortuna in Old French Literature,* Smith College Studies in Modern Languages, vol. 4, n° 4 [Paris: Champion, 1923]), analyzes and judges (pp. 28-29) the *Estrif* exclusively from Piaget's summary.

[7]See above, n. 1. Piaget was a student of Gaston Paris, who suggested the subject of the thesis and wrote a quite laudatory review of it in *Romania,* 18 (1889), 319-20.

[8]The title is incorrect. The "best" MSS do not repeat the preposition *de*. This syntactic modernization of the title will be used by Alphonse Bayot (see below, n. 12) and by many modern critics.

[9]Piaget speaks here about the "reprinting" of the *Estrif*, having in mind the three early printings: 1. *Incunabulum* without title, date, place, and printer's name. In all probability printed by Colard Mansion in Bruges in 1477; 2. *L'Estrif de Fortune et de Vertu.* (Paris: Michel Le Noir, 1506); 3. *Lestrif de fortune de vertu desquelz est souuairenement demontre. . .* (Paris: Michel Le Noir, 1519).

[10]It is the Brussels manuscript mentioned above in n. 2. There are at least twenty-nine other manuscripts extant. Roth analyzes them on pp. 17-76.

[11]In addition to his *Studien*, Roth has published two important articles on the relationship between Martin and Petrarch: "Martin Le Franc et le "De remediis" de Pétrarque," *Studi Francesi*, 15 (1971), 401-19; and "Martin Le Franc et les débuts de l'humanisme italien: Analyse des emprunts faits à Pétrarque," in *Il Petrarca ad Arquà: Atti del convegno di studi nel VI centenario. . .* ed. Giuseppe Billanovich and Giuseppe Frasso (Padova: Antenore, 1975), pp. 241-55.

[12]*Martin Le Franc: l'Estrif de Fortune et de Vertu. . .* (Bruxelles: Weckesser; Paris: Rousseau, 1928).

[13]This MS (*Bc*, according to the sigla established by Roth) is important chiefly for its beautiful execution and the miniature on its title page.

[14]D[avid] C[lark] Cabeen, gen'l ed., *A Critical Bibliography of French Literature*, vol. 1, *The Mediaeval Period*, ed. Urban T. Holmes (Syracuse, N. Y.: Syracuse University Press, 1947), p. 168. The enlarged edition (Syracuse, 1952), p. 168, repeats the error.

[15]Robert Bossuat, *Manuel bibliographique de la littérature française du moyen âge* (Melun: Argences, 1951), p. 453.

[16]I am now trying to remedy this situation and am preparing an edition of this text. Professor Roth of the Technische Universität Berlin has kindly communicated to me that he had planned to edit the whole text of the *Estrif* after the publication of his *Studien*, but other work and a growing interest in the sixteenth century have prevented him from carrying out his intention.

[17]In the review of Piaget's dissertation cited above, n. 7.

[18]*Martin Le Franc, Le Champion de Dames: première partie*, ed. Arthur Piaget, Mémoire et documents publiés par la Société d'Histoire de la Suisse Romande, troisième série, 7 (Lausanne: Payot, 1968), Léon Barbey in his *Martin Le Franc, prévôt de Lausanne et avocat de l'amour et de la femme au XVe siècle* (Fribourg: Editions Universitaires, 1985) presents a study of the contents of this edition. But he does not study the *Estrif*, "pour la bonne raison," as he says, that it "n'est accessible que dans ses manuscrits hors de notre portée" (p. 31). M. Robert Deschaux (from the University of Grenoble III) is preparing a new edition of the *Champion*.

[19]The "Complainte" published by Gaston Paris, "Un Poème inédit de Martin Le Franc," *Romania,* 16 (1887), 383-437. The text (of 472 octosyllables) was transcribed by Piaget, but Gaston Paris prepared a lengthy introduction and commentary. Before this Piaget-Paris venture, only some fragments of the *Champion,* as well as poem XIII and parts of poems XXIII and XI of the *Estrif* (the latter pertains to Martin's discussion of France), were published by André van Hasselt, *Essai sur l'histoire de la poésie française en Belgique,* Académie Royale des Sciences de Belgique: Mémoires Couronnés, 13 (Bruxelles: Hayez, 1838), pp. 114-19 and 200-18.

[20]L'abbé Claude-Pierre Goujet (1697-1767), polygraph and historian of literature particularly interested in ecclesiastical writers.

[21]Oskar Roth is not a victim of Piaget's peremptory judgments. His dissertation contains a chapter, "Fortuna und das gegenwärtige Frankreich" (pp. 341-403), devoted to examining not only Martin Le Franc's views on his contemporary France, but also, and above all (as in the rest of the *Studien*), to placing those views within the framework of the history of ideas. Roth published poem XI, which forms part of the discussion of the fifteenth-century French situation. I acknowledge my debt to Roth's work.

[22]Note that manuscript *B* uses here, as elsewhere, *-ez* for both tonic and atonic endings. I have transcribed, therefore, tonic *-ez* as *-éz.*

[23]This seems to indicate that the debate is taking place somewhere outside of France, probably at the court of the Duke of Burgundy.

[24]There is an obvious reference here to the *translatio imperii* topos.

[25]Martin is, of course, a highly traditional writer. He invented neither the method that he follows, nor the examples that he gives. His analogues and sources (in the case of this passage, Alain Chartier, his own *Champion de Dames,* etc.) have been studied by Oskar Roth (above, n. 2), especially pp. 385-403 and 481-86.

[26]Like most thinkers from about 1350 on, Martin expresses his belief in and desire for the restoration of chivalry. See Roth, and especially his section on "Le Franc und die burgundische Bewegung zur Erneuerung des Rittertums," pp. 377-83.

[27]"[S]on malheur deslie" (v. 1), cf. "destachier malheur [des liens]" (prose, fol. 49r and v. 17); for the discussion of the meaning of this phrase and its model in Boccaccio, see Roth, pp. 389ff.

[28]Here again, Martin follows a well-established tradition. Winthrop Wetherbee in his *Platonism and Poetry in the Twelfth Century: the Literary Influence of the School of Chartres* (Princeton, N. J.: Princeton University Press, 1972) notes that Boethius's poems have greater emotional undertones than his prose (for the discussion of the nature of inserted poems in *De Consolatione,* see pp. 74-82). I am grateful to my student, Michael Salda, for having drawn my attention to Wetherbee's discussion.

Rewriting Recognition
in Early Medieval Veridictory Drama

Donald Maddox

Despite its prominence in the critical lexicon of Aristotelian dramatic theory, "recognition" is not a term widely used with reference to medieval drama. This is hardly surprising in view of purely historical considerations. Aristotle's famous definition of anagnorisis ("recognition") as a "change from ignorance to knowledge" appears in the eleventh chapter of the *Poetics,* a treatise whose availability during the later Middle Ages was far more limited than other works in the Aristotelian corpus.[1] With regard to the *Organon,* for example, recent studies have detected among late twelfth-century vernacular poets a receptivity to the kinds of cognitive issues problematized in the contemporaneously rediscovered *Posterior Analytics, Topics,* and *Sophistical Refutations* as well as in their late classical and medieval commentaries.[2] While the *Poetics* also found its way into medieval critical theory, its relatively modest impact is of much later vintage and was considerably abetted by Averroes's twelfth-century commentary, in Arabic, translated into Latin by Hermannus Alemannus around 1250.[3] By the late fifteenth century the treatise and its commentary had come into greater prominence among theoreticians, though not among the craftsmen of late medieval dramatic spectacles.

While chronology would initially seem to obviate recognition as a valid problematic where medieval dramatic *practice* is concerned, a further complication—what Terence Cave has termed a "methodological problem"—derives from its being entertained in contexts other than that of its original usage: "The sense of the term 'anagnorisis' as used by Aristotle is determined by a tightly knit argument directed towards the analysis of a group of ancient Greek tragedies. . . . one might well ask whether recognition . . . can validly be used as the equivalent of anagnorisis, or whether either word can properly be used outside the context of Aristotelian theory and Greek dramatic practice."[4] While demonstrating that anagnorisis, properly speaking, remains anchored to a specific critical moment, Cave observes that modern European dramatic practice has invested the Aristotelian lexicon with "new and fruitful meanings" (p. 58). In his own analyses of recognition in Corneille's *Héraclius* and Shakespeare's *Twelfth Night,* he sustains in illuminating ways a productive "interplay" between his critical discourse and Aristotle's, showing how dramatic practice and the theory of drama both necessarily move beyond the *Poetics* during the very age that celebrated its rediscovery.

Yet what about an earlier age, in which it was virtually unknown? Should veneration, on these "historical" and "methodological" grounds, of a supposedly "primordial" notion of recognition as defined by the *Poetics* rule out study of the scope of related phenomena in "non-Aristotelian" medieval drama? Such an exclusion is certainly out of harmony with the Peripatetic's own theoretical assumptions. After all, in his evaluative description of the types of recognition in Greek tragedy (Chapter 16), Aristotle was rewriting, in his own critical idiom, the representational virtualities inscribed in specific dramatic works. At the same time, by identifying the tragic poet's essential role as being that of an "imitator" of "human action" (Chapter 6.5 *passim*), he was acknowledging that recognition in dramatic discourse is itself a rewriting of repertories already inscribed in human behavior. A hierarchy of rewritings thus obtains, one founded upon the cognitive comportments of mankind. It is this behavioral "proto-scripture" whose traces are rewritten into dramatic works, and these in turn shape Aristotle's—and our own—critical rewritings.[5] Far from being the products of a universalized abstraction, Aristotle's critical examples of recognition are derivative, their hypothetical variability determined by specific plays that variously imitate human action. Although the types of recognition described by Aristotle are thus determined by historical accident, he conceives of recognition itself as being fundamental to human cognition. Aristotelian recognition has in fact been defined as "the narrative pivot, of a cognitive order and . . . the passage from" an erroneous knowledge to "true" knowledge as constituted within a given discursive context, the same underlying cognitive phenomenon being reconfigured in narrative and dramatic works of every age.[6]

Including the Middle Ages. As discursive configurations of this phenomenon vary from one text to another, so, too, do our critical rewritings of them. Had Aristotle been writing the *Poetics* mindful of Arnoul Gréban instead of Sophocles, his predication of anagnorisis would also have varied accordingly. In the interplay between Aristotle's recognition as a discourse-specific moment of truth and our recognition of the value of studying such moments in medieval dramatic discourse, we may begin by asking how early French vernacular playwrights rewrote recognition.

As regards liturgical plays—the Latin "music-drama" of the medieval Church—the question has already been raised, in contrastive interplay with Aristotle. In Chapter 11 of the *Poetics,* we recall, Aristotle identifies three "organic parts" of the tragic plot: peripeteia, anagnorisis, and pathos. Together they constitute the critical nexus of a tragic action. Anagnorisis ideally coincides with a "reversal of the situation," as in *Oedipus,* and may involve a new awareness of previously unknown objects, deeds, situations, or identities. This pivotal movement occasions an affective response—"pity or fear"—and culminates in a "scene of suffering." Asserting a comparable relationship between "Christian rite and Christian drama" on the basis of their inverse development of this tragic pattern, O. B. Hardison, Jr., has suggested that the underlying ritual form of liturgical ceremonies characteristically involves a sequence of spiritual struggle, or agon, followed by a dramatic reversal accompanied by collective recognition and gaudium, or communal rejoicing.[7] The dysphoric affective curve in the Aristotelian tragic scheme is effectively reversed, so that the comprehensive movement of liturgical drama culminates in euphoria.[8] The shift is contextualized and validated by the moment of recognition centering salvation history, or *historia:* "The Resurrection," writes Hardison, "is both the peripeteia and the anagnorisis of the Christian mythos" (p. 43). This moment is explicitly signified in the Easter *Quem Quaeritis* trope whose metamorphoses and avatars recur for centuries in Latin and vernacular contexts.[9] As in the "dying and reviving god" pattern of ancient cultic drama, Christian drama takes as its primary locus of recognition the moment at which mediation of the most fundamental of all human contradictions, that between life and death, is ritually reactualized. If not actually replicated in liturgical and semiliturgical drama, it is either celebrated in its effects, as in saints' plays evoking the christological pattern as model, or else anticipated, as in the Fleury Herod plays and the *Raising of Lazarus.*[10]

The liturgical pattern that replaces pathos by gaudium consequent upon reversal and recognition also persists in the earliest French religious drama. Although the plaintive vernacular refrains of the otherwise Latin *Sponsus* and the long, effusive lament of Adam in the *Ordo representacionis Ade,* or *Jeu d'Adam,* emphasize pathos following recognition of alienation from grace, each reaffirms in its own way the optimistic futurity of *historia,* the *Sponsus* by symbolizing the correct alternative to exclusion from the Bridegroom's presence, the *Jeu d'Adam* by Adam's anachronistic allusions to an eventual Redeemer and the inchoate redemptive cyclicity suggested by the *Ordo prophetarum.*[11] As for the Passion, since its narrative recounts *the* reversal and *the* crucial recognition within the global context of *historia,* the pattern is fully in evidence in plays depicting all or part of this tradition, beginning with the fragmentary Anglo-Norman *Seincte Resurreccion* and culminating in the vast biblical cycles dating from the fifteenth century. The relatively late emergence of French Passion plays is anticipated by a long tradition of vernacular narratives, both of which affectively humanize gospel sources.[12] In the first-known of the vernacular Passion plays, the *Passion du Palatinus* (ca. 1300), the first half portrays events leading to the crucifixion, with the lengthy *planctus* of Mary and John at the foot of the Cross marking the center of the work. The second half moves from this scene of pathos to conventional moments of reversal—highlighted by the terrified guards as the tomb opens from within—and recognition. The latter features the three Marys' visit to a merchant of unguents and to the empty sepulchre where they learn of the resurrection, in emulation of precedents in the *Quem quaeritis* and *Visitatio sepulchri* traditions.[13] An ingenuously human Mary Magdalen, introduced early in the play, follows her recognition of the risen Christ with a final homiletic appeal to the audience to share in her prayer for righteousness and redemption. Despite the vernacular Passion play's frequent antagonism toward gospel and liturgical traditions, a sense of theological integrity is never wholly subverted.[14] To a considerable degree, this is maintained by retention of the same affective and cognitive rhythms already established in the liturgical tradition, with its emphasis on the positive outcome of reversal and recognition.

This continuity is further emphasized by a relatively consistent development of the theme of judgment. In tragic recognition, judgment brings a sudden awareness of the inevitability of a previously implausible situation.[15] At this moment of *veridiction,* or discovery of the "truth" as signified by the discourse, the tragic subject's formulation of a judgment sets him apart from all other parties, including the spectator. The latter's fear gives way to pity as the force of judgment is discovered and valorized by the subject.[16] In contrast, recognitions contextualized by the jubilatory teleology of *historia* achieve what could be called a "textuality of crisis" in three senses of this term. Within the subject, the cognitive severance (Gr. "krinein") from one order of knowledge stems from a veridictory judgment (Gr. "krisis") espousing the opposing order, the latter being qualified as a further affirmation of the New Law, founded by the pivotal crisis in salvation history.[17] Although this type of recognition is valorized in terms of its conformity with the operations of a divine plan moving inexorably through time, judgment is not depicted merely as the legacy of a transcendental agency communicated from on high by figures of veridiction, such as portents, dreams, visions, prophets, angels, and so on. As in tragic recognition, judgment occurs at the moment where the veridictory process is internalized. In diametrical contrast with tragic anagnorisis, however, ecclesiological recognition moves the dramatic subject from a previously eccentric cognitive position into sponsorship of a communal "re-cognition" of sacred verities. The spectator is invited to acknowledge the integrative perspective that has crystallized around the subject. Toward this end, the con-celebratory *Te Deum laudamus,* frequently sung at the end of the representation, seeks to neutralize all dissociation between the final affirmation of the play and the cognitive position of the spectator.

The comprehensive textuality of ecclesiological drama, whereby a cognitive crisis mediates a long dysphoric development and its compensatory, meliorative sequel, thus reconfigures and evokes, either as subject or as theme, the global morphology of *historia,* in which recognition and crisis also coincide.[18] One might well ask whether early vernacular plays that show a greater degree of independence from ecclesiological moorings contextualize recognition any differently. That question merits a brief look at three thirteenth-century plays of Arras. The *Jeu de Saint Nicolas* of Jehan Bodel, the anonymous *Courtois d'Arras,* and the *Jeu de la feuillée* of Adam de la Halle—the plays that constitute Artesian "tavern drama" because each features one or more tavern scenes—deal respectively with a saint's miracle, a parable, and the eve of a religious festival.[19] Despite their explicitly religious associations, these plays have been viewed as evidence of an unprecedented extension of "secular" concerns in medieval vernacular drama, whether as reflections of the influence of popular culture, the emergence of an urban—and urbane—middle class, or the intergeneric literary competence of their makers. At issue here are not the multiple causes of this discursive hybridization of vernacular drama but rather its *consequences* for the cognitive dimension of dramatic discourse as an embodiment of recognition.

The *Jeu de Saint Nicolas* imaginatively adapts a legendary tradition reflected much more modestly in the *Ludus super iconia sancti nicolai,* a brief Latin school play by Hilarius, and its counterpart from the Fleury play-book, the *Iconia sancti nicolai.*[20] As in these antecedents, Bodel's play makes conversion of an unbeliever consequent upon restitution of his stolen treasure through the saint's intercession, and Vincent has emphasized the play's "discernible debt to liturgical drama, especially that of the Fleury play-book."[21] The liturgical pattern moving from pathos to gaudium through reversal and recognition could be said to persist in Bodel's play, the miracle of the restored treasure being the climactic reversal by which the pagan Roi d'Afrique recognizes the efficacy of the saint's icon and the falsity of his former idol, Tervagant.

On the other hand, this pivotal moment is no longer the exclusive nexus of veridiction and is rivaled by other cognitive positions that relativize its traditional preeminence. After correctly foretelling the imminent massacre of the Christian warriors and guaranteeing their salvation (vv. 412-23; 428-35; 466-81), an angel informs the sole survivor that his future involvement in the conversion of the pagans will be successful:

LI ANGELES

> Preudons, soies joians, n'aies nule paour,
> Mais soies bien creans ens ou vrai Sauveour
>   Et en saint Nicolai,
> Que jou de verté sai que sen secours aras;
> Le roy convertiras et ses barons metras
> Fors de leur fole loy, et si tenront le foy
> Que tienent crestïen . . . de cuer vrai croi
>   . . . saint Nicolai.
>   (vv. 550-57)

While placing the conflict of ideologies under a transcendental aegis, this prolepsis also attentuates the dramatic impact of the later scene of recognition. In fact, recognition as a spontaneous, internalized assent to veridiction is all but elided, while emphasis is instead placed on the pagan king's lingering skepticism after he has already seen the results of the miracle.

LI ROIS

Or me di, crestïens, amis,
Crois tu dont qu'il le peüst faire?
Crois tu qu'i me puist desloier?
Crois tu qu'il me puist renvoier
Mon tresor? En iés tu si fers?

LI PREUDOM

A! rois, pour coi ne seroit kieles?
Il consilla les trois pucheles,
Si resuscita les trois clers;
Je croi bien qu'il te puist venquir
Et faire te loi relenquir,
Dont te dois estre a faus tenus.
En lui sont tout bien semenchié.

LI ROIS

Preudom, il a bien commenchié,
Car mes tresors est revenus;
Assés sont li miracle apert,
Puisqu'i fait avoir che c'on pert.
Mais je n'en creïsse nului!

LI ROIS

Senescaus, que vaurroit mentirs?
En lui est mes cuers si entirs
Que jamais ne querrai autrui.
                    (vv. 1418-37)

The role of the Preudom in this scene is twofold. In the first place, the king's anaphoric interrogation of his Christian captive is not exclusively a

test of the latter's heroism of faith under extreme duress.[22] For this
nonbeliever, the unanticipated return of his treasure is as much a mysterious
and unsettling implausibility as it is a matter of elation. The testimony of the
Preudom, who is well informed concerning the saint's miraculous efficacy,
provides—for the king and his entourage as well as for the audience—an
essential component of recognition, which is a means of ascribing plausibility to that which defies rational explanation.[23] Secondly, the Preudom
serves to identify the principal object of recognition, which is not that
Nicholas is to be venerated as the patron of those whose material wealth has
been jeopardized or purloined.[24] On the contrary, the saint's restitution of
the treasure is merely one manifestation of his far more consequential power
to "vanquish" the unbeliever and make him "relinquish" his law, a feat that
even epic warfare had been powerless to perform.

     In sum, we have here a recognition that goes well beyond the depic-
tion of purely mechanical assent to the miraculous implications of material
evidence. By making the Preudom a cognitive accessory to the king's
recognition, Bodel has greatly enhanced the psychological and ethical pro-
fundity of the moment.[25] Within the context of the entire play, however, he
has inscribed the traditional climactic point of recognition into a whole
network of cognitive perspectives. At one extreme lie the absolute
transcendental revelations of the angel, at the other the involuntary, forced
apostasy of the Amiraus d'Outre le Sec Arbre (vv. 1510 ff.).[26] In addition,
the three thieves, individualized embryonically in the Fleury version, now
fill nearly half of the play with their dicing, quaffing, and quarreling, and
ultimately fail to recognize the apparition of the saint as being other than a
terrifying "preudom" (vv. 1274 ff.). In contrast with the wholesale conversion of the pagan leaders after the miracle of the statue, the anthropomorphic
presence of Saint Nicholas himself inspires fear in these denizens of the
tavern but no antidote to their recidivism. Unlike the king perplexed by the
icon, they have no figure of veridiction equivalent to the Preudom to
motivate and condition their recognition. By showing in these various episodes that assent is relative, a matter of degree, and that it must be plausibly
motivated, the play moves closer to the broad cognitive spectrum of transac-
tional realism. At the same time, however, the formerly prominent nexus of
reversal and recognition as an affirmation of a transcendental signified now
marks only one of a number of relative degrees of cognitive and spiritual
proximity to discursive truth.

Courtois d'Arras is a dramatico-narrative adaptation of the parable of the Prodigal Son (Luke XV). The most explicit reference to the biblical text comes at the end of the play, as the father sums up the significance of his son's return in terms of the scriptural antecedent:

> Damesdieus, cho dist l'Escriture,
> d'un pecheor a gregnor joie,
> *qant il se connoist et ravoie,*
> que des autres nonante nuef.
> Bien en devons tuer no buef
> De joie k'il est revenus.
> Chantons *Te Deum laudamus.*
> (vv. 658-64)

By invoking the scriptural intertext in order to qualify the joyful return of Courtois, the father serves as the veridictory mediator between the play and the audience, while the *Te Deum laudamus* further inscribes this closure into the familiar context of celebration found in earlier liturgical and vernacular religious drama. The use of *sententiae* or proverbs as *epiphenomena* to produce a synthesizing conclusion was not uncommon in medieval texts, and a similar function could be ascribed to this closing evocation of biblical discourse, which retrospectively illuminates the foregoing action.[27]

The key term here is *se connoistre.* This reflexive verb reiterates a cognitive leitmotif that recurs throughout the play and marks the stages of Courtois's initial self-delusion and subsequent reorientation. Before his departure, the lad boasts that his winnings at the gaming tables will soon multiply the sixty *sous* from his share of his father's legacy, and he belittles those who hoard their wealth:

> Petit pris avoir ferloiet;
> celui tieng jo a emploiet
> dont on puet faire son conmant:
> *a la borse me reconnois.*
> (vv. 85-88)

After losing his purse and—literally—his shirt in the tavern, he evaluates his situation quite differently: his father had been correct all along; it was his own "fol sens" that undid him (vv. 433-39). His name is now "under erasure" from his father's will (v. 440)—he will close the stable, but the horse is already gone (v. 446).[28] In sum, it is now too late to make amends: *A tart me rechonois* (v. 445). His pessimism will turn out to have been unfounded, however, for his transition from a superficial self-identification with material wealth to an inwardly generated contrition is what enables his father to forgive him:

> Ton meffait ne pris une nois,
> *de puis que tu te reconnois,*
> et que tu as le mal laissié.
>   (vv. 621-23)

This iterative play on *self*-recognition ultimately converges with the initial *non*-recognition of the world-weary, bedraggled and starving Courtois by either the father or the older brother (vv. 590 ff.). These details are in no way anticipated by the parable, in which Jesus, as narrator, simply reports the return of the Prodigal Son without dwelling on the cognitive dimension involved while supplying the recognition beforehand, as part of his own metacommentary.[29]

Recognition in narrative can be supplemented in part by elements of the "frame" created by the narrative voices within the enunciation.[30] When it does not dispense with this dimension altogether, drama necessarily internalizes it, assimilating it, as commentary or metacommentary, to the perennial present of dramatic discourse.[31] Such is the case in the opening scene of the *Jeu de la feuillée,* where Adam narrates a lengthy, bittersweet, first-person commentary on his past absorption with Maroie, declaring his profound "disenchantment" with her and his intention to resume his studies in Paris (vv. 1-174). In defiance of the narrative logic of Aristotelian anagnorisis as a direct consequence of the action, Adam's recognition actually *precedes* the beginning of the play, and he now recounts to his companions the phases of this pre-diegetic discovery as part of his *congé,* or leave-taking, from Arras. Cave has suggested that "the precondition of recognition is cognitive error in the form of a kind of misreading." While "an initial error (hamartia) constitutes the fiction," recognition may involve "the exposure of the fallacy, the figure of a 'correct' reading . . ."[32] The protagonists of Artesian plays are preeminently misreaders, whether it be of the oracular prognostications of a Tervagant or of the tavern's decor as a blessed sanctuary of abundance (*Courtois,* vv. 114 ff.). The same is true of

Adam, as we learn from his clerkly "before-and-after" portrait of Maroie (vv. 81-174). The featured verb is *sanler,* occurring more than half a dozen times, first causatively—

> Mais Amours si le gent enoint
> Et cascune grasse enlumine
> En feme et *fait sanler* plus grande,
> Si c'on cuide d'une truande
> Bien ke che soit une roïne.
>
> (vv. 82-86)

—then in the imperfect (vv. 87, 100, 177, *passim*), through a long catalogue of physical features comprising the alluring "semblance" that held him spellbound. In his ecstasy, moreover, he had lost touch with his own selfhood:

> Et plus et plus fui en ardeur
> Pour s'amour *et mains me connui* . . .
>
> (vv. 161-62)

Finally the spell was broken:

> Car faitures n'ot pas si beles
> Comme Amours les me *fist sanler* . . .
>
> (vv. 167-68)

Having recognized the love-induced illusion for what it was, Adam now desires to avoid creating further local bondage for himself through procreation with his formerly winsome spouse and, at this early juncture in the play, says he will return to a Parisian life of the mind. *"S'est drois ke je me reconnoisse,"* he concludes (v. 171), in a manner reminiscent of Courtois at the onset of his recognition.[33]

While recognition unconventionally precedes—rather than developing logically from—the action, no clearly discernible action ensues, so that the balance of the play gives an appearance of being the inconsequential aftermath of recognition. Various ostensible figures of veridiction appear— the father, the physician, the monk, the fool, the three fairies, Fortune's wheel, and so on, yet each is less than promising as a potential accessory to

Adam's fulfillment of his scholarly vow. This secular *ordo* of inconclusive prophets leads finally to the tavern, which seems further emblematic of Adam's bondage to Arras. Like the protagonist in the *Jeu d'Adam,* this Adam bears the scars of his past transgression, but unlike his counterpart in the mystery, there is no prospect of a redeemer, least of all in the pathetic figure of the father. Though auspicious in the cognitive dimension, recognition opens onto ambiguity: are we to infer that Adam's insight will ensure his departure, or is it merely the inert product of an acknowledged need to escape the deleterious influence of Arras, vitiated by cynicism and an epidemic of avarice?[34] The play foreshadows modern drama in which tragedy turns upon recognition about which little or nothing can be done—no healing of the Fisher King, no reinvigoration of his lands. Negative in the extreme and apparently irremediable, life in avaricious Arras resembles life in an urban Waste Land.[35]

On balance, the Artesian tavern plays considerably broaden the field of medieval dramatic recognition. All three share a dominant tendency with earlier ecclesiological drama, which is to make recognition the moment where former deviation from an orderly world view becomes apparent, revealing the need for a compensatory change of direction, to find the "right way," as it were.[36] While preference for a "(re)integrative" recognition is marked only punctually in liturgical ceremonies, in these plays it gives rise to extended rational, analytic passages emphasizing motivation, plausibility, and ethical import. The *Jeu de Saint Nicolas* exteriorizes the justification of conversion in the Preudom's interpretation of material evidence; *Courtois d'Arras* develops a gradual, phased awakening within the protagonist, initially after his fleecing in the tavern (vv. 431 ff.) and then during his long monologue in which he decides to return, despite misgivings (vv. 486 ff.). In contrast with the pagan king's reliance on an interpretive adjuvant, Courtois's self-recognition emanates entirely from his progressive self-persuasion. As in Bodel's play, however, the object of recognition is not material—the mere gain or loss of treasure—but a conceptual, ideational verity that must be formulated by rhetorical artifice rather than simply signified by tangible signs.[37] Yet the deliberative, interpretive mentation of Courtois is more fully elaborated than the relatively modest persuasive discourse of Bodel's Preudom. This is also true of Adam's rhetorically amplified portrait of Maroie, which brilliantly blends the cognitive process leading to his recognition with the conventions of courtly portraiture. All three plays thus show a far greater concern than do liturgical ceremonies or even the more representational *Jeu d'Adam* with lending plausibility to the moment of discovery by laying bare the rational processes that motivate it. All three also avoid the tendency of some earlier medieval plays to make recognition the sole, or even the primary, locus of cognitive interest. Each play studies in its own way the psychological properties of recognition, but always within a broader cognitive spectrum dominated at one end by the delusive stratagems of the tavern and at the other by the incremental disclosure of a higher, spiritual consciousness.

The prominence of the tavern in all three plays illustrates in particular how valorization of space may catalyze audience recognition. As many critics have demonstrated, Bodel meticulously observes gaming and the reckoning of tavern bills, with emphasis on the seamier aspects of this environment. In *Courtois* the tavern is again an unredeemed, delusive milieu (see vv. 144 ff.). To adapt a phrase from the parable, Courtois "wastes his substance" in the kind of bibulous living never depicted in the source as he falls victim to the deceptive strategy of the two prostitutes.[38] Although less detailed, the tavern in the *Feuillée* has taken many of its cues from its congeners. In sum, this Artesian dramatic locus—or rather *lotus*—of spiritual oblivion harbors a corrupt world of hookers and hustlers—the urban embodiments of a noncourtly kind of *oisiveté*. In each play, recognition and veridiction occur outside the purview of the tavern and in direct opposition to it. Axiologically, the tavern is a mimetic displacement of Hellmouth, displaying a similar capacity to "turn" the righteous. The convention of nonneutrality of space deeply ingrained in Latin and vernacular ecclesiological drama conditions the reception of secular space as being inherently valorized, and in these plays the negative valence of the tavern contrastively signals the positive axiology of other secular loci, such as the newly converted African court or the paternal manor.[39] Even the closing tavern scene in the *Feuillée* is in opposition with the Shrine of the Virgin and consequently prevents that play from losing its symbolic disjunction of good and evil. The tavern's negative valorization of spatiality thus helps to orient the spectator's conceptualization of value-structures inherent in the semiosis of recognition.[40]

It will be apparent from the foregoing that the relationship between early French vernacular drama, as exemplified by the Artesian plays, and the antecedent ecclesiological norms of dramatic discourse is typified more by affinity than by discontinuity where recognition is concerned. The *Jeu de Saint Nicolas* and *Courtois d'Arras* both develop reversal and recognition in the transition from pathos to gaudium, in keeping with their respective liturgical and biblical sources, and in both the moment of recognition marks the corrective displacement of a harmful or negative ethical orientation within the dramatic subject. Along with this reaffirmation of a spiritual transcendence, there is, as we have seen, a new fascination with cognitive elements that momentarily defer or distract from the pattern's elaboration without subverting it. By suspending gaudium as an internalized product of recognition within the dramatic subject, the *Jeu de la feuillée* disrupts the pattern innovatively, particularly through the ironic foreclosure provided by the figures of a pseudo-veridiction. The delusive visage of Maroie as limned by Adam, the ineffectual father, the bogus relics of Saint Acaire, the fake remedies of the physician, the dubious magic of the fairies, all are symptomatic of a weakening in the medieval dramatic sign's connotation of transcendence in this play, such that recognition itself is ultimately called into question. Yet even in this remarkably atypical early play, we are still a very long way from losing all associations whatsoever with the transcendentally governed paradigm of *historia* and the related ethical opposition it conveys as part of a "textuality of crisis." Although the sacred shrine is now decentered, perhaps even off-scene, its appeal remains sufficiently compelling to empty the tavern of its clientele.

Robert Guiette insisted that liturgical drama relies for its effectiveness, not on the value-charged spatial elements of representation, but rather on the signification of symbolic liturgical accessories, such as the Cross, clerical vestments, and ritualized protocol. He also considered the transition from the modalities of liturgical signification to those of scenic representation to be a major development in the history of medieval drama.[41] The functioning of recognition in Artesian tavern drama would suggest that, as this transition slowly developed, there was no revolutionary rejection of the signifying norms of ecclesiological drama. Instead, as the foregoing discussion has indicated, these norms often served as the nuclei of representations that gave them renewed prominence by defamiliarizing them. Elsewhere I have suggested that in medieval *veridictory drama* "conditions of signification connote their equivalence to conditions of truth, both as a discourse-specific criterion and as a cultural value."[42] If one can atttribute the origin of medieval veridictory drama, in this double sense, to "the medieval Church and its rituals, which are veridictory of a mythopoeic, transcendental order,"[43] one must also acknowledge the persistent influence of these factors even as representational norms began to take shape.

The future of criticism devoted to medieval drama depends on its ability to delineate the ways in which playwrights began to explore the arbitrary nature of sign-functions, through exploitation of the breach between signifier and signified and development of the myriad possibilities for dramatizing, in interpretive behavior, the consistent risk—as well as the incomparable pleasure—of misreading. The study of recognition, adumbrated here within a limited but important corpus, is but one of many viable means of examining medieval drama's reluctant farewell to its ecclesiological affinities.

Notes

[1] See William F. Boggess, "Aristotle's *Poetics* in the Fourteenth Century," *Studies in Philology*, 67 (1970), 278-94. Citations of the *Poetics* are from the translation by S. H. Butcher, ed. F. Fergusson (New York: Harper, 1961), with reference to chapter numbers only.

[2] See Tony Hunt, "The Dialectic of *Yvain*," *Modern Language Review*, 72 (1977), 285-99, and "Aristotle, Dialectic, and Courtly Literature," *Viator*, 10 (1979), 96-102; Eugene Vance, *From Topic to Tale: Logic and Narrativity in the Middle Ages* (Minneapolis: Univ. of Minnesota Press, 1987); and my "Opérations cognitives et scandales romanesques" in *Farai chansonete novele: Essais sur la liberté créatrice (XIIe-XIIIe siècles)* [Mélanges J.-Ch. Payen] (Caen: Université de Caen, 1989).

[3] In addition to Boggess, see O. B. Hardison, Jr., "The Place of Averroes' Commentary on the *Poetics* in the History of Medieval Criticism," *Medieval and Renaissance Studies*, 4 (1970), 57-81; Judson Boyce Allen, "Hermann the German's Averroistic Aristotle and Medieval Poetic Theory," *Mosaic*, 9 (1976), 67-81; H. A. Kelly, "Aristotle-Averroes-Alemannus on Tragedy: The Influence of the *Poetics* on the Latin Middle Ages," *Viator*, 10 (1979), 161-209.

[4] Terence Cave, "Recognition and the Reader," *Comparative Criticism: A Yearbook*, ed. E. S. Shafer, vol. 2 (1980), pp. 49-69, sp. p. 50.

[5] I use the term "proto-scripture" mindful of the problematic of "écriture" and "archi-écriture" developed at length by Jacques Derrida, in *De la grammatologie* (Paris: Seuil, 1967).

[6] A. J. Greimas and Joseph Courtés, "The Cognitive Dimension of Narrative Discourse," *New Literary History*, 7 (1976), 433-47, sp. p. 440; see also, by Greimas, "The Veridiction Contract," *New Literary History* (forthcoming).

[7] O. B. Hardison, Jr., *Christian Rite and Christian Drama in the Middle Ages* (Baltimore: The Johns Hopkins Univ. Press, 1965), p. 40.

[8] The issue of affectivity and reception here becomes pertinent on a comparative basis. In the *Poetics*, tragedy entails release of pity and fear. See Gerald Else, *Aristotle's Poetics: The Argument* (Cambridge, Mass.: Howard Univ. Press, 1957), pp. 225 ff., and 433 ff. This doctrine was highly controversial during and after the Renaissance. See Baxter Hathaway, *The Age of Criticism* (Ithaca: Cornell Univ. Press, 1962), pp. 214 ff. According to Kathy Eden, "Aristotelian literary theory and Christian ethics share their concern with the same two emotions. . . . The transmission of fear and pity into Christian poetic theory and practice indirectly through Christian ethics, rather than directly through the domination of Aristotle's authority on literary matters, points to an even more profound continuity in the Aristotelian tradition. Even without the argument of the *Poetics*, fiction continues to share its peculiar psychology with the law and in particular with the relation between the Old and New Law." *Poetic and Legal Fiction in*

the Aristotelian Tradition (Princeton: Princeton Univ. Press, 1986), pp. 155-56; cf. p. 60n.

[9]See Johann Drumbl, *Quem Quaeritis: Teatro sacro dell'alto medioevo* (Rome: Bulzoni, 1981).

[10]See Karl Young, *The Drama of the Medieval Church*, 2 vols. (Oxford: The Clarendon Press, 1933), for texts of the *Quem quaeritis* tropes, plays from the Fleury collection, and other liturgical and semiliturgical texts.

[11]Larry S. Crist emphasizes contrasts between prospective elements in the *Jeu d'Adam* as opposed to the depictions of the Fall in later Passion plays, in "La Chute de l'homme sur la scène dans la France du XIIᵉ et du XVᵉ siècle," *Romania*, 99 (1978), 207-19.

[12]The earliest of these is a Franco-Provençal narrative known as the Clermont-Ferrand *Passion* (late eleventh century), recently analyzed by Stephen G. Nichols, Jr., in *Romanesque Signs: Early Medieval Narrative and Iconography* (New Haven & London: Yale Univ. Press, 1983), ch. 3. The nascent vernacular Passion play takes its cue from the twelfth-century *Passion des jongleurs*.

[13]Cf. this French Passion and the *Visitatio sepulchri* of Vich (Young, I, pp. 678-81), where the *Quem quaeritis* comes at the end of a lengthy development involving a Mercator and three individualized Marys. See also Drumbl, "Il genere e la storia. Appunti sulla tradizione drammatica nell'alto medioevo," *Teatro e Storia*, 3 (1987), 205-49, sp. pp. 230 ff.; on the amplification of the *Quem quaeritis* in the *Visitatio* ceremonies, see Hardison, p. 244.

[14]See my "1300—The *Passion du Palatinus* and Medieval Vernacular Drama," in *A New History of French Literature*, ed. Denis Hollier (Cambridge, Mass.: Harvard Univ. Press, 1989). See also Rainer Warning, "On the Alterity of Medieval Religious Drama," *New Literary History*, 10 (1979), 265-92, and his *Funktion und Struktur. Die Ambivalenzen des geistlichen Spiels* (Munich: Fink, 1974).

[15]The relationship between Aristotelian anagnorisis and forensic persuasion has been delineated by Eden, pp. 7 ff.

[16]Ibid., p. 61.

[17]Cf. my "The Semiosis of Assimilatio in Medieval Models of Time," *Style*, 20 (1986), 252-71.

[18]This temporal pattern is obviously the vehicle of an ethical bipartition. The latter has been likened to two types of imitation contrasted in Augustinian ethics: *imitatio Dei* and *imitatio Christi*, the latter substituting a model of Christian virtue for the former's malignant valorization of omnipotence. According to Eden, early Christian drama retains "in its own fashion the Aristotelian definition of tragedy as an imitation of action, the *imitatio Christi* and *Dei* [being] eventually converted to a dramatic . . . image inheriting the qualities of its ethical counterpart. Even without the theoretical instruction of the *Poetics*, . . . early Christian drama represents images of fear and pity; mystery play, morality, early *de casibus* tragedy all imitate dramatically the actions of these two

ethical types, usually in opposition to one another" (*Poetic and Legal Fiction*, pp. 124-41, cit. p. 139). For Augustine on the two types of imitation, see *De Trinitate*, 11.5.8 and the *Confessions*, 2.6.

[19]Reference is to the following editions: Jehan Bodel, *Le Jeu de Saint Nicolas*, ed. Albert Henry (Geneva: Droz, 1981); *Courtois d'Arras, Jeu du XIIIe siècle*, ed. Edmond Faral (Paris: Champion, 1980); Adam le Bossu, *Le Jeu de la feuillée*, ed. Ernest Langlois (Paris: Champion, 1978).

[20]For the texts, see Young, vol. 2.

[21]Patrick R. Vincent, *The 'Jeu de Saint Nicolas' of Jean Bodel of Arras, A Literary Analysis* (Baltimore: The Johns Hopkins Univ. Press, 1954), p. 377.

[22]This question is taken up by Michel Zink, "Le *Jeu de Saint Nicolas* de Jean Bodel, drame spirituel," *Romania*, 99 (1978), 31-46.

[23]On tragedy, plausibility, and the reader, see Cave, p. 55.

[24]The play's potential appeal to a middle-class audience is weighed by Tony Hunt, "A Note on the Ideology of Jean Bodel's *Jeu de Saint Nicolas*," *Studi Francesi*, 20 (1976), 67-72.

[25]In the context of Eden's observations concerning the *Poetics* as clarified by the *Rhetoric*, this recognition scene conforms to the type of dramatic discovery preferred by Aristotle. While in the *Rhetoric* he upholds forensic argumentation in preference to purely material evidence, in the *Poetics* he places recognitions combining persuasive artifice and inartificial signs above those featuring only the latter. *Poetic and Legal Fiction*, pp. 7-24.

[26]On this character see C. Horton, "The Role of the Emir d'Outre l'Arbre Sec in Jean Bodel's *Jeu de Saint Nicolas*," *Australian Journal of French Studies*, 14 (1977), 3-31.

[27]Paul Zumthor, "L'Epiphonème proverbial," *Revue des Sciences Humaines*, 41 (1976), 321-28; Hans Robert Jauss, "The Alterity and Modernity of Medieval Literature," *New Literary History*, 10 (1979), 218.

[28]On the interpretation of this proverbial utterance, see the nonetheless debatable conclusions of Knud Togeby, "Courtois d'Arras," in *Melanges Imbs, Travaux de Linguistique et de Littérature*, 11 (1973), 610.

[29]Citing the reflexive usage of *reconnoistre*, Charles Mela identifies the theme of self-recognition—"se ressaisir, revenir à soi après un égarement"—as the "principal theme" of the play. See *Blanchefleur et le saint homme, ou la semblance des reliques* (Paris: Seuil, 1979), pp. 85-86.

[30]John L. Grigsby, "The Narrator in *Partonopeu de Blois, Le Bel Inconnu*, and *Joufroi de Poitiers*," *Romance Philology*, 21 (1968), 536-43, and "Narrative Voices in Chrétien de Troyes, A Prolegomenon to Dissection," *Romance Philology*, 32 (1979), 261-73.

[31]Cf. Cesare Segre, *Teatro e romanzo: Due tipi di communicazione letteraria* (Turin: Einaudi, 1984), pp. 3-26.

[32]"Recognition and the Reader," pp. 65; 55.

[33]Noting the recurrence of *se reconnoistre* in this play, Mela maintains that it borrows its main theme—"the return to reason"—from *Courtois*. See *Blanchefleur,* pp. 98-99.

[34]The play's ambiguity is best reflected in the divergent interpretations by modern readers. Many critics have emphasized the failure of Adam's resolve from sporadic evidence that he will remain in Arras. Other interpretations have nuanced this view, recent contributions being those by Mela, pp. 116-22; Alexandre Leupin, "Le reasassement: sur le *Jeu de la feuillée* d'Adam de la Halle," *Le Moyen Age,* 93 (1983), 240-70; and Eugene Vance, "The Apple and the Feather," in *Mervelous Signals: Poetics and Sign Theory in the Middle Ages* (Lincoln, Nebr.: Univ. of Nebraska Press, 1986).

[35]On the other hand, the closing evocation of the bells of Saint Nicholas signaling the beginning of the festival venerating the shrine of the Virgin (cf. vv. 1077-80 and 1098-99) introduces, within the collectivity if not explicitly within the protagonist, a spiritual resonance. Cf. Mela, p. 122.

[36]This finds expression in such verbs as *avoier* and *ravoier,* as well as in Adam's identification of a "salutary" itinerary. (*JSN,* vv. 522, 1288; *CA,* v. 660; *JF,* v. 12).

[37]Whence in both plays a preference for a type of recognition considered by Aristotle to be superior to those stemming from inartificial devices. Cf. Eden, p. 20, and note 22 above.

[38]On the theme of the *gage* in *Courtois,* see Togeby, p. 609.

[39]On the signification of space in ecclesiological dramatic contexts, see Elie Königson, *L'Espace théatral médiéval* (Paris: CNRS, 1975).

[40]For related views, see Paul Verhuyck and A. Vermeer-Meyer, "La plus ancienne scène française," *Romania,* 100 (1979), 402-12, and my *Semiotics of Deceit: The Pathelin Era* (Lewisburg, Pa.: Bucknell Univ. Press, 1984), ch. 9.

[41]"Réflexions sur le drame liturgique," *Mélanges René Crozet* (Poitiers: C.E.S.C.M., 1966), I, 197-202.

[42]*Semiotics of Deceit,* p. 151.

[43]Ibid., p. 153.

Old French *nöer* (var. *naër*) 'to swim' and Its Congeners

Yakov Malkiel

The many uses that medieval French made of its oft-attested verb *nöer* 'to swim,' as well as of its variants, of its homonym *nöer* 'to knot, tie,' and of a whole phalanx of derivatives can be comfortably studied at present with the help of several carefully organized columns in Volume VI of Tobler-Lommatzsch's *Altfranzösisches Wörterbuch*.[1] In addition to the usual residue of philologically relevant questions, the rise and fall of that verb, almost entirely overlaid even in dialect speech at present, raises two important issues that a practitioner of historical linguistics must heed. The first has to some extent been answered, although some facets of the difficulty remain unsolved: There exists a basic agreement among authoritative scholars as to the reason for the decline and eventual extinction of *nöer*— namely its homonymic conflict with *no(u)er* 'to knot, tie, bind,' traceable to an entirely different source, namely **n ō d ā r e**, as against **n a t ā r e**.[2] The proponents of this hypothesis have not yet made it clear, however, why the verb for 'knotting' won out over its counterpart, namely the verb for 'swimming', nor is it entirely clear why the two homonyms could not be contextually distinguished and thus allowed to coexist peacefully, as in the parallel instance of Fr. *louer₁* 'to praise' < **l a u d ā r e** alongside its rival *louer₂* 'to rent' < **l o c ā r e**. Of course, there remains no further doubt about the eventual substitution of *nag(i)er,* originally 'to navigate,' 'to row,' for allegedly endangered *nöer* > *nouer*.

There prevails no unanimity of critical opinion, however, on the coinage, in provincial Folk Latin, of the by-form ***n ŏ t ā r e** which, apparently, underlies OFr. *nöer* and seems to have branched off from the adequately recorded standard form **n ă t ā r e;** as if to make things even more complicated, the classical form has likewise been transmitted into certain Romance vernaculars, witness Ptg. Sp. Prov. *nadar,* with a meager representation in Old French, too, judging from the sparingly recorded var. *näer.* Conversely, the area of ***n o t ā r e** transcends the territory of northern Gaul by a wide margin, as is immediately recognizable from It. (Tusc.) *nuotare.* Here, the discrepancy among the opinions of leading experts is alarmingly wide; suffice it to mention the fact that Wilhelm Meyer-Lübke, in perhaps the most stimulating if not most polished of his writings, suggested the remote possibility of some unidentified lexical blend; Ernst Gamillscheg, after decades of intensive thinking, preferred not to voice his opinion in a context clamoring for his decision; while Walther von Wartburg, repeatedly in the course of his "best years," came up with a conjecture of vowel dissimilation that simply makes little sense, as will be shown here at some length. This paper will advocate a radically different conjecture.[3]

The first problem here outlined concerns Old French viewed in isolation, although it is not lacking in implications for a future revised theory of the resolution of homonymic tensions and conflicts, which enters into the concerns and responsibilities of general linguistics. The second problem visibly transcends the realm of Old French, abounding in pan-Romanic dimensions, even though one is at liberty to stress somewhat more heavily the Old French material, for practical considerations. We shall start the more circumstantial part of our discussion with an analysis of VLat. ***n ŏ t ā r e** as an offshoot of Class. **n ă t ā r e.**

II.

As early as the middle of the past century it was perfectly clear to Friedrich Diez that, judging from the limited corpus of data available to him, there must have sprung into existence in Folk Latin, side by side with Class. **n ă t ā r e** 'to swim,' a by-form ***n ŏ t ā r e** unrecorded in the texts.[4] His slim evidence included OFr. *noer,* which he bracketed with It. *notare/nuoto;* with "Churwälsch" (i. e., Western Rhaeto-Romance, as spoken in the Swiss canton of Graubünden or Grisons) *nudar,* and with "Walachian" (i. e., Rumanian) *innotà,* an odd spelling for mod. *înotă.*[5] Diez was also aware of the existence of *not* in Albanian, which by implication he traced to the Latin strain of that language; he inferred from the pattern of geographic scattering the strikingly early rise ("uralt") of the baffling variant and invoked a plebeian or vernacular ("volksmäßig") coarsening ("Vergröberung") of the short *a*—a concept alien to modern linguistics.

The thrust of the efforts of his immediate successors was directed toward the approximate dating of the shift and, especially, toward the territorial delimitation of **n ă t ā r e** and ***n ŏ t ā r e** at the Romance level. In the late sixties, Hugo Schuchardt, in elaborating on his distinguished Bonn dissertation, spoke of a very early change ("sehr früh"), replaced "coarsening" by "darkening" of the vowel, and once more bracketed OFr. *noer* with the cognate languages already referred to by Diez.[6] Approximately twenty years later, Gustav Gröber produced the first tentative classification of the two branches: Classical **n ă t ā r e,** he argued persuasively, was represented by Sard. *nadare,* Sp. Ptg. *nadar,* OProv. *nadar,* and Neap. *natare;* conversely, OFr. *noer* was in the company not only of the four languages previously cited, but also of North Italian dialect speech, witness *nodà* in Bergamo and Milan.[7]

The following year, almost exactly a century ago, Wilhelm Meyer [-Lübke] turned his attention to the elusive problem, at first in collaboration with Francesco D'Ovidio,[8] later entirely on his own. The issue kept him busy for roughly a half-century, and in the process of revising his assessment he refined several statements made by his predecessors in reference to the respective areas occupied by the two rival types. Thus, a propos the closest congeners of OFr. *noer,* he made it clear that, within the Rhaeto-Romance domain, the Engadine Valley must be credited with *noder,* while Friulano displays *nodò.* Southern French, he discovered, is self-contradictory, with OProv. *nadar* joining Catalan, Spanish, and Portuguese, while certain modern patois (Dordogne, Haute Vienne) gravitate toward the original *langue d'oïl* preference (eventually overlaid by *nager*). While there was some measurable progress, at least, along that line, Meyer-Lübke's initial explicative attempt (undertaken, I repeat, in collaboration with D'Ovidio) apparently led nowhere, since by 1911 he himself bluntly declared: "Die -*o*-Form ist nicht erklärt," an eloquent admission of defeat.[9] Meyer-Lübke, at least, had the consolation of seeing that some of his former students and junior associates, in his lifetime, were pushing forward the discussion of the question, albeit merely along certain by-paths.[10]

The situation deteriorated dramatically where scholars have taken it upon themselves to identify the cause of the **n ă -** > ***n ŏ -** shift. Most of these aberrations Meyer-Lübke—in the end, an agnostic in this respect—

castigated mercilessly in §5846 of the revised version of his dictionary; but the participants in the debate also lashed out against one another in the free-for-all, with Peter (later Petar) Skok probably scoring best in ridiculing his rivals. D'Ovidio's and Puşcariu's heresies have already been parenthetically identified, above; in criticizing the eccentricity of **n a u t ā r e**, Meyer-Lübke, once a cosponsor of that thesis, in 1930-35 argued that even **n ŏ t a t** might have sufficed to have produced OFr. *no(u)e,* referring readers to his grammar.[11] F. Settegast toyed with a blend of **n ā t ā r e** and frequentative **m ō t ā r e** 'to move up and down,' adding for good measure a bit of influence from **m ŏ v ē r e**.[12] C. Merlo indirectly strengthened the position of the **n a -** branch by devising, out of whole cloth, the var. ***n a t i ā r e**, which, he argued, by way of alliance with the suffix **- i c ā r e**, gave rise to It. dial. *nazziká* and vars. 'to rock, dandle.'[13] P. Skok, starting from the correct premise that ***n ŏ t ā r e** must be old, i. e., pre-Romance, went too far by positing a pre-Latin form, operating with Indo-European reconstruction (point of departure: *SNO-T, as in Greek νότιος, in preference to *SNə-T.[14] R. Haberl visualized the process as, basically, another instance of vowel dissimilation at a distance, rashly bracketing OFr. *nöer* with *Noël* 'Christmas' < **n ā t ā l e,** *dommage* 'damage,' and *malotru* 'coarse, ill-bred, uncouth,' lit. 'born under an unlucky star.'[15] In the end, among scholars of that generation it was E. Schwan and D. Behrens who acted most judiciously by stopping at the point where they could project **n ă -** > ***n ŏ-** onto the level of Romanized Gaul.[16]

Since Haberl's thinking—absorbed either directly or via a detour, namely, through Meyer-Lübke's historical grammar of French (§228), of 1913 vintage—indirectly underlies W. von Wartburg's analysis, as proffered, again and again, at the very least between 1950 and 1968, it deserves much closer attention than the other hypotheses, half-forgotten by now. Of the five lexical items adduced, including the anthroponym **N o t a l i s** (on record since the eighth century), two are entirely inadmissible: *dommage,* accompanied by *dé-, en-dommager,* involves, as von Wartburg was the first to admit elsewhere, a blend of OFr. *damage* (as preserved in English) and *dongier* 'danger' and is, in consequence, as accurately traceable to **d o m i n u s** 'master' as it is to **d a m n u m** 'damage' and its Oïl reflex *dam.* What *malotru,* matching OProv. *malastru* and stemming from **m a l ĕ + a s t r u m + ū c u** (lit. 'born under an unlucky star'),[17] is expected to accomplish by way of exemplifying the schema of vowel dissimilation at a distance under study (*a—a > oa*) is not readily understandable. Finally, **n ă t ā r e** > OFr. *noer,* **n ā t ā l e** > *Noël,* and **N ā -** > post-Cl. Lat. **N ō - t ā l i s** indeed do belong together, exemplifying the Late Lat. confusion of **n ă t -** 'swimming' and **n ā t -** 'being born' (from **n ā s c ī**), of which more anon; but precisely on account of that close tie it would be circular and counterproductive to appeal to one of these formations in an effort to explain another member of the triad. What, conversely, might have been of help would be the availability of other Latin verbs in **- ā r e** truly comparable to **n a t ā r e** in structure and exhibiting the same pattern of vowel treatment. Unfortunately for R. Haberl and his late follower W. von Wartburg, the few verbs falling under this rubric show no tendency whatever to undergo such treatment: **b a t ā r e** 'to be open-mouthed' yielded OFr. *baer, beer* (cf. mod. *bayer aux corneilles, bouche-bée*); **p a r ā r e** 'to prepare, arrange' reappears as *parer,* even to the extent that it is not an Italianism; *ramer* 'to row,' rather than some verb based on **rom-,* involves a local blend of the **r ē m -** and the **r ā m -** families; all of which makes Haberl's conjecture untenable.

Because OFr. *noer* is, typologically (and, one is tempted to assume, also genetically), so closely akin to It. *nuotare,* one feels in this instance duty-bound to scrutinize the results of fairly recent research conducted by Italianists with considerable élan. Among authors of dictionaries, Bruno Migliorini (in collaboration with Aldo Duro), judicious as usual, remarks in a skeptical vein: "*Nuotare* . . . con alterazione non bene spiegata della vocale."[18] Giacomo Devoto, in sharp contrast, envisages a blend in Vulgar Latin of Class. **n ă t ā r e** with **r ŏ t ā r e** 'to turn (like a wheel).'[19] Carlo Battisti and Giovanni Alessio, with Maria Ines Martelli, invoke, not unlike von Wartburg, an old vowel dissimilation.[20] The latecomers Manlio Cortelazzo and Paolo Zolli simply place colloquial **n o t ā r e* alongside Class. **n a t ā r e.**[21] To round out the picture, one may quote Gerhard Rohlfs (cast in the role of a grammarian, for once) as joining the group of believers in the effect of vowel dissimilation; fortunately, he states his article of faith very cautiously: "Auch *a—a* scheint zur Dissimilation zu neigen, wenn auch mit verschiedenem Ergebnis." Not only do the (predominantly dialectal) instances he cites exhibit disquieting variety (among the results reached, *o—a* alternates with *e—a* and even *i—a*), but the motley material involves just a single *-are* verb and, consequently, has little, if any, bearing on the issue under investigation.

In summary, the hard-fact explorers, at least in this narrow field, have rendered present-day students a service distinctly greater than have those investigators who have indulged in unconvincing speculation. To intersperse the account with a few more names, one does not mind Jacqueline Picoche's studied silence;[23] one approves the sophisticated skepticism of a Migliorini; and one applauds the spare, if meticulous, listing of every ascertainable detail (dating, localization, etc.) by Jean Dubois and Henri Mitterand, the deft revisers of A. Dauzat's celebrated dictionary,[24] just as one admires Lommatzsch's skill in identifying—as he sailed in Tobler's wake—isolated traces of *näer* in almost solid *nöer* territory,[25] and, conversely, Meyer-Lübke's well-advised decision to point out vestiges of *n ŏ t ā r e in Southern France, an area otherwise committed to the tradition of n ă t ā r e. Italianists able to draw a fine dividing line between *notare* and *nuotare* in Tuscan have been as helpful as those who have singled out divergent Lombard and Neapolitan usage, or as Max Leopold Wagner through his discerning survey of Sardic and Corsican leanings.[26] But all of this still leaves the cause unaccounted for.

III.

Although the note that I have struck may sound a shade pessimistic, it is meant to involve an appeal to caution rather than to degenerate into a defeatist attitude. As a matter of fact, an acceptable explanatory hypothesis can, I believe, be formulated.

Insufficient stress, I am afraid, has so far been placed on a fact that presumably no one will want to dispute: the original form of the verb, to wit, n ă t ā r e, has basically been preserved by a cluster of daughter languages independently known for their lexical conservatism: those of the Iberian peninsula, Provençal, Sardic, and Southern Italian; to put it differently: the circum-Tyrrhenian languages, plus their westward prong toward the Atlantic. In territories Romanized at a later date, innovative *n ŏ t ā r e has prevailed instead. What major event of conceivable relevancy, so far as the history of spoken Latin is concerned, separates the two periods reflected in the above-mentioned geographic conditions?

The event alluded to has been familiar to generations of straight Latinists and Romance comparativists: the category of vowel quantity was given up, entailing a number of readjustments too well known to require tabulation. In particular, the contrast between long *a* and short *a,* so essential at the preceding time level, was completely abandoned.

One practical consequence of this reshuffling of the sound system was that the opposition of (a) **n ă t -,** as entering into the shape of the verb for 'swimming,' and (b) **n ā t -,** the past-participial stem of Class. **n ā s c ī** 'to be born,' was doomed to disappearance. Through a further twist of circumstances, this event coincided with a dramatic rise in numerical representation and in appeal to untutored speakers of (originally iterative) verbs in **- t ā r e / - s ā r e,** in severe competition with those in *** - t i ā r e.** With **n ă t ā r e,** all of a sudden, sounding as if it were a mere variation on **n ā s c e r e** (the form that deponential **n ā s c ī** had meanwhile assumed), speakers of Latin in newly acquired sections of the Empire where no solid tradition had meanwhile congealed may well have felt intensely uncomfortable about the collapse of **n ă t -** and **n ā t -** and the rising threat of ensuing ambiguity. So much for the disinclination of certain (geographically determined) groups of speakers to continue the long-unimpeded tradition of **n ă t ā r e.**

A question almost entirely unrelated and possibly more difficult to answer with comparable precision is the reason for the substitution of ***n ŏ t -** (in preference to, say, ***n ĕ t -** or ***n ĭ t -**) for semantically endangered **n ă t -.** The closest that we can, at present, expect to come to solving it is to remind ourselves that, in the centuries marking the transition from Late Latin to incipient Romance, a whole range of characteristic back vowels (Ŏ, Ō, Ŭ, Ū) entering into the stressed, free core syllables of words —more frequently, it is true, nouns than verbs—such as **n ō d u s** 'knot,' **n ū d u s** 'naked,' **n ŭ p t i a e** 'wedding,' **n ŭ r u s / *n ŭ r a** 'daughter-in-law,' **n ū t r ī r e** 'to nourish' (and **n ū t r ī x** 'wet nurse'), plus **n ŭ x** '(w)alnut,' have shown a striking degree of instability. Conceivably, a matter of sheer chance or coincidence was involved in this striking display of wavering, with N- invariably acting as a sort of common denominator. Thus, the switch from **n ū t r ī r e** to ***n ŭ t r ī r e,** which clearly underlies Fr. *nourrir* (cf. *nourrice*), OSp. *nodrecer* (cf. *nodriza*), etc. might well have been triggered by the verb's almost exact semantic opposite **p ŭ t r ī r e** for older **p ū t ē r e** 'to rot' alongside **p ŭ t e r** 'rotten.' Similarly, the pressure of **s ŏ c r u s,** V. Lat. **s ŏ c (e) r a** 'mother-in-law' could have transmuted **n ŭ r u s, - a** into ***n ŏ r a** (cf. OFr. *nuire* beside Gmc. *bru* and propitiatory *belle-fille,* It. *nuora,* Sp. *nuera,* etc.).[27] Whatever the concatenation of events, the protracted instability of several Romance words sharing *no-* or *nu-* as their usually stressed opening syllable could readily have suggested *n ŏ t a t '(s)he swims' as a substitute for awkwardly sounding n ă t a t.

Yet, despite the substantially narrowed range of possible remedial actions, there still remains the lingering uncertainty as to why speakers, in certain areas, deflected the verb for 'swimming' from its traditional course in the direction of *n ŏ - rather than, say, *n ō -, *n ŭ - , o r *n ū - t ā r e. Was the back vowel pressed into action to achieve that goal, by any chance, randomly chosen? Even though one must still work with a lacunary corpus of data and a far from complete ensemble of explicative hypotheses, it has nevertheless, of late, become clear that the imagerially understandable interplay of ē n ō d ā t u s and d ē n ū d ā t u s made it possible, in certain Romance offshoots of Latin, for n ō d u s to evolve into n ū d u s; that a specific case of lexical polarization, as explained, dragged n ū t r ī r e into the orbit of *n ŭ t r ī r e; but that n ŭ r a > n ŏ r a (a change, we recall, sparked by s ŏ c r u s) not only affected, presumably in close alliance with *n ŏ v i a 'bride,' the shape of n ŭ p t i a e, where semantic proximity could indeed have been operative (cf. Fr. *noces,* already medieval, and It. *nozze* < *n ŏ p t i a e), but also influenced n ŭ c e 'walnut' > *n ŏ c e, inferrable from Sp. *nuez,* Ptg. *nóz,* as well as, in a restricted territory, n ō d u 'knot' > Ast.-Leon. *nuedo, ñuedu.* To put it in broader terms, while n ŭ - and n ū - were secondarily arrived at only under a set of exceptionally favorable circumstances, with formal and semantic affinities lending mutual support, a gambit in the direc-tion of n ŏ - could be made without even any extra support from the side of content or meaning, on purely formal grounds. If this argument holds water, then the transmutation of n a t ā r e into *n o t ā r e rather than into anything else, under the peculiar set of circumstances previously expounded, indeed at long last emerges as the single fully understandable attempt at an escape from the menace of unwelcome ambiguity.

Incidentally, in the end the hazard was not completely averted. The temporary confusion of n ă t - and n ā t - in Gaul must, for a while, have been echoed by similar misunderstandings besetting n o t -; hence *Noël* 'Christmas' as against It. *Natale,* Ptg. (learnèd) *Natal,* etc.

IV.

To revert to the decline and eventual extinction of OFr. *nöer* 'to swim' in consequence of its protracted rivalry with *no(u)er* 'to knot, tie, bind': this oft-adduced explanation, however seductive, stands a chance of becoming truly persuasive, we recall, only after its advocates have demonstrated the superior strength of the descendant of **n ō d ā r e** over its assumed homonymic rival in this conflict, namely **n ă t ā r e**. Such proof, to the best of my knowledge, has not so far been presented by the various spokesmen for this otherwise attractive thesis.

To the extent that one can depend in such matters on the testimony of elaborate dictionary entries,[29] the verb for 'knotting, tying' was not used many times more frequently than its counterpart referring to 'swimming'; nor can it be claimed that the one was distinctly superior to the other as regards the numbers of derivational offshoots, whether suffixal or postverbal; as a matter of fact, if one discounts the dimension of incidence, it would seem that a higher number of lexical items had branched off, in Gallo-Latin, from the **n ă t -** than from the **n ō d -** nucleus (consider *noëment* 'swimming,' *nöeor* '[male] swimmer,' *nöer(r)esse* '[female] swimmer,' 'water snake,' *nöeure* 'fin,' *no* 'swimming,' comparable to Sp. *a nado*). In contrast, the relevant distinctive feature of the Old French verb for 'tying, binding' was its connection with *no, neu* 'knot' < **n ō d u**, i.e., the prototype of mod. *nœud*. That noun indeed boasted an extraordinary gamut of meanings, primary and figurative, bearing either on ropes, threads, and the like or on the tissue of a human's, or an animal's, body, including both domestic animals such as dogs, sheep, or horses, or the hunter's quarry, e.g., a stag, etc.[30] Most of the derivatives from the **n ō d -** kernel also happen to be denominal rather than deverbal: *no(i)el* 'knot, button, string, thread, thong, clasp, latch, buckle'; *nöellëiz* 'something connected';[31] *no(i)elet* '(small) knot'; *nöeillos* 'knotty, uneven, difficult to solve'; and, from there, a newly minted verb for 'tying' (used, e. g., in reference to shoes) took off: *nöeler*. It is the crushing weight of this noun *no/neu*, with which the verb *nöer* was doubtless as closely associated as are, in English, *(to) knot* with *(a) knot* and, in German, *knoten* with *Knoten*, that allowed Fr. *nouer*, at the conclusion of the Middle Ages, to emerge victorious from the contest with an otherwise equally powerful homonym as the unambiguous carrier of the meaning 'to tie.'

There is yet another vital feature of the late-medieval scene that even scholars endowed with a special flair for lexical conflicts have so far tended to overlook. Old French lexis also had a verb *noier/niier* 'to drown' (intr.), 'to send to the bottom' (tr.) which, through a subtle interplay of phonological and morphological conditions, before long developed the crucial variant *nöer*: the starting point there was ancestral **n e c ā r e** (cf. Sp. *anegar* 'to drown'). This verb was also surrounded by a number of satellites, albeit a more modest one: *noiement* 'drowning,' *nöerie* 'inundation,' *noiable* '(stretch of land) subject to flooding,' etc. Even in contexts where speakers and writers leaned toward avoiding ambiguity by clinging to *noer* for 'swimming' and to *noier* for 'drowning,' the mere proximity of these two verbs (serving to convey mutually contradictory messages) must have resulted in a major nuisance. Such a state of affairs, identifiable under the label of 'harmful near-homonymy,' independently cried out for some radical solution.

Lommatzsch quotes (s.v. *nöer* 'to swim') two particularly eloquent examples: one from G. Tilander's edition of *Les Livres du Roy Modus et de la Royne Ratio:* "Quant l'en voit le cerf aboier ou parmi un estanc *noier,*" where the stag, on contextual evidence, is portrayed as swimming rather than drowning in the pond; the other from G. *Guill:* "Les uns *noent* ['swim'], les autres *noient* ['drown'], / qui en assez poi d'eure afondent," where the line separating irreconcilable opposites in real life is phonically just too thin to have made the contemporary reader or listener feel comfortable—so far as one can venture to reconstruct the minds of past generations.[32]

Thus, toward the end of the Middle Ages the ill-fated Old French verb for 'swimming' was exposed to a sort of dual jeopardy: on the one hand, it conflicted, through full homonymy, with a verb semantically not very close, namely 'to knot, tie'; yet, on the other, it also collided, albeit—in most instances—solely on account of a state of near-homonymy, with a verb standing to it in dramatically direct semantic opposition: 'to swim [and survive]' vs. 'to drown [and perish]'. One can argue endlessly about which of these two confrontations involved the less easily bearable evil; what seems incontestable is the ensuing fact that a word placed inside such a combination of squeezes is foredoomed to perish.

Notes

[1]Adolf Tobler and Ernst Lommatzsch, *Altfranzösisches Wörterbuch*,VI (Wiesbaden: Franz Steiner, 1965), cols. 696-99; the relevant fascicle 54 appeared the year before. For *nöer* 'to knot' see cols. 699-701. There existed a third verb *nöer*, discernibly less frequent: a term of falconry; in documenting it (cols. 701-02), Lommatzsch derived it from **n ŏ t ā r e,** glossed it 'mit Flecken, Tüpfeln versehen,' and commented: 'vom Gefieder der Raubvögel.' As a noun, *nöer* functioned as a variant of *noier* 'walnut tree' (ibid., col. 706); see also fn. 32, below.

[2]**N ŏ d ā r e,** obviously, accompanied **n ŏ d u s** 'knot'; cf. Fr. *nœud/nouer*, Sp. *nudo/anudar* alongside *ñudo/añudar*, etc. Observe that, outside Gascony, the territory of France is free from the tendency—familiar to scholars from Catalan and Spanish evidence—for untutored speakers to raise the "etymological" *ŏ* of **n ŏ d u s** to an *ū*. The process must go back to Antiquity.

[3]Meyer-Lübke launched this idea, somewhat indecisively, in his *Einführung in das Studium der romanischen Sprachwissenschaft; see,* e. g., rev. 2d edn. (Heidelberg: Winter, 1909), p. 162. (To fully understand the encoded message of §153, one is well-advised to read first the preceding paragraph.) One detects not the slightest difference, on this score, between the messages conveyed by the otherwise divergent rev. 2d edn. of O. Bloch and W. von Wartburg, *Dictionnaire étymologique de la langue française* (Paris: Presses Universitaires de France, 1950), p. 405*a*, and by the 5th edn., p. 426 *ab*. Gamillscheg's statement has here been culled from the rev. 2d edn. of his *Etymologisches Wörterbuch der französischen Sprache* (Heidelberg: Winter, 1969), p. 642*b;* the original edn. of that book goes back to 1926.

[4]See F. Diez, *Etymologisches Wörterbuch der romanischen Sprachen* (Bonn: A. Marcus, 1853), pp. 240-41.

[5]Diez introduced no changes as late as the revised 3d edn. of his dictionary (1869-70), of which the concluding 5th edn. (1887) was a mere reprint. A. Scheler's appended Supplement to it contained no further information on *n ŏ t ā r e.

[6]H. Schuchardt, *Der Vokalismus des Vulgärlateins*, 3 vols. (Leipzig: B. G. Teubner, 1866-68), I, 173, 175; III, 89. The author provided evidence of scribal wavering between **n ā t u s** 'born' and **n ō t u s** 'known'; offered his share of Albanian evidence in Greek script; and culled, from MSS of the seventh to ninth centuries, sporadic instances of the graphy **n u t a u i t** for **n a t a u i t** 'swam.'

[7]"Vulgärlateinische Substrate romanischer Wörter," *Archiv für lateinische Lexikographie und Grammatik,* 4 (1887), 135, with yet another form adduced for Albanian.

[8]See their grammatical sketch "Die italienische Sprache," in G. Gröber, ed., *Grundriß der romanischen Philologie*, I (Straßburg: Karl J. Trübner, 1888), 489-560, at 501, where they characterize this process as "Entartung," i. e., 'degeneracy.'

[9]I have extracted this confession from the entry 5846 of the original edition of his *Romanisches etymologisches Wörterbuch* (Heidelberg: C. Winter, 1911-[20]). Originally, Meyer-Lübke and D'Ovidio wavered between two conjectures: either the assumption of confusion, in folk speech, of n ă t ā r e with n ŏ t ā r e 'to note,' a surmise allegedly supported by the disappearance of the latter, in its original meaning, from folk speech; or the posited rise of *n ā v i -, *n a u - t ā r e, supposedly parallel to n ā v i g ā r e 'to sail.' This is how Meyer-Lübke, in sad retrospect, by 1911 rated his 1888 *tour de force:* ". . . *n a u t ā r e wäre nur für das Französische möglich, ist aber auch hier nicht nötig, da die 3. sing. *noue* auf n ŏ t a t beruhen kann." Other noncommittal reactions by the Vienna and Bonn scholar will be found in: *Grammatik der romanischen Sprachen,* I: *Lautlehre* (Leipzig: Fues/Reisland, 1890), §274, and *Einführung. . .* , rev. 3d edn. (Heidelberg: C. Winter, 1920), p. 182, §172. In his *Historische Grammatik der französischen Sprache,* I: *Laut- und Flexionslehre,* 2d edn. (Heidelberg: C. Winter, 1913), §228, the author merely reports R. Haberl's attempt (see below) to combine the case of OFr. *nöer* with those of *Noël, dommage,* and *malotru.*

[10]Sextil Puşcariu, *Etymologisches Wörterbuch der rumänischen Sprache,* I: *Lateinisches Element* (Heidelberg: C. Winter, 1905), admitted the (older) spelling *înnot* as a variant of *înót;* cited Macedo-Rumanian *(a)not* and Italian dialect forms (e. g., Cerignolo *natä);* referred readers for details to O. Densusianu's *Histoire de la langue roumaine;* and, most important, tentatively advocated a blend of n ă t ō, -ā r e with n ō, n ā r e 'to swim, float' as the reason for the rise of *n ŏ t ā r e in folk speech. See further Matteo Bartoli, "Alle fonti del neolatino," *Miscellanea di studî in onore di Attilio Hortis* (Trieste, 1910), pp. 889-913, at 891 (an attempt to uphold the Italian nature of Istrian). Later, Bartoli reverted to the bifurcation of N Ă T Ā R E in his programmatic *Introduzione alla neolinguistica* (Genève: Olschki, 1925), p. 72.

[11]*Historische Grammatik der französischen Sprache,* I, §81: *roe* < r ŏ t a t, *loe* < l ŏ c a t, and the like.

[12]"Über einige Fälle von Wortverschmelzung (Kreuzung) im Romanischen," *ZRPh,* 37 (1913), 186-99, at 195-96. (Meyer-Lübke: ". . . ist mit dem romanischen - ọ - schwer vereinbar.")

[13]"Ital[iano] c[entro] -merid[ionale] *nnataká, nazziká* 'tentennare, barcollare, dondolarsi, cullare'," *ZRPh,* 37 (1913), 725-27. (Meyer-Lübke: "nirgends bezeugt," "bedenklich.")

[14]Zum Vulgärlatein," *Miscellanea linguistica dedicata a Hugo Schuchardt . . .* (Genève: Olschki, 1922; Bibl. dell' "Arch. Roman.," B3), pp. 126-33, at 130-31. (Meyer-Lübke: "Alter indogermanischer Ablaut?")

[15]*Zeitschrift für französische Sprache und Literatur,* 36 (1910), 302. (Meyer-Lübke: "Befriedigt auch nicht recht.")

[16]*Grammatik des Altfranzösischen,* rev. 8th edn. (Leipzig: O. R. Reisland, 1909), pp. 63, 316; noncommital as to cause.

[17]On the provenience and structural design of *malotru* see my paper, "Ancien français *faü, feü, malostru:* A la recherche de - ū c u s, suffixe latin et gallo-roman rare de la 'mauvaise fortune'," *Travaux de linguistique et de littérature,* 11: 1 (1973), 177-89 (= *Mélanges Paul Imbs*).

[18]*Prontuario etimologico della lingua italiana,* rev. 4th edn. (Torino, etc.: G. B. Paravia, 1964), s. vv. *natare* and *nuotare.*

[19]*Avviamento all' etimologia italiana: dizionario etimologico* (Firenze: Felice Le Monnier, 1966), p. 285*b,* with the remark that present-day usage has driven a wedge between monophthongized *notare* 'to record' and diphthongized *nuotare* 'to swim.'

[20]*Dizionario etimologico italiano,* 5 vols. (Firenze: Barbèra, 1950-57), IV, 2612*a.* The authors observe the continued use of *notare* for 'swimming' in contemporary substandard Italian.

[21]*Dizionario etimologico della lingua italiana* (Bologna: Zanichelli, 1983-), p. 814.

[22]*Historische Grammatik der italienischen Sprache und ihrer Mundarten,* 3 vols. (Bern: A. Francke, 1949-54), §330; see further §§14 ("besondere Fälle"), 108, 129, 538.

[23]*Nouveau dictionnaire étymologique du français* (Paris: Hachette-Tchou, 1971), s. vv. *nef* and *nœud* (pp. 452-53, 456).

[24]See the *Nouveau dictionnaire étymologique et historique,* rev. 4th edn. (Paris: Larousse, 1964, 1982), p. 486, whose search for causes wisely stops at the homonymic clash between *no(u)er*$_1$ 'nager' and *no(u)er*$_2$ 'faire un nœud.'

[25]In fairness to all parties, Lommatzsch freely admits how much his *AFW* owes to Frédéric Godefroy's *Dictionnaire de l'ancienne langue française,* V, 511*a,* to Meyer-Lübke's *REW*^{3}, and to W. von Wartburg's *FEW* (VII, 39*a*). *Näer* turns out to be conspicuously rare; where it does make its appearance, as when it is allowed to alternate with *nöer* (this is true of its use in the *Treatise of Walter of Bibblesworth,* ca. 1300, where *nager,* incidentally, stands for 'to row'), its 3. pres. ind. forms, as one would expect, are (sg.) *nëe* and (pl.) *nëent.*

[26]*Dizionario etimologico sardo,* 3 vols. (Heidelberg: Winter, [1957-64]: see II, 159*b;* the fascicle appeared in 1960). The author identified *natare* and *annatare* in the respective core dialects of Bitti and Siniscola; recorded *(an)naδare* in Logudoro (north-central) and -*ar* in Campidano (southern) while charging Sassari's preference for *annudà,* Gallura's for *nutà,* and Corsica's for *nutà, nudà* (beside *natá*) to superimposed Peninsular influence.

[27]This statement is based on the following research papers from my pen: "Trois exemples nouveaux de la 'polarisation lexicale' en roman: *nourrir* et *pourrir,*" *Romania,* 105 (1984), 411-61; "Los contactos entre las familias de n ō d u s y n ū d u s e n gascón, en catalán y en castellano," to appear in a testimonial volume in honor of Germán Colón; and "The Transmission into Romance of Latin n ō d u s, n ŭ p t i a e, n ŭ r u s, and n ŭ x: Diachronic Interplay of Phonetic and Semantic Analogies," to appear in *General Linguistics.* There is a slightly looser link between those three papers

and the following item, slated to appear in the *Nueva Revista de Filología Hispánica:* "La agonía del verbo *nozir, nuzir* 'dañar' en las postrimerías de la Edad Media española" (at issue is the descendant of **n o c ě r e**).

[28]By way of first orientation one may profitably consult Hans Rheinfelder: *Kultsprache und Profansprache in den romanischen Ländern* (Genève-Firenze: L. S. Olschki, 1933), pp. 440-43, with an important comment on the word's semantic scope.

[29]The use here of Vol. VI of Tobler-Lommatzsch's *AFW* has been the more fruitful as the younger partner in that team absorbed, with proper credit to various parties, all the bulk of the data previously assembled by Godefroy and von Wartburg.

[30]Lommatzsch's meticulous break-down of the total scale of *no/neu* into individual semantic nuances is so excellent as to deserve being quoted in full: 'Knoten,' 'Knoten zur Erinnerung,' 'Knoten am Gewande,' 'Minimalwert,' 'festes Band,' (physiol.) 'Knoten' (Mensch, Tier), 'Adamsapfel,' 'Wirbel des Rückgrats,' 'Schwanzwirbel des Hundes,' 'Knöchel am Gelenk,' 'Fleischwulst am Leibe des Pferdes,' 'Fleischstücke zwischen Hals und Schulter des erlegten Hirsches,' 'Lymphdrüsen am Hals des Hammels,' all of this in addition to idiosyncratic phraseological uses.

[31]On this derivational schema see my paper: "The Old French Verbal Abstracts in *-ëiz*," *ZRPh*, 102 (1986), 1-39.

[32]For all its apparent intricacy, the picture here pieced together in sober fact involves a gross oversimplification. I have deliberately left out *nöe* 'marshy meadow,' 'reedy river bank,' a word of Gaulish extraction; among lexical items traceable, in the last analysis, to **n ŭ x** '(wal)nut' and its derivatives, such as *noiel* 'hard core, nucleus' (cf. mod. *noyau*), let me place on record *noeloiz*, which Lommatzsch plausibly reinterprets as 'dry kernel,' positing as the standard form **noïeloiz*, while *noier ~ noer*, we recall, signify '(wal)nut tree,' cf. mod. *noisier*. Then again, there exist the genetically unrelated if homonymous verb *noiier ~ niier* 'to deny,' from **n e g ā r e** (mod. *nier*); plus *noiier ~ niier* 'to clean,' a close relative of *net* < **n ī t i d u.** See also n. 1, above.

The *Trois Savoirs* in Phillipps Manuscript 25970

Lenora D. Wolfgang

In 1908 Paul Meyer published excerpts of the Anglo-Norman poem the *Trois Savoirs* in *Romania,* 37, along with excerpts of four other works and the complete text of the two remaining works in Phillipps ms 25970.[1] In a footnote to his extracts of the *Trois Savoirs,* he says that Henri Omont, in the course of a trip to Cheltenham, had said he was willing to complete his transcription, although the *Romania* "Notice" was already in press.[2] Whether that transcription was ever made and whether Paul Meyer ever received it are not known.[3] However, as will be seen from the lines that I am presenting in this article, which will complete Paul Meyer's transcription of the *Trois Savoirs,* he undoubtedly had read the whole poem and had simply left out the passages he does not give in the "Notice," intending to publish them at some later time. Because the extracts of the *Trois Savoirs* in *Romania,* 37, do not have line numbers, and P. Meyer does not say how many lines the poem has, I have assigned the line numbers of the poem in this article. Of the 240 lines of the *Trois Savoirs,* P. Meyer gives 130: 1-14, 25-110, and 211-40. The most puzzling omission of text is in the middle of the poem, lines 111-210, where the so-called "three truths" of the title are given. In other words, the actual content of those "three truths" has been left to the reader's curiosity and imagination until now! Paul Meyer says that he had returned many times to Cheltenham to copy manuscripts, but he gives only two complete texts in his article.

The history of Phillipps 25970 is typical of the Phillipps collection in general. It had belonged to the Savile family in the sixteenth and seventeenth centuries, and it passed into the hands of Sir Thomas Phillipps at a sale in London in 1861 before the very eyes of Paul Meyer who complained with some bitterness of the inability of institutions to compete with rich collectors in the purchase of medieval manuscripts.[4] As the well-documented history by A. N. L. Munby of the formation and dispersal of the Phillipps library makes clear, Sir Thomas was not only rich but also was unscrupulous when it came to his obsession for collecting manuscripts.[5] After Sir Thomas's death in 1872 and the eventual breakup and piecemeal sales of his collection, Phillipps manuscript 25970 remained for some time in the hands of the Robinson brothers, London booksellers. It was subsequently sold, along with the remainder of the Phillipps manuscripts held by the Robinsons, to the New York bookdealer H. P. Kraus, in 1978. This sale was chronicled in the London *Times* with some of the same chagrin that had been expressed by Paul Meyer in 1861.[6]

My interest in this manuscript and in the text of the *Trois Savoirs* began as I was preparing an edition of the *Lai de l'Oiselet.*[7] The *Trois Savoirs* and a portion of the *Donnei des Amants* that is very similar to it[8] are two of the many analogues of the *Lai de l'Oiselet*. All of these poems tell a similar story and are consequently referred to in the literature, as Paul Meyer does in his "Notice," as "*Oiselet*-type" poems.[9] In turn, the "*Oiselet*-type" poems descend from two sources, exemplum no. 22 of the *Disciplina clericalis* of Petrus Alphonsi and the parable of the "*Oiselet*" in chapter ten of the Greek *Barlaam and Josaphat*.[10]

When Gaston Paris edited the *Lai de l'Oiselet* in 1884, he was unaware of the "*Oiselet*" passage in the *Donnei des Amants;* and when he edited the *Donnei* in 1896,[11] he was unaware of the poem of the *Trois Savoirs*. It was not until 1908 that Paul Meyer was able to compare these three analogous works, pointing out the close similarity of the *Trois Savoirs* and the *Donnei* and their relationship to the *Lai de l'Oiselet*.[12] Both Gaston Paris and Paul Meyer call the *Lai de l'Oiselet* an independent version of the *Disciplina* exemplum, and Gaston Paris went so far as to say that the similarities among the French "*Oiselet*-type" poems were merely "fortuites."[13] However, now that all these texts are available and can be compared, it is possible to discern a closer relationship among the French versions of the "*Oiselet*-type" poems than either Gaston Paris or Paul Meyer was in a position to realize. I reserve such a detailed comparison for elsewhere. My present purpose is to make the rest of the text of the *Trois Savoirs* available.

When I first made inquiries about the whereabouts of Phillipps 25970 (February, 1985), the general opinion was that it was "lost." The network of Phillipps manuscript watchers is a very good one, however, and concentrated effort finally unearthed it. My need of the missing parts of the poem had become acute, and my curiosity was totally aroused, since I had no other way of knowing what the "trois savoirs" actually contained in order to compare them with the corresponding passage in the *Lai de l'Oiselet*. The editors of the *Nouveau Recueil Complet des Fabliaux* had listed Phillipps 25970 in their vol. 1 (1983) and assigned it the siglum *s*, but they did not indicate the whereabouts of the manuscript.[14] An inquiry to the *IRHT* produced no answer. A letter to H. P. Kraus,[15] however, brought the prompt reply that Phillipps 25970 had been purchased from them in 1979 and was in a "private collection in this country," and they were forwarding my letter to the owner. Less than a week later a letter arrived from Princeton, informing me that the manuscript was now housed there in the Robert H. Taylor collection, where I was very welcome to come to see it any time I wished.[16]

The manuscript dates from the fourteenth century. It measures 240 x 155 mm, and contains 47 leaves. Leaves 42-47 are essentially blank, containing a scattered few lines of writing. There is one column of text to a page, 27 lines to the column. The text of the *Trois Savoirs* is on folios 22-26, numbered by Paul Meyer in pencil.[17] The *Trois Savoirs* has a large first initial "P," three lines high, decorated in blue. All the lines begin with a capital letter, and paragraph signs, decorated in red, appear at lines 25, 47, 55, 73, 81, 95, 99, 107, 117, 135, 155, 173, 195, and 205.

In order to facilitate an understanding of the poem as a whole, I include a brief summary of the portions of the text printed by Paul Meyer and a list of corrections of his transcription based on the manuscript readings. I also include a few textual notes and a brief glossary.[18]

Notes

[1]Paul Meyer, "Notice du ms. 25970 de la Bibliothèque Phillipps (Cheltenham)," *Romania,* 37 (1908), 209-35. The works published in this article are: 1. Pierre de Langtoft, three rhymed letters, translated from Latin, attributed to Pierre de Langtoft (pp. 210-12, excerpts); 2. *Les sept choses que Dieu hait* (pp. 212-15, complete text); 3. *La housse partie* (pp. 215-17, excerpts); 4. the *Trois Savoirs* (pp. 217-21, excerpts); 5. the *Doctrinal* (p. 221, excerpts); 6. *La Geste de Blancheflour et de Florence* (pp. 221-34, complete text); 7. *La lettre de l'Empereur Orgbille* (pp. 234-35, excerpts).

[2]*Ibid.,* p. 218, *n.* 5.

[3]There is no mention of such a transcription in the *Bibliographie des travaux de M. Henri Omont* (Paris, 1933).

[4]*Bibliothèque de l'Ecole des Chartes, Revue d'Erudition,* 21st year, series 5, tome 2 (Paris, 1861), "Vente des manuscrits de la Famille Savile," p. 278. The manuscript was no. 44 in the catalogue of the sale; cf. *Romania,* 37 (1908), 209-10.

[5]A. N. L. Munby, *Phillipps Studies,* 5 vols. (Cambridge: Cambridge University Press, 1951-60). An adaptation of these volumes was made by Nicolas Barker, *Portrait of an Obsession, the life of Sir Thomas Phillipps, the world's greatest book collector* (London: Constable, 1967).

[6]Friday, March 17, 1978, p. 1: "£1 m 'lucky dip' manuscripts sale: in 280 crates, some unopened." Professor Ruth J. Dean called this article to my attention. She also told me that she saw Phillipps 25970 for the first time in Cheltenham in 1933 and later in London at Messrs. Robinson, and she very kindly consented to read my transcription of it.

[7]*Le Lai de l'Oiselet, an Old French Poem of the Thirteenth Century: Edition and Critical Study* (forthcoming in the American Philosophical Society, *Transactions*).

[8]Lines 929-1160 edited by Gaston Paris, "Le Donnei des Amants," *Romania,* 25 (1896), 497- 541.

[9]P. Meyer, *Romania,* 37 (1908), 218, *n.* 5, refers to the *Trois Savoirs* as a "rédaction de l'*Oiselet*." This terminology makes for some confusion in discussions of these and other related works. I have tried to clarify such matters in the introduction to my forthcoming edition of the *Oiselet*.

[10]For an edition of the Greek *Barlaam,* see G. R. Woodward, H. Mattingly, and D. M. Lang, *St. John Damascene. Barlaam and Joasaph* (New York: Heinemann and Macmillan, 1983; Loeb Classical Library); for an edition of the *Disciplina clericalis,* see Alfons Hilka and Werner Söderhjelm, *Die Disciplina clericalis des Petrus Alfonsi* (Heidelberg: Winter, 1911).

[11]*Romania,* 25 (1896), 497-515. This poem is in Phillipps 3713, now Bodmer 82. For a complete description of this manuscript, see Françoise Vielliard, *Manuscrits français du Moyen Age, Bibliotheca Bodmeriana,* II (Cologny-Geneva: Fondation Martin Bodmer, 1975), 103-08.

[12]Pp. 217-18.

[13]*Romania*, 25 (1896), 541.

[14]Willem Noomen and Nico van den Boogaard, eds., *Nouveau Recueil Complet des Fabliaux,* 4 vols. (Assen, The Netherlands: Van Gorcum, 1983-).

[15]Professor William Roach suggested that I write to them.

[16]I had the good fortune to meet Mr. Taylor on my second visit to his collection on April 17, 1985, and the pleasure of explaining to him my interest in his manuscript. He very kindly granted me permission to have a microfilm made of the manuscript. But before I could receive it, and before I could send him the letter in which I was writing down all that I had told him about his manuscript, I read in the *New York Times* on May 9 of his untimely death in Princeton on May 5. By the end of the year the estate was settled, and the microfilm he had authorized was sent to me.

[17]*Romania,* 37 (1908), 210, *n.* 1.

[18]I have consulted the following works: *the Anglo-Norman Dictionary,* ed. William Rothwell, et al. (London: Modern Humanities Research Association, 1977-88), 5 fascicles to date (to the letter "*q*"); Johan Vising, *Anglo-Norman Language and Literature* (London: Oxford University Press, 1923), *Etude sur le dialecte anglo-normand du XIIe siècle* (Upsala, 1882), *Sur la versification anglo-normande* (Upsala, 1884), ed., *La Plainte d'amour* (Göteborg, 1905); M. K. Pope, *From Latin to Modern French* (Manchester, 1934, pp. 462-85); Lucy Toulmin Smith and Paul Meyer, eds., *Les Contes Moralisés de Nicole Bozon* (Paris: SATF, 1889); and various editions in the series published by the Anglo-Norman Text Society.

The Text

Although no attempt will be made here to give a systematic study of the language of the text, the following are examples from the *Trois Savoirs* of Anglo-Norman features listed by Johan Vising in his *Anglo-Norman Language and Literature* (pp. 27-33): *Continental traits—phonology o* or *u* for *ou, eu* (p. 27) *totes* 5, *plusores* 8, *lur* 64; *ain, ein* confusion (p. 28) *fonteine* 7, *feim* 85, *mein(s)* 144, 156; *ie* for *e* (p. 28) *chief* 9, *piert* 42, *ciertes* 56, *pierte* 131, *lieve* 158; *Continental traits—morphology -om, -on* for *-oms, -ons* (p. 28) *avom* 204; *Insular traits—phonology u* and *o* confusion (p. 29) *umbre* 15, *pur* 44; *ei* and *ai* confusion (p. 29) *solaille* 16, *pleisir* 71; *aun* and *oun* for *an, on* (p. 29) *ensaumple* 2, *dount* 6, 25, *founteine* 7, *chaunta* 19, *taunt* 27, 93, 171, *respount, ataunt* 40, *prisoun(e)* 59, 92, *noun* 60, *saunz* 66, *suspecioun* 103, *traisoun* 104, *covenaunt* 105, *dotaunt* 106, etc.; final *d* for *t* (p. 30)*ad* 35, 36, etc.; *Insular traits— morphology lu, lui* as definite article *lui vilain* 37, etc.; *lui oiselet* 81, etc.; transfer to *-er* conjugation (p. 30) *tyene* 14, *aparceiver* 143; *Sigmatic perfects (late) parust* 12, *fist* 21, *conust* 116, *dist* 118, *pustes* 143, *eustes* 144, *eust* 153; *-et* for *-ez coveitisset* 199; *Substitute forms of subjunctive for forms of indicative oie* 155, *coveitisset* 199; *Syntax* use of tonic instead of atonic pers. pro. (p. 30) *De lui prendre* 115, *de moi mangier* 86; *Use of 'aveir' with intrans. and refl. verbs* (p. 31) *a mountez* 33; *Orthography oe* for *eu* (p. 31) *voet* 238, *estoet* 43; *aa* and *ee estee* 13, *plentee* 14, *baas* 20, *veet, priveement* 30, *avisee* 31, *perchee* 32, *mees* 82, *peerte* 133, *maluree* 161; *Vocabulary* words of Latin origin (p. 31) *eindegree* 107; *Use of English words* (p. 31) *of* 117, 225, 226; *noise* 158. Other Anglo-Norman traits are the presence of atonic *e* that may or may not be counted in the verse: *trope* 128, 132, 210, *soire, pierte* 208, etc.

The following list gives readings in Paul Meyer's text followed by the correct manuscript readings: *title* treis > trois   14 Tyeve > Tyene   28 conmu > commu   29 coveita > coveite   46 n'avrez > n'averez (cf. 82)   46, 57, 211 que > qe   59 Si > Ni (?)   78 Le > De   85 estainchier > estauncher   93 estais > estaus   107 Donque > Donqe   234 trop > trope   235 as > al   237 trop > trope.

Abbreviations in the text are solved the following way: *m͞t = mout* (cf. 38, 52, 82, etc., but *mult* 175); *g͞nt = grant; car', kar', chier', voir' = care, kare, chiere, voire; av'ez = averez* (cf. 82); *i = j; vo' = vous* (cf. 72,

106, 129, etc.); *donq' = donqe* (cf. 187); *qñt = qant; p = par; oūt = ount; coñu = commu.*

The poem begins on folio 22*r* at the top of the page. I give the title and the first three lines of the poem that are also in P. Meyer, but otherwise I summarize the portions of the poem that he printed.

De Trois Savoirs

22*r*   Pieres Aumfurs en ceo liveret
          Un ensaumple retret e met
          D'un vilein q'out beau vergier

Lines 4-14. The garden has many different trees, and its spring (*founteine*) has healing waters that are cold as ice in summer and plentiful in winter.

(*22r*)   Si i avoit l'umbre d'un lorer
            Qe le solaille ne pout damagier.   16
            Sur ceo lorer vint a coustume
            Un oisel de jaune plume
            Qe si chaunta doucement,
            Haut e baas diversement,   20
            Qe au vilein fist joie e heit,
            Qe cuer de caillowe avoit,
            Qe quer de vilein rien commue;
            Miracle fait e grant vertue.   24

Lines 25-110. Because of the bird's beautiful singing, the villein covets him and sets up a trap to catch him. Caught in the snare, the bird chides the villein for being so joyful over catching such a small prey. The villein replies that, on the contrary, he will have much service from the bird since he will put him in a cage and have him sing for his pleasure. The bird replies that he will never sing in a cage, but, if the villein lets him go, he will willingly come three or four times a day to the garden (68), and the villein has only to call him to have him sing. The villein dismisses these words as a ruse (*feintise*), and says that either he will have singing or the bird will go to the kitchen (80). The bird says that his cooked flesh won't amount to much, but, if the villein lets him go, he will tell him three valuable truths [worth the] meat of "trois veals" (94). Thereupon the villein opens his hands, and the bird flies off.

(24r)   Sur ceo lorer est haut assis.
        Huimés ne creit ses enemis,   112
        Care du vilein fu si hastez:
        A touz jours mes ert plus aviseez
        De lui prendre n'ad il mes rien.
        Lasceon e glu conust il bien.   116
        L'oiselet of grant nobloi
        Dist au vilein: "Entendez a moi,
        Si vous dirroi huimés pur voire
        Tot par ordre chascon savoir   120
        De ceaux qe jeo vous ai premis.
        Le primer est, beau douz amis,
        Ne creez pas quant qe l'em dist.
        Ceo sen ne tenez a petit,   124
        Greinour est qe ne l'entendez.
        L'autre sen tantost orrez:
        Ceo qe aver ne poez nient,
        Ne coveitez trope durement.   128
        Deus savoirs dit vous ai,
        Le tierce apres vous dirroi:
        Ja por pierte qe vous eietz,
        De chatel trope ne dolousez;   132
        De plorer peerte n'ad mestier
        Qant mes n'i ad nul recoverir."
        Qant l'oiselet out dit taunt,
24v   Si recomence haut son chaunt.   136
        En son corage pense au plein
        De soi vengier du vilein.
        Pense de faire lui tristour,
        Car il lui out mis en grant pour.   140
        "Vilein," fait il, "Dieu loé soit,
        Qe les oelz coverez vous tenoit,
        Qe aparceiver rien ne pustes
        Quele chose vous en mein eustes   144
        Kaunt vous m'aviez tot a estrus.
        Tresore eustes mout precious:
        Souz ciel n'ad argent ni or
        Qe countrevaille tien tresor.   148
        Mes Dieux eit graces e los,
        Qe si les euz vous tenoit clos.
        Dedeinz mon corps ad une jagounce,

Qe de fin or peise un unce.   152
Ke cele eust en sa baillie
Ne serroit poures jor de sa vie."
Qant ceo oie lui fous vileins,
Tire cheveuz e tort ses meins,   156
A terre chiet e rount son piz,
Lieve noise e braeiz e criz,
Plure e deult a demesure,
E dit qe de sa vie n'ad cure: 160
"Allas," fait il, "jeo maluree!
Lui ors q'avoie m'est emblee!

25r   Taunt fu riches e ne savoi mie,
Qant tieu tresor ei en baillie.   164
Allas," fait il, "dolent frarin,
Jeo mesmes ai fait ceu larcin!
Ceu larcin, ceste folie,
Jeo me sui mesmes honie!   168
L'em me deveroit bien a reisoun
Pendre plus haut qe nul laroun!"
Taunt est dolent, taunt est irrez,
A poi q'il n'ad les euz crevez.   172
Qant lui oiselet ad ceo veu,
Q'il est si dolent e irascu,
Mult richement se tint paié,
E de ses maus bien vengee.   176
Mes neqedent puis au darein
Dist l'oiselet au fou vilein:
"Taunt estes dure por aprendre,
Por lesceoun lire e entendre;   180
Mout avez oblié par temps
Le primer de voz trois sens
Qe un poi devaunt vous oi apris.
Por nient estes a lesceon mis.   184
Ne vous di jeo primes saunz respit
'Ne creez pas qant qe l'em dit'?
A quei vousistes vous donqe creoire
Ceo qe jeo dis come chose voire   188
De la jagounce dedenz moi?

25v   Qe quidez vous en bone foi?
Coment purroit une jagounce
Qe de fin or peisast un unce   192

Dedenz mon ventre estre manaunt
Qant tot mon corps ne peise taunt?
Le primer sen est obliez;
Et de l'autre poi retenez: 196
Ceo vi jeo par ton marrement.
Dit vous avoi apertement
Qe ja ne coveitisset por voir
Chose qe vous ne poez avoir.   200
Jagounce avez desiree,
Qe ja ni ert par vous conquesté
Ne retenuz tot a estrous;
Kar ne l'avom ne moi ne vous.   204
Le tierce savoir tot ensement
Retenistes mout malement:
Jeo vous defendi au darein,
Qe ja por piert, soire ne mein,   208
Ou recoverir ne poessez avoir,
Ne deussez pas trope dolouseir.

Lines 211-40. The bird concludes his admonition to the villein by saying
that he has forgotten all three of the truths he has just been told, and so it is
a waste of time to teach an "asne a harper" (216). The villein can take it to
court if he wants; but now he has neither jewel nor bird! The bird flies
away, leaving the villein "gabez"; and the poem ends with the reminder that,
despite what the villein believes, the three truths will serve well the one who
uses them "de cuer parfit."

Textual Notes

1   *Pieres Aumfurs* refers to Petrus Alfonsi, that is, the author of the *Disciplina
         clericalis.*

112   Ms has *creent* that I change to the singular *creit:* "From now on he will not
         believe his enemies," because the villein (an enemy) proceeds to try to recapture
         him. The efforts of the villein to recapture the bird are a little out of place here,
         since the villein does not yet know how valuable a prize he has let go, nor the
         content of the three truths.

155   *oie* The ps. subj. 3 is used here for the ps. indic. This is a characteristic AN
         trait.

157   *rount* Changed from *tount,* a dittography from 156 where there is a similar
         context: *e tort ses* (156), *e tount son* (157).

199   *coveitisset* The impf. subj. 3 is used for the imperative and the *-et* ending is
       substituted for the *-ez* ending. Both of these are characteristic AN traits.

Glossary

aver 127 to have; *ind ps 1* **ei** 164, **oi** 183, *3* **ad** 35, 36, 115, etc.; *sbj 5* **eietz** 131;
    imper or sbj 3 **eit** 149, *5* **eiez** 103
aviseez 114 minded
baillie 153 possession
braeiz 158 howls
caillowe 22 flint
care 113 for
chare 91, 94 flesh
chatel 132 property
commue 23 moved
countrevaille 148 comparable to
coveitisset 199 *imper sbj 5* of "to covet"
darein *loc* **au darein** 177, 207 finally
dirroi *fut 1* 76, 90 of "to say"
diversement 19 in different ways
dolouseir 210 to lament
e 249, etc., and
ei *v.* **aver**
eietz *v.* **aver**
eit *v.* **aver**
em 123, 169, 186 one
emblee 162 stolen
ensement *loc* **tot ensement** 205 in the same way
estaus *loc* 93 **prendre e.** to take a firm stand
estrus *loc* **a estrus** 145, **a estrous** 203 outright, entirely
euz 150, 172 eyes
frarin 165 needy one, poor wretch
froi 52 *fut 1, fut 2* **fras** 54 of "to make"
glu 116 birdlime
hastez 113 harrassed, pressed
heit 21 gladness, happiness
huimés 112 from now on, 119 now
issi 75, 96 thus
jagounce 151, 189, 191, 201 hyacinth (precious stone, jewel)
kar 204 in that case

kaunt 145 when
ke 153 he, the one who
larcin 166, 167 theft
laroun 170 thief
lorer 15, 17 laurel tree
lui 95, 107, 155, 173, etc. the
maluree 161 coward, weakling
manaunt 193 have abode, dwell
marrement 197 distress
mein *loc* 208 **soire ne mein** evening nor morning; 144, 156 hand(s)
mes *loc with imper* 149; **m. ne** 134 no longer; **m. a touz jours** 98, 114 forever more; **il n'ad mes rien** 115 he had no other desire
mestier *loc* **aver m.** 133 to be useful
ne 204 neither, nor
neqedent 177 nevertheless
nobloi *loc* **of grant nobloi** 117 with great intrepidity, arrogance
oelz 142 eyes
oie 155 *ps sbj 3* **oie,** *pp* oié 95 of "to hear"
paié *loc* **se tenir paié** 175 to be satisfied
plein *loc* **au plein** 137 completely
pour 140 fear
poures 154 poor
purroi 61 *cond 1* of "to be able"
qe 19, 21, 22, 142, 148, 150, 152 who, which; 16, 28, 121, 123, 125, 127 that; 23, 143, 190 for
quei *loc* 187 **a quei** why, for what reason
quidez 190 *ps ind 5* of "to believe"
recoverir *subst* 134 recovery
reisoun *loc* 169 **a reisoun** with reason, cause
rount 157 *ps ind 1* of "to tear"
serroi 84 *fut 1* of "to be"
si 15, 119 and
soire 208 evening
taunt 135, 194 so much
temps *loc* 181 **par temps** soon
teil 49, **tien** 148, **tieu** 164 such (a)
tresore 146 treasure
vendroi 67, 71 *cond 1, fut 2* **vendras** 80 of "to come"
vertue 24 wonder, miracle
voire *loc* **pur voire** 119 truly

Notes on Contributors

R. Howard Bloch serves as Chair of the French Department at the University of California, Berkeley. He is the author of *Medieval French Literature and Law* (California, 1977), *Etymologies and Genealogies: A Literary Anthropology of the French Middle Ages* (Chicago, 1983), *The Scandal of the Fabliaux* (Chicago, 1986), and a recent novel, *Moses in the Promised Land* (Peregrine Smith Books, 1988). He is currently working on a book entitled *Medieval Misogyny and the Invention of Western Romantic Love.*

Gerard J. Brault is Professor of French at The Pennsylvania State University. He holds a Ph.D. from the University of Pennsylvania and taught at Bowdoin College and at Pennsylvania before moving to Penn State in 1965. He is the author of seven books—including *Early Blazon* (1972), *The Song of Roland: An Analytical Edition,* 2 vols. (1978), and *The French-Canadian Heritage in New England* (1986)—and of numerous articles on medieval and Renaissance French language and literature, medieval heraldry, and French-Canadian language and culture.

Keith Busby is Professor of French and Chair of the Department of Modern Languages at the University of Oklahoma. He has published *Gauvain in Old French Literature* (1980), *Two Old French Didactic Poems* (1983), *The Lais of Marie de France* (translation, with Glyn S. Burgess, 1986), and many studies in scholarly journals. He is also a coeditor of *The Legacy of Chrétien de Troyes* (1987-88) and is presently completing a critical edition of Chrétien de Troyes's *Perceval.*

William Calin is Graduate Research Professor at the University of Florida; he has previously taught at Dartmouth, Stanford, the University of Oregon, and the University of Poitiers, and has been Visiting Fellow, Clare Hall, Cambridge. He has published eight books and over fifty articles on French and Occitan literature and has held NEH, ACLS, Fulbright, and Guggenheim Fellowships. His most recent volumes are *A Muse for Heroes: Nine Centuries of the Epic in France* (Toronto) and *In Defense of French Poetry: An Essay in Revaluation* (Penn State). His current project is a synthesis entitled "The French Literary Tradition and Medieval England."

Larry S. Crist, whose Ph.D. is from Princeton, is Professor of French and former Chair of French and Italian at Vanderbilt University. His main field of research is the *chanson de geste,* especially the second cycle of the Crusades. Among his publications are *Le deuxième cycle de la croisade: deux études sur son développement* (Geneva, 1972; with Robert F. Cook) and his edition of the *Saladin* (Geneva, 1972). He has recently completed work on the 26,000-line *Baudouin de Sebourc,* edited in collaboration with Robert Cook. The present article is his second on the fabliaux.

Peter F. Dembowski, Professor of French at the University of Chicago, received his Doctorat de l'Université de Paris in Slavic philology and the Ph.D. from the University of California, Berkeley, in Old French language and literature. Besides his activities as an editor of Old French texts, he published *La Chronique de Robert de Clari* (Toronto, 1963) and *Jean Froissart and his Meliador* (Lexington, 1986). He taught in British Columbia and in Toronto before coming to Chicago.

Joseph J. Duggan teaches French, Comparative Literature, and Romance Philology at the University of California, Berkeley. He was Editor-in-Chief of *Romance Philology,* 1982-87. His publications include the *Song of Roland: Formulaic Style and Poetic Craft* (1973), *A Guide to Studies on the Chanson de Roland* (1976), and *A New Fragment of Les Enfances Vivien* (1985). His study *The Cantar de mio Cid: Poetic Creation in its Economic and Social Contexts* will be published this year by Cambridge University Press.

Peter Haidu is Professor of French at UCLA, where he teaches medieval literature, textual theory, and issues in semiotics. His publications include *Aesthetic Distance in Chrétien de Troyes: Irony and Comedy in "Cligès" and "Perceval"* (Droz, 1968) and *Lion-queue-coupée: l'écart symbolique chez Chrétien de Troyes* (Droz, 1972), and he edited *Approaches to Medieval Romance* (*Yale French Studies,* No. 51). He is completing a semiotic study of medieval narrative as historical phenomenon and working out a theory of historical semiotics.

William L. Hendrickson, an Associate Professor at Arizona State University, previously taught at Brown University and at Washington University, where he was a colleague of John L. Grigsby's. Hendrickson is the coeditor of the *Jean Misrahi Memorial Volume,* which contains his article "Toward an Edition of *Garin de Monglane,*" and of *Studies on the Seven Sages of Rome and Other Essays in Medieval Literature.*

James F. Jones, Jr., has chaired the Department of Romance Languages and Literatures at Washington University since 1982 and was recently the Senior Visitor for the Hilary Term at Oxford. He has written a book on utopia in Rousseau's *La Nouvelle Héloïse* and many articles on eighteenth-century French literature, has translated one of Prévost's novels, and has recently completed a book on Rousseau's *Dialogues.*

Hans-Erich Keller teaches medieval French and Occitan literatures and languages at The Ohio State University. He has published several studies of Wace, and his new edition of Wace's *Vie de Sainte Marguerite* will appear in 1989. His other principal field of inquiry concerns the *chansons de geste,* an area in which his extensive contributions include "La Version dionysienne de la *Chanson de Roland*" (1975) and "La Conversion de Bramimonde" (1974); he also edited *Romance Epic* (1987), which includes eighteen studies by specialists in the field.

Douglas Kelly is Julian E. Harris Professor of French at the University of Wisconsin-Madison. His books include: *'Sens' and 'Conjointure' in the "Chevalier de la Charrette"* (Mouton, 1966); *Chrétien de Troyes: An Analytical Bibliography* (Grant & Cutler, 1976), *Medieval Imagination* (Wisconsin, 1978); he is an editor of *The Romances of Chrétien de Troyes: A Symposium* (French Forum, 1985) and *The Legacy of Chrétien de Troyes* (Rodopi, 1987). He has a forthcoming monograph on *The Arts of Poetry and Prose,* and he is completing a book on *The Art of Medieval Romance.*

William W. Kibler is the Superior Oil—Linward Shivers Centennial Professor of Medieval Studies at the University of Texas, Austin. He has worked extensively on the *chansons de geste* and is currently editor of *Olifant,* the journal of the American-Canadian Branch of the Société Rencesvals. His recent publications include *An Introduction to Old French* (MLA, 1984) and *Guillaume de Machaut: Le Jugement du roy de Behaigne and Remede de Fortune* (Georgia, 1988; with James I. Wimsatt). He is currently preparing an edition of the Lyon MS. of the *Chanson de Roland.*

Norris J. Lacy recently moved from the University of Kansas to succeed John L. Grigsby as medievalist at Washington University. He is author or editor of a number of volumes, including *The Craft of Chrétien de Troyes* (1980), *The Arthurian Encyclopedia* (1986), *The Legacy of Chrétien de Troyes* (1987-88), *The Arthurian Handbook* (1988), and Béroul's *Tristran* (1989). He is currently serving as general editor for a translation of the complete Old French "Lancelot-Grail" cycle, to be issued by Garland Publishing.

Donald Maddox is Professor of French and Comparative Literature at the University of Connecticut, Storrs. He previously taught at Duke, the University of California, Santa Barbara, and Boston College, and was a three-year Mellon Fellow in Medieval Studies at Brandeis. His books include *Structure and Sacring: The Systematic Kingdom in Chrétien's "Erec et Enide"* (1978), *Semiotics of Deceit: The Pathelin Era* (1984), and his just-completed study of early Arthurian narrative, *Once and Future Fictions.* He has also published numerous studies on medieval literature and literary theory and is currently at work on a study dealing with medieval textualities and narrative genres.

Yakov Malkiel has been associated with the Berkeley Campus of the University of California since 1942, teaching historical linguistics as well as history of linguistics under the aegis of the Romance Philology Program and, after 1966, also in the Department of Linguistics. He was the founding editor of the *Romance Philology* quarterly (1947-82). His principal publications include *Essays on Linguistic Themes* (1968) and *From Particular to General Linguistics: Essays 1965-78* (1983).

John F. Plummer, Associate Professor of English at Vanderbilt University, studied Chrétien de Troyes with John L. Grigsby at Washington University while earning his Ph.D. in Comparative Literature. He has published studies of Chrétien, Malory, medieval lyrics, and Chaucer, and is currently completing an edition of Chaucer's *Summoner's Tale* for the Variorum Chaucer.

Hans R. Runte holds the Ph.D. from the University of Kansas and has been teaching French and comparative medieval literature at Dalhousie University (Halifax) since 1971. He edited *Li Ystoire de la male marastre* (Tübingen, 1974) and has written on the *Roman des sept sages de Rome,* Chrétien de Troyes, and Marie de France, as well as on contemporary French-Canadian literature. He is the founder (1975) of the Society of the Seven Sages and editor of its annual Newsletter, treasurer of the International Arthurian Society, and editor of *Dalhousie French Studies.*

Barbara Nelson Sargent-Baur is Professor of French and Director of the Medieval and Renaissance Studies Program at the University of Pittsburgh. She has published numerous articles on Chrétien de Troyes, Béroul, Villon, and Andreas Capellanus. Her books include *Le Livre du Roy Rambaux de Frise* and (with Robert F. Cook) *Aucassin et Nicolete: A Critical Bibliography.* She recently completed a monograph on François Villon and the legend of Job and is engaged on a long study of Chrétien's *Conte du Graal.*

Gloria Torrini-Roblin has her Ph.D. from Washington University (1987), where she was the last doctoral candidate to complete the degree under the direction of John L. Grigsby. Her dissertation, "The Semiotics of the *Roman courtois:* The Hypotextual Relationship Between the *Conte du Graal* and the *First Continuation*," reflects her research interests in genre theory, semiotics, and textual pragmatics.

Colette-Anne Van Coolput, born in Bruges, studied Romance Philology at the Université de Louvain (KUL), where in 1982 she defended her doctoral thesis on the *Tristan en prose,* published under the title *Aventures querant et le sens du monde* (Louvain Univ. Press, 1986). She is preparing a book on anthropomorphic representations (statues, paintings, embroideries) in narrative texts of the twelfth and thirteenth centuries. She teaches at the Vlaamse Economische Hogeschool (Brussels).

Lenora D. Wolfgang holds her Ph.D. from the University of Pennsylvania, where her thesis director was William Roach. She taught at Pennsylvania and at Temple University before assuming her present position at Lehigh University, where she is Professor of French. She is the editor of *Bliocadran: A Prologue to the Perceval of Chrétien de Troyes* (Tübingen, 1976) and has contributed to *Romance Philology, Speculum, French Review, Oliphant,* and *The Arthurian Encyclopedia.*

OTHER MEDIEVAL STUDIES
from
Summa Publications

Cynthia Brown, *The Shaping of History and Poetry in Late Medieval France*	US $18.95
Barbara Craig, *The Evolution of a Mystery Play: Le Sacrifice d'Abraham*	24.00
David Fein, *A Reading of Villon's Testament*	10.95
Norris Lacy, *L'Istoyre de Jehan Coquault: A Literary Forgery*	11.95
Norris Lacy/Jerry Nash, eds., *Essays in Early French Literature presented to Barbara M. Craig*	24.00
Richard O'Gorman, *Les Braies au cordelier: An Anonymous Fabliau of the Thirteenth Century*	16.00
Elizabeth Poe, *From Poetry to Prose in Old Provençal*	16.95
Hans Runte, Henri Niedszielski, William Hendrickson, eds., *Jean Misrahi Memorial Volume*, vol. 1	18.95
David Schenck, *The Myth of Guillaume: Poetic Consciousness in the Guillaume d'Orange Cycle*	19.95
Margaret Winters, *Jean Renart's Le Lai de l'ombre* (critical edition)	16.95
Atie Zuurdeeg, *Narrative Techniques and Their Effects in La Mort Le Roi Artu*	9.95

TRANSLATIONS

Samuel Danon/Samuel Rosenberg, *Ami and Amile*	11.95
Mary Lou Martin, *The Fables of Marie de France*	23.95
Jean-Louis Picherit, *The Journey of Charlemagne*	12.95

RENAISSANCE STUDIES

Barbara Bowen, *One Hundred Renaissance Jokes*	21.95
Christine Raffini, *The Second Sequence in Maurice Scève's Délie*	24.95
Régine Reynolds-Cornell, *Witnessing an Era: Georgette de Montenay and The Emblèmes ou Devises Chrestiennes*	19.95
Tilde Sankovitch, *Jodelle et la création du masque: Etude structurale et normative de l'Eugène*	13.95

P.O. Box 20725 • Birmingham, AL 35216 • USA